THE SCARLET LETTER

NEW RIVERSIDE EDITIONS

Series Editor for the American Volumes
Paul Lauter

For a complete listing of our American and British New Riverside Editions, visit our web site at **http://college.hmco.com.**

NEW RIVERSIDE EDITIONS
Series Editor for the American Volumes
Paul Lauter, Trinity College

NATHANIEL HAWTHORNE

The Scarlet Letter

Complete Text with Introduction
Historical Contexts • *Critical Essays*

Edited by Rita K. Gollin

STATE UNIVERSITY NEW YORK AT GENESEO

Houghton Mifflin Company

BOSTON • NEW YORK

FOR MY HUSBAND, OUR GRANDCHILDREN, AND THEIR PARENTS

Sponsoring Editor: Michael Gillespie
Editorial Associate: Bruce Cantley
Senior Project Editor: Tracy Patruno
Senior Cover Design Coordinator: Deborah Azerrad Savona
Manufacturing Manager: Florence Cadran
Marketing Manager: Cindy Graff Cohen
Cover image: © Corbis

Printed in the U.S.A.

Library of Congress Control Number: 2001090569
ISBN: 0-618-10734-7
1 2 3 4 5 6 7 8 9-FFG-05 04 03 02 01

As part of Houghton Mifflin's ongoing
commitment to the environment, this text
has been printed on recycled paper.

CONTENTS

LIST OF ILLUSTRATIONS

ABOUT THIS SERIES
Paul Lauter

The Riverside name dates back well over a century. Readers of this book may have seen—indeed, may own—Riverside Editions of works by the best-known nineteenth-century American writers, such as Emerson, Thoreau, Lowell, Longfellow, and Hawthorne. Houghton Mifflin and its predecessor, Ticknor & Fields, were the primary publishers of the New England authors who constituted much of the undisputed canon of American literature until well into the twentieth century. The Riverside Editions of works by these writers, and of some later writers such as Amy Lowell, became benchmarks for distinguished and useful editions of standard American authors for home, library, and classroom.

In the 1950s and 1960s, the Riverside name was used for another series of texts, primarily for the college classroom, of well-known American and British literary works. These paperback volumes, edited by distinguished critics of that generation, were among the most widely used and appreciated of their day. They provided carefully edited texts in a handsome and readable format, with insightful critical introductions. They were books one kept beyond the exam, the class, or even the college experience.

In the last quarter century, however, ideas about the American literary canon have changed. Many scholars want to see a canon that reflects a broader American heritage, including significant literary works by previously marginalized writers, many of them women or men of color. These changes began to be institutionalized in curricula as well as in textbooks such as *The Heath Anthology of American Literature*, which Houghton Mifflin started publishing in 1998. The older Riverside series, excellent in its day, ran the risk of appearing outdated; the editors were long retired or deceased, and the authors were viewed by some as too exclusive.

Yet the name Riverside and the ideas behind it continued to have appeal. The name stood for distinction and worth in the publication of America's literary heritage. Houghton Mifflin's New Riverside Series, initiated in the year 2000, is designed to uphold the Riverside reputation for excellence while offering a more inclusive range of authors. The Series also provides today's reader with books that contain, in addition to notable literary works, introductions by influential critics, as well as a variety of stimulating materials that bring alive the debates, the conversations, the social and cultural movements within which America's literary classics were formed.

Thus emerged the book you have in hand. Each volume of the New Riverside Editions will contain the basic elements that we think today's readers find interesting and useful: important literary works by significant authors, incisive introductions, and a variety of contextual materials to make the literary text fully engaging. These books will be useful in many kinds of classrooms, but they are also designed to offer the casual reader the enjoyment of a good read in a fresh and accessible format. Among the first group of New Riverside Editions are familiar titles, such as Henry David Thoreau's *Walden* and Mark Twain's *Adventures of Huckleberry Finn.* There are also works in fresh new combinations, such as the collection of early captivity narratives and the volume that pairs texts by Ralph Waldo Emerson and Margaret Fuller. And there are well known works in distinctively interesting formats, such as the volume containing Edith Wharton's *The Age of Innocence* and the volume of writings by Stephen Crane. Future books will include classics as well as works drawing renewed attention.

The New Riverside Editions will provide discriminating readers with a wide range of important literary works, contextual materials that vividly illuminate those works, and the best of recent critical commentary and analysis. And because we have not confined our editors to a single monotonous format, we think our readers will find that each volume in this new series has a character appropriate to the literary work it presents.

We expect the New Riverside Editions to bring to the twenty-first century the same literary publishing distinction of its nineteenth- and twentieth-century predecessors.

Portrait of Nathaniel Hawthorne (1850) by Cephas Giovanni Thompson

INTRODUCTION
Rita K. Gollin

I send you, at last, the manuscript portion of my volume,"
Nathaniel Hawthorne told the Boston publisher James T. Fields
on 15 January 1850; "not quite all of it, however, for there are
three chapters still to be written of 'The Scarlet Letter.'" Soliciting Fields's
judgment, Hawthorne asked him to read the introductory essay first. He
also offered a confidence: "In the process of writing, all political and official
turmoil has subsided within me" (*Letters, 1843–1853* 305).

Hawthorne had endured that turmoil since March 1849, when he
learned that local Whigs planned a "strong effort" to oust him as surveyor
of revenue for the port of Salem. In March 1846, he had been appointed to
that post by President Polk, a Democrat. In March 1849, however, when the
victorious Whig candidate Zachary Taylor became president, leaders of
Salem's Whig Party wanted to have Hawthorne replaced with a man of
their own. "I do not think that this ought to be done," Hawthorne told his
friend George Hillard, "for I was not appointed to office as a reward for
political services, nor have I acted as a politician since." In a tone at once
self-defensive, self-deprecatory, and vitriolic, he argued that "an inoffensive man of letters—having obtained a pitiful little office on no other plea
than his pitiful little literature—ought not to be left to the mercy of these
thick-skulled and no-hearted ruffians" (*Letters, 1843–1853* 263–64). But he
was dismissed in June.

His case went public through an assault on him in one Whig newspaper
and his refutation of it in another. After a stream of newspaper editorials
and letters to Washington echoed Hawthorne's arguments, reinstatement
seemed possible. Then in July, Salem's Whig leaders stepped up their attack. In a long, truth-stretching "memorial" to the secretary of the treasury, they depicted Surveyor Hawthorne as an active Democrat and a tool
of his party. "My surveyorship is lost," he told his brother-in-law Horace
Mann in early August (*Letters, 1843–1853* 269–71). All charges against him

were false, he insisted. But he no longer expected or even desired to regain his post.

At the height of his public shaming in July, Hawthorne had also endured the deeply private anguish of his mother's terminal illness. Kneeling at her bedside, he pondered the "sort of coldness between us, such as is apt to come between persons of strong feelings, if they are not managed rightly." He took her hand, shook with sobs, and then thought, "Oh what a mockery, if what I saw were all." But the intolerable bitterness of that thought provoked a strong testament of faith: "God would not have made the close so dark and wretched, if there were nothing beyond [. . .]" (*American Notebooks* 429). Hawthorne had survived what he called the darkest hour of his life. But its emotional and philosophical turmoil, intermingling with the "political and official turmoil" that he had endured for months, would permeate *The Scarlet Letter* (*Letters, 1843–1853* 305).

Hawthorne had fought his ouster as surveyor because he wanted to defeat his Whig assailants, to clear his name, and to keep what he thought was rightly his—a relatively undemanding but respected job that helped him support his wife and children and even house his mother and two sisters. His role as surveyor, however, dulled his creative imagination. Therefore, as he attested in "The Custom-House," his "decapitation" was fortunate. In the wake of his public shaming and his mother's death, the forty-five-year-old Hawthorne "opened his long-disused literary desk, and was again a literary man." *The Scarlet Letter* was the result.

Twenty-four years earlier, at the age of twenty-one, Hawthorne had graduated from Bowdoin College, returned to his family's home in Salem, and labored to establish himself as "a literary man." He read widely, wrote diligently, placed dozens of tales and sketches in periodicals and gift books, edited a short-lived magazine, and produced a children's history book. But throughout what he called his "twelve lonely years," his earnings were slim, and his publications went unsigned.

Then in 1837, his collection of *Twice-Told Tales* appeared with his name on the cover (though only after his college friend Horatio Bridge secretly guaranteed the publisher against loss). Reviewers praised it, his Bowdoin classmate Henry Wadsworth Longfellow among them. Another consequence was meeting an amateur artist named Sophia Peabody, who also lived in Salem; at the end of 1838, they became secretly engaged. But because his income remained small, in January 1839 he accepted a patronage appointment as measurer of salt and coal at the Boston Custom House. During the next two years, those uncongenial duties proved so stultifying that he produced only a few children's books. He quit in January 1841.

That April, Hawthorne embarked on an experiment he later called "the most romantic episode" of his life (*Blithedale Romance* 2). He joined the new utopian community of Brook Farm, founded on Emersonian principles of self-trust and self-fulfillment. At first he thought it might be the perfect place to pursue his literary career and to begin married life with Sophia, but farm drudgery left him too exhausted to write fiction, and he returned to Salem in November.

A remarkably idyllic period began the following July when he married Sophia and settled into the comfortable Old Manse in Concord. Adored by his wife, befriended by stimulating neighbors including Henry David Thoreau and Ralph Waldo Emerson, and master of his own time, Hawthorne wrote prolifically, continued to publish everything he wrote, and began preparing a second volume of stories that he would title *Mosses from an Old Manse*. Even so, his income did not cover his expenses, a problem that became increasingly serious after his first daughter, Una, was born in 1844. He enlisted friends in the Democratic Party to find him a second suitable patronage job; in April 1846 he became surveyor of the Salem Custom House.

Two other milestones came two months later: His *Mosses* was published, and his son, Julian, was born. His literary reputation was high, his home life was happy, and his work at the Custom House occupied only his mornings. Yet, as at the Boston Custom House, routine work dulled his imagination, and he wrote only a handful of tales during the next three years. After his ouster from the Salem Custom House and the grief of his mother's death, however, Hawthorne emerged from despair into the most creative period of life. By the end of September, Sophia could report that he was "writing immensely."

James T. Fields, the "literary" partner in the eminent Boston publishing firm of Ticknor, Reed, and Fields, came to visit and offered immediate publication of any new Hawthorne book. Hawthorne initially denied having anything to show; but just as Fields was about to leave for the railroad station, Hawthorne handed him a roll of manuscript, saying, "It is either very good or very bad, I don't know which" (qtd. Fields 50). Fields read "the germ of 'The Scarlet Letter'" on his way home and sent Hawthorne a note of glowing praise that same night, then returned to secure the story for publication. On December 29, he began advertising "a new volume by Hawthorne."[1] From then on, Fields was Hawthorne's sole American publisher as well as his literary adviser and publicist, his agent for publication in England, his banker, and his devoted friend.

---

[1] Fields's often-quoted account of the episode first appeared in the *Atlantic Monthly* and then in his *Yesterdays with Authors*. But Sophia Hawthorne, angrily disputing his account, said that Edwin Whipple had accompanied Fields to Salem and helped persuade Hawthorne that his story was excellent (Fisk "The Profession of Authorship").

At first, both the author and the publisher thought Hawthorne's new volume would be a third collection of tales. But in mid-January when Hawthorne sent Fields "The Custom-House" and most of *The Scarlet Letter*, Fields urged that they be published separately in one volume, so the tale would be perceived as a novel, which was more marketable than a collection of stories. Fields's list was short on novels, and at a time when the only American novelist to enjoy national renown was James Fenimore Cooper, publishing Hawthorne's first novel would be a marketing coup and a signal cultural event.

Despite his reluctance to stake the success of his new volume on a single story, especially such a somber one, Hawthorne deferred to Field's judgment. He even proposed a "piquant and appropriate" way of attracting readers: by printing his title—*The Scarlet Letter*—in red ink on the title page. Fields gladly agreed and put his typesetters to work. "I finished my book only yesterday," Hawthorne told his friend Horatio Bridge on February 4, "one end being in the press in Boston, while the other was in my head here in Salem." He added that when he read his final pages to Sophia, they "broke her heart and sent her to bed with a grievous headache—which I took as a triumphant success!" (*Letters, 1843–1853* 430).

On March 16, Hawthorne began enjoying other forms of success. *The Scarlet Letter* went on sale, sold out within days, and received wide though not unanimous praise. Predictably, conservative readers felt offended by his "scandalous" subject and by his two main characters, the heroic adulteress and the hypocritical Puritan minister who had fathered her child. Also predictably, many Salemites were infuriated by his introductory essay, particularly by his contemptuous sketches of Custom House officials. But other readers were amused, and only two weeks after the book was published, Hawthorne seized the opportunity for a bit of gloating by writing a mock-innocent preface for the second edition. "The Custom-House" could not have been written "in a better or a kindlier spirit, nor [. . .] with a livelier effect of truth," he claimed, and therefore he was republishing it "without the change of a word" (85 in this volume).

Later that spring, Hawthorne left Salem forever. During the next year and a half, while living in a Berkshire cottage, he produced a novel set in Salem (*The House of the Seven Gables*), a third collection of short stories (*The Snow-Image*), and several collections of children's stories. He also formed a deep friendship with Herman Melville, who was then writing *Moby-Dick*, which he would dedicate to Hawthorne "In Token of my admiration for his genius." Hawthorne's daughter Rose was born in 1851; in 1852 he produced a novel based on his Brook Farm experience, entitled *The Blithedale Romance*, bought the house in Concord he called the Wayside (the only house he ever owned), and wrote a campaign biography for his college friend Franklin Pierce. When Pierce became president, Hawthorne accepted what would be his third and last political appointment—as American consul to Liverpool. His most intense period of literary productivity was over. During his four years in England, his notebook entries were virtually his only literary productions. Then during a subsequent sixteen months in Italy, he drafted what would become his final novel— *The Marble Faun.*

Hawthorne returned to Concord in June 1860, added a tower study to the Wayside, and embarked on three "romances" that he would never complete. Encouraged by Fields, he prepared a lively eyewitness essay about wartime Washington for the firm's new periodical, the *Atlantic Monthly,* as well as a series of well-paid and well-received sketches drawn from his English notebooks that were separately published as *Our Old Home* (1863). But he brooded about the Civil War and about his stagnant imagination while nonetheless struggling to write, and his health became seriously impaired. He died in his sleep on 19 May 1864.

From the day it was published, *The Scarlet Letter* was acclaimed as a major novel. Many reviewers, including Fields's and Hawthorne's friend Edwin Whipple, praised it as a powerful and provocative story about America's Puritan past, a work of "perfect unity" that presented "a severe but wholesome moral"; their friend Evert Duyckinck called it a "psychological romance" that offered deep insights into the human soul.[2] Predictably, Orestes Brownson and other Christian moralists objected to Hawthorne's sympathetic treatment of the adulteress Hester Prynne, his unsympathetic treatment of her judges, and his depiction of a conflicted Puritan minister as Hester's unacknowledged partner in sin. Yet even Brownson praised Hawthorne's narrative power and his felicitous style. Responses to "The Custom-House" ranged from fury to pleasure in its caricatures of doddering office holders. Many readers admired his wry self-presentation, and some even preferred the essay to the novel. But no one explored the many connections between the essay and the novel, and no one suspected that Hawthorne's account of discovering a mysterious scarlet letter in the Custom House was entirely fictitious.

Over the next century and a half, *The Scarlet Letter* was repeatedly called Hawthorne's finest work, America's finest novel, and a historical romance of profound originality. It has been ranked with the greatest novels of his

---

[2] See the reviews by Whipple and Duyckinck in Part Three.

contemporaries—including those of Charles Dickens and George Eliot, Fyodor Dostoyevsky and Ivan Turgenev, Honoré de Balzac and Gustave Flaubert; it has been classed with Greek tragedy and Dante's *Divine Comedy* and even called the greatest book ever written in the Western Hemisphere. Even critics who reject the elitism of such claims acknowledge the book's preeminence. It has never gone out of print; it has generated volumes of criticism, as well as plays, operas, and films; it is a staple of high school and college courses on American literature; and allusions to it have become staples of popular culture. In each successive decade, readers have found that the novel and its author mirror their own concerns: a 1930s introduction to the novel discusses Hawthorne's need to support his family, a 1950s introduction talks about witch-hunts, and a 1980s introduction presents an author and a heroine who are victimized by society yet triumph over it.

Yet in every decade, distinguished critics have perceived the novel differently. In his influential *Hawthorne* (1879), the ambitious young novelist Henry James called *The Scarlet Letter* Hawthorne's masterpiece and "the finest piece of imaginative writing yet put forth in the country," but he complained of its gloom, its philosophical abstractness, and its "superficial" symbolism, concluding that the author himself was limited by the thinness of American culture and his own sensibility (284–86 in this volume). Turn-of-the-century biographers and critics who succeeded James echoed his superlatives but voiced none of his complaints.[3]

In 1941 F. O. Matthiessen's discussion of *The Scarlet Letter* in his *American Renaissance* inaugurated over two decades of primarily formalist criticism. Concentrating on Hawthorne's artistry, Matthiessen acclaimed his tight plot and symmetrical design, his intertwined and psychologically complex characters, his powerful symbols, and his device of "multiple choice" (289 in this volume). So did the many so-called New Critics who flourished during the postwar years when American literature courses proliferated, training readers to explore the novel as a closed system—to decode its symbols and images, to locate ironies and ambiguities, to elucidate the functions of the scaffold and other settings, and to schematize Hawthorne's interdependent characters.[4]

Other midcentury concerns included grappling with Hawthorne's definition of *The Scarlet Letter* as a romance and himself as a romancer (rather

---

[3] George M. Woodberry, for example, praised the "great and unique romance" for its moral profundity and potent symbols, the letter *A* in particular (189–91).
[4] The long list of such studies includes Leland Schubert's *Hawthorne the Artist: Fine Art Devices in Fiction* and Richard Harter Fogle's *Hawthorne's Fiction: The Light and the Dark.* (See For Further Reading.)

than a novelist).[5] More recent approaches include those of psychoanalytic critics (whether they focus on Hawthorne's conflicted relationships with members of his family or on his characters' entanglements of guilt and desire), reader-response critics (who focus on ways the text "constructs" its readers), poststructuralists (including semiologists who analyze the ways in which Hester's *A* and her child Pearl are invested with meaning), and gender critics (whose interrogations include the construction of femininity in Hester and masculinity in her author). Additional scholarly approaches include investigations of its sources, its antecedents in Hawthorne's own stories and notebook entries, and its influence on such twentieth-century writers as Jorge Luis Borges, Flannery O'Connor, and John Updike. The 1962 Centenary Edition of *The Scarlet Letter*, the first volume of the definitive edition of Hawthorne's complete works, provoked fresh attention to the book as a cultural production—for example, to Field's marketing strategies and those of subsequent editors.

The most important recent critics include those whose work appears in this volume. Many of them focus on gender constraints and power structures in *The Scarlet Letter* and in Hawthorne's own experience. Exploring the connections between "The Custom-House" and the novel, most of them see Hawthorne's indictments of Puritan New England as informed by the ideologies of antebellum America, particularly the conflicting ideologies of self-fulfillment and social constraint. In the process, most of them also discuss Hawthorne's elusive narrative voice and—more broadly—the ways he constructed and defined himself as narrator while reaching out to his readers. Each enriches the reader's response to the novel.

As Hawthorne declared in "The Custom-House," his "best definition of happiness" was "to live throughout the whole range of his faculties and sensibilities." During his stultifying years as surveyor, that was impossible. Not even when he sat alone in his moonlit and firelit parlor could he enter "a neutral territory, somewhere between the real world and fairyland, where the Actual and the Imaginary may meet, and each imbue itself with the nature of the other," the place where his creative imagination could generate his romances. Only after leaving the Custom House could he regain access to all his "faculties and sensibilities" and thus to that "neutral territory" where *The Scarlet Letter* came to life.

---

[5] In *The American Novel and Its Tradition,* Richard Chase expanded on Hawthorne's definition of *The Scarlet Letter* as a romance to differentiate American from English novelistic "traditions," a definition and differentiation variously addressed by subsequent critics including Michael Bell, Evan Carton, Emily Budick, Richard Brodhead, and Richard Millington. (See Chase vii–xii, 12–13, 18–19.)

By claiming in "The Custom-House" that he was merely the editor "or very little more" of manuscripts found in the building, and by describing the gold-embroidered letter found with them and the "burning heat" he felt when he placed it on his breast, Hawthorne prepared his readers to admire Hester Prynne and to ponder the "deep meaning, most worthy of interpretation," of this "mystic symbol." But he also identified with Hester. His own ancestors haunted him as persecutors, men who, like Hester's persecutors in *The Scarlet Letter*, had "all the Puritanic traits, both good and evil." William Hathorne, "who came so early, with his Bible and his sword," had been a "bitter persecutor" of Quakers, and William's son John was a judge in Salem's notorious witchcraft trials.

Though Hawthorne imagined the contempt these ancestors would feel for an "idler" like himself, a mere "writer of story-books," *The Scarlet Letter* demonstrates that "strong traits of their nature have intertwined themselves with mine." His tightly plotted, densely symbolic, and psychologically probing story of concealed and revealed sin in seventeenth-century Boston is both his most serious work of moral and cultural history and his most consummate work of art. By writing a tightly constructed novel that nonetheless invites conflicting critical interpretations, Hawthorne, like Hester, resisted his own conformist society. As he said in the opening paragraph of "The Custom-House," he had cast "his leaves forth upon the wind," addressing "not the many who will fling aside his volume, or never take it up, but the few who will understand him [. . .]." As he both warned and informed such readers, his "inmost Me" remains veiled. But from his time to ours, readers who seek to understand *The Scarlet Letter: A Romance* enlarge themselves.

A NOTE ON THE TEXT
Rita K. Gollin

The first edition of *The Scarlet Letter* was published in Boston on 16 March 1850 by Ticknor, Reed, and Fields. That edition of 2,500 quickly sold out. On March 30, Hawthorne prepared his preface to the second edition, a printing of 2,500 books, which appeared on April 22. Many other editions followed. (See Michael Winship's article, 68–76 in this volume, for a detailed publishing history.)

In 1962, Ohio University Press published its definitive *Centenary Edition of the Works of Nathaniel Hawthorne,* of which *The Scarlet Letter* was volume one. The editors regularized the anomalous spellings and punctuation of the first edition to conform with Hawthorne's regular practice and included Hawthorne's preface to the second edition. The text of this New Riverside Edition follows that of the Centenary Edition. All notes are provided by the present volume editor.

Part One

CONTEXTS

STORIES AND NOTEBOOKS

Hawthorne's source material for *The Scarlet Letter* includes three of his own narratives of the 1830s and the notebook entries of the 1840s that appear in Part One of this volume. "Mrs. Hutchinson" (1830)—one of six biographical sketches Hawthorne published in the Salem *Gazette*—centers on the trial of Ann Hutchinson (1591–1643) for preaching the "obnoxious" antinomian doctrine that God's grace rather than good works is the route to salvation. The proud woman "of extraordinary talent and strong imagination" whose Puritan judges banish her from Boston anticipates the fictional Hester Prynne, whose Puritan judges exact punishment for a very different kind of threat to their community. The sketch begins by disparaging "public women" for ignoring the "strong division lines of nature" but then sympathetically dramatizes Mrs. Hutchinson's stalwart self-sufficiency, anticipating Hawthorne's modulated sympathy for Hester's proud self-sufficiency and the two allusions to Mrs. Hutchinson in his novel (120 and 204). Hester is also foreshadowed by the beautiful woman who appears briefly in "Endicott and the Red Cross" (1837)—an adulteress sentenced to wear a scarlet letter on her gown who has so skillfully embroidered it in gold thread "that the A might have been thought to mean Admirable, or any thing rather than Adulteress." And Parson Hooper, the protagonist of "The Minister's Black Veil" (1836), anticipates the minister Arthur Dimmesdale in his obsession with "secret sin" that precludes earthly happiness but transforms him from a good preacher into a great one.

Many of Hawthorne's notebook entries of the 1840s also contain the germs of characters and ideas that his first novel would develop. Three anticipate Chillingworth's destructive relationship with Arthur Dimmesdale. In one, a cold-hearted "investigator" pries into the dark depths of the human soul, "content that it should be wicked"; in another, one man reduces another to "slavery and dependence on him" but discovers that the enslavement is reciprocal. In a third entry, Hawthorne contemplates writing a story about the diabolizing effects of revenge. An 1844 entry speculates about the life of a woman condemned "by old colony law" to wear a scarlet *A* on her dress. For the creation of Hester's daughter Pearl, Hawthorne relied heavily on his 1849 notebook entries that not only describe his daughter Una but also speculate about her inner life.

MRS. HUTCHINSON

The character of this female suggests a train of thought which will form as natural an introduction to her story as most of the prefaces to Gay's Fables[1] or the tales of Prior,[2] besides that the general soundness of the moral may excuse any want of present applicability. We will not look for a living resemblance of Mrs. Hutchinson, though the search might not be altogether fruitless. — But there are portentous indications, changes gradually taking place in the habits and feelings of the gentle sex, which seem to threaten our posterity with many of those public women, whereof one was a burthen too grievous for our fathers. The press, however, is now the medium through which feminine ambition chiefly manifests itself, and we will not anticipate the period, (trusting to be gone hence ere it arrive,) when fair orators shall be as numerous as the fair authors of our own day. The hastiest glance may show, how much of the texture and body of cis-atlantic literature is the work of those slender fingers, from which only a light and fanciful embroidery has heretofore been required, that might sparkle upon the garment without enfeebling the web. Woman's intellect should never give the tone to that of man, and even her morality is not exactly the material for masculine virtue. A false liberality which mistakes the strong division lines of Nature for arbitrary distinctions, and a courtesy, which might polish criticism but should never soften it, have done their best to add a girlish feebleness to the tottering infancy of our literature. The evil is likely to be a growing one. As yet, the great body of American women are a domestic race; but when a continuance of ill-judged incitements shall have turned their hearts away from the fireside, there are obvious circumstances which will render female pens more numerous and more prolific than those of men, though but equally encouraged; and (limited of course by the scanty support of the public, but increasing indefinitely within those limits) the ink-stained Amazons will expel their rivals by actual pressure,

From *Miscellaneous Prose and Verse*. Ed. Thomas Woodson, Claude M. Simpson, and L. Neal Smith. Columbus: Ohio State UP, 1994. (First published in the *Salem Gazette* 7 Dec. 1830.)

[1] John Gay (1688–1732), English poet and playwright, author of *The Beggar's Opera*. [ED.]
[2] Matthew Prior (1664–1721), English poet, essayist, and diplomat. [ED.]

and petticoats wave triumphant over all the field. But, allowing that such forebodings are slightly exaggerated, is it good for woman's self that the path of feverish hope, of tremulous success, of bitter and ignominious disappointment, should be left wide open to her? Is the prize worth her having if she win it? Fame does not increase the peculiar respect which men pay to female excellence, and there is a delicacy, (even in rude bosoms, where few would think to find it) that perceives, or fancies, a sort of impropriety in the display of woman's naked mind to the gaze of the world, with indications by which its inmost secrets may be searched out. In fine, criticism should examine with a stricter, instead of a more indulgent eye, the merits of females at its bar, because they are to justify themselves for an irregularity which men do not commit in appearing there; and woman, when she feels the impulse of genius like a command of Heaven within her, should be aware that she is relinquishing a part of the loveliness of her sex, and obey the inward voice with sorrowing reluctance, like the Arabian maid who bewailed the gift of Prophecy. Hinting thus imperfectly at sentiments which may be developed on a future occasion, we proceed to consider the celebrated subject of this sketch.

Mrs. Hutchinson was a woman of extraordinary talent and strong imagination, whom the latter quality, following the general direction taken by the enthusiasm of the times, prompted to stand forth as a reformer in religion. In her native country, she had shown symptoms of irregular and daring thought, but, chiefly by the influence of a favorite pastor, was restrained from open indiscretion. On the removal of this clergyman, becoming dissatisfied with the ministry under which she lived, she was drawn in by the great tide of Puritan emigration, and visited Massachusetts within a few years after its first settlement. But she bore trouble in her own bosom, and could find no peace in this chosen land. —She soon began to promulgate strange and dangerous opinions, tending, in the peculiar situation of the colony, and from the principles which were its basis and indispensable for its temporary support, to eat into its very existence. We shall endeavor to give a more practical idea of this part of her course.

It is a summer evening. The dusk has settled heavily upon the woods, the waves, and the Trimontane peninsula, increasing that dismal aspect of the embryo town which was said to have drawn tears of despondency from Mrs. Hutchinson, though she believed that her mission thither was divine. The houses, straw-thatched and lowly roofed, stand irregularly along streets that are yet roughened by the roots of the trees, as if the forest, departing at the approach of man, had left its reluctant foot prints behind. Most of the dwellings are lonely and silent; from a few we may hear the reading of some sacred text, or the quiet voice of prayer; but nearly all the sombre life of the scene is collected near the extremity of the village. A crowd of hooded women, and of men in steeple-hats and close cropt hair, are assembled at the door and open windows of a house newly built. An earnest expression glows in every face, and some press inward as if the bread of life were to be dealt forth, and they feared to lose their share, while others would fain hold them back, but enter with them since they may not be restrained. We also will go in, edging through the thronged doorway to an apartment which occupies the whole breadth of the house. At the upper end, behind a table on which are placed the Scriptures and two glimmering lamps, we see a woman, plainly attired as befits her ripened years; her hair, complexion, and eyes are dark, the latter somewhat dull and heavy, but kindling up with a gradual brightness. Let us look round upon the hearers. At her right hand, his countenance suiting well with the gloomy light which discovers it, stands Vane the youthful governor, preferred by a hasty judgment of the people over all the wise and hoary heads that had preceded him to New-England. In his mysterious eyes we may read a dark enthusiasm, akin to that of the woman whose cause he has espoused, combined with a shrewd worldly foresight, which tells him that her doctrines will be productive of change and tumult, the elements of his power and delight. On her left, yet slightly drawn back so as to evince a less decided support, is Cotton, no young and hot enthusiast, but a mild, grave man in the decline of life, deep in all the learning of the age, and sanctified in heart and made venerable in feature by the long exercise of his holy profession. He also is deceived by the strange fire now laid upon the altar, and he alone among his brethren is excepted in the denunciation of the new Apostle, as sealed and set apart by Heaven to the work of the ministry. Others of the priesthood stand full in front of the woman, striving to beat her down with brows of wrinkled iron, and whispering sternly and significantly among themselves, as she unfolds her seditious doctrines and grows warm in their support. Foremost is Hugh Peters, full of holy wrath, and scarce containing himself from rushing forward to convict her of damnable heresies; there also is Ward, meditating a reply of empty puns, and quaint antitheses, and tinkling jests that puzzle us with nothing but a sound. The audience are variously affected, but none indifferent. On the foreheads of the aged, the mature, and strong-minded, you may generally read steadfast disapprobation, though here and there is one, whose faith seems shaken in those whom he had trusted for years; the females, on the other hand, are shuddering and weeping, and at times they cast a desolate look of fear around them; while the young men lean forward, fiery and impatient, fit instruments for whatever rash deed may be suggested. And what is the eloquence that gives rise to all these passions? The woman tells them, (and cites texts from the Holy Book to prove her words,) that they have put their trust in unregenerated and uncommissioned men, and have followed them into the wilderness for naught. Therefore their hearts are turning from those whom they had chosen to lead them to Heaven, and they feel like children who have been enticed far from home, and see the features of their guides change all at once, assuming a fiendish shape in some frightful solitude.

These proceedings of Mrs. Hutchinson could not long be endured by the provincial government. The present was a most remarkable case, in which religious freedom was wholly inconsistent with public safety, and where the principles of an illiberal age indicated the very course which must have been pursued by worldly policy and enlightened wisdom. Unity of faith was the star that had guided these people over the deep, and a diversity of sects would either have scattered them from the land to which they had as yet so few attachments, or perhaps have excited a diminutive civil war among those who had come so far to worship together. The opposition to what may be termed the established church had now lost its chief support, by the removal of Vane from office and his departure for England, and Mr. Cotton began to have that light in regard to his errors, which will sometimes break in upon the wisest and most pious men, when their opinions are unhappily discordant with those of the Powers that be. A Synod, the first in New England, was speedily assembled, and pronounced its condemnation of the obnoxious doctrines. Mrs. Hutchinson was next summoned before the supreme civil tribunal, at which, however, the most eminent of the clergy were present, and appear to have taken a very active part as witnesses and advisers. We shall here resume the more picturesque style of narration.

It is a place of humble aspect where the Elders of the people are met, sitting in judgment upon the disturber of Israel. The floor of the low and narrow hall is laid with planks hewn by the axe, —the beams of the roof still wear the rugged bark with which they grew up in the forest, and the hearth is formed of one broad unhammered stone, heaped with logs that roll their blaze and smoke up a chimney of wood and clay. A sleety shower beats fitfully against the windows, driven by the November blast, which comes howling onward from the northern desert, the boisterous and unwelcome herald of a New England winter. Rude benches are arranged across the apartment and along its sides, occupied by men whose piety and learning might have entitled them to seats in those high Councils of the ancient Church, whence opinions were sent forth to confirm or supersede the Gospel in the belief of the whole world and of posterity.—Here are collected all those blessed Fathers of the land, who rank in our veneration next to the Evangelists of Holy Writ, and here also are many, unpurified from the fiercest errors of the age and ready to propagate the religion of peace by violence. In the highest place sits Winthrop, a man by whom the innocent and the guilty might alike desire to be judged, the first confiding in his integrity and wisdom, the latter hoping in his mildness. Next is Endicott, who would stand with his drawn sword at the gate of Heaven, and resist to the death all pilgrims thither, except they travelled his own path. The infant eyes of one in this assembly beheld the faggots blazing round the martyrs, in bloody Mary's time; in later life he dwelt long at Leyden, with the first who went from England for conscience sake; and now, in his weary age, it matters little where he lies down to die. There are others whose hearts were smitten in the high meridian of ambitious hope, and whose dreams still tempt them with the pomp of the old world and the din of its crowded cities, gleaming and echoing over the deep. In the midst, and in the centre of all eyes, we see the Woman. She stands loftily before her judges, with a determined brow, and, unknown to herself, there is a flash of carnal pride half hidden in her eye, as she surveys the many learned and famous men whom her doctrines have put in fear. They question her, and her answers are ready and acute; she reasons with them shrewdly, and brings Scripture in support of every argument; the deepest controversialists of that scholastic day find here a woman, whom all their trained and sharpened intellects are inadequate to foil. But by the excitement of the contest, her heart is made to rise and swell within her, and she bursts forth into eloquence. She tells them of the long unquietness which she had endured in England, perceiving the corruption of the church, and yearning for a purer and more perfect light, and how, in a day of solitary prayer, that light was given; she claims for herself the peculiar power of distinguishing between the chosen of man and the Sealed of Heaven, and affirms that her gifted eye can see the glory round the foreheads of the Saints, sojourning in their mortal state. She declares herself commissioned to separate the true shepherds from the false, and denounces present and future judgments on the land, if she be disturbed in her celestial errand. Thus the accusations are proved from her own mouth. Her judges hesitate, and some speak faintly in her defence; but, with a few dissenting voices, sentence is pronounced, bidding her go out from among them, and trouble the land no more.

Mrs. Hutchinson's adherents throughout the colony were now disarmed, and she proceeded to Rhode Island, an accustomed refuge for the exiles of Massachusetts, in all seasons of persecution. Her enemies believed that the anger of Heaven was following her, of which Governor Winthrop does not disdain to record a notable instance, very interesting in a scientific point of view, but fitter for his old and homely narrative than for modern repetition. In a little time, also, she lost her husband, who is mentioned in history only as attending her footsteps, and whom we may conclude to have been (like most husbands of celebrated women) a mere insignificant appendage of his mightier wife. She now grew uneasy among the Rhode-Island colonists, whose liberality towards her, at an era when liberality was not esteemed a Christian virtue, probably arose from a comparative inso-licitude on religious matters, more distasteful to Mrs. Hutchinson than even the uncompromising narrowness of the Puritans. Her final move-ment was to lead her family within the limits of the Dutch Jurisdiction, where, having felled the trees of a virgin soil, she became herself the virtual head, civil and ecclesiastical, of a little colony.

Perhaps here she found the repose, hitherto so vainly sought. Secluded from all whose faith she could not govern, surrounded by the dependents over whom she held an unlimited influence, agitated by none of the tu-multuous billows which were left swelling behind her, we may suppose, that, in the stillness of Nature, her heart was stilled. But her impressive story was to have an awful close. Her last scene is as difficult to be portrayed as a shipwreck, where the shrieks of the victims die unheard along a deso-late sea, and a shapeless mass of agony is all that can be brought home to the imagination. The savage foe was on the watch for blood. Sixteen per-sons assembled at the evening prayer; in the deep midnight, their cry rang through the forest; and daylight dawned upon the lifeless clay of all but one. It was a circumstance not to be unnoticed by our stern ancestors, in considering the fate of her who had so troubled their religion, that an infant daughter, the sole survivor amid the terrible destruction of her mother's household, was bred in a barbarous faith, and never learned the way to the Christian's Heaven. Yet we will hope, that there the mother and the child have met.

THE MINISTER'S BLACK VEIL

A Parable[1]

The sexton stood in the porch of Milford[2] meetinghouse, pulling lustily at the bell rope. The old people of the village came stooping along the street. Children, with bright faces, tript merrily beside their parents, or mimicked a graver gait, in the conscious dignity of their Sunday clothes.

From *Twice-Told Tales*. Ed. Bill Ellis and Claude M. Simpson. Columbus: Ohio State UP, 1974. (First published in the *Token* [1836] and included in *Twice-Told Tales* [1837].)

[1] "Another clergyman in New England, Mr. Joseph Moody, of York, Maine, who died about eighty years since, made himself remarkable by the same eccentricity that is here related of the Reverend Mr. Hooper. In his case, however, the symbol had a different im-port. In early life he had accidentally killed a beloved friend; and from that day till the hour of his own death, he hid his face from men." [Hawthorne's note.]
[2] A town southwest of Boston. [ED.]

Spruce bachelors looked sidelong at the pretty maidens, and fancied that the Sabbath sunshine made them prettier than on weekdays. When the throng had mostly streamed into the porch, the sexton began to toll the bell, keeping his eye on the Reverend Mr. Hooper's door. The first glimpse of the clergyman's figure was the signal for the bell to cease its summons.

"But what has good Parson Hooper got upon his face?" cried the sexton in astonishment.

All within hearing immediately turned about, and beheld the semblance of Mr. Hooper, pacing slowly his meditative way towards the meeting-house. With one accord they started, expressing more wonder than if some strange minister were coming to dust the cushions of Mr. Hooper's pulpit.

"Are you sure it is our parson?" inquired Goodman Gray of the sexton.

"Of a certainty it is good Mr. Hooper," replied the sexton. "He was to have exchanged pulpits with Parson Shute of Westbury; but Parson Shute sent to excuse himself yesterday, being to preach a funeral sermon."

The cause of so much amazement may appear sufficiently slight. Mr. Hooper, a gentlemanly person of about thirty, though still a bachelor, was dressed with due clerical neatness, as if a careful wife had starched his band, and brushed the weekly dust from his Sunday's garb. There was but one thing remarkable in his appearance. Swathed about his forehead, and hanging down over his face, so low as to be shaken by his breath, Mr. Hooper had on a black veil. On a nearer view, it seemed to consist of two folds of crape, which entirely concealed his features, except the mouth and chin, but probably did not intercept his sight, farther than to give a darkened aspect to all living and inanimate things. With this gloomy shade before him, good Mr. Hooper walked onward, at a slow and quiet pace, stooping somewhat and looking on the ground, as is customary with abstracted men, yet nodding kindly to those of his parishioners who still waited on the meeting-house steps. But so wonder-struck were they, that his greeting hardly met with a return.

"I can't really feel as if good Mr. Hooper's face was behind that piece of crape," said the sexton.

"I don't like it," muttered an old woman, as she hobbled into the meeting-house. "He has changed himself into something awful, only by hiding his face."

"Our parson has gone mad!" cried Goodman Gray, following him across the threshold.

A rumor of some unaccountable phenomenon had preceded Mr. Hooper into the meeting-house, and set all the congregation astir. Few could refrain from twisting their heads towards the door; many stood upright, and turned directly about; while several little boys clambered upon the seats, and came down again with a terrible racket. There was a general bustle, a rustling of the women's gowns and shuffling of the men's feet, greatly at variance with that hushed repose which should attend the entrance of the minister. But Mr. Hooper appeared not to notice the perturbation of his people. He entered with an almost noiseless step, bent his head mildly to the pews on each side, and bowed as he passed his oldest parishioner, a white haired great-grandsire, who occupied an arm-chair in the centre of the aisle. It was strange to observe, how slowly this venerable man became conscious of something singular in the appearance of his pastor. He seemed not fully to partake of the prevailing wonder, till Mr. Hooper had ascended the stairs, and showed himself in the pulpit, face to face with his congregation, except for the black veil. That mysterious emblem was never once withdrawn. It shook with his measured breath as he gave out the psalm; it threw its obscurity between him and the holy page, as he read the Scriptures; and while he prayed, the veil lay heavily on his uplifted countenance. Did he seek to hide it from the dread Being whom he was addressing?

Such was the effect of this simple piece of crape, that more than one woman of delicate nerves was forced to leave the meeting-house. Yet perhaps the pale-faced congregation was almost as fearful a sight to the minister, as his black veil to them.

Mr. Hooper had the reputation of a good preacher, but not an energetic one: he strove to win his people heavenward, by mild persuasive influences, rather than to drive them thither, by the thunders of the Word. The sermon which he now delivered, was marked by the same characteristics of style and manner, as the general series of his pulpit oratory. But there was something, either in the sentiment of the discourse itself, or in the imagination of the auditors, which made it greatly the most powerful effort that they had ever heard from their pastor's lips. It was tinged, rather more darkly than usual, with the gentle gloom of Mr. Hooper's temperament. The subject had reference to secret sin, and those sad mysteries which we hide from our nearest and dearest, and would fain conceal from our own consciousness, even forgetting that the Omniscient can detect them. A subtle power was breathed into his words. Each member of the congregation, the most innocent girl, and the man of hardened breast, felt as if the preacher had crept upon them, behind his awful veil, and discovered their hoarded iniquity of deed or thought. Many spread their clasped hands on their bosoms. There was nothing terrible in what Mr. Hooper said; at least, no violence; and yet, with every tremor of his melancholy voice, the hearers quaked. An unsought pathos came hand in hand with awe. So sensible were the audience of some unwonted attribute in their minister, that they longed for a breath of wind to blow aside the veil, almost believing that a stranger's visage would be discovered, though the form, gesture, and voice were those of Mr. Hooper.

At the close of the services, the people hurried out with indecorous confusion, eager to communicate their pent-up amazement, and conscious of lighter spirits, the moment they lost sight of the black veil. Some gathered in little circles, huddled closely together, with their mouths all whispering in the centre; some went homeward alone, wrapt in silent meditation; some talked loudly, and profaned the Sabbath-day with ostentatious laughter. A few shook their sagacious heads, intimating that they could penetrate the mystery; while one or two affirmed that there was no mystery at all, but only that Mr. Hooper's eyes were so weakened by the midnight lamp, as to require a shade. After a brief interval, forth came good Mr. Hooper also, in the rear of his flock. Turning his veiled face from one group to another, he paid due reverence to the hoary heads, saluted the middle-aged with kind dignity, as their friend and spiritual guide, greeted the young with mingled authority and love, and laid his hands on the little children's heads to bless them. Such was always his custom on the Sabbath-day. Strange and bewildered looks repaid him for his courtesy. None, as on former occasions, aspired to the honor of walking by their pastor's side. Old Squire Saunders, doubtless by an accidental lapse of memory, neglected to invite Mr. Hooper to his table, where the good clergyman had been wont to bless the food, almost every Sunday since his settlement. He returned, therefore, to the parsonage, and, at the moment of closing the door, was observed to look back upon the people, all of whom had their eyes fixed upon the minister. A sad smile gleamed faintly from beneath the black veil, and flickered about his mouth, glimmering as he disappeared.

"How strange," said a lady, "that a simple black veil, such as any woman might wear on her bonnet, should become such a terrible thing on Mr. Hooper's face!"

"Something must surely be amiss with Mr. Hooper's intellects," observed her husband, the physician of the village. "But the strangest part of the affair is the effect of this vagary, even on a sober-minded man like myself. The black veil, though it covers only our pastor's face, throws its influence over his whole person, and makes him ghost-like from head to foot. Do you not feel it so?"

"Truly do I," replied the lady; "and I would not be alone with him for the world. I wonder he is not afraid to be alone with himself!"

"Men sometimes are so," said her husband.

The afternoon service was attended with similar circumstances. At its conclusion, the bell tolled for the funeral of a young lady. The relatives and friends were assembled in the house, and the more distant acquaintances stood about the door, speaking of the good qualities of the deceased, when their talk was interrupted by the appearance of Mr. Hooper, still covered with his black veil. It was now an appropriate emblem. The clergyman stepped into the room where the corpse was laid, and bent over the coffin, to take a last farewell of his deceased parishioner. As he stooped, the veil hung straight down from his forehead, so that, if her eye-lids had not been closed for ever, the dead maiden might have seen his face. Could Mr. Hooper be fearful of her glance, that he so hastily caught back the black veil? A person, who watched the interview between the dead and living, scrupled not to affirm, that, at the instant when the clergyman's features were disclosed, the corpse had slightly shuddered, rustling the shroud and muslin cap, though the countenance retained the composure of death. A superstitious old woman was the only witness of this prodigy. From the coffin, Mr. Hooper passed into the chamber of the mourners, and thence to the head of the staircase, to make the funeral prayer. It was a tender and heart-dissolving prayer, full of sorrow, yet so imbued with celestial hopes, that the music of a heavenly harp, swept by the fingers of the dead, seemed faintly to be heard among the saddest accents of the minister. The people trembled, though they but darkly understood him, when he prayed that they, and himself, and all of mortal race, might be ready, as he trusted this young maiden had been, for the dreadful hour that should snatch the veil from their faces. The bearers went heavily forth, and the mourners followed, saddening all the street, with the dead before them, and Mr. Hooper in his black veil behind.

"Why do you look back?" said one in the procession to his partner.

"I had a fancy," replied she, "that the minister and the maiden's spirit were walking hand in hand."

"And so had I, at the same moment," said the other.

That night, the handsomest couple in Milford village were to be joined in wedlock. Though reckoned a melancholy man, Mr. Hooper had a placid cheerfulness for such occasions, which often excited a sympathetic smile, where livelier merriment would have been thrown away. There was no quality of his disposition which made him more beloved than this. The company at the wedding awaited his arrival with impatience, trusting that the strange awe, which had gathered over him throughout the day, would now be dispelled. But such was not the result. When Mr. Hooper came, the first thing that their eyes rested on was the same horrible black veil, which had added deeper gloom to the funeral, and could portend nothing but evil to the wedding. Such was its immediate effect on the guests, that a cloud seemed to have rolled duskily from beneath the black crape, and dimmed the light of the candles. The bridal pair stood up before the minister. But the bride's cold fingers quivered in the tremulous hand of the bridegroom, and her deathlike paleness caused a whisper, that the maiden who had been buried a few hours before, was come from her grave to be married. If ever another wedding were so dismal, it was that famous one, where they tolled the wedding-knell.[3] After performing the ceremony, Mr. Hooper raised a glass of wine to his lips, wishing happiness to the new-married couple, in a strain of mild pleasantry that ought to have brightened the features of the guests, like a cheerful gleam from the hearth. At that instant, catching a glimpse of his figure in the looking-glass, the black veil involved his own spirit in the horror with which it overwhelmed all others. His frame shuddered—his lips grew white—he spilt the untasted wine upon the carpet—and rushed forth into the darkness. For the Earth, too, had on her Black Veil.

The next day, the whole village of Milford talked of little else than Parson Hooper's black veil. That, and the mystery concealed behind it, supplied a topic for discussion between acquaintances meeting in the street, and good women gossiping at their open windows. It was the first item of news that the tavern-keeper told to his guests. The children babbled of it on their way to school. One imitative little imp covered his face with an old black handkerchief, thereby so affrighting his playmates, that the panic seized himself, and he well nigh lost his wits by his own waggery.

It was remarkable, that, of all the busy-bodies and impertinent people in the parish, not one ventured to put the plain question to Mr. Hooper, wherefore he did this thing. Hitherto, whenever there appeared the slightest call for such interference, he had never lacked advisers, nor shown himself averse to be guided by their judgment. If he erred at all, it was by so painful a degree of self-distrust, that even the mildest censure would lead him to consider an indifferent action as a crime. Yet, though so well acquainted with this amiable weakness, no individual among his parishioners chose to make the black veil a subject of friendly remonstrance. There was a feeling of dread, neither plainly confessed nor carefully concealed, which caused each to shift the responsibility upon another, till at length it was found expedient to send a deputation of the church, in order to deal with Mr. Hooper about the mystery, before it should grow into a scandal. Never did an embassy so ill discharge its duties. The minister received them with friendly courtesy, but became silent, after they were seated, leaving to his visiters the whole burthen of introducing their important business. The topic, it might be supposed, was obvious enough. There was the black veil, swathed round Mr. Hooper's forehead, and concealing every feature above

---

[3] Hawthorne's story "The Wedding Knell," also published in the 1836 *Token* and included in *Twice-Told Tales.* [ED.]

his placid mouth, on which, at times, they could perceive the glimmering of a melancholy smile. But that piece of crape, to their imagination, seemed to hang down before his heart, the symbol of a fearful secret between him and them. Were the veil but cast aside, they might speak freely of it, but not till then. Thus they sat a considerable time, speechless, confused, and shrinking uneasily from Mr. Hooper's eye, which they felt to be fixed upon them with an invisible glance. Finally, the deputies returned abashed to their constituents, pronouncing the matter too weighty to be handled, except by a council of the churches, if, indeed, it might not require a general synod.

But there was one person in the village, unappalled by the awe with which the black veil had impressed all beside herself. When the deputies returned without an explanation, or even venturing to demand one, she, with the calm energy of her character, determined to chase away the strange cloud that appeared to be settling round Mr. Hooper, every moment more darkly than before. As his plighted wife, it should be her privilege to know what the black veil concealed. At the minister's first visit, therefore, she entered upon the subject, with a direct simplicity, which made the task easier both for him and her. After he had seated himself, she fixed her eyes steadfastly upon the veil, but could discern nothing of the dreadful gloom that had so overawed the multitude: it was but a double fold of crape, hanging down from his forehead to his mouth, and slightly stirring with his breath.

"No," said she aloud, and smiling, "there is nothing terrible in this piece of crape, except that it hides a face which I am always glad to look upon. Come, good sir, let the sun shine from behind the cloud. First lay aside your black veil: then tell me why you put it on."

Mr. Hooper's smile glimmered faintly.

"There is an hour to come," said he, "when all of us shall cast aside our veils. Take it not amiss, beloved friend, if I wear this piece of crape till then."

"Your words are a mystery too," returned the young lady. "Take away the veil from them, at least."

"Elizabeth, I will," said he, "so far as my vow may suffer me. Know, then, this veil is a type and a symbol, and I am bound to wear it ever, both in light and darkness, in solitude and before the gaze of multitudes, and as with strangers, so with my familiar friends. No mortal eye will see it withdrawn. This dismal shade must separate me from the world: even you, Elizabeth, can never come behind it!"

"What grievous affliction hath befallen you," she earnestly inquired, "that you should thus darken your eyes for ever?"

"If it be a sign of mourning," replied Mr. Hooper, "I, perhaps, like most other mortals, have sorrows dark enough to be typified by a black veil."

"But what if the world will not believe that it is the type of an innocent sorrow?" urged Elizabeth. "Beloved and respected as you are, there may be whispers, that you hide your face under the consciousness of secret sin. For the sake of your holy office, do away this scandal!"

The color rose into her cheeks, as she intimated the nature of the rumors that were already abroad in the village. But Mr. Hooper's mildness did not forsake him. He even smiled again — that same sad smile, which always appeared like a faint glimmering of light, proceeding from the obscurity beneath the veil.

"If I hide my face for sorrow, there is cause enough," he merely replied; "and if I cover it for secret sin, what mortal might not do the same?"

And with this gentle, but unconquerable obstinacy, did he resist all her entreaties. At length Elizabeth sat silent. For a few moments she appeared lost in thought, considering, probably, what new methods might be tried, to withdraw her lover from so dark a fantasy, which, if it had no other meaning, was perhaps a symptom of mental disease. Though of a firmer character than his own, the tears rolled down her cheeks. But, in an instant, as it were, a new feeling took the place of sorrow: her eyes were fixed insensibly on the black veil, when, like a sudden twilight in the air, its terrors fell around her. She arose, and stood trembling before him.

"And do you feel it then at last?" said he mournfully.

She made no reply, but covered her eyes with her hand, and turned to leave the room. He rushed forward and caught her arm.

"Have patience with me, Elizabeth!" cried he passionately. "Do not desert me, though this veil must be between us here on earth. Be mine, and hereafter there shall be no veil over my face, no darkness between our souls! It is but a mortal veil — it is not for eternity! Oh! you know not how lonely I am, and how frightened to be alone behind my black veil. Do not leave me in this miserable obscurity for ever!"

"Lift the veil but once, and look me in the face," said she.

"Never! It cannot be!" replied Mr. Hooper.

"Then, farewell!" said Elizabeth.

She withdrew her arm from his grasp, and slowly departed, pausing at the door, to give one long, shuddering gaze, that seemed almost to penetrate the mystery of the black veil. But, even amid his grief, Mr. Hooper smiled to think that only a material emblem had separated him from happiness, though the horrors which it shadowed forth, must be drawn darkly between the fondest of lovers.

From that time no attempts were made to remove Mr. Hooper's black veil, or, by a direct appeal, to discover the secret which it was supposed to hide. By persons who claimed a superiority to popular prejudice, it was reckoned merely an eccentric whim, such as often mingles with the sober

actions of men otherwise rational, and tinges them all with its own semblance of insanity. But with the multitude, good Mr. Hooper was irreparably a bugbear. He could not walk the streets with any peace of mind, so
conscious was he that the gentle and timid would turn aside to avoid him,
and that others would make it a point of hardihood to throw themselves in
his way. The impertinence of the latter class compelled him to give up his
customary walk, at sunset, to the burial ground; for when he leaned pen-
sively over the gate, there would always be faces behind the grave-stones,
peeping at his black veil. A fable went the rounds, that the stare of the dead
people drove him thence. It grieved him, to the very depth of his kind
heart, to observe how the children fled from his approach, breaking up
their merriest sports, while his melancholy figure was yet afar off. Their instinctive dread caused him to feel, more strongly than aught else, that a
preternatural horror was interwoven with the threads of the black crape. In
truth, his own antipathy to the veil was known to be so great, that he never
willingly passed before a mirror, nor stooped to drink at a still fountain,
lest, in its peaceful bosom, he should be affrighted by himself. This was
what gave plausibility to the whispers, that Mr. Hooper's conscience tortured him for some great crime, too horrible to be entirely concealed, or
otherwise than so obscurely intimated. Thus, from beneath the black veil,
there rolled a cloud into the sunshine, an ambiguity of sin or sorrow, which
enveloped the poor minister, so that love or sympathy could never reach
him. It was said, that ghost and fiend consorted with him there. With self-
shudderings and outward terrors, he walked continually in its shadow,
groping darkly within his own soul, or gazing through a medium that saddened the whole world. Even the lawless wind, it was believed, respected his
dreadful secret, and never blew aside the veil. But still good Mr. Hooper
sadly smiled, at the pale visages of the worldly throng as he passed by.

Among all its bad influences, the black veil had the one desirable effect,
of making its wearer a very efficient clergyman. By the aid of his mysterious emblem — for there was no other apparent cause — he became a man of
awful power, over souls that were in agony for sin. His converts always regarded him with a dread peculiar to themselves, affirming, though but figuratively, that, before he brought them to celestial light, they had been with
him behind the black veil. Its gloom, indeed, enabled him to sympathize
with all dark affections. Dying sinners cried aloud for Mr. Hooper, and
would not yield their breath till he appeared; though ever, as he stooped to
whisper consolation, they shuddered at the veiled face so near their own.
Such were the terrors of the black veil, even when Death had bared his visage! Strangers came long distances to attend service at his church, with the
mere idle purpose of gazing at his figure, because it was forbidden them to
behold his face. But many were made to quake ere they departed! Once,

during Governor Belcher's administration, Mr. Hooper was appointed to preach the election sermon.[4] Covered with his black veil, he stood before the chief magistrate, the council, and the representatives, and wrought so deep an impression, that the legislative measures of that year, were characterized by all the gloom and piety of our earliest ancestral sway.

In this manner Mr. Hooper spent a long life, irreproachable in outward act, yet shrouded in dismal suspicions; kind and loving, though unloved, and dimly feared; a man apart from men, shunned in their health and joy, but ever summoned to their aid in mortal anguish. As years wore on, shedding their snows above his sable veil, he acquired a name throughout the New-England churches, and they called him Father Hooper. Nearly all his parishioners, who were of mature age when he was settled, had been borne away by many a funeral: he had one congregation in the church, and a more crowded one in the church-yard; and having wrought so late into the evening, and done his work so well, it was now good Father Hooper's turn to rest.

Several persons were visible by the shaded candlelight, in the death-chamber of the old clergyman. Natural connections he had none. But there was the decorously grave, though unmoved physician, seeking only to mitigate the last pangs of the patient whom he could not save. There were the deacons, and other eminently pious members of his church. There, also, was the Reverend Mr. Clark, of Westbury, a young and zealous divine, who had ridden in haste to pray by the bed-side of the expiring minister. There was the nurse, no hired handmaiden of death, but one whose calm affection had endured thus long, in secresy, in solitude, amid the chill of age, and would not perish, even at the dying hour. Who, but Elizabeth! And there lay the hoary head of good Father Hooper upon the death-pillow, with the black veil still swathed about his brow and reaching down over his face, so that each more difficult gasp of his faint breath caused it to stir. All through life that piece of crape had hung between him and the world: it had separated him from cheerful brotherhood and woman's love, and kept him in that saddest of all prisons, his own heart; and still it lay upon his face, as if to deepen the gloom of his darksome chamber, and shade him from the sunshine of eternity.

For some time previous, his mind had been confused, wavering doubtfully between the past and the present, and hovering forward, as it were, at

---

[4]Jonathan Belcher (1682–1757) was Governor of both Massachusetts and New Hampshire between 1730 and 1741, which sets Hawthorne's story during the period of religious fervor known as "The Great Awakening." The annual election sermon was delivered by an eminent minister to solemnize the inauguration of a newly elected governor. [Ed.]

intervals, into the indistinctness of the world to come. There had been feverish turns, which tossed him from side to side, and wore away what little strength he had. But in his most convulsive struggles, and in the wildest vagaries of his intellect, when no other thought retained its sober influence, he still showed an awful solicitude lest the black veil should slip aside. Even if his bewildered soul could have forgotten, there was a faithful woman at his pillow, who, with averted eyes, would have covered that aged face, which she had last beheld in the comeliness of manhood. At length the death-stricken old man lay quietly in the torpor of mental and bodily exhaustion, with an imperceptible pulse, and breath that grew fainter and fainter, except when a long, deep, and irregular inspiration seemed to prelude the flight of his spirit.

The minister of Westbury approached the bedside.

"Venerable Father Hooper," said he, "the moment of your release is at hand. Are you ready for the lifting of the veil, that shuts in time from eternity?"

Father Hooper at first replied merely by a feeble motion of his head; then, apprehensive, perhaps, that his meaning might be doubtful, he exerted himself to speak.

"Yea," said he, in faint accents, "my soul hath a patient weariness until that veil be lifted."

"And is it fitting," resumed the Reverend Mr. Clark, "that a man so given to prayer, of such a blameless example, holy in deed and thought, so far as mortal judgment may pronounce; is it fitting that a father in the church should leave a shadow on his memory, that may seem to blacken a life so pure? I pray you, my venerable brother, let not this thing be! Suffer us to be gladdened by your triumphant aspect, as you go to your reward. Before the veil of eternity be lifted, let me cast aside this black veil from your face!"

And thus speaking, the Reverend Mr. Clark bent forward to reveal the mystery of so many years. But, exerting a sudden energy, that made all the beholders stand aghast, Father Hooper snatched both his hands from beneath the bed-clothes, and pressed them strongly on the black veil, resolute to struggle, if the minister of Westbury would contend with a dying man.

"Never!" cried the veiled clergyman. "On earth, never!"

"Dark old man!" exclaimed the affrighted minister, "with what horrible crime upon your soul are you now passing to the judgment?"

Father Hooper's breath heaved; it rattled in his throat; but, with a mighty effort, grasping forward with his hands, he caught hold of life, and held it back till he should speak. He even raised himself in bed; and there he sat, shivering with the arms of death around him, while the black veil hung down, awful, at that last moment, in the gathered terrors of a

life-time. And yet the faint, sad smile, so often there, now seemed to glimmer from its obscurity, and linger on Father Hooper's lips.

"Why do you tremble at me alone?" cried he, turning his veiled face
round the circle of pale spectators. "Tremble also at each other! Have men
avoided me, and women shown no pity, and children screamed and fled,
only for my black veil? What, but the mystery which it obscurely typifies,
has made this piece of crape so awful? When the friend shows his inmost
heart to his friend; the lover to his best-beloved; when man does not vainly
shrink from the eye of his Creator, loathsomely treasuring up the secret of
his sin; then deem me a monster, for the symbol beneath which I have
lived, and die! I look around me, and, lo! on every visage a Black Veil!"

While his auditors shrank from one another, in mutual affright,
Father Hooper fell back upon his pillow, a veiled corpse, with a faint smile
lingering on the lips. Still veiled, they laid him in his coffin, and a veiled
corpse they bore him to the grave. The grass of many years has sprung up
and withered on that grave, the burial-stone is moss-grown, and good
Mr. Hooper's face is dust; but awful is still the thought, that it mouldered
beneath the Black Veil!

From ENDICOTT AND THE RED CROSS

At noon of an autumnal day, more than two centuries ago, the English colors were displayed by the standard-bearer of the Salem trainband, which
had mustered for martial exercise under the orders of John Endicott. It was
a period, when the religious exiles were accustomed often to buckle on
their armour, and practise the handling of their weapons of war. Since the
first settlement of New England, its prospects had never been so dismal.
The dissensions between Charles the First and his subjects were then, and
for several years afterwards, confined to the floor of Parliament. The measures of the King and ministry were rendered more tyrannically violent by
an opposition, which had not yet acquired sufficient confidence in its own
strength, to resist royal injustice with the sword. The bigoted and haughty
primate, Laud, Archbishop of Canterbury, controlled the religious affairs
of the realm, and was consequently invested with powers which might have
wrought the utter ruin of the two Puritan colonies, Plymouth and Massachusetts. There is evidence on record, that our forefathers perceived their

---

From *Twice-Told Tales*. Ed. Bill Ellis and Claude M. Simpson. Columbus:
Ohio State UP, 1974. (First published in the 1838 *Token* and republished in
the second edition of *Twice-Told Tales* [1842]).

danger, but were resolved that their infant country should not fall without a struggle, even beneath the giant strength of the King's right arm.

Such was the aspect of the times, when the folds of the English banner, with the Red Cross in its field, were flung out over a company of Puritans. Their leader, the famous Endicott, was a man of stern and resolute countenance, the effect of which was heightened by a grizzled beard that swept the upper portion of his breastplate. This piece of armour was so highly polished, that the whole surrounding scene had its image in the glittering steel. The central object, in the mirrored picture, was an edifice of humble architecture, with neither steeple nor bell to proclaim it, —what nevertheless it was, —the house of prayer. A token of the perils of the wilderness was seen in the grim head of a wolf, which had just been slain within the precincts of the town, and, according to the regular mode of claiming the bounty, was nailed on the porch of the meetinghouse. The blood was still plashing on the door-step. There happened to be visible, at the same noontide hour, so many other characteristics of the times and manners of the Puritans, that we must endeavour to represent them in a sketch, though far less vividly than they were reflected in the polished breastplate of John Endicott.

In close vicinity to the sacred edifice appeared that important engine of Puritanic authority, the whipping-post, —with the soil around it well trodden by the feet of evil-doers, who had there been disciplined. At one corner of the meetinghouse was the pillory, and at the other the stocks; and, by a singular good fortune for our sketch, the head of an Episcopalian and suspected Catholic was grotesquely encased in the former machine; while a fellow-criminal, who had boisterously quaffed a health to the King, was confined by the legs in the latter. Side by side, on the meetinghouse steps, stood a male and a female figure. The man was a tall, lean, haggard personification of fanaticism, bearing on his breast this label, —A Wanton Gospeller, —which betokened that he had dared to give interpretations of Holy Writ, unsanctioned by the infallible judgment of the civil and religious rulers. His aspect showed no lack of zeal to maintain his heterodoxies, even at the stake. The woman wore a cleft stick on her tongue, in appropriate retribution for having wagged that unruly member against the elders of the church; and her countenance and gestures gave much cause to apprehend, that, the moment the stick should be removed, a repetition of the offence would demand new ingenuity in chastising it.

The abovementioned individuals had been sentenced to undergo their various modes of ignominy, for the space of one hour at noonday. But among the crowd were several, whose punishment would be life-long; some, whose ears had been cropt, like those of puppy-dogs; others, whose cheeks had been branded with the initials of their misdemeanors; one, with his nostrils slit and seared; and another, with a halter about his neck, which he was forbidden ever to take off, or to conceal beneath his garments. Methinks he must have been grievously tempted to affix the other end of the rope to some convenient beam or bough. There was likewise a young woman, with no mean share of beauty, whose doom it was to wear the letter A on the breast of her gown, in the eyes of all the world and her own children. And even her own children knew what that initial signified. Sporting with her infamy, the lost and desperate creature had embroidered the fatal token in scarlet cloth, with golden thread, and the nicest art of needle-work; so that the capital A might have been thought to mean Admirable, or any thing rather than Adulteress.

Let not the reader argue, from any of these evidences of iniquity, that the times of the Puritans were more vicious than our own, when, as we pass along the very street of this sketch, we discern no badge of infamy on man or woman. It was the policy of our ancestors to search out even the most secret sins, and expose them to shame, without fear or favor, in the broadest light of the noonday sun. Were such the custom now, perchance we might find materials for a no less piquant sketch than the above.[. . .]

From THE AMERICAN NOTEBOOKS

[ca 27 July 1844]

The Unpardonable Sin might consist in a want of love and reverence for the Human Soul; in consequence of which, the investigator pried into its dark depths, not with a hope or purpose of making it better, but from a cold philosophical curosity, — content that it should be wicked in what ever kind or degree, and only desiring to study it out. Would not this, in other words, be the separation of the intellect from the heart?

[ca 27 July 1844]

Sketch of a person, who, by strength of character, or assistant circumstances, has reduced another to absolute slavery and dependence on him. Then show, that the person who appears to be the master, must inevitably be at least as much a slave, if not more, than the other. All slavery is reciprocal, on the supposition most favorable to the rulers.

From *The American Notebooks*. Ed. Claude M. Simpson. Columbus: Ohio State UP, 1972.

[ca 27 July 1844]

The life of a woman, who, by the old colony law, was condemned always to wear the letter A, sewed on her garment, in token of her having committed adultery.

[17 November 1847]

A story of the effects of revenge, in diabolizing him who indulges in it.

[28 January 1849]

[Una's] natural bent is towards the passionate and tragic. Her life, at present, is a tempestuous day, with blinks of sunshine gushing between the rifts of cloud; she is as full oftentimes of acerbity as an unripe apple, that may be perfected to a mellow deliciousness hereafter [...].

Her beauty is the most flitting, transitory, most uncertain and unaccountable affair, that ever had a real existence; it beams out when nobody expects it; it has mysteriously passed away, when you think yourself sure of it—if you glance sideways at her, you perhaps think it is illuminating her face, but, turning full round to enjoy it, it is gone again.... When really visible, it is rare and precious as the vision of an angel; it is a transfiguration—a grace, delicacy, an ethereal fineness, which, at once, in my secret soul, makes me give up all severe opinions that I may have begun to form respecting her. It is but fair to conclude, that, on these occasions, we see her real soul; when she seems less lovely, we merely see something external. But, in truth, one manifestation belongs to her as much as another; for, before the establishment of principles, what is character but the series and succession of moods? [...]

[30 July 1849]

[...] But, to return to Una, there is something that almost frightens me about the child—I know not whether elfish or angelic, but, at all events, supernatural. She steps so boldly into the midst of everything, shrinks from nothing, has such a comprehension of everything, seems at times to have but little delicacy, and anon shows that she possesses the finest essence of it; now so hard, now so tender; now so perfectly unreasonable, soon again so wise. In short, I now and then catch an aspect of her, in which I cannot believe her to be my own human child, but a spirit strangely mingled with good and evil, haunting the house where I dwell. [...]

LETTERS

In the first of the four letters excerpted in this section, Hawthorne tried to prevent his dismissal as chief executive officer of the Salem custom house following the Whigs' access to political power in March 1849. Writing to his friend George Hillard, a Boston lawyer and an influential Whig, Hawthorne made the case for his retention on the grounds that he had been hired as a man of letters and not a politician, an argument that he asked Hillard to disseminate. In its cannily selective self-presentation, the letter anticipates not only Hawthorne's subsequent campaign to retain his job but also his account of the entire episode in "The Custom-House."

The next three letters concern the final shaping of *The Scarlet Letter* and Hawthorne's ambivalence about its reception. The letter of 15 January 1850 to his publisher James T. Fields reveals that he wrote "The Custom-House" before completing the long narrative that he thought would make up about half of a new collection of stories. Though the subject of his new tale was "delicate," he thought his treatment of it precluded "objections on that score." Five days later, he yielded to Fields's arguments for separate publication of what would thus become his first novel. He worried about the reception of his dark story but shrewdly suggested that printing the title in red would be "piquant and appropriate." Two weeks later, he told his college friend Horatio Bridge that he had just completed his novel, gloated that its conclusion broke his wife's heart, and rightly antipicated that some readers would enjoy his introductory sketch more than his somber story.

From LETTER TO GEORGE S. HILLARD

Salem, March 5th 1849

Dear Hillard,

[. . .]I am informed that there is to be a strong effort among the politicians here to remove me from office, and that my successor is already marked out. I do not think that this ought to be done; for I was not appointed to office as a reward for political services, nor have I acted as a politician since. A large portion of the local Democratic party look coldly on me, for not having used the influence of my position to obtain the removal of whigs — which I might have done, but which I in no case did. [. . .] Nor can any charge of inattention to duty, or other official misconduct, be brought against me; or, if so, I could easily refute it. There is therefore no ground for disturbing me, except on the most truculent party system. [. . .]

But it seems to me that an inoffensive man of letters — having obtained a pitiful little office on no other plea than his pitiful little literature — ought not to be left to the mercy of these thick-skulled and no-hearted ruffians. It is for this that I now write to you. There are men in Boston — Mr. Rufus Choate,[1] for instance — whose favorable influence with the administration would make it impossible to remove me, and whose support and sympathy might fairly be claimed in my behalf — not on the ground that I am a very good writer, but because I gained my position, such as it is, by my literary character, and have done nothing to forfeit that tenure. I do not think that you can have any objection to bringing this matter under the consideration of such men; but if you do so object, I am sure it will be for some good reason, and therefore beg you not to stir in it. I do not want any great fuss to be made; the whole thing is not worth it; but I should like to have the Administration enlightened by a few such testimonials as would take my name out of the list of ordinary officeholders, and at least prevent any hasty action. I think, too, that the letters (if you obtain any) had better

---

From *The Letters, 1843–1853*. Ed. Thomas Woodson, L. Neal Smith, and Norman Pearson. Columbus: Ohio State UP, 1985.

[1] "(1799–1859) a famous lawyer who had been an organizer of the Whig party in Massachusetts and had served as a congressman, 1830–34, and U.S. senator, 1841–45. [. . .] Hillard, a Whig, persuaded Choate to write on NH's behalf to Secretary Meredith immediately after his dismissal, on June 9. Choate characterized NH as "a writer of rare beauty, & merit & fame, a person of the purest character, & in politics perfectly quiet & silent" (MS, National Archives. [. . .])." [Woodson's note.]

contain no allusion to the proposed attack on me, as it may possibly fall through of itself. Certainly, the general feeling here in Salem would be in my favor; but I have seen too much of the modes of political action to lay any great stress on that. [. . .]

> Your friend,
>
> Nath¹ Hawthorne

From LETTER TO JAMES T. FIELDS

> Salem, Jan. 15th 1850

My dear Fields,

I send you, at last, the manuscript portion of my volume; not quite all of it, however, for there are three chapters still to be written of "The Scarlet Letter." I have been much delayed by illness in my family and other interruptions. Perhaps you will not like the book nor think well of its prospects with the public. If so (I need not say) I shall not consider you under any obligation to publish it. "The Scarlet Letter" is rather a delicate subject to write upon, but in the way in which I have treated it, it appears to me there can be no objections on that score. The article entitled "Custom House" is introductory to the volume, so please read it first. In the process of writing, all political and official turmoil has subsided within me, so that I have not felt inclined to execute justice on any of my enemies. I have not yet struck out a title, but may possibly hit on one before I close the package. If not, there need be no running title of the book over each page, but only of the individual articles. Calculating the page of the new volume at the size of that of the "Mosses," I can supply 400 and probably more. "The Scarlet Letter," I suppose, will make half of that number; otherwise, the calculation may fall a little short, though I think not.

> Very truly yours,
>
> Nath¹ Hawthorne

From *The Letters, 1843–1853.* Ed. Thomas Woodson, L. Neal Smith, and Norman Pearson. Columbus: Ohio State UP, 1985.

From LETTER TO JAMES T. FIELDS

Salem, January 20th, 1850

My dear Fields,

I am truly glad that you like the introduction; for I was rather afraid that it might appear absurd and impertinent to be talking about myself, when no-body, that I know of, has requested any information on that subject.

As regards the size of the book, I have been thinking a good deal about it. Considered merely as a matter of taste and beauty, the form of publication which you recommend seems to me much preferable to that of the *Mosses*. In the present case, however, I have some doubts of the expediency; because, if the book is made up entirely of *The Scarlet Letter*, it will be too sombre. I found it impossible to relieve the shadows of the story with so much light as I would gladly have thrown in. Keeping so close to its point as the tale does, and diversified no otherwise than by turning different sides of the same dark idea to the reader's eye, it will weary very many people, and disgust some. Is it safe, then, to stake the fate of the book entirely on this one chance? A hunter loads his gun with a bullet and several buck-shot; and, following his sagacious example, it was my purpose to conjoin the one long story with half a dozen shorter ones; so that, failing to kill the public outright with my biggest and heaviest lump of lead, I might have other chances with the smaller bits, individually and in the aggregate.

However, I am willing to leave these considerations to your judgment, and should not be sorry to have you decide for the separate publication.

In this latter event, it appears to me that the only proper title for the book would be "The Scarlet Letter"; for "The Custom House" is merely introductory—an entrance-hall to the magnificent edifice which I throw open to my guests. It would be funny, if, seeing the further passages so dark and dismal, they should all choose to stop there!

If "The Scarlet Letter" is to be the title, would it not be well to print it on the title-page in red ink? I am not quite sure about the good taste of so doing; but it would certainly be piquant and appropriate—and, I think, attractive to the great gull whom we are endeavoring to circumvent.

Very truly Yours,

Nath¹ Hawthorne

From *The Letters, 1843–53*. Ed. Thomas Woodson, L. Neal Smith, and Norman Pearson. Columbus: Ohio State UP, 1985.

[An undated draft of the January 20 letter to James T. Fields]
As regards the book, I have been thinking and considering—I was rather afraid that it appears sagacious absurd and impertinent to have some doubts, of the introduction to the book, which you recommend. I have found it impossible to relieve the shadows of the story with so much light as I would gladly stake the fate of the book entirely on the public. However, I am willing to leave these considerations to your judgment, and should not be sorry to have you decide for the separate publication.

If the Judgment Letter is to be the title—print it on the title page in red ink. I think that the only proper title for the book would be the Scarlet Letter. I am quite sure about the taste of so doing. I think it is attractive and appropriate—

From LETTER TO HORATIO BRIDGE

Salem, Feb 4th 1850

Dear Bridge,

I finished my book only yesterday; one end being in the press in Boston, while the other was in my head here in Salem—so that, as you see, the story is at least fourteen miles long. [. . .]

My book, the publisher tells me, will not be out before April. He speaks of it in tremendous terms of approbation; so does Mrs. Hawthorne, to whom I read the conclusion, last night. It broke her heart and sent her to bed with a grievous headache—which I look upon as triumphant success! Judging from its effect on her and the publisher, I may calculate on what bowlers call a "ten-strike." Yet I do not make any such calculation. Some portions of the book are powerfully written; but my writings do not, nor ever will, appeal to the broadest class of sympathies, and therefore will not attain a very wide popularity. Some like them very much; others care nothing for them, and see nothing in them. There is an introduction to this book—giving a sketch of my Custom-House life, with an imaginative

From *The Letters, 1843–53.* Ed. Thomas Woodson, L. Neal Smith, and Norman Pearson. Columbus: Ohio State UP, 1985.

From *The Letters, 1843–53.* Ed. Thomas Woodson, L. Neal Smith, and Norman Pearson. Columbus: Ohio State UP, 1985.

touch here and there—which perhaps may be more widely attractive than the main narrative. The latter lacks sunshine. To tell you the truth it is— (I hope Mrs. Bridge is not present)—it is positively a h–ll-fired story, into which I found it almost impossible to throw any cheering light. [. . .]

Truly Your friend,

Nath[l] Hawthorne

HISTORICAL BACKGROUND

The following three essays variously place Hawthorne's book in its historical settings. Charles Ryskamp discusses the sources Hawthorne drew on for his novel's colonial background and his relatively few divergences from historical fact. Larry J. Reynolds discusses the many ways in which *The Scarlet Letter* is informed by European revolutions, recent and otherwise. And Michael Winship discusses the publication, marketing, and reception of Hawthorne's novel from the time it first appeared until the end of the nineteenth century.

The New England Sources
of *The Scarlet Letter*

Charles Ryskamp

After all the careful studies of the origins of Hawthorne's tales and the extensive inquiry into the English sources of *The Scarlet Letter*,[1] it is surprising that the American sources for the factual background of his most famous novel have been largely unnoticed. As would seem only natural,

American Literature 31 (1959): 257–72.

[1] I shall make no reference to the English sources of *The Scarlet Letter* which have been investigated by Alfred S. Reid in *The Yellow Ruff and The Scarlet Letter* (Gainesville, 1955) and in his edition of *Sir Thomas Overbury's Vision . . . and Other English Sources of Nathaniel Hawthorne's "The Scarlet Letter"* (Gainesville, 1957). Most of this article was written before the publication of Reid's books. It may serve, however, as a complement or corrective to the central thesis put forth by Reid: "that accounts of the murder of Sir Thomas Overbury were Hawthorne's principal sources in composing *The Scarlet Letter*" (*The Yellow Ruff*, p. 112).

Hawthorne used the most creditable history of Boston available to him at that time, and one which is still an important source for the identification of houses of the early settlers and for landmarks in the city. The book is Dr. Caleb H. Snow's *History of Boston*. Study and comparison of the many histories read by Hawthorne reveal his repeated use of it for authentication of the setting of *The Scarlet Letter*. Consequently, for the most part this article will be concerned with Snow's book.

If we are to see the accurate background Hawthorne created, some works other than Snow's must also be mentioned, and the structure of time as well as place must be established. Then it will become apparent that although Hawthorne usually demanded authentic details of colonial history, some small changes were necessary in his portrayal of New England in the 1640's. These were not made because of lack of knowledge of the facts, nor merely by whim, but according to definite purposes—so that the plot would develop smoothly to produce the grand and simple balance of the book as we know it.

During the "solitary years," 1825–37, Hawthorne was "deeply engaged in reading everything he could lay his hands on. It was said in those days that he had read every book in the Athenaeum. . . ."[2] Yet no scholar has studied his notebooks without expressing surprise at the exceptionally few remarks there on his reading. Infrequently one will find a bit of "curious information, sometimes with, more often without, a notation of the source; and some of these passages find their way into his creative work."[3] But for the most part Hawthorne did not reveal clues concerning the books he read and used in his own stories. About half of his writings deal in some way with colonial American history, and Professor Turner believes that "Hawthorne's indebtedness to the history of New England was a good deal larger than has ordinarily been supposed."[4] Certainly in *The Scarlet Letter* the indebtedness was much more direct than has hitherto been known.

Any work on the exact sources would have been almost impossible if it had not been for Hawthorne's particular use of the New England annals. Most of these are similar in content. The later historian builds on those preceding, who, in turn, must inevitably base all history on the chronicles, diaries, and records of the first settlers. Occasionally an annalist turns up a hitherto unpublished fact, a new relationship, a fresh description. It is

---

[2] James T. Fields, *Yesterdays with Authors* (Boston, 1900) p. 47. For a list of books which Hawthorne borrowed from the Salem Athenaeum, see Marion L. Kesselring, *Hawthorne's Reading 1828–1850* (New York, 1949). All of my sources are included in this list, except the second edition (1845) of Felt's *Annals of Salem*.

[3] *The American Notebooks*, ed. Randall Stewart (New Haven, 1932), p. xxxii.

[4] H. Arlin Turner, "Hawthorne's Literary Borrowings," *PMLA*, LI, 545 (June 1936).

these that Hawthorne seizes upon for his stories, for they would, of course, strike the mind of one who had read almost all the histories, and who was intimate with the fundamentals of colonial New England government.

As a young bachelor in Salem Hawthorne, according to his future sister-in-law, Elizabeth Peabody, "made himself thoroughly acquainted with the ancient history of Salem, and especially with the witchcraft era."[5] This meant that he studied Increase Mather's *Illustrious Providences* and Cotton Mather's *Magnalia Christi Americana*. He read the local histories of all the important New England towns. He read—and mentioned in his works— Bancroft's *History of the United States*, Hutchinson's *History of Massachusetts*, Snow's *History of Boston*, Felt's *Annals of Salem*, and Winthrop's *Journal*.[6] His son reported that Hawthorne pored over the daily records of the past: newspapers, magazines, chronicles, English state trials, "all manner of lists of things. . . . The forgotten volumes of the New England Annalists were favorites of his, and he drew not a little material from them."[7] He used these works to establish verisimilitude and greater materiality for his own books. His reading was perhaps most often chosen to help him— as he wrote to Longfellow—"give a life-like semblance to such shadowy stuff"[8] as formed his romances. Basically it was an old method of achieving reality, most successfully accomplished in his own day by Scott; but for Hawthorne the ultimate effects were quite different. Here and there Hawthorne reported actual places, incidents, and people—historical facts— and these were united with the creations of his mind. His explicitly stated aim in *The Scarlet Letter* was that "the Actual and the Imaginary may meet, and each imbue itself with the nature of the other." His audience should recognize "the authenticity of the outline" of the novel, and this would help them to accept the actuality of the passion and guilt which it contained. For the author himself, the strongest reality of outline or scene was in the past, especially the history of New England.

The time scheme of the plot of *The Scarlet Letter* may be dated definitely.

---

[5] Moncure D. Conway, *Life of Nathaniel Hawthorne* (New York, 1890), p. 31.

[6] Edward Dawson, *Hawthorne's Knowledge and Use of New England History: A Study of Sources* (Nashville, Tenn., 1939), pp. 5–6; Turner, p. 551.

[7] Julian Hawthorne, *Hawthorne Reading* (Cleveland, 1902), pp. 107–108, 111, 132. Hawthorne's sister Elizabeth wrote to James T. Fields: "There was [at the Athenaeum] also much that related to the early History of New England. . . . I think if you looked over a file of old Colonial Newspapers you would not be surprised at the fascination my brother found in them. There were a few volumes in the Salem Athenaeum; he always complained because there were no more" (Randall Stewart, "Recollections of Hawthorne by His Sister Elizabeth," *American Literature*, XVI, 324, 330, Jan., 1945).

[8] *The American Notebooks*, p. xlii.

In Chapter xii, "The Minister's Vigil," the event which brings the various characters together is the death of Governor Winthrop. From the records we know that the old magistrate died on March 26, 1649.[9] However, Hawthorne gives the occasion as Saturday, "an obscure night of early May." Some suggestions may be made as reasons for changing the date. It would be difficult to have a night-long vigil in the cold, blustery month of March without serious plot complications. The rigidly conceived last chapters of the book require a short period of time to be dramatically and psychologically effective. The mounting tension in the mind and heart of the Reverend Mr. Dimmesdale cries for release, for revelation of his secret sin. Hawthorne realized that for a powerful climax, not more than a week, or two weeks at the most, should elapse between the night of Winthrop's death, when Dimmesdale stood on the scaffold, and the public announcement of his sin to the crowd on Election Day. The Election Day and the Election Sermons (253)[10] were well-known and traditionally established in the early colony in the months of May or June.[11] (The election of 1649, at which John Endicott became governor, was held on May 2.) Consequently Hawthorne was forced to choose between two historical events, more than a month apart. He wisely selected May, rather than March, 1649, for the time of the action of the last half of the book (Chapters xii–xxiii).

The minister's expiatory watch on the scaffold is just seven years after Hester Prynne first faced the hostile Puritans on the same platform. Therefore, the first four chapters of *The Scarlet Letter* may be placed in June, 1642.

---

[9] William Allen, *An American Biographical and Historical Dictionary* (Cambridge, Mass., 1809), p. 616; Caleb H. Snow, *A History of Boston* (Boston, 1825), p. 104; Thomas Hutchinson, *The History of Massachusetts* (Salem, 1795), I, 142.

[10] All page references to *The Scarlet Letter* are to this New Riverside Edition. [ED.]

[11] John Winthrop, *The History of New England from 1630 to 1649* (Boston, 1825–1826), II, 31, 218 (a note on p. 31 states that the charter of 1629 provided for a general election on "the last Wednesday in Easter term yearly"; after 1691, on the last Wednesday of May); also Daniel Neal, *The History of New-England . . . to . . . 1700* (London, 1747), II, 252. Speaking of New England festivals, Neal writes: "their Grand Festivals are the Day of the annual Election of Magistrates at Boston, which is the latter End of *May;* and the Commencement at *Cambridge,* which is the last *Wednesday* in *July,* when business is pretty much laid aside, and the People are as chearful among their Friends and Neighbours, as the *English* are at *Christmas.*" Note Hawthorne's description of Election Day (*The Scarlet Letter,* 249): "Had they followed their hereditary taste, the New England settlers would have illustrated all events of public importance by bonfires, banquets, pageantries of processions. . . . There was some shadow of an attempt of this kind in the mode of celebrating the day on which the political year of the colony commenced. The dim reflection of a remembered splendor, a colorless and manifold diluted repetition of what they had beheld in proud old London . . . might be traced in the customs which our forefathers instituted, with reference to the annual installation of magistrates."

Hawthorne says that at this time Bellingham was governor. Again one does not find perfect historical accuracy; if it were so, then Winthrop would have been governor, for Bellingham had finished his term of office just one month before.[12] A possible reason for Hawthorne's choice of Bellingham will be discussed later.

The next major scene—that in which Hester Prynne goes to the mansion of Bellingham—takes place three years later (1645).[13] Hawthorne correctly observes: "though the chances of a popular election had caused this former ruler to descend a step or two from the highest rank, he still held an honorable and influential place among the colonial magistracy."[14] From the description of the garden of Bellingham's house we know that the time of the year was late summer.

With these references to time, as Edward Dawson has suggested,[15] we can divide the major action of the novel as follows:

ACT ONE

i. Chapters I–III. The Market-Place, Boston. A June morning, 1642.

ii. Chapter IV. The Prison, Boston. Afternoon of the same day. ⋅

ACT TWO

Chapters VII–VIII. The home of Richard Bellingham, Boston. Late summer, 1645.

ACT THREE

i. Chapter XII. The Market-Place. Saturday night, early May, 1649.

ii. Chapters XIV–XV. The sea coast, "a retired part of the peninsula." Several days later.

iii. Chapters XVI–XIX. The forest. Several days later.

---

[12] Winthrop, II, 31: June 2, 1641, Richard Bellingham elected governor. Winthrop, II, 63: May 18, 1642, John Winthrop elected governor.

[13] *The Scarlet Letter*, 165: "Pearl, therefore, so large were the attainments of her three years' lifetime, could have borne a fair examination in the New England Primer, or the first column of the Westminster Catechisms, although unacquainted with the outward form of either of those celebrated works." The Westminster Catechisms were not formulated until 1647; the New England Primer was first brought out ca. 1690.

[14] Winthrop, II, 220: on May 14, 1645, Thomas Dudley had been elected governor.

[15] I am largely indebted to Dawson, p. 17, for this time scheme.

ACT FOUR

Chapters xxi–xxiii. The Market-Place. Three days later.

The place of each action is just as carefully described as is the time. Hawthorne's picture of Boston is done with precise authenticity. A detailed street-by-street and house-by-house description of the city in 1650 is given by Snow in his *History of Boston*. It is certainly the most complete history of the early days in any work available to Hawthorne. Whether he had an early map of Boston cannot be known, but it is doubtful that any existed from the year 1650. However, the City of Boston Records, 1634–1660, and

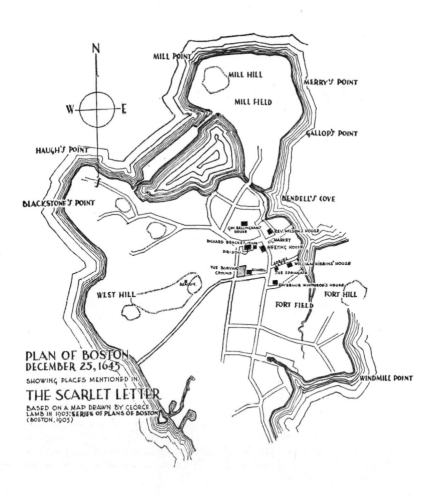

N

W—E

MILL POINT

MILL HILL

MERRY'S POINT

MILL FIELD

GALLOP'S POINT

HAUGH'S POINT

BLACKSTONE'S POINT

BENDELL'S COVE

GOV. BELLINGHAM'S HOUSE

REV. WILSON'S HOUSE

RICHARD BRACKET, JAILER

MARKET
MEETING HOUSE

PRISON

THE BURYING GROUND

SCHOOL

WILLIAM HIBBINS' HOUSE

THE SPRINGATE

BEACON

GOVERNOR WINTHROP'S HOUSE

WEST HILL

FORT HILL

FORT FIELD

PLAN OF BOSTON
DECEMBER 25, 1645

SHOWING PLACES MENTIONED IN

THE SCARLET LETTER

BASED ON A MAP DRAWN BY GEORGE
LAMB IN 1903: SERIES OF PLANS OF BOSTON
(BOSTON, 1905)

WINDMILL POINT

the "Book of Possessions" with the reconstructed maps (made in 1903–1905 by George Lamb, based on the original records)[16] prove conclusively the exactness of the descriptions written by Snow and Hawthorne. Hawthorne locates the first scene of *The Scarlet Letter* in this way:

> ... it may safely be assumed that the forefathers of Boston had built the first prison-house somewhere in the vicinity of Cornhill, almost as seasonably as they marked out the first burial-ground, on Isaac Johnson's lot, and round about his grave, which subsequently became the nucleus of all the congregated sepulchres in the old churchyard of King's Chapel.[17]

> It was no great distance, in those days, from the prison-door to the market-place.... Hester Prynne ... came to a sort of scaffold, at the western extremity of the market-place. It stood nearly beneath the eaves of Boston's earliest church, and appeared to be a fixture there.[18]

Snow says that in 1650 Governor Bellingham and the Rev. John Wilson lived on one side of the Market-Place and Church Square (Snow, p. 117). Near Spring Lane on the other side of the Square (mentioned by Hawthorne when little Pearl says, "I saw her, the other day, bespatter the Governor himself with water, at the cattle trough in Spring Lane") was the home of Governor Winthrop (Snow, p. 108). All the action of *The Scarlet Letter* set in Boston is thus centered in the heart of the city. This, as Snow takes great pains to point out, was where all the leading townsmen lived. He writes:

> It has been so often repeated that it is now generally believed the north part of the town was at that period the most populous. We are convinced that the idea is erroneous.... The book of possessions records the estates of about 250, the number of their houses, barns, gardens, and sometimes the measurement of their lands. It seems to embrace the pe-

---

[16] For the drawing of the map reproduced with this article, I am grateful to Professor W. F. Shellman, Jr., of the School of Architecture, Princeton University.

[17] Concerning Isaac Johnson, Snow writes: "According to his particular desire expressed on his death bed, he was buried at the Southwest corner of the lot, and the people exhibited their attachment to him, by ordering their bodies to be buried near him. This was the origin of the first burying place, at present the Chapel burial ground" (p. 37).

[18] Justin Winsor, in *The Memorial History of Boston* (Boston, 1881), I, 506, 539, writes: "The whipping-post appears as a land-mark in the Boston records in 1639, and the frequent sentences to be whipped must have made the post entirely familiar to the town. It stood in front of the First Church, and was probably thought to be as necessary to good discipline as a police-station now is.... The stocks stood sometimes near the whipping-post.... And here, at last, before the very door of the sanctuary, perhaps to show that the Church and State went hand-in-hand in precept and penalty, stood the first whipping-post—no unimportant adjunct of Puritan life."

riod from 1640 to 1650, and we conclude, gives us the names of almost, if not quite, all the freemen of Boston. They were settled through the whole length of the main street on both sides. . . . It is evident too, that most of the wealthy and influential characters lived in what is now the centre of the town. We discover only about thirty names of residents north of the creek.

A clear instance of Hawthorne's borrowing a fact from Snow is in the naming of "Master Brackett, the jailer." Few colonial historians mention a jailer in Boston at this time, and if they do, they give his name as Parker. But Snow, alone it would seem, gives this information about Brackett, after writing about the property of John Leverett: "His next neighbour on the south was Richard Parker or Brackett, whose name we find on the colony records as prison keeper so early as 1638. He had '*the market stead*' on the east, the prison yard west, and the meeting house on the south" (Snow, p. 116). This last sentence taken from Snow gives the exact location of the action of the early chapters of *The Scarlet Letter*.

Another example of Hawthorne's use of Snow is shown in the description of Governor Bellingham's house. Here Hawthorne builds a vivid image of the old mansion. He writes of Hester and Pearl:

> Without further adventure, they reached the dwelling of Governor Bellingham. This was a large wooden house, built in a fashion of which there are specimens still extant in the streets of our older towns. . . . It had, indeed, a very cheery aspect; the walls being overspread with a kind of stucco, in which fragments of broken glass were plentifully intermixed; so that, when the sunshine fell aslantwise over the front of the edifice, it glittered and sparkled as if diamonds had been flung against it by the double handful. . . . It was further decorated with strange and seemingly cabalistic figures and diagrams, suitable to the quaint taste of the age, which had been drawn in the stucco when newly laid on, and had now grown hard and durable, for the admiration of after times.[19]

There are almost no representations of the first settlers' houses in the New England annals. But Snow on one occasion does print an old plate showing an "Ancient building at the corner of Ann-Street and Market-Square" (p. 166). And he describes the house in a way which bears a remarkable resemblance to the sketch written by Hawthorne twenty-five years later:

> This, says a description furnished by a friend, is perhaps the only wooden building now standing in the city to show what was considered

---

[19] Hawthorne also accurately noted that Governor Bellingham was "bred a lawyer." Snow writes of Bellingham: "He was by education a lawyer" (p. 159).

elegance of architecture here, a century and a half ago. . . . The outside is covered with plastering, or what is commonly called rough-cast. But instead of pebbles, which are generally used at the present day to make a hard surface on the mortar, broken glass was used. This glass appears like that of common junk bottles, broken into pieces of about half an inch diameter. . . . This surface was also variegated with ornamental squares, diamonds and flowers-de-luce. (p. 167)[20]

Snow is also the only historian who tells the story of Mrs. Sherman's pig in order to bring out its effect upon the early Massachusetts government.[21] Hawthorne, with his characteristic interest in the unusual fact from the past, refers to this strange incident:

At that epoch of pristine simplicity, however, matters of even slighter public interest, and of far less intrinsic weight, than the welfare of Hester and her child, were strangely mixed up with the deliberations of legislators and acts of state. The period was hardly, if at all, earlier than that of our story, when a dispute concerning the right of property in a pig not only caused a fierce and bitter contest in the legislative body of the colony, but resulted in an important modification of the framework itself of the legislature.

In his version of the story Snow said that the incident "gave rise to a change also in regard to the Assistants" (p. 95) and that because of the confusion and dissatisfaction over the decision of the court, "provision was made for some cases in which, if the two houses differed, it was agreed that the major vote of the whole should be decisive. This was the origin of our present Senate" (p. 96).

The characters named in *The Scarlet Letter*—other than Hester, Pearl, Chillingworth, and Dimmesdale, for whom we can find no real historical bases—were actual figures in history. The fictional protagonists of the action move and gain their being in part through their realistic meetings with well-known people of colonial Boston. Even the fantastic Pearl grows somewhat more substantial in the light of the legend and story of her primitive world. She is seen, for example, against the silhouette of the earlier Mr. Blackstone. When describing Bellingham's garden Hawthorne relates:

---

[20] For a possible source for details concerning the interior of Bellingham's house, the front door, knocker, etc., see Joseph B. Felt, *Annals of Salem* (2nd ed.; Salem, 1845). I, 403–406.

[21] Snow, pp. 95–96. Hutchinson, I, 135–136, also refers to the incident, but not in this particular way.

"There were a few rose-bushes, however, and a number of apple-trees, probably the descendants of those planted by the Reverend Mr. Blackstone, the first settler of the peninsula; that half-mythological personage, who rides through our early annals, seated on the back of a bull." Snow had said:

> By right of previous possession, Mr. Blackstone had a title to proprietorship in the whole peninsula. It was in fact for a time called Blackstone's neck. . . . Mr. Blackstone was a very eccentrick character. He was a man of learning, and had received episcopal ordination in England. . . . It was not very long before Mr. Blackstone found that there might be more than one kind of nonconformity, and was virtually obliged to leave the remainder of his estate here. . . . Let the cause of his removal have been what it may, certain it is that he went and settled by the Pawtucket river. . . . At this his new plantation he lived uninterrupted for many years, and there raised an orchard, the first that ever bore apples in Rhode Island. He had the first of the sort called yellow sweetings, that were ever in the world, and is said to have planted the first orchard in Massachusetts also. . . . Though he was far from agreeing in opinion with Roger Williams, he used frequently to go to Providence to preach the gospel; and to encourage his younger hearers, while he gratified his own benevolent disposition, he would give them of his apples, which were the first they ever saw. It was said that when he grew old and unable to travel on foot, not having any horse, he used to ride on a bull, which he had tamed and tutored to that use. (pp. 50–53)

This account is taken virtually word for word from a series of articles called "The Historical Account of the Planting and Growth of Providence" published in the Providence *Gazette* (January 12 to March 30, 1765).[22] However, Snow adds to this narrative the application to Boston, which would be of special interest to Hawthorne (the phrase, "and is said to have planted the first orchard in Massachusetts also").

The only minor characters that are developed to such an extent that they become in any way memorable figures are Mrs. Hibbins and the Rev. John Wilson. Hawthorne's use of Mrs. Hibbins shows again a precise interest in the byways of Boston history. He describes the costume of the "reputed witch-lady" carefully. He refers to her as "Governor Bellingham's bitter-tempered sister, . . . the same who, a few years later, was executed as a witch." And again, during the minister's vigil, Hawthorne writes that

---

[22] These were reprinted in the Massachusetts Historical Society's *Collections*, 2nd Ser., IX, 166–203 (1820).

Dimmesdale beheld "at one of the chamber-windows of Governor Bellingham's mansion . . . the appearance of the old magistrate himself. . . . At another window of the same house, moreover, appeared old Mistress Hibbins, the Governor's sister. . . ." In Snow's book there is this account of
Mrs. Ann Hibbins:

> The most remarkable occurrence in the colony in the year 1655 was the
> trial and condemnation of Mrs. Ann Hibbins of Boston for witchcraft.
> Her husband, who died July 23, 1654, was an agent for the colony in Eng-
> land, several years one of the assistants, and a merchant of note in the
> town; but losses in the latter part of his life had reduced his estate, and
> increased the natural crabbedness of his wife's temper, which made her
> turbulent and quarrelsome, and brought her under church censures,
> and at length rendered her so odious to her neighbours as to cause some
> of them to accuse her of witchcraft. The jury brought her in guilty, but
> the magistrates refused to accept the verdict; so the cause came to the
> general court, where the popular clamour prevailed against her, and the
> miserable old lady was condemned and executed in June 1656. (p. 140)[23]

There seems to be only one source for Hawthorne's reference to
Mrs. Hibbins as Bellingham's sister. That is in a footnote by James Savage
in the 1825 edition of John Winthrop's *History of New England*, and it
was this edition that Hawthorne borrowed from the Salem Athenaeum.[24]
Savage writes that Mrs. Hibbins "suffered the punishment of death, for
the ridiculous crime, the year after her husband's decease; her brother,
Bellingham, not exerting, perhaps, his highest influence for her preservation."[25] Hawthorne leads the reader to assume that Mrs. Hibbins, nine
years before the death of her husband, is living at the home of her brother.
Hawthorne uses this relationship between Bellingham and Mrs. Hibbins in
order to have fewer stage directions and explanations. It helps him to establish a more realistic unity in the tale. It partially explains the presence of
the various people at the Market-Place the night of the minister's vigil,
since Bellingham's house was just north of the scaffold. It also suggests why

---

[23] This is almost a literal copy from Hutchinson, I, 173. See also William Hubbard,
"A General History of New England," *Massachusetts Historical Society Collections*,
2nd Ser., V, 574 (1815); Winthrop, I, 321.
[24] Kesselring, p. 64.
[25] Winthrop, I, 321 n. This contradicts Julian Hawthorne's observation: "As for Mistress
Hibbins, history describes her as Bellingham's relative, but does not say that she was his
sister, as is stated in the 'Romance'" ("Scenes of Hawthorne's Romances," *Century
Magazine*, XXVIII, 391, July 1884).

Bellingham is the governor chosen for the opening scenes of the novel, to prevent the plot from becoming encumbered with too many minor figures.

The Reverend John Wilson's description is sympathetically done, and it is for the most part historically accurate. Hawthorne presents him as "the reverend and famous John Wilson, the eldest clergyman of Boston, a great scholar, like most of his contemporaries in the profession, and withal a man of kind and genial spirit." Cotton Mather,[26] William Hubbard,[27] and Caleb Snow testify to his remarkable "compassion for the distressed and . . . affection for all" (Snow, p. 156). William Allen, in his *American Biographical and Historical Dictionary*, writes that "Mr. Wilson was one of the most humble, pious, and benevolent men of the age, in which he lived. Kind affections and zeal were the prominent traits in his character. . . . Every one loved him. . . ."[28] Hawthorne, to gain dramatic opposition to Dimmesdale, makes the preacher seem older than he really was. He pictures the man of fifty-seven as "the venerable pastor, John Wilson . . . [with a] beard, white as a snow-drift"; and later, as the "good old minister."

Hawthorne's description of Puritan costuming has been substantiated by twentieth-century research. Although the elders of the colonial church dressed in "sad-colored garments, and gray, steeple-crowned hats"[29] and preached simplicity of dress, Hawthorne recognized that "the church attendants never followed that preaching."[30] "Lists of Apparell" left by the old colonists in their wills, inventories of estates, ships' bills of lading, laws telling what must *not* be worn, ministers' sermons denouncing excessive ornamentation in dress, and portraits of the leaders prove that "little of the extreme Puritan is found in the dress of the first Boston colonists."[31] Alice

---

[26] *Magnalia Christi Americana* (London, 1702), bk. III, p. 46.

[27] Hubbard, p. 604.

[28] Allen, p. 613. The Reverend John Wilson was born in 1588; he died in 1667.

[29] The phrase, "steeple-crowned hats," is used by Hawthorne each time he describes the dress of the Puritan elders (*The Scarlet Letter*, pp. 119, 126, 251). The only source that I have been able to find for this particular phrase is in an essay on hats in a series of articles on clothing worn in former times: Joseph Moser, "Vestiges, Collected and Recollected, Number XXIV," *European Magazine*, XLV, 409–415 (1804). The Charge-Books of the Salem Athenaeum show that Hawthorne read the magazine in which this article appeared. Moser wrote about the "elevated and solemn beavers of the Puritans" (p. 414) and the "high and steeple-crowned hats, probably from an idea, that the conjunction of Church and State was necessary to exalt their archetype in the manner that it was exalted" (p. 411).

[30] Alice Morse Earle, *Two Centuries of Costume in America* (New York, 1903), I, 8.

[31] Earle, I, 13.

Morse Earle, after going over the lists of clothing brought by the Puritans, concludes:

> From all this cheerful and ample dress, this might well be a Cavalier emigration; in truth, the apparel supplied as an outfit to the Virginia planters (who are generally supposed to be far more given over to rich dress) is not as full nor as costly as this apparel of Massachusetts Bay. In this as in every comparison I make, I find little to indicate any difference between Puritan and Cavalier in quantity of garments, in quality, or cost—or, indeed, in form. The differences in England were much exaggerated in print; in America they often existed wholly in men's notions of what a Puritan must be. (I, 34)

Hawthorne's descriptions agree with the early annals. The embroideries and bright colors worn by Pearl, the silks and velvets of Mrs. Hibbins, Hester's needlework—the laces, "deep ruffs . . . and gorgeously embroidered gloves"—were, as he said, "readily allowed to individuals dignified by rank or wealth, even while sumptuary laws forbade these and similar extravagances to the plebeian order." The Court in 1651 had recorded "its utter detestation and dislike that men or women of mean condition should take upon them the garb of Gentlemen, by wearing gold or silver lace . . . which, though allowable to persons of greater Estates or more liberal Education, yet we cannot but judge it intolerable in persons of such like condition." [32] Hawthorne's attempt to create an authentic picture of the seventeenth century is shown in *The American Notebooks* where he describes the "Dress of an old woman, 1656." [33] But all of Hawthorne's description is significant beyond the demands of verisimilitude. In *The Scarlet Letter* he is repeating the impressions which are characteristic of his tales: the portrayal of color contrasts for symbolic purposes, the play of light and dark, the rich color of red against black, the brilliant embroideries [34] on the sable background of the "sad-colored garments."

So far there has been slight mention of the influence of Cotton Mather's writings on *The Scarlet Letter*. These surely require our attention in any study such as this one. Professor Turner believes that certain elements of Mather's *Magnalia Christi Americana*, "and in particular the accounts of God's judgment on adulterers [in II, 397–398], may also have influenced *The Scarlet Letter*. Mather relates [II, 404–405] that a woman who had

---

[32] Winsor, I, 484–485. Hawthorne had read the *Acts and Laws . . . of the Massachusetts-Bay in New-England* (Boston, 1726)—see Kesselring, p. 56.
[33] *The American Notebooks*, p. 109.
[34] One of Hawthorne's favorite words—for example, see *The American Notebooks*, p. 97.

killed her illegitimate child was exhorted by John Wilson and John Cotton to repent while she was in prison awaiting execution. In like manner, as will be recalled, John Wilson joins with Governor Bellingham and Arthur Dimmesdale in admonishing Hester Prynne to reveal the father of her child."[35] It is possible that an echo of the witch tradition in the *Magnalia Christi Americana* may also be found in *The Scarlet Letter*. "The proposal by Mistress Hibbins that Hester accompany her to a witch meeting is typical of the Mather witch tradition, which included, in accordance with the well known passage in *The Scarlet Letter*, the signing in the devil's book with an iron pen and with blood for ink. . . ."[36] The Black Man mentioned so often by Hawthorne was familiar to the Puritan settlers of New England. Pearl tells her mother "a story about the Black Man. . . . How he haunts this forest, and carries a book with him, —a big, heavy book, with iron clasps; and how this ugly Black Man offers his book and an iron pen to everybody that meets him here among the trees; and they are to write their names with their own blood." Concerning the Black Man, Cotton Mather had written: "These *Tormentors* tendred unto the afflicted a *Book*, requiring them to *Sign* it, or *Touch* it at least, in token of their consenting to be Listed in the Service of the *Devil;* which they refusing to do, the *Spectres* under the Command of that *Blackman*, as they called him, would apply themselves to Torture them with prodigious Molestations."[37]

Even the portent in the sky, the great red letter A, which was seen on the night of the revered John Winthrop's death (and Dimmesdale's vigil), would not have seemed too strange to Puritan historians. To them it would certainly not have been merely an indication of Hawthorne's gothic interests. Snow had related that when John Cotton had died on Thursday, December 23, 1652, "strange and alarming signs appeared in the heavens, while his body lay, according to the custom of the times, till the Tuesday following" (p. 133).

The idea of the scarlet A had been in Hawthorne's mind for some years before he wrote the novel. In 1844 he had made this comment in his notebooks as a suggestion for a story: "The life of a woman, who, by the old

---

[35] Turner, p. 550; Turner is using the Hartford (1855) edition of the *Magnalia Christi Americana*. (See *The Scarlet Letter*, 132–35.)

[36] Turner, p. 546—see *The Scarlet Letter* (170) and *Magnalia Christi Americana*, bk. VI, p. 81: "It was not long before M. L. . . . confess'd that *She* rode with her Mother to the said Witch-meeting. . . . At another time M. L. *junior*, the Granddaughter, aged about 17 Years . . . declares that . . . they . . . rode on a Stick or Pole in the *Air* . . . and that they set their Hands to the Devil's Book. . . ."

[37] *Magnalia Christi Americana*, bk. II, p. 60; see also Massachusetts Historical Society *Collections*, V. 64 (1708); Neal, II, 131, 133–135, 144, 150, 158, 160, 169.

colony law, was condemned always to wear the letter A, sewed on her garment, in token of her having committed adultery."[38] Before that, in "Endicott and the Red Cross," he had told of a "woman with no mean share of beauty" who wore a scarlet A. It has commonly been accepted that the "old colony law" which he had referred to in his notebooks had been found in Felt's *Annals of Salem*, where we read under the date of May 5, 1694: "Among such laws, passed this session, were two against Adultery and Polygamy. Those guilty of the first crime, were to sit an hour on the gallows, with ropes about their necks — be severely whipt not above 40 stripes; and forever after wear a capital A, two inches long, cut out of cloth coloured differently from their clothes, and sewed on the arms, or back parts of their garments so as always to be seen when they were about."[39]

Exactly when Hawthorne began writing *The Scarlet Letter* is not known, but by September 27, 1849, he was working on it throughout every day. It was finished by February 3, 1850.[40] In the novel there is the same rapid skill at composition which is typical of the notebooks. From the multitude of historical facts he knew he could call forth with severe economy only a few to support the scenes of passion or punishment. Perhaps it does not seem good judgment to claim that Hawthorne wrote *The Scarlet Letter* with a copy of Snow's *History of Boston* on the desk. But it does not appear believable that all these incidental facts from New England histories, the exacting time scheme, the authentic description of Boston in the 1640's, should have remained so extremely clear and perfect in his mind when he was under the extraordinary strain of writing the story. Here the studies of Hawthorne's literary borrowings made by Dawson, Turner, and others must be taken into account. They have shown that in certain of his tales, he "seems to have written with his original open before him."[41] To claim a firm dependence upon certain New England histories for the background of *The Scarlet Letter* should therefore not seem unreasonable.

The incidents, places, and persons noticed in this article are the principal New England historical references in *The Scarlet Letter*. A study like this of Hawthorne's sources shows something of his thorough method of reading; it reveals especially his certain knowledge of colonial history and his interest in the unusual, obscure fact. But these are side lights of an author's mind. His steady determination was to make the romances of his imagination as real as the prison-house and the grave.

---

[38] *The American Notebooks*, p. 107.
[39] Joseph B. Felt, *The Annals of Salem, from Its First Settlement* (Salem, 1827), p. 317.
[40] Randall Stewart, *Nathaniel Hawthorne* (New Haven, 1948), pp. 93–95.
[41] Turner, p. 547.

It would be unfair to leave the study of Hawthorne's historical approach here. His final concern in history was the attempt to find the "spiritual significance"[42] of the facts. As his sister Elizabeth had said of the young man: "He was not very fond of history in general."[43] Hawthorne stated concretely his conception of history and the novel in a review (1846) of W. G. Simms's *Views and Reviews in American History:*

> . . . we cannot help feeling that the real treasures of his subject have escaped the author's notice. The themes suggested by him, viewed as he views them, would produce nothing but historical novels, cast in the same worn out mould that has been in use these thirty years, and which it is time to break up and fling away. To be the prophet of Art requires almost as high a gift as to be a fulfiller of the prophecy. Mr. Simms has not this gift; he possesses nothing of the magic touch that should cause new intellectual and moral shapes to spring up in the reader's mind, peopling with varied life what had hitherto been a barren waste.[44]

With the evocation of the spirit of the colonial past, and with a realistic embodiment of scene, Hawthorne repeopled a landscape wherein new intellectual and moral shapes could dwell. The new fiction of Hester Prynne and the old appearances of Mrs. Hibbins could not be separated. Time past and time present became explicable as they were identified in the same profound moral engagement.

The Scarlet Letter and Revolutions Abroad

Larry J. Reynolds

When Hawthorne wrote *The Scarlet Letter* in the fall of 1849, the fact and idea of revolution were much on his mind. In "The Custom-House" sketch, while forewarning the reader of the darkness in the story to follow, he explains that "this uncaptivating effect is perhaps due to the period of hardly accomplished revolution and still seething turmoil, in which the story shaped itself" (116).[1] His explicit reference is to his recent ouster

---

American Literature 57 (1985): 44–67.

[42] Julian Hawthorne, *Hawthorne Reading*, p. 100.
[43] "Recollections of Hawthorne by His Sister Elizabeth," p. 324.
[44] Stewart, "Hawthorne's Contributions to *The Salem Advertiser*," *American Literature*, V, 331–332 (Jan. 1934).
[1] All parenthetical references are to this New Riverside Edition. [ED.]

from the Salem Custom House, his "beheading" as he calls it, but we know that the death of his mother and anxiety about where and how he would support his family added to his sense of upheaval. Lying behind all these referents, however, are additional ones that have gone unnoticed: actual revolutions, past and present, which Hawthorne had been reading about and pondering for almost twenty consecutive months. These provided the political context for *The Scarlet Letter* and shaped the structure, characterizations, and themes of the work.

I

ROME YET UNCONQUERED! FRANCE TRANQUIL. LEDRU-ROLLIN NOT TAKEN. THE HUNGARIANS TRIUMPH! GREAT BATTLE NEAR RAAB! THE AUSTRIANS AND RUSSIANS BEATEN. CONFLICTS AT PETERWARDEIN AND JORDANOW. SOUTHERN GERMANY REPUBLICAN. BATTLE WITH THE PRUSSIANS AT MANHEIM. RESULT UNDECIDED. These are the headlines of the *New York Tribune* for 5 July 1849; and because they are typical, they suggest the excitement and interest generated in America by the wave upon wave of revolution that swept across Europe during the years 1848 and 1849. [. . .] By the fall of 1849, all of the fledgling republics had been crushed by conservative and reactionary forces, and this fact explains in part why the influence of the revolutions upon *The Scarlet Letter* in particular and the American literary renaissance in general has been overlooked. [. . .]

Although Margaret Fuller's former devotee Sophia Hawthorne [. . .] expressed approval of the republican successes in Europe as they were occurring in 1848, her husband most likely shared neither her optimism nor the enthusiasm of their literary friends, particularly Fuller. In fact, the book that he wrote in the wake of the revolutions in 1849 indicates that they reaffirmed his scepticism about revolution and reform and inspired a strong reactionary spirit which underlies the work.

[. . .] [I]n "The Custom-House" sketch, Hawthorne presents himself as the victim of [a] "bloodthirsty" mob, the Whigs, who, acting out of a "fierce and bitter spirit of malice and revenge," have struck off his head with the political guillotine and ignominiously kicked it about. This presentation, humorous in tone but serious in intent, gives *The Scarlet Letter* its alternate title of "The Posthumous Papers of a Decapitated Surveyor" and foreshadows the use and treatment of revolutionary imagery in the novel proper.

This imagery, of course, is drawn from the French Revolution of 1789. [. . .] Predictably, the American press drew careless comparisons between the European revolutions and the American political scene. When Zachary

Taylor began his series of political appointments in the spring and summer of 1849, they were reported in the Democratic papers as revolutionary acts, as symbolic beheadings of Democratic party members. Some seven times in May and June, for example, the *Boston Post* printed, in conjunction with the announcement of a political appointment and removal, a small drawing presumably of General Taylor standing beside a guillotine, puffing a cigar, surrounded by heads (presumably of Democrats) at his feet. One of these drawings appeared on 11 June and on the following day, a letter to the editor appeared objecting to Hawthorne's removal from the Salem Custom House. "This is one of the most heartless acts of this heartless administration," the anonymous writer declared. "The head of the poet and the scholar is stricken off to gratify and reward some greedy partizan! . . . There stands, at the guillotine, beside the headless trunk of a pure minded, faithful and well deserving officer, sacrificed to the worth of party proscription, Gen. Zachary Taylor, now President." As Arlin Turner has pointed out, this letter was probably a source of Hawthorne's "beheading" metaphor;[2] however, behind the reference were two years of revolutionary events in Europe, two years of revolutionary rhetoric and imagery.

II

Such rhetoric and imagery appeared not only in the newspapers, of course, but also in contemporary books, some of which dealt with revolution in a serious historical manner. Although *The Scarlet Letter* has often been praised for its fidelity to New England history, the central setting of the novel, the scaffold, is, I believe, an historical inaccuracy intentionally used by Hawthorne to develop the theme of revolution. The Puritans occasionally sentenced a malefactor to stand upon a shoulder-high block or upon the ladder of the gallows, [. . .] but in none of the New England histories Hawthorne used as sources [. . .] are these structures called scaffolds. [. . .] The common instruments of punishment in the Massachusetts Bay Colony were, as Hawthorne shows in "Endicott and the Red Cross," the whipping post, the stocks, and the pillory. [. . .] Although Hawthorne in his romance identifies the scaffold as part of the pillory, his narrator and his characters refer to it by the former term alone some twenty-six times, calling it the scaffold of the pillory only four times and the pillory only once.

As early as 1557 and then later with increasing frequency during the first French Revolution, the word "scaffold" served as a synecdoche for a public beheading—by the executioner's axe or the guillotine. And, because of

---

[2] *Nathaniel Hawthorne: A Biography* (New York: Oxford UP, 1980), 181.

its role in the regicides of overthrown kings, the word acquired powerful political associations, which it still retains. When King Charles I was beheaded with an axe following the successful rebellion led by Cromwell, Andrew Marvell in his "An Horation Ode" used the word in the following tribute to his king:

> . . . thence the royal actor born
> The tragic scaffold might adorn:
> While round the armed bands
> Did clap their bloody hands.
> *He* nothing common did or mean
> Upon that memorable scene:
> But bowed his comely head
> Down, as upon a bed.

One hundred and forty-four years later, when Louis XVI became a liability to the new French republic, he too, of course, mounted what was termed the "scaffold" and there became one of the victims of the new device being advocated by Dr. Guillotin. The association of a scaffold with revolution and beheading, particularly the beheading of Charles I and Louis XVI, explains, I think, why Hawthorne uses it as his central and dominant setting. It links the narrator of "The Custom-House" sketch with the two main characters in the romance proper, and it raises their common predicaments above the plane of the personal into the helix of history.

Hawthorne's desire to connect his narrative with historic revolutions abroad is further shown by the time frame he uses. The opening scenes of the novel take place in May 1642 and the closing ones in May 1649. These dates coincide almost exactly with those of the English Civil War fought between King Charles I and his Puritan Parliament. Hawthorne was familiar with histories of this subject and had recently (June 1848) checked out of the Salem Atheneum Francois Guizot's *History of the English Revolution of 1640, Commonly Called the Great Rebellion*.[3] Guizot, Professor of Modern History of the Sorbonne when he wrote this work, became, of course, Louis Philippe's Prime Minister whose policies provoked the French Revolution of 1848. During the spring of 1848 Guizot's name became familiar to Americans, and probably the man's recent notoriety led Hawthorne to a reading of his work in the summer of 1848.

Examination of the simultaneity between fictional events in *The Scarlet*

---

[3] Marion L. Kesselring, *Hawthorne's Reading, 1828–1850* (1949; rpt. New York: Norwood, 1976), 52.

Letter and historical events in America and England verifies that the 1642–1649 time frame for events in the romance was carefully chosen to enhance the treatment of revolutionary themes. When Hester Prynne is led from the prison by the beadle who cries, "Make way, good people, make way, in the King's name," less than a month has passed since Charles's Puritan Parliament had sent him what amounted to a declaration of war. Five months later, in October, 1642, the first battle between Round-heads and Cavaliers was fought at Edgehill, and word of the open hostilities reached America in December. Then and in the years that followed, the Bay Colony fasted and prayed for victory by Parliament, but these became times of political anxiety and stress in America as well as England. According to one of Hawthorne's sources, Felt's *Annals of Salem,* in November 1646 the General Court (presided over by Messrs. Bartholomew and Hathorne) ordered "a fast on Dec. 24th, for the hazardous state of England . . . and difficulties of Church and State among themselves, both of which, say they, some strive to undermine."[4] By the final scenes of the novel, when Arthur is deciding to die as a martyr, Charles I has just been beheaded (on 30 January 1649); thus, when Chillingworth sarcastically thanks Arthur for his prayers, calling them "golden recompense" and "the current gold coin of the New Jerusalem, with the King's own mint-mark on them" (246), Hawthorne adds to Chillingworth's irony with his own. Furthermore, given the novel's time frame, the tableau of Arthur bowing "his head forward on the cushions of the pulpit, at the close of his Election Sermon" (261), while Hester stands waiting beside the scaffold, radiates with ominous import, particularly when one recalls that Arthur is not a graduate of Cambridge, as most of the Puritan ministers of New England were, but rather of Oxford, . . . the place of refuge for King Charles during the Revolution.

By thus setting events in an age when "men of the sword had overthrown nobles and kings" (204), Hawthorne provides a potent historical backdrop for the revolutionary and counter-revolutionary battles fought, with shifting allegiances, among the four main characters and the Puritan leadership. Furthermore, his battle imagery, such as Governor Bellingham's armor and Pearl's simulated slaying of the Puritan children, draws upon and reflects the actual warfare abroad and thus illuminates the struggles being fought on social, moral, and metaphysical grounds in Boston.

Bearing upon the novel perhaps even more than its connections with

---

[4] Joseph B. Felt, *The Annals of Salem, from Its First Settlement* (Salem: W. & S. B. Ives, 1827), 175.

the English "Rebellion" and its attendant regicide are its connections with the first French Revolution and the execution of Louis XVI. In the romance itself, Hawthorne first alludes to one tie when he describes the scaffold in the opening scenes; "it constituted," he writes, "a portion of a penal machine, which . . . was held, in the old time, to be as effectual an agent in the promotion of good citizenship, as ever was the guillotine among the terrorists of France" (124–25). This allusion may be derived from the imagery appearing, . . . in the contemporary press; but it is also shaped, in a more profound way, by an overlooked source of *The Scarlet Letter*, Alphonse de Lamartine's *History of the Girondists*, a history of the first French Revolution published in France in 1847, translated into English by H. T. Ryde and published in the United States in three volumes in 1847–48.

[. . .][Lamartine's] account of the first French Revolution is an imaginative and dramatic construct that gains much of its power from its sympathetic treatment of Louis XVI and its suspenseful narrative structure, which includes a tableau at the scaffold [where he is beheaded] as its climactic scene. [. . .] Lamartine's stirring treatment of revolutionary events and political martyrdom and especially his unprecedented use of the scaffold as both a dramatic setting and a unifying structural device lead one to speculate that Hawthorne may have read this work before he wrote *The Scarlet Letter;* however, speculation is unnecessary. He did. The records of the Salem Atheneum reveal that on 13 September 1849, he checked out the first two volumes of Lamartine's *History*. Moreover, Sophia Hawthorne's letters to her sister and mother, combined with Hawthorne's notebook entries, reveal, as no biographer has yet pointed out, that it was about ten days later, most likely between 21 September and 25 September, that Hawthorne began work in earnest on *The Scarlet Letter*.[5] On 27 September he checked out the third volume of Lamartine's *History*, and on that date Sophia, in an often-quoted letter, informed her mother, "Mr. Hawthorne

---

[5] Hawthorne and his wife spent much of the last half of August and the first part of September househunting, first on the Atlantic shore near Kittery Point, and then in the Berkshires near Lenox. Hawthorne may have worked on *The Scarlet Letter* during the second week in September after Sophia returned from Lenox, but if he did, it was not with the commitment he later displayed, for on 17 September he set out with his friend Ephraim Miller on a leisurely three-day journey to Temple, New Hampshire. Assuming he rested on the 20th, the day after his return, and knowing it was the 27th when Sophia first said he was writing "immensely" mornings and afternoons, it seems likely that between 21 September and 25 September he became absorbed in the writing of his romance. All of the letters from Sophia Hawthorne to her mother Elizabeth P. Peabody and her sister Mary Mann are quoted with the kind permission of the Henry W. and Albert A. Berg Collection, The New York Public Library, Astor, Lenox and Tilden Foundation.

is writing morning & afternoon. . . . He writes immensely—I am almost frightened about it—But he is well now & looks very shining."[6] (He returned the first two volumes of the *History* 6 November and the third volume 12 November.) This correlation in dates plus Hawthorne's allusions to the terrorists of France suggests that what has become one of the most celebrated settings in American literature, the scaffold of *The Scarlet Letter*, was taken from the Place de la Révolution of eighteenth-century Paris, as described by Lamartine, and transported to the Marketplace of seventeenth-century Boston, where it became the focal point of Hawthorne's narrative. Along with it came, most likely, a reinforced scepticism about violent reform.

III

Recognition that revolutionary struggle stirred at the front of Hawthorne's consciousness as he wrote *The Scarlet Letter* not only accounts for many structural and thematic details in the novel but also explains some of the apparent inconsistencies in his treatment of his characters, especially Hester and Arthur. [. . .] I think the revolutionary context of events provides a key for sorting out Hawthorne's sympathies, or more accurately those of his narrator (whose biases closely resemble Hawthorne's). The narrator, as a member of a toppled established order, an *ancien régime* so to speak, possesses instincts that are conservative and antirevolutionary, consistently so, but the individuals he regards undergo considerable change, thus evoking inconsistent attitudes on his part. Specifically, when Hester or Arthur battle to maintain or regain their rightful place in the social or spiritual order, the narrator sympathizes with them; when they become revolutionary instead and attempt to overthrow an established order, he becomes unsympathetic.[7] The scaffold serves to clarify the political and spiritual issues raised by events in the novel, and the decapitated surveyor of the Custom House, not surprisingly, identifies with whoever becomes a martyr upon it.

Hawthorne's use of the scaffold as a structural device has long been recognized. [. . .] The way in which the scaffold serves as a touchstone for the

---

[6] Letter to Elizabeth P. Peabody (mother); Berg Collection, New York Public Library.
[7] Nina Baym in her discussion of "The Custom-House" sketch posits that "like Hester, [Hawthorne] becomes a rebel because he is thrown out of society, by society. . . . The direct attack of 'The Custom-House' on some of the citizens of Salem adds a fillip of personal revenge to the theoretical rebellion that it dramatizes" (348 in this volume). Hawthorne's attack, I think, can be more accurately termed a counterattack and seen as dramatizing not a rebellion but his reaction to a rebellion.

narrator's sympathies, however, has not been fully explored, particularly with reference to the matter of revolution.

As every reader notices, at the beginning of the story, Hester is accorded much sympathy. Her beauty, her courage, her pride, all receive emphasis; and the scaffold, meant to degrade her, elevates her, figuratively as well as literally. The narrator presents her as an image of Divine Maternity, and more importantly, as a member of the old order of nobility suffering at the hands of a vulgar mob. Her recollection of her paternal home, "poverty-stricken," but "retaining a half-obliterated shield of arms over the portal" (126) establishes her link to aristocracy. Furthermore, although she has been sentenced by the Puritan magistrates, her worst enemies are the coarse, beefy, pitiless "gossips" who surround the scaffold and argue that she should be hanged or at least branded on the forehead. The magistrates, whom Hawthorne characterizes as "good men, just, and sage" have shown clemency in their sentence, and that clemency is unpopular with the chorus of matrons who apparently speak for the people.

Through the first twelve chapters, half of the book, the narrator's sympathies remain with Hester, for she continues to represent, like Charles I, Louis XVI, and Surveyor Hawthorne, a fallen aristocratic order struggling in defense of her rights against an antagonistic populace. The poor, the well-to-do, adults, children, laymen, clergy, all torment her in various ways; but she, the narrator tells us, "was patient—a martyr, indeed" (146). It is Pearl, of course, who anticipates what Hester will become—a revolutionary—and reveals the combative streak her mother possesses. "The warfare of Hester's spirit," Hawthorne writes, "was perpetuated in Pearl" (150), and this is shown by Pearl's throwing stones at the Puritan children ("the most intolerant brood that ever lived" [152]), her smiting and uprooting the weeds that represent these children, and her splashing the Governor himself with water. "She never created a friend, but seemed always to be sowing broadcast the dragon's teeth, whence sprung a harvest of armed enemies, against whom she rushed to battle" (154). [. . .]

Hester's own martial spirit comes to the fore in the confrontation with Bellingham, but here she fights only to maintain the *status quo* and thus keeps the narrator's sympathies. She visits the Governor not to attack him in any way but to defend her right to raise Pearl. Undaunted by Bellingham's shining armor, which "was not meant for mere idle show," Hester triumphs, because she has the natural order upon her side and because Arthur comes to her aid. Drawing Pearl forcibly into her arms, she confronts "the old Puritan magistrate with almost a fierce expression"; and Arthur, prompted into action by Hester's veiled threats, responds like a valiant Cavalier. His voice, as he speaks on her behalf, is "sweet, tremulous, but powerful, insomuch that the hall reechoed, and the hollow armour rang with it" (166, 168).

In the central chapters of the novel, when the narrator turns his attention toward Arthur and evidences antipathy toward him, it is not only because of the minister's obvious hypocrisy but also because of the intellectual change that he has undergone at Chillingworth's hands. Subtly, Arthur becomes radicalized and anticipates Hester's ventures into the realm of speculative and revolutionary thought. "There was a fascination for the minister," Hawthorne writes, "in the company of the man of science, in whom he recognized an intellectual cultivation of no moderate depth or scope; together with a range and freedom of ideas, that he would have vainly looked for among the members of his own profession" (174). And if Arthur is the victim of the leech's herbs and poisons, he is also a victim of more deadly intellectual brews as well. The central scene of the novel, Arthur's "vigil" on the scaffold, is inspired, apparently, by the "liberal views" he has begun to entertain. "On one of those ugly nights," we are told, "the minister started from his chair. A new thought had struck him" (191). This thought is to stand on the scaffold in the middle of the night, but by so doing he joins the ranks of Satan's rebellious legions. As he indulges in "the mockery of penitence" upon the scaffold, his guilt becomes "heaven-defying" and reprehensible, in the narrator's eyes. Rather than seeking to reestablish his moral force, which has been "abased into more than childish weakness," Arthur, in his imagination, mocks the Reverend Wilson, the people of Boston, and God himself. [. . .] The blazing A in the sky, which Arthur sees "addressed to himself alone," marks Governor Winthrop's death, according to the townspeople, and thus further emphasizes (by its reference to Winthrop's famous leadership and integrity) the nadir Arthur has reached by his indulgence in defiant thought and behavior.

The transformation Hester undergoes in the middle of the novel (which only appears to be from sinner to saint) is a stronger version of that which Arthur has undergone at her husband's hands; she too becomes, like the French revolutionaries of 1789 and the Italian revolutionaries of 1849, a radical thinker engaged in a revolutionary struggle against an established political–religious order. And as such, she loses the narrator's sympathies (while gaining those of most readers). The transformation begins with her regaining, over the course of seven years, the goodwill of the public, which "was inclined to show its former victim a more benign countenance than she cared to be favored with, or, perchance, than she deserved" (202). The rulers of the community, who "were longer in acknowledging the influence of Hester's good qualities than the people," become, as time passes, not her antagonists but rather the objects of her antagonism. We first see her impulse to challenge their authority when Chillingworth tells her that the magistrates have discussed allowing her to remove the scarlet letter from her bosom. "It lies not in the pleasure of the magistrates to take off this badge" (207), she tells him. Similarly, when she meets Arthur in the forest several days later, she subversively asks, "What hast thou to do with all these iron men and their opinions? They have kept thy better part in bondage too long already!" (227).

The new direction Hester's combativeness has taken is political in nature and flows from her isolation and indulgence in speculation. In a passage often quoted, but seldom viewed as consistent with the rest of the novel, because of its unsympathetic tone, the narrator explains that Hester Prynne "had wandered, without rule or guidance, in a moral wilderness. . . . Shame, Despair, Solitude! These had been her teachers,—stern and wild ones,— and they had made her strong, but taught her much amiss" (228). Hester's ventures into new areas of thought link her, significantly, with the overthrow of governments and the overthrow of "ancient prejudice, wherewith was linked much of ancient principle." "She assumed," the narrator points out, "a freedom of speculation, then common enough on the other side of the Atlantic, but which our forefathers, had they known of it, would have held to be a deadlier crime than that stigmatized by the scarlet letter" (204). Referring for the second time to the antinomian Anne Hutchinson, whom Hawthorne in another work had treated with little sympathy, the narrator speculates that if Pearl had not become the object of her mother's devotion, Hester "might, and not improbably would, have suffered death from the stern tribunals of the period, for attempting to undermine the foundations of the Puritan establishment" (204).[8]

Although Hester does not lead a political–religious revolt against the Puritan leadership, these speculations are quite relevant to the action which follows, for Hawthorne shows her radicalism finding an outlet in her renewed relationship with Arthur, which assumes revolutionary form. When they hold their colloquy in the forest, during which she reenacts her role as Eve the subversive temptress, we learn that "the whole seven years of outlaw and ignominy had been little other than a preparation for this very hour" (229). What Hester accomplishes during this hour (other than raising the reader's hopes) is once again to overthrow Arthur's system and

---

[8] For excellent discussions of Hawthorne's attitudes toward women activists, see Neal F. Doubleday, "Hawthorne's Hester and Feminism," *PMLA*, 54 (1939), 825–28; Morton Cronin, "Hawthorne on Romantic Love and the Status of Women," *PMLA*, 69 (1954), 89–98; and Darrel Abel, "Hawthorne on the Strong Dividing Lines of Nature," *American Transcendental Quarterly*, No. 14 (1972), 23–31.

undermine his loyalty to the Puritan community and the Puritan God. She establishes a temporary provisional government within him, so to speak, which fails to sustain itself. Although Hester obviously loves Arthur and seeks only their happiness together, her plan, which most readers heartily endorse, challenges, in the narrator's eyes, the social order of the community and the spiritual order of the universe, and thus earns his explicit disapproval.

When Hester tells Arthur that the magistrates have kept his better part in bondage, the narrator makes it clear that it is Arthur's better part that has actually kept his worse and lawless self imprisoned. For some time the prison has proved sound, but "the breach which guilt has once made into the human soul is never, in this mortal state, repaired," the narrator declares. "It may be watched and guarded; so that the enemy shall not force his way again into the citadel. . . . But there is still the ruined wall" (229). Thus, as Hawthorne draws upon the popular revolutionary imagery of 1848–49 to present Hester as a goddess of Liberty leading a military assault, she prevails; however, her victory, like that of the first Bastille day, sets loose forces of anarchy and wickedness. Arthur experiences "a glow of strange enjoyment" after he agrees to flee with her, but to clarify the moral dimensions of this freedom, Hawthorne adds, "It was the exhilarating effect—upon a prisoner just escaped from the dungeon of his own heart—of breathing the wild, free atmosphere of an unredeemed, unchristianized, lawless region" (229–30).

Unlike the earlier struggle that Hester and Arthur had fought together to maintain the *status quo*—the traditional relationship between mother and child—this struggle accomplishes something far more pernicious: "a revolution in the sphere of thought and feeling." And because it does, it receives unsympathetic treatment. "In truth," Hawthorne writes, "nothing short of a total change of dynasty and moral code, in that interior kingdom, was adequate to account for the impulses now communicated to the unfortunate and startled minister. At every step he was incited to do some strange, wild, wicked thing or other, with a sense that it would be at once involuntary and intentional" (241).

[. . .] Arthur's impulses to blaspheme, curse, and lead innocence astray are a stronger version of those seen during his vigil, and they confirm the narrator's assertion that the minister has acquired "sympathy and fellowship with wicked mortals and the world of perverted spirits" (244). It is important to notice also that the success of Arthur's sermon, which is so eloquent, so filled with compassion and wisdom, depends ultimately not upon his new revolutionary impulses but upon older counter-revolutionary sources that are spiritually conservative. He draws upon the "energy—or say, rather, the inspiration which had held him up, until he should have delivered the sacred message that brought its own strength along with it from heaven" (262).

The final change of heart and spirit that Arthur undergoes and that leads him to his death on the scaffold is foreshadowed by events in the marketplace prior to his sermon. There the exhibition of broadswords upon the scaffold plus Pearl's sense of "impending revolution" suggests that while the minister's better self has been overthrown, it will reassert itself shortly. The procession in which Arthur appears dramatizes the alternative to the lawless freedom Hester has offered. Here, as Michael Davitt Bell has observed, we have "the greatest tribute in all of Hawthorne's writing to the nobility of the founders."[9] The people, we are told, had bestowed their reverence "on the white hair and venerable brow of age; on long-tried integrity; on solid wisdom and sad-colored experience; on endowments of that grave and weighty order, which gives the idea of permanence, and comes under the general definition of respectability" (254). These are the qualities that distinguish Bradstreet, Endicott, Dudley, Bellingham, and their compeers. And, although we are not told who the new governor is (it was Endicott), we know that his election represents orderly change, in contrast to the rebellion and regicide that has recently occurred in England. "Today," Hester tells Pearl, "a new man is beginning to rule over them," and, in harmony with this event, Arthur acts to reestablish his place within the order of the community and within the order of the kingdom of God.

During the sermon Arthur seems to regain some of his spiritual stature and is described as an angel, who, "in his passage to the skies, had shaken his bright wings over the people for an instant, —at once a shadow and a splendor." Because Arthur is still a hypocrite, considerable irony exists within this description; however, when the minister walks to and mounts the scaffold, the narrator's irony turns to sincerity. Arthur attempts, before he dies, to regain God's favor, and as he nears the scaffold, where Hester and Chillingworth will both oppose his effort to confess, we are told that "it was hardly a man with life in him, that tottered on his path so nervelessly, yet tottered, and did not fall!" (262). The exclamation mark indicates the double sense of "fall" Hawthorne wishes to suggest, and at the end Arthur seems to escape from the provisional control over him that both Chillingworth and Hester have had.

"Is not this better than what we dreamed of in the forest?" he asks Hester, and although she replies "I know not! I know not!" the revolu-

---

[9] *Hawthorne and the Historical Romance of New England* (Princeton: Princeton Univ. Press, 1971), 140.

tionary context of the novel, the bias toward restoration and order, indicate we are supposed to agree that it is.[10] Arthur's final scene upon the scaffold mirrors Hester's first scene there, even though he proceeds from the church whereas she had proceeded from the prison. But, unlike Hester, Arthur through humility and faith seems to achieve peace, whereas she, through "the combative energy of her character," had achieved only "a kind of lurid triumph" (142). In the final scaffold scene, Pearl acts as an ethical agent once again and emphasizes Hawthorne's themes about peace and battle, order and revolt. At the moment of his death, Arthur kisses Pearl, and the tears she then sheds are "the pledge that she would grow up amid human joy and sorrow, nor for ever do battle with the world, but be a woman in it" (267). In what seems to be a reward for her docility, she marries into European nobility (thereby accomplishing a restoration of the ties with aristocracy her maternal relatives once enjoyed); similarly, Hester at last, we are told in a summary, forsakes her radicalism and recognizes that the woman who would lead the reform movements of the future and establish women's rights must be less "stained with sin," less "bowed down with shame" than she. This woman must be "lofty, pure, and beautiful, and wise, moreover, not through dusky grief, but the ethereal medium of joy" (271).

More than one reader has correctly surmised that this ending to the novel constitutes a veiled compliment to Hawthorne's little Dove, Sophia, and a veiled criticism of Margaret Fuller, America's foremost advocate of women's rights and, at the time, one suffering from a sullied reputation due to gossip about her child and questionable marriage. Hawthorne's long and ambivalent relationship with Fuller and his response to her activities as a radical and revolutionary in 1849 had a decided effect upon the novel. There are several parallels which indicate Fuller served as a model for Hester: both had the problem of facing a Puritan society encumbered by a child of questionable legitimacy; both were concerned with social reform and the role of woman in society; both functioned as counsellor and comforter to women; and both had children entitled to use the armorial seals of a non-English noble family. [. . .]

In [. . .] *The Scarlet Letter* [Hawthorne] drew upon the issues and rhetoric he was encountering in the present, especially those relating to himself as a public figure. Moreover, he responded strongly and creatively to accounts of foreign revolutions and revolutionaries that he found in the

---

[10] A number of critics have read this scene as ironic and seen Dimmesdale as deluded or damned; however, the *Pietà* tableau, Arthur's Christlike forgiveness of Chillingworth, and Hawthorne's own emotional response to the scene (when he read it to Sophia) make it difficult to agree with such a reading.

newspapers, the periodicals, and books new to the libraries. Although to most of his countrymen the overthrow of kings and the triumph of republicanism were exhilarating events, to a man of Hawthorne's temperament, the violence, the bloodshed, the extended chaos that accompanied the revolutions of 1848–49 were deeply disturbing. [. . .]

Publishing *The Scarlet Letter* in the Nineteenth-Century United States

Michael Winship

Besides, America is now wholly given over to a d___d mob of scribbling women, and I should have no chance of success while the public taste is occupied with their trash — and should be ashamed of myself if I did succeed. What is the mystery of these innumerable editions of the Lamplighter, and other books neither better nor worse? — worse they could not be, and better they need not be, when they sell by 100.000.[1]

It may well be that no single passage written by Nathaniel Hawthorne is better known than this or, at least over the past few decades, more widely quoted. An extraordinary possibility, especially as the passage comes from the middle of a rather long private letter, written to his publisher and friend, William D. Ticknor, on 19 January 1855, and first published in 1910.[2] Nevertheless, this passage has resonated through recent discussions of American literary history, for it raises questions that are key to our understandings of that tradition: What is the relationship between popular success and literary quality? What role do gender politics play in our assessment of a work? In what ways have the economic factors facing authors and publish-

Adapted from a paper delivered at the National Hawthorne Conference on *The Scarlet Letter*, Boston, June 2000. (A slightly longer version appeared in *Studies in American Fiction* 29 [2001]: 3–13.)

[1] Letter to William D. Ticknor, 19 Jan. 1855, Nathaniel Hawthorne, *The Letters, 1853–1856*, ed. Thomas Woodson, L. Neal Smith, and Norman Holmes Pearson (Columbus: Ohio State University Press, 1987), 304. The original letter is in the Berg Collection in the New York Public Library.

[2] Hawthorne, *Letters of Hawthorne to William D. Ticknor, 1851–1864* (New York: Cateret Book Club, 1910), 73–76. Rpt. Caroline Ticknor, *Hawthorne and His Publisher* (Boston: Houghton Mifflin, 1913), 14.

ers fostered or discouraged authorship in the United States? And how is it that during the 1850s, a decade that came to be dubbed as the "American Renaissance," sentimental novels could enjoy popular success while the "classics" by Hawthorne, Melville, Thoreau, and Whitman did not?

Although he could hardly have thought in such terms, Hawthorne was clearly bothered by these issues as he pondered in what direction to continue his literary career. He returned to the subject in his very next letter to Ticknor, but here at least he selects one of that "scribbling mob," Fanny Fern, for praise.[3] His original outburst had been directed specifically at the work of another, Maria Susannah Cummins, whose best-selling novel *The Lamplighter* was making a tremendous success. Published in early March 1854, this work is reported to have sold 20,000 copies in twenty days and 40,000 copies in eight weeks. By year's end, nearly 75,000 copies had been produced; by the end of the decade, total sales in the United States were somewhere around 90,000.[4] Nevertheless, Hawthorne clearly exaggerated when in exasperation he claimed that books written by women were selling by the hundred thousands. Although sales of *The Lamplighter* approached that figure, its success was exceptional, and its sales were not matched by other novels of the decade. The exception, of course, was Harriet Beecher Stowe's *Uncle Tom's Cabin*, which indeed did sell in the hundred thousands—around 310,000 copies during the 1850s.[5]

Hawthorne's frustration is understandable. Consider his most popular work, *The Scarlet Letter*, which was published in March 1850: only 11,800 copies had been produced by 1860. For the short term at least, sales of his works had to be reckoned in the thousands instead of tens of thousands, much less hundreds of thousands. But as we mark this year the sesquicentennial of the original publication of *The Scarlet Letter*, it pays to look at the longer term. What was the publication history of the work for the remainder of the nineteenth century? And how does this history compare to that of *Uncle Tom's Cabin*? What can the comparison tell us about the subsequent histories and reputations of these works?

---

[3] Letter to Ticknor, 2 Feb. 1855, *Letters, 1853–1856*, 307–08.

[4] See advertisements and notices in *Norton's Literary Gazette* (1 April 1854, 1 May 1854, 15 Dec. 1854). The total sales are difficult to know precisely. The work's publisher, John P. Jewett, lists the 89,000 in his catalog dated 1 April 1858; *American Publisher's Circular* gives the total as 90,000. These figures do not account for the many thousands that must have been produced and sold in Great Britain.

[5] The following totals for American fiction: Stowe's *Uncle Tom's Cabin* (1852), 310,000; Cummins's *The Lamplighter* (1854), 90,000; Fanny Fern's *Fern Leaves* (1853), 70,000, and *Ruth Hall* (1855), 55,000; Martha Stone Hubble's *The Shady Side* (1853), 42,000; Marion Harland's *Alone* (1854), *The Hidden Path* (1855), and *Moss Side* (1857)—25,000 each (*American Publisher's Circular*).

The story of the composition and original publication of *The Scarlet Letter* is well known.[6] Hawthorne, an established writer of short stories and sketches, began work on the manuscript sometime—probably late summer—during 1849, the same year that he was dismissed from his job at the Salem Custom House. Before year's end, Boston publisher James T. Fields called on Hawthorne in Salem and came away with a draft of "The Scarlet Letter," which Hawthorne imagined as one of several stories in a collection to be called *Old-Time Legends* (or possibly *The Custom-House*). Fields encouraged Hawthorne to consider expanding the work for separate publication, and Hawthorne eventually agreed. On 15 January 1850, Hawthorne sent the revised manuscript to Fields, including the introductory "Custom-House" sketch but missing three chapters, which were sent on to Boston on February 3. In the meantime, Fields had gone ahead with production, putting typesetters to work, and by February 18 he was able to include the sheets "as far as printed" in a parcel sent to the London publisher Richard Bentley. On March 16, the first edition of 2,500 copies, bound in the characteristic Ticknor and Fields binding of brown-ribbed T-cloth, appeared at a retail price of seventy-five cents.

As Fields had hoped but to Hawthorne's apparent surprise, the work was both well received and a moderate success.[7] A second edition of 2,500 copies was issued on April 22, containing a new preface by Hawthorne dated 30 March 1850; a third edition of 1,000 copies, for the first time printed from stereotype plates, followed on September 9. By year's end, Hawthorne had earned $663.75 in royalties—his royalty was 15 percent of the retail price—and the publisher's profits came to roughly nine hundred dollars, even after paying for the cost of the stereotype plates. These results were due in part to Fields's talents as a publisher who was skilled at managing the publicity of announcements, advertisements, and a network of sympathetic reviewers to push his firm's publications.[8]

---

[6] The following account is based on William Charvat, Introduction, *The Scarlet Letter* (Columbus: Ohio State University Press, 1962), xv–xxviii, supplemented with information from *The Cost Books of Ticknor and Fields and Their Predecessors, 1832–1858*, ed. Warren S. Tryon and William Charvat (New York: Bibliographical Society of America, 1949) and C. E. Frazer Clark, *Nathaniel Hawthorne: A Descriptive Bibliography* (Pittsburgh: University of Pittsburgh Press, 1978).

[7] The reception history of *The Scarlet Letter* can be found in *The Critical Response to Nathaniel Hawthorne's The Scarlet Letter*, ed. Gary Scharnhorst (New York: Greenwood, 1992). For a more general discussion of Hawthorne's reputation over time, see Richard H. Brodhead, *The School of Hawthorne* (New York: Oxford University Press, 1986).

[8] Tryon and Charvat, entries A173a, A79a, A189a; see also William Charvat, "James T. Fields and the Beginnings of Book Promotion," in *The Profession of Authorship in America, 1800–1870: The Papers of William Charvat*, ed. Matthew J. Bruccoli (Columbus: Ohio State University Press, 1968), 168–89.

In one regard, though, Fields fell short, for in rushing the work into publication, he failed to allow time for arrangements for an authorized English edition. British copyright law required that such an edition appear before or simultaneously with the American edition, but by the time that Bentley—the London publisher whom Fields had approached—received the entire text, it had already been published in Boston. Bentley reported that two other firms were preparing unauthorized editions and declined to publish the work. Though imported copies of the American sheets had been available earlier, it was not reprinted in England until May 1851.

The wish to rush the work into publication may also explain in part why the firm printed the first two editions from type rather than from stereotype plates, though this is not as surprising as it may at first appear. Although the firm's standard practice only a few years later was to print most of its new publications from plates, in 1850 only four of its eighteen new works were stereotyped for the first printing. The reason may have been financial—the firm was in the process of expanding its list and may have wished to avoid the extra investment that plates entailed. The cost of producing stereotype plates nearly doubled the cost of composition: In the case of *The Scarlet Letter,* composition for the first two editions came to $130.11 and $121.57, respectively, whereas the cost of composition and stereotyping for the third was $233.39. Clearly, producing the plates immediately would have been more economical, but the firm may not have expected the work to have such success.[9]

Despite these oversights, Hawthorne was surely pleased with Fields's handling of the work's publication; over the next several years, Fields's firm—Ticknor and Fields—reissued many of Hawthorne's earlier works and published his new works as they were finished. Hawthorne himself formed close personal ties with both partners, and Ticknor and Fields and its successor firms remained Hawthorne's primary publisher for the rest of the century. Hawthorne's works formed a key part of the core list of canonical American literary works—including those of Emerson and Thoreau—that modern scholars have come to associate with Houghton Mifflin Company, the firm into which Ticknor and Fields evolved.

Harriet Beecher Stowe was less fortunate in her original choice of publisher for *Uncle Tom's Cabin,* Boston's John P. Jewett. Despite the work's

---

[9] Tryon and Charvat (entries A173a, A179a, A189a). For a general discussion of the firm's practice in regard to printing from plates, see Michael Winship, *American Literary Publishing in the Mid-Nineteenth Century. The Business of Ticknor and Fields* (Cambridge: Cambridge University Press, 1995), 103–10, 142–47. The relatively large press runs for the first two editions reflect the fact that they were printed from type instead of plates.

tremendous initial success and despite the skillful promotional efforts of its publisher, demand fell off markedly after little over a year. Shortly thereafter, Stowe fell out with Jewett over contract terms, and for future works she turned to another Boston firm, Phillips, Sampson and Company, which had originally declined to publish her antislavery masterpiece. After the break with Stowe, Jewett remained the publisher of *Uncle Tom's Cabin*, but he nearly failed during the Panic of 1857; in 1860 he dissolved his publishing business. In 1859 Stowe's chief publishers, Phillips, Sampson and Company, also went out of business; consequently, she approached Fields to act as her publisher. In 1860, when Stowe's works joined those of Hawthorne on the list of Ticknor and Fields, *Uncle Tom's Cabin* had been, for all intents and purposes, out of print for many years.[10]

In the meantime, *The Scarlet Letter* had remained happily in print with steady sales, which declined only slightly as time passed. The investment in stereotype plates for the third edition in September 1850 allowed the firm to produce small impressions over time as demand required. A second printing from these plates—the fourth printing of the work overall—of 800 copies was produced in June 1851; between then and Hawthorne's death on 19 May 1864, the plates were used for thirteen impressions of 500 copies each, a total of 6,500 copies at an average of one impression per year.[11]

Hawthorne's death occurred a little over a month after that of William Ticknor, the senior partner of Ticknor and Fields, which had occurred on 10 April 1864 while he and Hawthorne were on a vacation trip to the South that was hoped to revive Hawthorne's failing health. Inevitably, these deaths affected the publication of Hawthorne's works, including *The Scarlet Letter*. Hawthorne's business relations with Ticknor and Fields had been complicated, based on a series of oral agreements setting the royalties on his works at varying terms, 10 percent of the retail price for some and 15 percent for others. Once the firm was reorganized with Fields firmly in charge as senior partner, he arranged to regularize matters; it was agreed that the firm would in future pay a flat sum of 12 cents for each copy sold of any of Hawthorne's works.[12]

---

[10] Fields was in no hurry to rush it back into print; his firm's first printing, a mere 270 copies, was not completed until November 1862. For the history of the publication of *Uncle Tom's Cabin*, see Michael Winship, "'The Greatest Book of Its Kind': A Publishing History of *Uncle Tom's Cabin*," *Proceedings of the American Antiquarian Society* 109 (1999).

[11] Ticknor and Fields, Cost Books, fair, A–D, in the Houghton Library, Harvard University.

[12] For this and the following paragraph, see Ellen Ballou, *The Building of the House: Houghton Mifflin's Formative Years* (Boston: Houghton Mifflin, 1970), 143–56, 242; Warren S. Tryon, *Parnassus Corner: A Life of James T. Fields, Publisher to the Victorians* (Bos-

The fairness of this new arrangement is difficult to assess. At the time, it certainly seemed generous, for 12 cents a copy represented an increase in a royalty on *The Scarlet Letter,* from 11¼ cents to 12 cents. Similarly, it meant an increase in royalties for all of Hawthorne's other works except *The House of the Seven Gables* and *Our Old Home,* which were earning 15 cents per copy under the old arrangement. The problem, however, arises from the shift in the method of determining royalties from a percentage basis to a flat fee. Retail prices for books had remained remarkably stable throughout the 1840s and 1850s, but the Civil War had brought about a period of inflation and consequent increase in book production costs, which in turn inevitably led to an increase in retail prices, a result that Fields must have foreseen. By the late 1860s, retail prices on all of Hawthorne's works had risen to $1.50 or $2.00, which meant that the royalty on *The Scarlet Letter,* for example, would have risen under the old agreement to 30 cents a copy. From this perspective, Fields had struck a very hard bargain indeed!

Conflict was inevitable. Hawthorne's widow, Sophia, raising three children alone, found herself strapped financially and sensed that perhaps Hawthorne's royalties were less than they should be. Her suspicions seemed confirmed in 1868, when Gail Hamilton, another Ticknor and Fields author whose royalty terms had been changed in 1864 in a manner similar to Hawthorne's, began to raise questions. Upset, Sophia Hawthorne went so far as to threaten to transfer future rights in her husband's works to another firm. Fields reacted quickly: He prepared an explanation, backed by figures, and offered to submit the matter to arbitration. Eventually, Sophia's sister, Elizabeth Peabody, intervened. After examining the firm's accounts, she concluded that, despite several clerical errors and other carelessness, the firm's records were consistent with one another; however, she also noted that demand had been such that neither author nor firm had received as much as $1,000 per year on average from Hawthorne's books. Ticknor and Fields was technically vindicated, but relations were soured. In an attempt to placate Sophia Hawthorne, Fields offered to pay in future a royalty of 10 percent on all of Hawthorne's works. These terms were agreed to and remained in force until 1875, when apparently Hawthorne's heirs accepted the firm's offer of a regular annuity of $2,000 in lieu of royalties.[13]

Hawthorne's death in 1864 was to have another important impact on the

---

ton: Houghton Mifflin, 1963), 333–49; and Carl J. Weber, *The Rise and Fall of James Ripley Osgood* (Waterville: Colby College Press, 1959), 135–137.

[13] Ballou states that the offer was not accepted due to wrangling among Hawthorne's children (242), but the firm's records indicate otherwise; see Agreement No. 2, 1 May

publication of *The Scarlet Letter,* for in the fall of that year the firm issued the first collected edition of Hawthorne's works. *The Scarlet Letter,* printed from the 1850 plates, appeared as the sixth volume of fourteen volumes in this Tinted Edition. A second collected edition was issued in 1871, and the same plates were used for *The Scarlet Letter,* which appeared bound with *The Blithedale Romance* as the fourth volume in the twelve-volume Illustrated Library Edition. This trend continued; when new plates for *The Scarlet Letter* were finally cast in 1875, they were used in the twenty-three-volume Little Classic Edition of Hawthorne's collected works. A third set of plates, cast in 1883, was prepared for the Riverside Edition, where *The Scarlet Letter* appeared, again bound with *The Blithedale Romance,* as the fifth volume of twelve volumes. These sets of Hawthorne's collected works, expanded as posthumous works, were repackaged and reissued in a variety of formats and bindings at a range of prices, over the years. For the rest of the century, *The Scarlet Letter* was generally marketed as part of Hawthorne's collected works, not singly as his greatest masterpiece.[14]

Hawthorne and Stowe shared the same publisher from 1860, but the pattern of publication of their works was different. *Uncle Tom's Cabin* clearly stood out among Stowe's works, not only in terms of importance but also in income. By the end of the 1880s, her earnings from *Uncle Tom's Cabin* equaled nearly two and a half times the royalties on all her other books combined. Unlike *The Scarlet Letter,* which had been chiefly available as part of a set of Hawthorne's collected works since his death in 1864, *Uncle Tom's Cabin* was chiefly sold by itself. Stowe, who survived Hawthorne by over thirty years, continued to produce new works through the 1870s, but no collected edition of Stowe's works appeared until after her death in 1896.

What of the sales of the two works? *The Scarlet Letter* started out at considerable disadvantage, but as time passed and sales increased, the difference grew less striking. During the 1860s, roughly 6,500 copies of *The Scarlet Letter* were produced, compared with 8,000 copies of *Uncle Tom's Cabin;* during the 1870s, roughly 20,000 copies were produced, compared with 26,000 copies of *Uncle Tom's Cabin.*[15] In 1878, with the formation of a new business partnership, the stereotype plates of the two works were inventoried and valued, a figure that served as a guide to estimating the worth

---

1875, in the uncataloged Houghton Mifflin contract files in the Houghton Library, Harvard University.

[14] See C. E. Frazer Clark, *Nathaniel Hawthorne: A Descriptive Bibliography* (Pittsburgh: University of Pittsburgh Press, 1978) for details.

[15] These figures are based on the Ticknor and Fields and Houghton, Osgood and Co. Sheet Stock Books in the Houghton Library, Harvard University.

of the rights to their publication: The plates of *The Scarlet Letter* were valued at \$4,792.38 and those for *Uncle Tom's Cabin* at \$4,524.60.[16]

Although *The Scarlet Letter* was chiefly marketed as part of Hawthorne's collected works, it was also issued from time to time in separate editions. In late 1877, as the end of the original copyright term of twenty-eight years approached, James R. Osgood and Company, a successor firm to Ticknor and Fields, issued the first new separate edition of *The Scarlet Letter*. With rather lavish illustrations by Mary Hallock Foote, this was an expensive volume at four dollars in cloth, nine dollars in leather. The illustrations may have been intended to support the firm's claims in the work, though the copyright in the text could be and was renewed and protected for a further fourteen years. In 1879 Houghton, Osgood and Company, another successor firm, issued for ten dollars F. O. C. Darley's *Compositions in Outline from Hawthorne's* Scarlet Letter, a series of twelve illustrated prints, each accompanied by a page of text extracted from Hawthorne's work.[17]

In early 1892, Houghton Mifflin Company, the final inheritor of the rights to Hawthorne's works, again prepared new separate editions of *The Scarlet Letter*, all printed from plates already in use for collected editions. In their spring announcement issued in March, the firm listed two new separate editions: the Universal Edition (printed from plates of the Riverside Edition),[18] which cost 50 cents in cloth, 25 cents in paper; and an even cheaper Salem Edition (printed from the plates of the Little Classic Edition), at 30 cents in cloth, 15 cents in paper. These were followed in May by an expensive edition, illustrated with photogravures based on Darley's outline drawings: The Trade Edition cost \$2.50 (printed from plates of the Riverside Edition), and a special Large Paper Edition (limited to 200 numbered copies and bound in vellum) cost \$7.50. These joined the Popular Edition of *The Scarlet Letter* (printed from the plates of the Riverside Edition), the only other separate edition that had been issued, which had been in print since 1885 and was priced at \$1 in cloth, 50 cents in paper. As the work entered the public domain, its authorized publisher—Houghton Mifflin Company—made sure that it was available separately in a range of formats and prices that appealed to as broad a market as possible.[19]

---

[16] Ticknor and Fields, Plate Inventory (1873–77) in the Houghton Library, Harvard University.

[17] For a full discussion of the illustrated editions of *The Scarlet Letter*, see Rita K. Gollin, "*The Scarlet Letter*" in "From Cover to Cover: The Presentation of Hawthorne's Major Romances," *Essex Institute Historical Collections*, 127 (1991): 12–30.

[18] This "edition" is not listed in Frazer Clark, but most likely it is that listed as A16.13.f.

[19] Houghton Mifflin seems to have believed that the copyright term on the work of forty-two years expired on 15 November 1892, though this is almost surely an error on their

The copyright on *Uncle Tom's Cabin* was scheduled to expire on 12 May 1893. As with *The Scarlet Letter*, the firm issued a range of new editions, both cheap and expensive, in an attempt to maintain their hold over the market. After *The Scarlet Letter* and *Uncle Tom's Cabin* entered the public domain, however, both were quickly reprinted in unauthorized editions. By century's end, separate editions of *The Scarlet Letter* were available from many of the firms that specialized in cheap publishing—Altemus, Bay View, Burt, Caldwell, Coates, Crowell, Donohue, Hill, Hurst, Lupton, McKay, Mershon, Ogilvie, Page, Rand, Stokes, Truslove, Warne, Ziegler—a list closely matching that for *Uncle Tom's Cabin*.[20] Houghton Mifflin Company continued as an important publisher of both works but was no longer able to control the ways that they were packaged and marketed.

For much of the twentieth century, critical opinion of the two works followed different paths. *Uncle Tom's Cabin* came to be viewed as flawed, overly sentimental, and frankly racist, in fact an embarrassment—an assessment that has only recently been revised. In the meanwhile, *The Scarlet Letter* emerged, along with Melville's *Moby-Dick*, as one of the "two most nearly undisputed classics of American fiction."[21] Clearly, reception history cannot be explained only by a work's publication and marketing, but it is interesting to speculate on the extent they have influenced the critical understanding of the importance of *The Scarlet Letter* in Hawthorne's oeuvre—for as the twentieth century dawned, it was for the first time readily and widely available to readers not as one volume from his collected works but as a distinct and separate work.

---

part. At that time, legal copyright in a work was established when it was registered and a prepublication title page was filed in the district court clerk's office; surely this must have been done in late 1849, not 1850.

[20] See *The United States Catalog: Books in Print, 1899* (Part 1: Author Index), ed. George Flavel Danforth and Marion E. Potter (Minneapolis: H. W. Wilson, 1900), 290, 631.

[21] See Charvat, Introduction xv.

Part Two

THE SCARLET LETTER

The Scarlet Letter

Nathaniel Hawthorne

The Scarlet Letter;

a

Romance.

By Nathaniel Hawthorne.

Facsimile of Hawthorne's original title page for *The Scarlet Letter*. The title page and the table of contents (opposite) are the only surviving pages from Hawthorne's original manuscript.

Contents.

Introductory

The Custom House.

CONTENTS OF
THE SCARLET LETTER

PREFACE

To the Second Edition

Much to the author's surprise, and (if he may say so without additional of-fence) considerably to his amusement, he finds that his sketch of official life, introductory to *The Scarlet Letter*, has created an unprecedented ex-citement in the respectable community immediately around him. It could hardly have been more violent, indeed, had he burned down the Custom-House, and quenched its last smoking ember in the blood of a certain venerable personage, against whom he is supposed to cherish a peculiar malevolence. As the public disapprobation would weigh very heavily on him, were he conscious of deserving it, the author begs leave to say, that he has carefully read over the introductory pages, with a purpose to alter or expunge whatever might be found amiss, and to make the best reparation in his power for the atrocities of which he has been adjudged guilty. But it appears to him, that the only remarkable features of the sketch are its frank and genuine good-humor, and the general accuracy with which he has conveyed his sincere impressions of the characters therein described. As to enmity, or ill-feeling of any kind, personal or political, he utterly disclaims such motives. The sketch might, perhaps, have been wholly omitted, with-out loss to the public, or detriment to the book; but, having undertaken to write it, he conceives that it could not have been done in a better or a kind-lier spirit, nor, so far as his abilities availed, with a livelier effect of truth.

The author is constrained, therefore, to republish his introductory sketch without the change of a word.

Salem, March 30, 1850

The Scarlet Letter. Centenary Edition. Vol. 1. Columbus: Ohio UP, 1962. (All notes are by the present editor.)

The Custom-House by Mary Hallock Foote, engraved by A. V. S. Anthony. Originally appeared in the 1877 Osgood and Company edition of the novel.

THE CUSTOM-HOUSE

Introductory to The Scarlet Letter

It is a little remarkable, that—though disinclined to talk overmuch of myself and my affairs at the fireside, and to my personal friends—an autobiographical impulse should twice in my life have taken possession of me, in addressing the public. The first time was three or four years since, when I favored the reader—inexcusably, and for no earthly reason, that either the indulgent reader or the intrusive author could imagine—with a description of my way of life in the deep quietude of an Old Manse.[1] And now—because, beyond my deserts, I was happy enough to find a listener or two on the former occasion—I again seize the public by the button, and talk of my three years' experience in a Custom-House. The example of the famous "P. P., Clerk of this Parish," was never more faithfully followed.[2] The truth seems to be, however, that, when he casts his leaves forth upon the wind, the author addresses, not the many who will fling aside his volume, or never take it up, but the few who will understand him, better than most of his schoolmates and lifemates. Some authors, indeed, do far more than this, and indulge themselves in such confidential depths of revelation as could fittingly be addressed, only and exclusively, to the one heart and mind of perfect sympathy; as if the printed book, thrown at large on the wide world, were certain to find out the divided segment of the writer's own nature, and complete his circle of existence by bringing him into communion with it. It is scarcely decorous, however, to speak all, even where we speak impersonally. But—as thoughts are frozen and utterance benumbed, unless the speaker stand in some true relation with his audience—it may be pardonable to imagine that a friend, a kind and apprehensive, though not the closest friend, is listening to our talk; and then, a native reserve being thawed by this genial consciousness, we may prate of the circumstances that lie around us, and even of ourself, but still keep the inmost Me behind its veil. To this extent and within these limits, an author, methinks, may be autobiographical, without violating either the reader's rights or his own.

It will be seen, likewise, that this Custom-House sketch has a certain propriety, of a kind always recognized in literature, as explaining how a large portion of the following pages came into my possession, and as offering proofs of the authenticity of a narrative therein contained. This, in fact,—

---

[1] The introduction to *Mosses from an Old Manse* (1846), entitled "The Author Makes the Reader Acquainted with His Abode."

[2] An anonymous English parody of Bishop Gilbert Burnet's tedious autobiography written around 1715 by Alexander Pope and John Gay.

a desire to put myself in my true position as editor, or very little more, of the most prolix among the tales that make up my volume, —this, and no other, is my true reason for assuming a personal relation with the public.[3] In accomplishing the main purpose, it has appeared allowable, by a few extra touches, to give a faint representation of a mode of life not heretofore described, together with some of the characters that move in it, among whom the author happened to make one.

In my native town of Salem, at the head of what, half a century ago, in the days of old King Derby,[4] was a bustling wharf, —but which is now burdened with decayed wooden warehouses, and exhibits few or no symptoms of commercial life; except, perhaps, a bark or brig, half-way down its melancholy length, discharging hides; or, nearer at hand, a Nova Scotia schooner, pitching out her cargo of fire-wood, —at the head, I say, of this dilapidated wharf, which the tide often overflows, and along which, at the base and in the rear of the row of buildings, the track of many languid years is seen in a border of unthrifty grass, —here, with a view from its front windows adown this not very enlivening prospect, and thence across the harbour, stands a spacious edifice of brick. From the loftiest point of its roof, during precisely three and a half hours of each forenoon, floats or droops, in breeze or calm, the banner of the republic; but with the thirteen stripes turned vertically, instead of horizontally, and thus indicating that a civil, and not a military post of Uncle Sam's government, is here established. Its front is ornamented with a portico of half a dozen wooden pillars, supporting a balcony, beneath which a flight of wide granite steps descends towards the street. Over the entrance hovers an enormous specimen of the American eagle, with outspread wings, a shield before her breast, and, if I recollect aright, a bunch of intermingled thunderbolts and barbed arrows in each claw. With the customary infirmity of temper that characterizes this unhappy fowl, she appears, by the fierceness of her beak and eye and the general truculency of her attitude, to threaten mischief to the inoffensive community; and especially to warn all citizens, careful of their safety, against intruding on the premises which she overshadows with her wings. Nevertheless, vixenly as she looks, many people are seeking, at this very moment, to shelter themselves under the wing of the federal eagle; imagining, I presume, that her bosom has all the softness and snugness of an

---

[3] When "The Custom-House" was typeset in January 1850, Hawthorne expected that it would introduce a group of tales he had already published, as well as the long story he had not yet completed, but his publisher James T. Fields persuaded him to let *The Scarlet Letter* stand alone. See notes 24 and 29.

[4] E. H. Derby (1739–99), a wealthy Salem merchant and ship owner.

eider-down pillow. But she has no great tenderness, even in her best of moods, and, sooner or later,—oftener soon than late,—is apt to fling off her nestlings with a scratch of her claw, a dab of her beak, or a rankling wound from her barbed arrows.

The pavement round about the above-described edifice—which we may as well name at once as the Custom-House of the port—has grass enough growing in its chinks to show that it has not, of late days, been worn by any multitudinous resort of business. In some months of the year, however, there often chances a forenoon when affairs move onward with a livelier tread. Such occasions might remind the elderly citizen of that period, before the last war with England,[5] when Salem was a port by itself; not scorned, as she is now, by her own merchants and ship-owners, who permit her wharves to crumble to ruin, while their ventures go to swell, needlessly and imperceptibly, the mighty flood of commerce at New York or Boston. On some such morning, when three or four vessels happen to have arrived at once,— usually from Africa or South America,—or to be on the verge of their departure thitherward, there is a sound of frequent feet, passing briskly up and down the granite steps. Here, before his own wife has greeted him, you may greet the sea-flushed ship-master, just in port, with his vessel's papers under his arm in a tarnished tin box. Here, too, comes his owner, cheerful or sombre, gracious or in the sulks, accordingly as his scheme of the now accomplished voyage has been realized in merchandise that will readily be turned to gold, or has buried him under a bulk of incommodities, such as nobody will care to rid him of. Here, likewise,—the germ of the wrinkle-browed, grizzly-bearded, careworn merchant,—we have the smart young clerk, who gets the taste of traffic as a wolf-cub does of blood, and already sends adventures in his master's ships, when he had better be sailing mimic boats upon a mill-pond. Another figure in the scene is the outward-bound sailor, in quest of a protection; or the recently arrived one, pale and feeble, seeking a passport to the hospital. Nor must we forget the captains of the rusty little schooners that bring firewood from the British provinces; a rough-looking set of tarpaulins, without the alertness of the Yankee aspect, but contributing an item of no slight importance to our decaying trade.

Cluster all these individuals together, as they sometimes were, with other miscellaneous ones to diversify the group, and, for the time being, it made the Custom-House a stirring scene. More frequently, however, on ascending the steps, you would discern—in the entry, if it were summer time, or in their appropriate rooms, if wintry or inclement weather—a row of venerable figures, sitting in old-fashioned chairs, which were tipped on

---

[5] The War of 1812.

their hind legs back against the wall. Oftentimes they were asleep, but occasionally might be heard talking together, in voices between speech and a snore, and with that lack of energy that distinguishes the occupants of alms-houses, and all other human beings who depend for subsistence on charity, on monopolized labor, or any thing else but their own independent exertions. These old gentlemen—seated, like Matthew, at the receipt of custom, but not very liable to be summoned thence, like him, for apostolic errands[6]—were Custom-House officers.

Furthermore, on the left hand as you enter the front door, is a certain room or office, about fifteen feet square, and of a lofty height; with two of its arched windows commanding a view of the aforesaid dilapidated wharf, and the third looking across a narrow lane, and along a portion of Derby Street. All three give glimpses of the shops of grocers, block-makers, slop-sellers, and ship-chandlers; around the doors of which are generally to be seen, laughing and gossiping, clusters of old salts, and such other wharf-rats as haunt the Wapping[7] of a seaport. The room itself is cobwebbed, and dingy with old paint; its floor is strewn with gray sand, in a fashion that has elsewhere fallen into long disuse; and it is easy to conclude, from the general slovenliness of the place, that this is a sanctuary into which womankind, with her tools of magic, the broom and mop, has very infrequent access. In the way of furniture, there is a stove with a voluminous funnel; an old pine desk, with a three-legged stool beside it; two or three wooden-bottom chairs, exceedingly decrepit and infirm; and,—not to forget the library,—on some shelves, a score or two of volumes of the Acts of Congress, and a bulky Digest of the Revenue Laws. A tin pipe ascends through the ceiling, and forms a medium of vocal communication with other parts of the edifice. And here, some six months ago,—pacing from corner to corner, or lounging on the long-legged stool, with his elbow on the desk, and his eyes wandering up and down the columns of the morning newspaper,—you might have recognized, honored reader, the same individual who welcomed you into his cheery little study, where the sunshine glimmered so pleasantly through the willow branches, on the western side of the Old Manse. But now, should you go thither to seek him, you would inquire in vain for the Loco-foco Surveyor.[8] The besom[9] of reform has swept him out of office; and a worthier successor wears his dignity and pockets his emoluments.

---

[6] Matthew was a custom-house officer before becoming a disciple of Jesus (Matthew 9.9).
[7] London's dockside slum district; thus, any such area.
[8] Nickname for the Democrats, derived from the friction matches or "locofocos" that the radical faction used to reilluminate Tammany Hall in 1835 after the conservatives extinguished the lamps.
[9] Broom.

This old town of Salem—my native place, though I have dwelt much away from it, both in boyhood and maturer years—possesses, or did possess, a hold on my affections, the force of which I have never realized during my seasons of actual residence here. Indeed, so far as its physical aspect is concerned, with its flat, unvaried surface, covered chiefly with wooden houses, few or none of which pretend to architectural beauty,—its irregularity, which is neither picturesque nor quaint, but only tame,—its long and lazy street, lounging wearisomely through the whole extent of the peninsula, with Gallows Hill and New Guinea at one end, and a view of the alms-house at the other,—such being the features of my native town, it would be quite as reasonable to form a sentimental attachment to a disarranged checkerboard. And yet, though invariably happiest elsewhere, there is within me a feeling for old Salem, which, in lack of a better phrase, I must be content to call affection. The sentiment is probably assignable to the deep and aged roots which my family has struck into the soil. It is now nearly two centuries and a quarter since the original Briton, the earliest emigrant of my name,[10] made his appearance in the wild and forest-bordered settlement, which has since become a city. And here his descendants have been born and died, and have mingled their earthy substance with the soil; until no small portion of it must necessarily be akin to the mortal frame wherewith, for a little while, I walk the streets. In part, therefore, the attachment which I speak of is the mere sensuous sympathy of dust for dust. Few of my countrymen can know what it is; nor, as frequent transplantation is perhaps better for the stock, need they consider it desirable to know.

But the sentiment has likewise its moral quality. The figure of that first ancestor, invested by family tradition with a dim and dusky grandeur, was present to my boyish imagination, as far back as I can remember. It still haunts me, and induces a sort of home-feeling with the past, which I scarcely claim in reference to the present phase of the town. I seem to have a stronger claim to a residence here on account of this grave, bearded, sable-cloaked, and steeple-crowned progenitor,—who came so early, with his Bible and his sword, and trod the unworn street with such a stately port, and made so large a figure, as a man of war and peace,—a stronger claim than for myself, whose name is seldom heard and my face hardly known. He was a soldier, legislator, judge; he was a ruler in the Church; he had all the Puritanic traits, both good and evil. He was likewise a bitter persecutor; as witness the Quakers, who have remembered him in their histories, and relate an incident of his hard severity towards a woman of their sect,

---

[10] William Hathorne (c. 1607–81), who arrived in Massachusetts in 1630, served as a major in the Salem militia, a speaker in the state legislature, and a magistrate who ordered punishment of Quakers.

which will last longer, it is to be feared, than any record of his better deeds, although these were many. His son, too, inherited the persecuting spirit, and made himself so conspicuous in the martyrdom of the witches, that their blood may fairly be said to have left a stain upon him.[11] So deep a stain, indeed, that his old dry bones, in the Charter Street burial-ground, must still retain it, if they have not crumbled utterly to dust! I know not whether these ancestors of mine bethought themselves to repent, and ask pardon of Heaven for their cruelties; or whether they are now groaning under the heavy consequences of them, in another state of being. At all events, I, the present writer, as their representative, hereby take shame upon myself for their sakes, and pray that any curse incurred by them—as I have heard, and as the dreary and unprosperous condition of the race, for many a long year back, would argue to exist—may be now and henceforth removed.

Doubtless, however, either of these stern and black-browed Puritans would have thought it quite a sufficient retribution for his sins, that, after so long a lapse of years, the old trunk of the family tree, with so much venerable moss upon it, should have borne, as its topmost bough, an idler like myself. No aim, that I have ever cherished, would they recognize as laudable; no success of mine—if my life, beyond its domestic scope, had ever been brightened by success—would they deem otherwise than worthless, if not positively disgraceful. "What is he?" murmurs one gray shadow of my forefathers to the other. "A writer of storybooks! What kind of a business in life,—what mode of glorifying God, or being serviceable to mankind in his day and generation,—may that be? Why, the degenerate fellow might as well have been a fiddler!" Such are the compliments bandied between my great-grandsires and myself, across the gulf of time! And yet, let them scorn me as they will, strong traits of their nature have intertwined themselves with mine.

Planted deep, in the town's earliest infancy and childhood, by these two earnest and energetic men, the race has ever since subsisted here; always, too, in respectability; never, so far as I have known, disgraced by a single unworthy member; but seldom or never, on the other hand, after the first two generations, performing any memorable deed, or so much as putting forward a claim to public notice. Gradually, they have sunk almost out of sight; as old houses, here and there about the streets, get covered half-way to the eaves by the accumulation of new soil. From father to son, for above a hundred years, they followed the sea; a gray-headed shipmaster, in each generation, retiring from the quarter-deck to the homestead, while a boy

---

[11] John Hathorne (1641–1717), a magistrate and one of the three judges in the Salem witchcraft trials of 1692.

of fourteen took the hereditary place before the mast, confronting the salt spray and the gale, which had blustered against his sire and grandsire. The boy, also, in due time, passed from the forecastle to the cabin, spent a tempestuous manhood, and returned from his world-wanderings, to grow old, and die, and mingle his dust with the natal earth. This long connection of a family with one spot, as its place of birth and burial, creates a kindred between the human being and the locality, quite independent of any charm in the scenery or moral circumstances that surround him. It is not love, but instinct. The new inhabitant—who came himself from a foreign land, or whose father or grandfather came—has little claim to be called a Salemite; he has no conception of the oyster-like tenacity with which an old settler, over whom his third century is creeping, clings to the spot where his successive generations have been imbedded. It is no matter that the place is joyless for him; that he is weary of the old wooden houses, the mud and dust, the dead level of site and sentiment, the chill eastwind, and the chillest of social atmospheres;—all these, and whatever faults besides he may see or imagine, are nothing to the purpose. The spell survives, and just as powerfully as if the natal spot were an earthly paradise. So has it been in my case. I felt it almost as a destiny to make Salem my home; so that the mould of features and cast of character which had all along been familiar here—ever, as one representative of the race lay down in his grave, another assuming, as it were, his sentry-march along the Main Street—might still in my little day be seen and recognized in the old town. Nevertheless, this very sentiment is an evidence that the connection, which has become an unhealthy one, should at last be severed. Human nature will not flourish, any more than a potato, if it be planted and replanted, for too long a series of generations, in the same worn-out soil. My children have had other birthplaces, and, so far as their fortunes may be within my control, shall strike their roots into unaccustomed earth.

On emerging from the Old Manse, it was chiefly this strange, indolent, unjoyous attachment for my native town, that brought me to fill a place in Uncle Sam's brick edifice, when I might as well, or better, have gone somewhere else. My doom was on me. It was not the first time, nor the second, that I had gone away—as it seemed, permanently,—but yet returned, like the bad half-penny; or as if Salem were for me the inevitable centre of the universe. So, one fine morning, I ascended the flight of granite steps, with the President's commission in my pocket, and was introduced to the corps of gentlemen who were to aid me in my weighty responsibility, as chief executive officer of the Custom-House.

I doubt greatly—or rather, I do not doubt at all—whether any public functionary of the United States, either in the civil or military line, has ever had such a patriarchal body of veterans under his orders as myself. The whereabouts of the Oldest Inhabitant was at once settled, when I looked at them. For upwards of twenty years before this epoch, the independent position of the Collector had kept the Salem Custom-House out of the whirlpool of political vicissitude, which makes the tenure of office generally so fragile. A soldier,—New England's most distinguished soldier,—he stood firmly on the pedestal of his gallant services; and, himself secure in the wise liberality of the successive administrations through which he had held office, he had been the safety of his subordinates in many an hour of danger and heart-quake. General Miller [12] was radically conservative; a man over whose kindly nature habit had no slight influence; attaching himself strongly to familiar faces, and with difficulty moved to change, even when change might have brought unquestionable improvement. Thus, on taking charge of my department, I found few but aged men. They were ancient sea-captains, for the most part, who, after being tost on every sea, and standing up sturdily against life's tempestuous blast, had finally drifted into this quiet nook; where, with little to disturb them, except the periodical terrors of a Presidential election, they one and all acquired a new lease of existence. Though by no means less liable than their fellow-men to age and infirmity, they had evidently some talisman or other that kept death at bay. Two or three of their number, as I was assured, being gouty and rheumatic, or perhaps bed-ridden, never dreamed of making their appearance at the Custom-House, during a large part of the year; but, after a torpid winter, would creep out into the warm sunshine of May or June, go lazily about what they termed duty, and, at their own leisure and convenience, betake themselves to bed again. I must plead guilty to the charge of abbreviating the official breath of more than one of these venerable servants of the republic. They were allowed, on my representation, to rest from their arduous labors, and soon afterwards—as if their sole principle of life had been zeal for their country's service; as I verily believe it was—withdrew to a better world. It is a pious consolation to me, that, through my interference, a sufficient space was allowed them for repentance of the evil and corrupt practices, into which, as a matter of course, every Custom-House officer must be supposed to fall. Neither the front nor the back entrance of the Custom-House opens on the road to Paradise.

The greater part of my officers were Whigs. [13] It was well for their venerable brotherhood, that the new Surveyor was not a politician, and, though

---

[12] Gen. James F. Miller (1776–1851), a hero of the War of 1812 and of later battles against the British, who was the first territorial Governor of Arkansas (1819–25) and later chief officer of the Port of Salem (1825–49).
[13] Members of the conservative political party formed to oppose the Democrats (1834–52).

a faithful Democrat in principle, neither received nor held his office with any reference to political services. Had it been otherwise,—had an active politician been put into this influential post, to assume the easy task of making head against a Whig Collector, whose infirmities withheld him from the personal administration of his office,—hardly a man of the old corps would have drawn the breath of official life, within a month after the exterminating angel had come up the Custom House steps. According to the received code in such matters, it would have been nothing short of duty, in a politician, to bring every one of those white heads under the axe of the guillotine. It was plain enough to discern, that the old fellows dreaded some such discourtesy at my hands. It pained, and at the same time amused me, to behold the terrors that attended my advent; to see a furrowed cheek, weather-beaten by half a century of storm, turn ashy pale at the glance of so harmless an individual as myself; to detect, as one or another addressed me, the tremor of a voice, which, in long-past days, had been wont to bellow through a speaking-trumpet, hoarsely enough to frighten Boreas[14] himself to silence. They knew, these excellent old persons, that, by all established rule,—and, as regarded some of them, weighted by their own lack of efficiency for business,—they ought to have given place to younger men, more orthodox in politics, and altogether fitter than themselves to serve our common Uncle. I knew it too, but could never quite find in my heart to act upon the knowledge. Much and deservedly to my own discredit, therefore, and considerably to the detriment of my official conscience, they continued, during my incumbency, to creep about the wharves, and loiter up and down the Custom-House steps. They spent a good deal of time, also, asleep in their accustomed corners, with their chairs tilted back against the wall; awaking, however, once or twice in a forenoon, to bore one another with the several thousandth repetition of old sea-stories, and mouldy jokes, that had grown to be pass-words and countersigns among them.

The discovery was soon made, I imagine, that the new Surveyor had no great harm in him. So, with lightsome hearts, and the happy consciousness of being usefully employed,—in their own behalf, at least, if not for our beloved country,—these good old gentlemen went through the various formalities of office. Sagaciously, under their spectacles, did they peep into the holds of vessels! Mighty was their fuss about little matters, and marvellous, sometimes, the obtuseness that allowed greater ones to slip between their fingers! Whenever such a mischance occurred,—when a wagon-load of valuable merchandise had been smuggled ashore, at noonday, perhaps, and directly beneath their unsuspicious noses,—nothing could exceed the

---

[14] In Greek mythology, the god of the North Wind.

vigilance and alacrity with which they proceeded to lock, and double-lock, and secure with tape and sealing-wax, all the avenues of the delinquent vessel. Instead of a reprimand for their previous negligence, the case seemed rather to require an eulogium on their praiseworthy caution, after the mischief had happened; a grateful recognition of the promptitude of their zeal, the moment that there was no longer any remedy!

Unless people are more than commonly disagreeable, it is my foolish habit to contract a kindness for them. The better part of my companion's character, if it have a better part, is that which usually comes uppermost in my regard, and forms the type whereby I recognize the man. As most of these old Custom-House officers had good traits, and as my position in reference to them, being paternal and protective, was favorable to the growth of friendly sentiments, I soon grew to like them all. It was pleasant, in the summer forenoons, — when the fervent heat, that almost liquefied the rest of the human family, merely communicated a genial warmth to their half-torpid systems, — it was pleasant to hear them chatting in the back entry, a row of them all tipped against the wall, as usual; while the frozen witticisms of past generations were thawed out, and came bubbling with laughter from their lips. Externally, the jollity of aged men has much in common with the mirth of children; the intellect, any more than a deep sense of humor, has little to do with the matter; it is, with both, a gleam that plays upon the surface, and imparts a sunny and cheery aspect alike to the green branch, and gray, mouldering trunk. In one case, however, it is real sunshine; in the other, it more resembles the phosphorescent glow of decaying wood.

It would be sad injustice, the reader must understand, to represent all my excellent old friends as in their dotage. In the first place, my coadjutors were not invariably old; there were men among them in their strength and prime, of marked ability and energy, and altogether superior to the sluggish and dependent mode of life on which their evil stars had cast them. Then, moreover, the white locks of age were sometimes found to be the thatch of an intellectual tenement in good repair. But, as respects the majority of my corps of veterans, there will be no wrong done, if I characterize them generally as a set of wearisome old souls, who had gathered nothing worth preservation from their varied experience of life. They seemed to have flung away all the golden grain of practical wisdom, which they had enjoyed so many opportunities of harvesting, and most carefully to have stored their memories with the husks. They spoke with far more interest and unction of their morning's breakfast, or yesterday's, to-day's, or to-morrow's dinner, than of the shipwreck of forty or fifty years ago, and all the world's wonders which they had witnessed with their youthful eyes.

The father of the Custom-House — the patriarch, not only of this little squad of officials, but, I am bold to say, of the respectable body of tidewaiters[15] all over the United States—was a certain permanent Inspector.[16] He might truly be termed a legitimate son of the revenue system, dyed in the wool, or rather, born in the purple; since his sire, a Revolutionary colonel, and formerly collector of the port, had created an office for him, and appointed him to fill it, at a period of the early ages which few living men can now remember. This Inspector, when I first knew him, was a man of fourscore years, or thereabouts, and certainly one of the most wonderful specimens of winter-green that you would be likely to discover in a lifetime's search. With his florid cheek, his compact figure, smartly arrayed in a bright-buttoned blue coat, his brisk and vigorous step, and his hale and hearty aspect, altogether, he seemed—not young, indeed—but a kind of new contrivance of Mother Nature in the shape of man, whom age and infirmity had no business to touch. His voice and laugh, which perpetually reechoed through the Custom-House, had nothing of the tremulous quaver and cackle of an old man's utterance; they came strutting out of his lungs, like the crow of a cock, or the blast of a clarion. Looking at him merely as an animal,—and there was very little else to look at,—he was a most satisfactory object, from the thorough healthfulness and wholesomeness of his system, and his capacity, at that extreme age, to enjoy all, or nearly all, the delights which he had ever aimed at, or conceived of. The careless security of his life in the Custom-House, on a regular income, and with but slight and infrequent apprehensions of removal, had no doubt contributed to make time pass lightly over him. The original and more potent causes, however, lay in the rare perfection of his animal nature, the moderate proportion of intellect, and the very trifling admixture of moral and spiritual ingredients; these latter qualities, indeed, being in barely enough measure to keep the old gentleman from walking on all-fours. He possessed no power of thought, no depth of feeling, no troublesome sensibilities; nothing, in short, but a few commonplace instincts, which, aided by the cheerful temper that grew inevitably out of his physical well-being, did duty very respectably, and to general acceptance, in lieu of a heart. He had been the husband of three wives, all long since dead; the father of twenty children, most of whom, at every age of childhood or maturity, had likewise returned to dust. Here, one would suppose, might have been sorrow enough to imbue the sunniest disposition, through and through, with a sable tinge. Not so with our old Inspector! One brief sigh sufficed to carry off the entire burden of

---

[15] Customs officials who boarded incoming ships to oversee the unloading of cargo.
[16] This satirical portrait of William Lee (1771–1851) and the descriptions of other indolent officials provoked a public outcry in Salem, to which Hawthorne responded in his preface to the second edition of *The Scarlet Letter*, disingenuously declaring that "the only remarkable features of the sketch are its frank and genuine good-humor."

these dismal reminiscences. The next moment, he was as ready for sport as any unbreeched infant; far readier than the Collector's junior clerk, who at nineteen years, was much the elder and graver man of the two.

I used to watch and study this patriarchal personage with, I think, livelier curiosity than any other form of humanity there presented to my notice. He was, in truth, a rare phenomenon; so perfect in one point of view; so shallow, so delusive, so impalpable, such an absolute nonentity, in every other. My conclusion was that he had no soul, no heart, no mind; nothing, as I have already said, but instincts; and yet, withal, so cunningly had the few materials of his character been put together, that there was no painful perception of deficiency, but, on my part, an entire contentment with what I found in him. It might be difficult—and it was so—to conceive how he should exist hereafter, so earthy and sensuous did he seem; but surely his existence here, admitting that it was to terminate with his last breath, had been not unkindly given; with no higher moral responsibilities than the beasts of the field, but with a larger scope of enjoyment than theirs, and with all their blessed immunity from the dreariness and duskiness of age.

One point, in which he had vastly the advantage over his four-footed brethren, was his ability to recollect the good dinners which it had made no small portion of the happiness of his life to eat. His gourmandism was a highly agreeable trait; and to hear him talk of roast-meat was as appetizing as a pickle or an oyster. As he possessed no higher attribute, and neither sacrificed nor vitiated any spiritual endowment by devoting all his energies and ingenuities to subserve the delight and profit of his maw, it always pleased and satisfied me to hear him expatiate on fish, poultry, and butcher's meat, and the most eligible methods of preparing them for the table. His reminiscences of good cheer, however ancient the date of the actual banquet, seemed to bring the savor of pig or turkey under one's very nostrils. There were flavors on his palate, that had lingered there not less than sixty or seventy years, and were still apparently as fresh as that of the mutton-chop which he had just devoured for his breakfast. I have heard him smack his lips over dinners, every guest at which, except himself, had long been food for worms. It was marvellous to observe how the ghosts of bygone meals were continually rising up before him; not in anger or retribution, but as if grateful for his former appreciation, and seeking to reduplicate an endless series of enjoyment, at once shadowy and sensual. A tenderloin of beef, a hind-quarter of veal, a sparerib of pork, a particular chicken, or a remarkably praiseworthy turkey, which had perhaps adorned his board in the days of the elder Adams,[17] would be remembered; while all

---

[17] John Adams (1735–1826), second president of the United States.

the subsequent experience of our race, and all the events that brightened or darkened his individual career, had gone over him with as little permanent effect as the passing breeze. The chief tragic event of the old man's life, so far as I could judge, was his mishap with a certain goose, which lived and died some twenty or forty years ago; a goose of most promising figure, but which, at table, proved so inveterately tough that the carving-knife would make no impression on its carcass; and it could only be divided with an axe and handsaw.

But it is time to quit this sketch; on which, however, I should be glad to dwell at considerably more length, because, of all men whom I have ever known, this individual was fittest to be a Custom-House officer. Most persons, owing to causes which I may not have space to hint at, suffer moral detriment from this peculiar mode of life. The old Inspector was incapable of it, and, were he to continue in office to the end of time, would be just as good as he was then, and sit down to dinner with just as good an appetite.

There is one likeness, without which my gallery of Custom-House portraits would be strangely incomplete; but which my comparatively few opportunities for observation enable me to sketch only in the merest outline. It is that of the Collector, our gallant old General, who, after his brilliant military service, subsequently to which he had ruled over a wild Western territory, had come hither, twenty years before, to spend the decline of his varied and honorable life. The brave soldier had already numbered, nearly or quite, his threescore years and ten, and was pursuing the remainder of his earthly march, burdened with infirmities which even the martial music of his own spirit-stirring recollections could do little towards lightening. The step was palsied now, that had been foremost in the charge. It was only with the assistance of a servant, and by leaning his hand heavily on the iron balustrade, that he could slowly and painfully ascend the Custom-House steps, and, with a toilsome progress across the floor, attain his customary chair beside the fireplace. There he used to sit, gazing with a somewhat dim serenity of aspect at the figures that came and went; amid the rustle of papers, the administering of oaths, the discussion of business, and the casual talk of the office; all which sounds and circumstances seemed but indistinctly to impress his senses, and hardly to make their way into his inner sphere of contemplation. His countenance, in this repose, was mild and kindly. If his notice was sought, an expression of courtesy and interest gleamed out upon his features; proving that there was light within him, and that it was only the outward medium of the intellectual lamp that obstructed the rays in their passage. The closer you penetrated to the substance of his mind, the sounder it appeared. When no longer called upon to speak, or listen, either of which operations cost him an evident effort, his face would briefly subside into its former not uncheerful quietude. It was not painful to behold this look; for, though dim, it had not the imbecility of decaying age. The framework of his nature, originally strong and massive, was not yet crumbled into ruin.

To observe and define his character, however, under such disadvantages, was as difficult a task as to trace out and build up anew, in imagination, an old fortress, like Ticonderoga, from a view of its gray and broken ruins. Here and there, perchance, the walls may remain almost complete; but elsewhere may be only a shapeless mound, cumbrous with its very strength, and overgrown, through long years of peace and neglect, with grass and alien weeds.

Nevertheless, looking at the old warrior with affection,—for, slight as was the communication between us, my feeling towards him, like that of all bipeds and quadrupeds who knew him, might not improperly be termed so,—I could discern the main points of his portrait. It was marked with the noble and heroic qualities which showed it to be not by a mere accident, but of good right, that he had won a distinguished name. His spirit could never, I conceive, have been characterized by an uneasy activity; it must, at any period of his life, have required an impulse to set him in motion; but, once stirred up, with obstacles to overcome, and an adequate object to be attained, it was not in the man to give out or fail. The heat that had formerly pervaded his nature, and which was not yet extinct, was never of the kind that flashes and flickers in a blaze, but, rather, a deep, red glow, as of iron in a furnace. Weight, solidity, firmness; this was the expression of his repose, even in such decay as had crept untimely over him, at the period of which I speak. But I could imagine, even then, that, under some excitement which should go deeply into his consciousness,—roused by a trumpet-peal, loud enough to awaken all of his energies that were not dead, but only slumbering,—he was yet capable of flinging off his infirmities like a sick man's gown, dropping the staff of age to seize a battlesword, and starting up once more a warrior. And, in so intense a moment, his demeanour would have still been calm. Such an exhibition, however, was but to be pictured in fancy; not to be anticipated, nor desired. What I saw in him—as evidently as the indestructible ramparts of Old Ticonderoga, already cited as the most appropriate simile—were the features of stubborn and ponderous endurance, which might well have amounted to obstinacy in his earlier days; of integrity, that, like most of his other endowments, lay in a somewhat heavy mass, and was just as unmalleable and unmanageable as a ton of iron ore; and of benevolence, which, fiercely as he led the bayonets on at Chippewa or Fort Erie, I take to be of quite as genuine a stamp as what actuates any or all the polemical philanthropists of the age. He had slain men with his own hand, for aught I know;—certainly, they had fallen, like blades of grass at the sweep of the scythe, before the charge to which his spirit imparted its triumphant energy; — but, be that as it might, there was never in his heart so much cruelty as would have brushed the down off a butterfly's wing. I have not known the man, to whose innate kindliness I would more confidently make an appeal.

Many characteristics — and those, too, which contribute not the least forcibly to impart resemblance in a sketch — must have vanished, or been obscured, before I met the General. All merely graceful attributes are usually the most evanescent; nor does Nature adorn the human ruin with blossoms of new beauty, that have their roots and proper nutriment only in the chinks and crevices of decay, as she sows wall-flowers over the ruined fortress of Ticonderoga. Still, even in respect of grace and beauty, there were points well worth noting. A ray of humor, now and then, would make its way through the veil of dim obstruction, and glimmer pleasantly upon our faces. A trait of native elegance, seldom seen in the masculine character after childhood or early youth, was shown in the General's fondness for the sight and fragrance of flowers. An old soldier might be supposed to prize only the bloody laurel on his brow; but here was one, who seemed to have a young girl's appreciation of the floral tribe.

There, beside the fireplace, the brave old General used to sit; while the Surveyor — though seldom, when it could be avoided, taking upon himself the difficult task of engaging him in conversation — was fond of standing at a distance, and watching his quiet and almost slumberous countenance. He seemed away from us, although we saw him but a few yards off; remote, though we passed close beside his chair; unattainable, though we might have stretched forth our hands and touched his own. It might be, that he lived a more real life within his thoughts, than amid the unappropriate environment of the Collector's office. The evolutions of the parade; the tumult of the battle; the flourish of old, heroic music, heard thirty years before; — such scenes and sounds, perhaps, were all alive before his intellectual sense. Meanwhile, the merchants and ship-masters, the spruce clerks, and uncouth sailors, entered and departed; the bustle of this commercial and Custom-House life kept up its little murmur roundabout him; and neither with the men nor their affairs did the General appear to sustain the most distant relation. He was as much out of place as an old sword — now rusty, but which had flashed once in the battle's front, and showed still a bright gleam along its blade — would have been, among the inkstands, paper-folders, and mahogany rulers, on the Deputy Collector's desk.

There was one thing that much aided me in renewing and re-creating the stalwart soldier of the Niagara frontier, — the man of true and simple energy. It was the recollection of those memorable words of his, — "I'll try, Sir!" — spoken on the very verge of a desperate and heroic enterprise, and breathing the soul and spirit of New England hardihood, comprehending all perils, and encountering all. If, in our country, valor were rewarded by heraldic honor, this phrase—which it seems so easy to speak, but which only he, with such a task of danger and glory before him, has ever spoken— would be the best and fittest of all mottoes for the General's shield of arms.

It contributes greatly towards a man's moral and intellectual health, to be brought into habits of companionship with individuals unlike himself, who care little for his pursuits, and whose sphere and abilities he must go out of himself to appreciate. The accidents of my life have often afforded me this advantage, but never with more fulness and variety than during my continuance in office. There was one man, especially, the observation of whose character gave me a new idea of talent. His gifts were emphatically those of a man of business; prompt, acute, clear-minded; with an eye that saw through all perplexities, and a faculty of arrangement that made them vanish, as by the waving of an enchanter's wand. Bred up from boyhood in the Custom-House, it was his proper field of activity; and the many intricacies of business, so harassing to the interloper, presented themselves before him with the regularity of a perfectly comprehended system. In my contemplation, he stood as the ideal of his class. He was, indeed, the Custom-House in himself; or, at all events, the main-spring that kept its variously revolving wheels in motion; for, in an institution like this, where its officers are appointed to subserve their own profit and convenience, and seldom with a leading reference to their fitness for the duty to be performed, they must perforce seek elsewhere the dexterity which is not in them. Thus, by an inevitable necessity, as a magnet attracts steel-filings, so did our man of business draw to himself the difficulties which everybody met with. With an easy condescension, and kind forbearance towards our stupidity,—which, to his order of mind, must have seemed little short of crime,—would he forthwith, by the merest touch of his finger, make the incomprehensible as clear as daylight. The merchants valued him not less than we, his esoteric friends. His integrity was perfect; it was a law of nature with him, rather than a choice or a principle; nor can it be otherwise than the main condition of an intellect so remarkably clear and accurate as his, to be honest and regular in the administration of affairs. A stain on his conscience, as to any thing that came within the range of his vocation, would trouble such a man very much in the same way, though to a far greater degree, than an error in the balance of an account, or an ink-blot on the fair page of a book of record. Here, in a word,—and it is a rare instance in my life,—I had met with a person thoroughly adapted to the situation which he held.

Such were some of the people with whom I now found myself connected. I took it in good part at the hands of Providence, that I was thrown into a position so little akin to my past habits; and set myself seriously to gather from it whatever profit was to be had. After my fellowship of toil and impracticable schemes, with the dreamy brethren of Brook Farm; after living for three years within the subtile influence of an intellect like Emerson's; after those wild, free days on the Assabeth, indulging fantastic speculations beside our fire of fallen boughs, with Ellery Channing; after talking with Thoreau about pine-trees and Indian relics, in his hermitage at Walden; after growing fastidious by sympathy with the classic refinement of Hillard's culture, after becoming imbued with poetic sentiment at Longfellow's hearth-stone; — it was time, at length, that I should exercise other faculties of my nature, and nourish myself with food for which I had hitherto had little appetite. Even the old Inspector was desirable, as a change of diet, to a man who had known Alcott.[18] I looked upon it as an evidence, in some measure, of a system naturally well balanced, and lacking no essential part of a thorough organization, that, with such associates to remember, I could mingle at once with men of altogether different qualities, and never murmur at the change.

Literature, its exertions and objects, were now of little moment in my regard. I cared not, at this period, for books; they were apart from me. Nature, — except it were human nature, — the nature that is developed in earth and sky, was, in one sense, hidden from me; and all the imaginative delight, wherewith it had been spiritualized, passed away out of my mind. A gift, a faculty, if it had not departed, was suspended and inanimate within me. There would have been something sad, unutterably dreary, in all this, had I not been conscious that it lay at my own option to recall whatever was valuable in the past. It might be true, indeed, that this was a life which could not, with impunity, be lived too long; else, it might make me permanently other than I had been, without transforming me into any shape which it would be worth my while to take. But I never considered it as other than a transitory life. There was always a prophetic instinct, a low whisper in my ear, that, within no long period, and whenever a new change of custom should be essential to my good, a change would come.

Meanwhile, there I was, a Surveyor of the Revenue, and, so far as I have been able to understand, as good a Surveyor as need be. A man of thought, fancy, and sensibility, (had he ten times the Surveyor's proportion of those

---

[18] After leaving the utopian community of Brook Farm, Hawthorne married and moved to Concord, near the Assabeth River (a tributary of the Concord), where his neighbors included the leading Transcendentalists Ralph Waldo Emerson (1803–82), Henry David Thoreau (1817–62), Ellery Channing (1818 1901), and Bronson Alcott (1799–1888). Two of his most supportive friends were the Boston lawyer George Stillman Hillard (1808–79) and the Harvard professor and popular poet Henry Wadsworth Longfellow (1806–82).

qualities,) may, at any time, be a man of affairs, if he will only choose to give himself the trouble. My fellow-officers, and the merchants and sea-captains with whom my official duties brought me into any manner of connection, viewed me in no other light, and probably knew me in no other character. None of them, I presume, had ever read a page of my inditing, or would have cared a fig the more for me, if they had read them all; nor would it have mended the matter, in the least, had those same unprofitable pages been written with a pen like that of Burns or of Chaucer, each of whom was a Custom-House officer in his day, as well as I.[19] It is a good lesson — though it may often be a hard one — for a man who has dreamed of literary fame, and of making for himself a rank among the world's dignitaries by such means, to step aside out of the narrow circle in which his claims are recognized, and to find how utterly devoid of significance, beyond that circle, is all that he achieves, and all he aims at. I know not that I especially needed the lesson, either in the way of warning or rebuke; but, at any rate, I learned it thoroughly; nor, it gives me pleasure to reflect, did the truth, as it came home to my perception, ever cost me a pang, or require to be thrown off in a sigh. In the way of literary talk, it is true, the Naval Officer — an excellent fellow, who came into office with me, and went out only a little later — would often engage me in a discussion about one or the other of his favorite topics, Napoleon or Shakespeare. The Collector's junior clerk, too, — a young gentleman who, it was whispered, occasionally covered a sheet of Uncle Sam's letter-paper with what, (at the distance of a few yards,) looked very much like poetry, — used now and then to speak to me of books, as matters with which I might possibly be conversant. This was my all of lettered intercourse; and it was quite sufficient for my necessities.

No longer seeking nor caring that my name should be blazoned abroad on title-pages, I smiled to think that it had now another kind of vogue. The Custom-House marker imprinted it, with a stencil and black paint, on pepper-bags, and baskets of anatto,[20] and cigar-boxes, and bales of all kinds of dutiable merchandise, in testimony that these commodities had paid the impost, and gone regularly through the office. Borne on such queer vehicle of fame, a knowledge of my existence, so far as a name conveys it, was carried where it had never been before, and, I hope, will never go again.

But the past was not dead. Once in a great while, the thoughts, that had

---

[19] The Scottish poet Robert Burns (1759–96) was an excise collector for two years; the English poet Geoffrey Chaucer (1340?–1400) was London's controller of customs for twelve years.

[20] Annatto was a reddish yellow dye. Hawthorne's name stenciled on imported goods signified that the import tax had been paid.

seemed so vital and so active, yet had been put to rest so quietly, revived again. One of the most remarkable occasions, when the habit of bygone days awoke in me, was that which brings it within the law of literary propriety to offer the public the sketch which I am now writing.

In the second story of the Custom-House, there is a large room, in which the brick-work and naked rafters have never been covered with panelling and plaster. The edifice — originally projected on a scale adapted to the old commercial enterprise of the port, and with an idea of subsequent prosperity destined never to be realized — contains far more space than its occupants know what to do with. This airy hall, therefore, over the Collector's apartments, remains unfinished to this day, and, in spite of the aged cobwebs that festoon its dusky beams, appears still to await the labor of the carpenter and mason. At one end of the room, in a recess, were a number of barrels, piled one upon another, containing bundles of official documents. Large quantities of similar rubbish lay lumbering the floor. It was sorrowful to think how many days, and weeks, and months, and years of toil, had been wasted on these musty papers, which were now only an encumbrance on earth, and were hidden away in this forgotten corner, never more to be glanced at by human eyes. But, then, what reams of other manuscripts — filled, not with the dullness of official formalities, but with the thought of inventive brains and the rich effusion of deep hearts — had gone equally to oblivion; and that, moreover, without serving a purpose in their day, as these heaped-up papers had, and — saddest of all — without purchasing for their writers the comfortable livelihood which the clerks of the Custom-House had gained by these worthless scratchings of the pen! Yet not altogether worthless, perhaps, as materials of local history. Here, no doubt, statistics of the former commerce of Salem might be discovered, and memorials of her princely merchants, — old King Derby, — old Billy Gray, — old Simon Forrester,[21] and many another magnate in his day; whose powdered head, however, was scarcely in the tomb, before his mountain-pile of wealth began to dwindle. The founders of the greater part of the families which now compose the aristocracy of Salem might here be traced, from the petty and obscure beginning of their traffic, at periods generally much posterior to the Revolution, upward to what their children look upon as long-established rank.

Prior to the Revolution, there is a dearth of records; the earlier documents and archives of the Custom-House having, probably, been carried

---

[21] Like E. H. Derby (see note 4), William Gray (1750–1825) and Simon Forrester (1776–1825) were wealthy Salem merchants and ship owners; Forrester had married one of Hawthorne's aunts.

off to Halifax, when all the King's officials accompanied the British army in its flight from Boston.[22] It has often been a matter of regret with me; for, going back, perhaps, to the days of the Protectorate, those papers must have contained many references to forgotten or remembered men, and to antique customs, which would have affected me with the same pleasure as when I used to pick up Indian arrow-heads in the field near the Old Manse.

But, one idle and rainy day, it was my fortune to make a discovery of some little interest. Poking and burrowing into the heaped-up rubbish in the corner; unfolding one and another document, and reading the names of vessels that had long ago foundered at sea or rotted at the wharves, and those of merchants, never heard of now on 'Change, nor very readily decipherable on their mossy tombstones; glancing at such matters with the saddened, weary, half-reluctant interest which we bestow on the corpse of dead activity, — and exerting my fancy, sluggish with little use, to raise up from these dry bones an image of the old town's brighter aspect, when India was a new region, and only Salem knew the way thither, — I chanced to lay my hand on a small package, carefully done up in a piece of ancient yellow parchment. This envelope had the air of an official record of some period long past, when clerks engrossed their stiff and formal chirography on more substantial materials than at present. There was something about it that quickened an instinctive curiosity, and made me undo the faded red tape, that tied up the package, with the sense that a treasure would here be brought to light. Unbending the rigid folds of the parchment cover, I found it to be a commission, under the hand and seal of Governor Shirley, in favor of one Jonathan Pue,[23] as Surveyor of his Majesty's Customs for the port of Salem, in the Province of Massachusetts Bay. I remembered to have read (probably in Felt's Annals) a notice of the decease of Mr. Surveyor Pue, about fourscore years ago; and likewise, in a newspaper of recent times, an account of the digging up of his remains in the little grave-yard of St. Peter's Church, during the renewal of that edifice. Nothing, if I rightly call to mind, was left of my respected predecessor, save an imperfect skeleton, and some fragments of apparel, and a wig of majestic frizzle; which, unlike the head that it once adorned, was in very satisfactory preservation.

---

[22] When Washington's troops besieged Boston in January 1776, General Howe evacuated British troops to Nova Scotia.

[23] William Shirley (1694–1771) was governor of Massachusetts 1741 to 1749 and from 1753 to 1756. Jonathan Pue was appointed surveyor of customs in Salem in 1752 and died in 1760, as recorded in Joseph B. Felt's *The Annals of Salem, from its First Settlement* (1827), a text Hawthorne often used for historical background. But Pue's "small package" is entirely fictitious.

But, on examining the papers which the parchment commission served to envelop, I found more traces of Mr. Pue's mental part, and the internal operations of his head, than the frizzled wig had contained of the venerable skull itself.

They were documents, in short, not official, but of a private nature, or, at least, written in his private capacity, and apparently with his own hand. I could account for their being included in the heap of Custom-House lumber only by the fact, that Mr. Pue's death had happened suddenly; and that these papers, which he probably kept in his official desk, had never come to the knowledge of his heirs, or were supposed to relate to the business of the revenue. On the transfer of the archives to Halifax, this package, proving to be of no public concern, was left behind, and had remained ever since unopened.

The ancient Surveyor—being little molested, I suppose, at that early day, with business pertaining to his office—seems to have devoted some of his many leisure hours to researches as a local antiquarian, and other inquisitions of a similar nature. These supplied material for petty activity to a mind that would otherwise have been eaten up with rust. A portion of his facts, by the by, did me good service in the preparation of the article entitled "Main Street," included in the present volume.[24] The remainder may perhaps be applied to purposes equally valuable, here after; or not impossibly may be worked up, so far as they go, into a regular history of Salem, should my veneration for the natal soil ever impel me to so pious a task. Meanwhile, they shall be at the command of any gentleman, inclined, and competent, to take the unprofitable labor off my hands. As a final disposition, I contemplate depositing them with the Essex Historical Society.[25]

But the object that most drew my attention, in the mysterious package, was a certain affair of fine red cloth, much worn and faded. There were traces about it of gold embroidery, which, however, was greatly frayed and defaced; so that none, or very little, of the glitter was left. It had been wrought, as was easy to perceive, with wonderful skill of needlework; and the stitch (as I am assured by ladies conversant with such mysteries) gives evidence of a now forgotten art, not to be recovered even by the process of picking out the threads. This rag of scarlet cloth,—for time, and wear, and a sacrilegious moth, had reduced it to little other than a rag,—on careful examination, assumed the shape of a letter. It was the capital letter A. By an

---

[24] This had been Hawthorne's original intention, but the sketch, which had first appeared in Elizabeth Peabody's *Aesthetic Papers* (1849), would be included in *The Snow Image and other Twice-Told Tales* (1852).

[25] Now the Peabody Essex Museum.

accurate measurement, each limb proved to be precisely three inches and a quarter in length. It had been intended, there could be no doubt, as an ornamental article of dress; but how it was to be worn, of what rank, honor, and dignity, in by-past times, were signified by it, was a riddle which (so evanescent are the fashions of the world in these particulars) I saw little hope of solving. And yet it strangely interested me. My eyes fastened themselves upon the old scarlet letter, and would not be turned aside. Certainly, there was some deep meaning in it, most worthy of interpretation, and which, as it were, streamed forth from the mystic symbol, subtly communicating itself to my sensibilities, but evading the analysis of my mind.

While thus perplexed, — and cogitating, among other hypotheses, whether the letter might not have been one of those decorations which the white men used to contrive, in order to take the eyes of Indians, — I happened to place it on my breast. It seemed to me, — the reader may smile, but must not doubt my word, — it seemed to me, then, that I experienced a sensation not altogether physical, yet almost so, as of burning heat; and as if the letter were not of red cloth, but red-hot iron. I shuddered, and involuntarily let it fall upon the floor.

In the absorbing contemplation of the scarlet letter, I had hitherto neglected to examine a small roll of dingy paper, around which it had been twisted. This I now opened, and had the satisfaction to find, recorded by the old Surveyor's pen, a reasonably complete explanation of the whole affair. There were several foolscap sheets, containing many particulars respecting the life and conversation of one Hester Prynne, who appeared to have been rather a noteworthy personage in the view of our ancestors. She had flourished during a period between the early days of Massachusetts and the close of the seventeenth century. Aged persons, alive in the time of Mr. Surveyor Pue, and from whose oral testimony he had made up his narrative, remembered her in their youth, as a very old, but not decrepit woman of a stately and solemn aspect. It had been her habit from an almost immemorial date, to go about the country as a kind of voluntary nurse, and doing whatever miscellaneous good she might; taking upon herself, likewise, to give advice in all matters, especially those of the heart; by which means, as a person of such propensities inevitably must, she gained from many people the reverence due to an angel, but, I should imagine, was looked upon by others as an intruder and a nuisance. Prying farther into the manuscript, I found the record of other doings and sufferings of this singular woman, for the most of which the reader is referred to the story entitled "The Scarlet Letter"; and it should be borne carefully in mind, that the main facts of that story are authorized and authenticated by the document of Mr. Surveyor Pue. The original papers, together with the scarlet letter itself,—a most curious relic,—are still in my possession, and shall be freely exhibited to whomsoever, induced by the great interest of the narrative, may desire a sight of them.[26] I must not be understood as affirming, that, in the dressing up of the tale, and imagining the motives and modes of passion that influenced the characters who figure in it, I have invariably confined myself within the limits of the old Surveyor's half a dozen sheets of foolscap. On the contrary, I have allowed myself, as to such points, nearly or altogether as much license as if the facts had been entirely of my own invention. What I contend for is the authenticity of the outline.

This incident recalled my mind, in some degree, to its old track. There seemed to be here the groundwork of a tale. It impressed me as if the ancient Surveyor, in his garb of a hundred years gone by, and wearing his immortal wig,—which was buried with him, but did not perish in the grave,—had met me in the deserted chamber of the Custom-House. In his port was the dignity of one who had borne his Majesty's commission, and who was therefore illuminated by a ray of the splendor that shone so dazzlingly about the throne. How unlike, alas! the hang-dog look of a republican official, who, as the servant of the people, feels himself less than the least, and below the lowest, of his masters. With his own ghostly hand, the obscurely seen, but majestic, figure had imparted to me the scarlet symbol, and the little roll of explanatory manuscript. With his own ghostly voice, he had exhorted me, on the scared consideration of my filial duty and reverence towards him,—who might reasonably regard himself as my official ancestor,—to bring his mouldy and moth-eaten lucubrations before the public. "Do this," said the ghost of Mr. Surveyor Pue, emphatically nodding the head that looked so imposing within its memorable wig, "do this, and the profit shall be all your own! You will shortly need it; for it is not in your days as it was in mine, when a man's office was a life-lease, and oftentimes an heirloom. But, I charge you, in this matter of old Mistress Prynne, give to your predecessor's memory the credit which will be rightfully its due!" And I said to the ghost of Mr. Surveyor Pue,—"I will!"

On Hester Prynne's story, therefore, I bestowed much thought. It was the subject of my meditations for many an hour, while pacing to and fro across my room, or traversing, with a hundredfold repetition, the long extent from the front-door of the Custom-House to the side-entrance, and

---

[26] This account of discovering the scarlet letter wrapped in Pue's papers is a conventional fiction based on information derived from Felt and other historical sources. In "Endicott and the Red Cross" (1838), Hawthorne had briefly described a beautiful adulteress wearing a gold-embroidered scarlet *A*, and a later notebook passage speculates on the life of such a woman. See the notebook entries in Part One.

back again. Great were the weariness and annoyance of the old Inspector and the Weighers and Gaugers, whose slumbers were disturbed by the unmercifully lengthened tramp of my passing and returning footsteps. Remembering their own former habits, they used to say that the Surveyor was walking the quarter-deck. They probably fancied that my sole object — and, indeed, the sole object for which a sane man could ever put himself into voluntary motion — was, to get an appetite for dinner. And to say the truth, an appetite, sharpened by the east-wind that generally blew along the passage, was the only valuable result of so much indefatigable exercise. So little adapted is the atmosphere of a Custom-House to the delicate harvest of fancy and sensibility, that, had I remained there through ten Presidencies yet to come, I doubt whether the tale of "The Scarlet Letter" would ever have been brought before the public eye. My imagination was a tarnished mirror. It would not reflect, or only with miserable dimness, the figures with which I did my best to people it. The characters of the narrative would not be warmed and rendered malleable, by any heat that I could kindle at my intellectual forge. They would take neither the glow of passion nor the tenderness of sentiment, but retained all the rigidity of dead corpses, and stared me in the face with a fixed and ghastly grin of contemptuous defiance. "What have you to do with us?" that expression seemed to say. "The little power you might once have possessed over the tribe of unrealities is gone! You have bartered it for a pittance of the public gold. Go, then, and earn your wages!" In short, the almost torpid creatures of my own fancy twitted me with imbecility, and not without fair occasion.

It was not merely during the three hours and a half which Uncle Sam claimed as his share of my daily life, that this wretched numbness held possession of me. It went with me on my sea-shore walks and rambles into the country, whenever — which was seldom and reluctantly — I bestirred myself to seek that invigorating charm of Nature, which used to give me such freshness and activity of thought, the moment that I stepped across the threshold of the Old Manse. The same torpor, as regarded the capacity for intellectual effort, accompanied me home, and weighed upon me in the chamber which I most absurdly termed my study. Nor did it quit me, when, late at night, I sat in the deserted parlour, lighted only by the glimmering coal-fire and the moon, striving to picture forth imaginary scenes, which, the next day, might flow out on the brightening page in many-hued description.

If the imaginative faculty refused to act at such an hour, it might well be deemed a hopeless case. Moonlight, in a familiar room, falling so white upon the carpet, and showing all its figures so distinctly, — making every object so minutely visible, yet so unlike a morning or noontide visibility, — is a medium the most suitable for a romance-writer to get acquainted with his illusive guests. There is the little domestic scenery of the well-known apartment; the chairs, with each its separate individuality; the centre-table, sustaining a work-basket, a volume or two, and an extinguished lamp; the sofa; the book-case; the picture on the wall; all these details, so completely seen, are so spiritualized by the unusual light, that they seem to lose their actual substance, and become things of intellect. Nothing is too small or too trifling to undergo this change, and acquire dignity thereby. A child's shoe; the doll, seated in her little wicker carriage; the hobby-horse;—whatever, in a word, has been used or played with, during the day, is now invested with a quality of strangeness and remoteness, though still almost as vividly present as by daylight. Thus, therefore, the floor of our familiar room has become a neutral territory, somewhere between the real world and fairy-land, where the Actual and the Imaginary may meet, and each imbue itself with the nature of the other. Ghosts might enter here, without affrighting us. It would be too much in keeping with the scene to excite surprise, were we to look about us and discover a form, beloved, but gone hence, now sitting quietly in a streak of this magic moonshine, with an aspect that would make us doubt whether it had returned from afar, or had never once stirred from our fireside.

The somewhat dim coal-fire has an essential influence in producing the effect which I would describe. It throws its unobtrusive tinge throughout the room, with a faint ruddiness upon the walls and ceiling, and a reflected gleam from the polish of the furniture. This warmer light mingles itself with the cold spirituality of the moonbeams, and communicates, as it were, a heart and sensibilities of human tenderness to the forms which fancy summons up. It converts them from snow-images into men and women. Glancing at the looking-glass, we behold—deep within its haunted verge—the smouldering glow of the half-extinguished anthracite, the white moonbeams on the floor, and a repetition of all the gleam and shadow of the picture, with one remove farther from the actual, and nearer to the imaginative. Then, at such an hour and with this scene before him, if a man, sitting all alone, cannot dream strange things, and make them look like truth, he need never try to write romances.

But, for myself, during the whole of my Custom-House experience, moonlight and sunshine, and the glow of firelight, were just alike in my regard; and neither of them was of one whit more avail than the twinkle of a tallow-candle. An entire class of susceptibilities, and a gift connected with them,—of no great richness or value, but the best I had,—was gone from me.

It is my belief, however, that, had I attempted a different order of composition, my faculties would not have been found so pointless and inefficacious. I might, for instance, have contented myself with writing out the narratives of a veteran shipmaster, one of the Inspectors, whom I should be most ungrateful not to mention; since scarcely a day passed that he did not stir me to laughter and admiration by his marvellous gifts as a story-teller. Could I have preserved the picturesque force of his style, and the humorous coloring which nature taught him how to throw over his descriptions, the result, I honestly believe, would have been something new in literature. Or I might readily have found a more serious task. It was a folly, with the materiality of this daily life pressing so intrusively upon me, to attempt to fling myself back into another age; or to insist on creating the semblance of a world out of airy matter, when, at every moment, the impalpable beauty of my soap-bubble was broken by the rude contact of some actual circumstance. The wiser effort would have been, to diffuse thought and imagination through the opaque substance of to-day, and thus to make it a bright transparency; to spiritualize the burden that began to weigh so heavily; to seek, resolutely, the true and indestructible value that lay hidden in the petty and wearisome incidents, and ordinary characters, with which I was now conversant. The fault was mine. The page of life that was spread out before me seemed dull and commonplace, only because I had not fathomed its deeper import. A better book than I shall ever write was there; leaf after leaf presenting itself to me, just as it was written out by the reality of the flitting hour, and vanishing as fast as written, only because my brain wanted the insight and my hand the cunning to transcribe it. At some future day, it may be, I shall remember a few scattered fragments and broken paragraphs, and write them down, and find the letters turn to gold upon the page.

These perceptions have come too late. At the instant, I was only conscious that what would have been a pleasure once was now a hopeless toil. There was no occasion to make much moan about this state of affairs. I had ceased to be a writer of tolerably poor tales and essays, and had become a tolerably good Surveyor of the Customs. That was all. But, nevertheless, it is any thing but agreeable to be haunted by a suspicion that one's intellect is dwindling away; or exhaling, without your consciousness, like ether out of a phial; so that, at every glance, you find a smaller and less volatile residuum. Of the fact, there could be no doubt; and, examining myself and others, I was led to conclusions in reference to the effect of public office on the character, not very favorable to the mode of life in question. In some other form, perhaps, I may hereafter develop these effects. Suffice it here to say, that a Custom-House officer, of long continuance, can hardly be a very praiseworthy or respectable personage, for many reasons; one of them, the tenure by which he holds his situation, and another, the very nature of his business, which — though, I trust, an honest one — is of such a sort that he does not share in the united effort of mankind.

An effect—which I believe to be observable, more or less, in every individual who has occupied the position—is, that, while he leans on the mighty arm of the Republic, his own proper strength departs from him. He loses, in an extent proportioned to the weakness or force of his original nature, the capability of self-support. If he possess an unusual share of native energy, or the enervating magic of place do not operate too long upon him, his forfeited powers may be redeemable. The ejected officer—fortunate in the unkindly shove that sends him forth betimes, to struggle amid a struggling world—may return to himself, and become all that he has ever been. But this seldom happens. He usually keeps his ground just long enough for his own ruin, and is then thrust out, with sinews all unstrung, to totter along the difficult footpath of life as he best may. Conscious of his own infirmity,—that his tempered steel and elasticity are lost,—he for ever afterwards looks wistfully about him in quest of support external to himself. His pervading and continual hope—a hallucination, which, in the face of all discouragement, and making light of impossibilities, haunts him while he lives, and, I fancy, like the convulsive throes of the cholera, torments him for a brief space after death—is, that, finally, and in no long time, by some happy coincidence of circumstances, he shall be restored to office. This faith, more than any thing else, steals the pith and availability out of whatever enterprise he may dream of undertaking. Why should he toil and moil, and be at so much trouble to pick himself up out of the mud, when, in a little while hence, the strong arm of his Uncle will raise and support him? Why should he work for his living here, or go to dig gold in California, when he is so soon to be made happy, at monthly intervals, with a little pile of glittering coin out of his Uncle's pocket? It is sadly curious to observe how slight a taste of office suffices to infect a poor fellow with this singular disease. Uncle Sam's gold—meaning no disrespect to the worthy old gentleman—has, in this respect, a quality of enchantment like that of the Devil's wages. Whoever touches it should look well to himself, or he may find the bargain to go hard against him, involving, if not his soul, yet many of its better attributes; its sturdy force, its courage and constancy, its truth, its self-reliance, and all that gives the emphasis to manly character.

Here was a fine prospect in the distance! Not that the Surveyor brought the lesson home to himself, or admitted that he could be so utterly undone, either by continuance in office, or ejectment. Yet my reflections were not the most comfortable. I began to grow melancholy and restless; continually prying into my mind, to discover which of its poor properties were gone, and what degree of detriment had already accrued to the remainder. I endeavoured to calculate how much longer I could stay in the Custom-House, and yet go forth a man. To confess the truth, it was my greatest apprehension,—as it would never be a measure of policy to turn out so quiet an individual as myself, and it being hardly in the nature of a public officer to resign, — it was my chief trouble, therefore, that I was likely to grow gray and decrepit in the Surveyorship, and become much such another animal as the old Inspector. Might it not, in the tedious lapse of official life that lay before me, finally be with me as it was with this venerable friend, — to make the dinner-hour the nucleus of the day, and to spend the rest of it, as an old dog spends it, asleep in the sunshine or the shade? A dreary look-forward this, for a man who felt it to be the best definition of happiness to live throughout the whole range of his faculties and sensibilities! But, all this while, I was giving myself very unnecessary alarm. Providence had meditated better things for me than I could possibly imagine for myself.

A remarkable event of the third year of my Surveyorship—to adopt the tone of "P. P."—was the election of General Taylor to the Presidency.[27] It is essential, in order to form a complete estimate of the advantages of official life, to view the incumbent at the in-coming of a hostile administration. His position is then one of the most singularly irksome, and, in every contingency, disagreeable, that a wretched mortal can possibly occupy; with seldom an alternative of good, on either hand, although what presents itself to him as the worst event may very probably be the best. But it is a strange experience, to a man of pride and sensibility, to know that his interests are within the control of individuals who neither love nor understand him, and by whom, since one or the other must needs happen, he would rather be injured than obliged. Strange, too, for one who has kept his calmness throughout the contest, to observe the blood-thirstiness that is developed in the hour of triumph, and to be conscious that he is himself among its objects! There are few uglier traits of human nature than this tendency—which I now witnessed in men no worse than their neighbours—to grow cruel, merely because they possessed the power of inflicting harm. If the guillotine, as applied to office-holders, were a literal fact, instead of one of the most apt of metaphors, it is my sincere belief, that the active members of the victorious party were sufficiently excited to have chopped off all our heads, and have thanked Heaven for the opportunity! It appears to me—who have been a calm and curious observer, as well in

---

[27] In the summer of 1849, after the victorious Whig candidate Zachary Taylor (1784–1850) became president, Hawthorne was ousted from office as a consequence of the spoils system. Although he claimed that as a man of letters he was above politics and asked friends to campaign for his reinstatement, opponents produced evidence that he had abetted the Democrats. His relaxed tone masks his feelings of outrage and humiliation, as well as the anguish intensified by his mother's death. See the Introduction to this volume, 1–8.

victory as defeat—that this fierce and bitter spirit of malice and revenge has never distinguished the many triumphs of my own party as it now did that of the Whigs. The Democrats take the offices, as a general rule, because they need them, and because the practice of many years has made it the law of political warfare, which, unless a different system be proclaimed, it were weakness and cowardice to murmur at. But the long habit of victory has made them generous. They know how to spare, when they see occasion; and when they strike, the axe may be sharp, indeed, but its edge is seldom poisoned with ill-will; nor is it their custom ignominiously to kick the head which they have just struck off.

In short, unpleasant as was my predicament, at best, I saw much reason to congratulate myself that I was on the losing side, rather than the triumphant one. If, heretofore, I had been none of the warmest of partisans, I began now, at this season of peril and adversity, to be pretty acutely sensible with which party my predilections lay; nor was it without something like regret and shame, that, according to a reasonable calculation of chances, I saw my own prospect of retaining office to be better than those of my Democratic brethren. But who can see an inch into futurity, beyond his nose? My own head was the first that fell!

The moment when a man's head drops off is seldom or never, I am inclined to think, precisely the most agreeable of his life. Nevertheless, like the greater part of our misfortunes, even so serious a contingency brings its remedy and consolation with it, if the sufferer will but make the best, rather than the worst, of the accident which has befallen him. In my particular case, the consolatory topics were close at hand, and, indeed, had suggested themselves to my meditations a considerable time before it was requisite to use them. In view of my previous weariness of office, and vague thoughts of resignation, my fortune somewhat resembled that of a person who should entertain an idea of committing suicide, and, altogether beyond his hopes, meet with the good hap to be murdered. In the Custom-House, as before in the Old Manse, I had spent three years; a term long enough to rest a weary brain; long enough to break off old intellectual habits, and make room for new ones; long enough, and too long, to have lived in an unnatural state, doing what was really of no advantage nor delight to any human being, and withholding myself from toil that would, at least, have stilled an unquiet impulse in me. Then, moreover, as regarded his unceremonious ejectment, the late Surveyor was not altogether ill-pleased to be recognized by the Whigs as an enemy; since his inactivity in political affairs,—his tendency to roam, at will, in that broad and quiet field where all mankind may meet, rather than confine himself to those narrow paths where brethren of the same household must diverge from one another,—had sometimes made it questionable with his brother Democrats whether he was a friend. Now, after he had won the crown of martyrdom, (though with no longer a head to wear it on,) the point might be looked upon as settled. Finally, little heroic as he was, it seemed more decorous to be overthrown in the downfall of the party with which he had been content to stand, than to remain a forlorn survivor, when so many worthier men were falling; and, at last, after subsisting for four years on the mercy of a hostile administration, to be compelled then to define his position anew, and claim the yet more humiliating mercy of a friendly one.

Meanwhile, the press had taken up my affair, and kept me, for a week or two, careering through the public prints, in my decapitated state, like Irving's Headless Horseman;[28] ghastly and grim, and longing to be buried, as a politically dead man ought. So much for my figurative self. The real human being, all this time, with his head safely on his shoulders, had brought himself to the comfortable conclusion, that every thing was for the best; and, making an investment in ink, paper, and steel-pens, had opened his long-disused writing-desk, and was again a literary man.

Now it was, that the lucubrations of my ancient predecessor, Mr. Surveyor Pue, came into play. Rusty through long idleness, some little space was requisite before my intellectual machinery could be brought to work upon the tale, with an effect in any degree satisfactory. Even yet, though my thoughts were ultimately much absorbed in the task, it wears, to my eye, a stern and sombre aspect; too much ungladdened by genial sunshine; too little relieved by the tender and familiar influences which soften almost every scene of nature and real life, and, undoubtedly, should soften every picture of them. This uncaptivating effect is perhaps due to the period of hardly accomplished revolution, and still seething turmoil, in which the story shaped itself. It is no indication, however, of a lack of cheerfulness in the writer's mind; for he was happier, while straying through the gloom of these sunless fantasies, than at any time since he had quitted the Old Manse. Some of the briefer articles, which contribute to make up the volume, have likewise been written since my involuntary withdrawal from the toils and honors of public life, and the remainder are gleaned from annuals and magazines, of such antique date that they have gone round the circle, and come back to novelty again.[29] Keeping up the metaphor of the political

---

[28] The enterprising practical joker in Washington Irving's "The Legend of Sleepy Hollow" (1820).

[29] "At the time of writing this article, the author intended to publish, along with 'The Scarlet Letter,' several shorter tales and sketches. These it has been thought advisable to defer." [Hawthorne's note.] See notes 3 and 24.

guillotine, the whole may be considered as the *Posthumous Papers of a Decapitated Surveyor*; and the sketch which I am now bringing to a close, if too autobiographical for a modest person to publish in his lifetime, will readily be excused in a gentleman who writes from beyond the grave. Peace be with all the world! My blessing on my friends! My forgiveness to my enemies! For I am in the realm of quiet!

The life of the Custom-House lies like a dream behind me. The old Inspector—who, by the by, I regret to say, was overthrown and killed by a horse, some time ago; else he would certainly have lived for ever,—he, and all those other venerable personages who sat with him at the receipt of custom, are but shadows in my view; white-headed and wrinkled images, which my fancy used to sport with, and has now flung aside for ever. The merchants,—Pingree, Phillips, Shepard, Upton, Kimball, Bertram, Hunt,—these, and many other names, which had such a classic familiarity for my ear six months ago,—these men of traffic, who seemed to occupy so important a position in the world,—how little time has it required to disconnect me from them all, not merely in act, but recollection! It is with an effort that I recall the figures and appellations of these few. Soon, likewise, my old native town will loom upon me through the haze of memory, a mist brooding over and around it; as if it were no portion of the real earth, but an overgrown village in cloud-land, with only imaginary inhabitants to people its wooden houses, and walk its homely lanes, and the unpicturesque prolixity of its main street. Henceforth, it ceases to be a reality of my life. I am a citizen of somewhere else. My good townspeople will not much regret me; for—though it has been as dear an object as any, in my literary efforts, to be of some importance in their eyes, and to win myself a pleasant memory in this abode and burial-place of so many of my forefathers—there has never been, for me, the genial atmosphere which a literary man requires, in order to ripen the best harvest of his mind. I shall do better amongst other faces; and these familiar ones, it need hardly be said, will do just as well without me.

It may be, however,—O, transporting and triumphant thought!—that the great-grandchildren of the present race may sometimes think kindly of the scribbler of bygone days, when the antiquary of days to come, among the sites memorable in the town's history, shall point out the locality of The Town-Pump![30]

---

[30] Hawthorne's popular sketch "A Rill from the Town-Pump" (1835) describes everyday Salem life from the pump's point of view.

The Prison Door by Mary Hallock Foote, engraved by A. V. S. Anthony. Originally appeared in the 1877 Osgood and Company edition of the novel.

I
The Prison-Door

A throng of bearded men, in sad-colored garments and gray, steeple-crowned hats, intermixed with women, some wearing hoods, and others bareheaded, was assembled in front of a wooden edifice, the door of which was heavily timbered with oak, and studded with iron spikes.

The founders of a new colony, whatever Utopia of human virtue and happiness they might originally project, have invariably recognized it among their earliest practical necessities to allot a portion of the virgin soil as a cemetery, and another portion as the site of a prison. In accordance with this rule, it may safely be assumed that the forefathers of Boston had built the first prison-house, somewhere in the vicinity of Cornhill, almost as seasonably as they marked out the first burial-ground, on Isaac Johnson's lot, and round about his grave, which subsequently became the nucleus of all the congregated sepulchres in the old church-yard of King's Chapel.[1] Certain it is, that, some fifteen or twenty years after the settlement of the town,[2] the wooden jail was already marked with weather-stains and other indications of age, which gave a yet darker aspect to its beetle-browed and gloomy front. The rust on the ponderous iron-work of its oaken door looked more antique than any thing else in the new world. Like all that pertains to crime, it seemed never to have known a youthful era. Before this ugly edifice, and between it and the wheel-track of the street, was a grass-plot, much overgrown with burdock, pig-weed, apple-peru, and such unsightly vegetation, which evidently found something congenial in the soil that had so early borne the black flower of civilized society, a prison. But, on one side of the portal, and rooted almost at the threshold, was a wild rose-bush, covered, in this month of June, with its delicate gems, which might be imagined to offer their fragrance and fragile beauty to the prisoner as he went in, and to the condemned criminal as he came forth to his doom, in token that the deep heart of Nature could pity and be kind to him.

This rose-bush, by a strange chance, has been kept alive in history; but whether it had merely survived out of the stern old wilderness, so long after the fall of the gigantic pines and oaks that originally overshadowed it, — or whether, as there is fair authority for believing, it had sprung up under

---

[1] Isaac Johnson (1601–1630), a wealthy Puritan who died soon after emigrating to Massachusetts in 1630, bequeathing his land for public use. King's Chapel, built in 1688, was the first Anglican church in Boston.

[2] The novel's main events occur between 1642 and 1647.

the footsteps of the sainted Ann Hutchinson,[3] as she entered the prison-door,—we shall not take upon us to determine. Finding it so directly on the threshold of our narrative, which is now about to issue from that inauspicious portal, we could hardly do otherwise than pluck one of its flowers and present it to the reader. It may serve, let us hope, to symbolize some sweet moral blossom, that may be found along the track, or relieve the darkening close of a tale of human frailty and sorrow.

I I

The Marketplace

The grass-plot before the jail, in Prison Lane, on a certain summer morning, not less than two centuries ago, was occupied by a pretty large number of the inhabitants of Boston; all with their eyes intently fastened on the iron-clamped oaken door. Amongst any other population, or at a later period in the history of New England, the grim rigidity that petrified the bearded physiognomies of these good people would have augured some awful business in hand. It could have betokened nothing short of the anticipated execution of some noted culprit, on whom the sentence of a legal tribunal had but confirmed the verdict of public sentiment. But, in that early severity of the Puritan character, an inference of this kind could not so indubitably be drawn. It might be that a sluggish bond-servant, or an undutiful child, whom his parents had given over to the civil authority, was to be corrected at the whipping-post. It might be, that an Antinomian, a Quaker, or other heterodox religionist, was to be scourged out of the town, or an idle and vagrant Indian, whom the white man's fire-water had made riotous about the streets, was to be driven with stripes into the shadow of the forest. It might be, too, that a witch, like old Mistress Hibbins,[4] the bitter-tempered widow of the magistrate, was to die upon the gallows. In either case, there was very much the same solemnity of demeanour on the part of the spectators; as befitted a people amongst whom religion and law were almost identical, and in whose character both were so thoroughly interfused, that the mildest and the severest acts of public discipline were

---

[3] Anne Hutchinson (1591–1643) was imprisoned and then banished from Massachusetts for preaching antinomianism (that is, salvation results from God's grace, experienced within, and independent of the obligation to obey God's laws and to perform good works). Hawthorne's sympathetic yet conflicted sketch of "Mrs. Hutchinson" had appeared in the *Salem Gazette* in 1830. (See pages 14–19 in this volume.)
[4] Ann Hibbens (?–1656), the widow of a wealthy Bostonian, was condemned as a witch in 1655 and hanged the following year. One of Hawthorne's sources identified her as Bellingham's sister.

alike made venerable and awful. Meagre, indeed, and cold, was the sympathy that a transgressor might look for, from such bystanders at the scaffold. On the other hand, a penalty which, in our days, would infer a degree of mocking infamy and ridicule, might then be invested with almost as stern a dignity as the punishment of death itself.

It was a circumstance to be noted, on the summer morning when our story begins its course, that the women, of whom there were several in the crowd, appeared to take a peculiar interest in whatever penal infliction might be expected to ensue. The age had not so much refinement, that any sense of impropriety restrained the wearers of petticoat and farthingale[5] from stepping forth into the public ways, and wedging their not unsubstantial persons, if occasion were, into the throng nearest to the scaffold at an execution. Morally, as well as materially, there was a coarser fibre in those wives and maidens of old English birth and breeding, than in their fair descendants, separated from them by a series of six or seven generations; for, throughout that chain of ancestry, every successive mother has transmitted to her child a fainter bloom, a more delicate and briefer beauty, and a slighter physical frame, if not a character of less force and solidity, than her own. The women, who were now standing about the prison-door, stood within less than half a century of the period when the man-like Elizabeth[6] had been the not altogether unsuitable representative of the sex. They were her countrywomen; and the beef and ale of their native land, with a moral diet not a whit more refined, entered largely into their composition. The bright morning sun, therefore, shone on broad shoulders and well-developed busts, and on round and ruddy cheeks, that had ripened in the far-off island, and had hardly yet grown paler or thinner in the atmosphere of New England. There was, moreover, a boldness and rotundity of speech among these matrons, as most of them seemed to be, that would startle us at the present day, whether in respect to its purport or its volume of tone.

"Goodwives," said a hard-featured dame of fifty, "I'll tell ye a piece of my mind. It would be greatly for the public behoof, if we women, being of mature age and church-members in good repute, should have the handling of such malefactresses as this Hester Prynne. What think ye, gossips?[7] If the hussy stood up for judgment before us five, that are now here in a knot together, would she come off with such a sentence as the worshipful magistrates have awarded? Marry, I trow not!"[8]

---

[5] A hoop skirt.
[6] Elizabeth I (1533–1603), Queen of England from 1558 to 1603.
[7] Friends.
[8] "Indeed, I think not."

"People say," said another, "that the Reverend Master Dimmesdale, her godly pastor, takes it very grievously to heart that such a scandal should have come upon his congregation."

"The magistrates are God-fearing gentlemen, but merciful overmuch, — that is a truth," added a third autumnal matron. "At the very least, they should have put the brand of a hot iron on Hester Prynne's forehead. Madam Hester would have winced at that, I warrant me. But she, — the naughty baggage, — little will she care what they put upon the bodice of her gown! Why, look you, she may cover it with a brooch, or such like heathenish adornment, and so walk the streets as brave as ever!"

"Ah, but," interposed, more softly, a young wife, holding a child by the hand, "let her cover the mark as she will, the pang of it will be always in her heart."

"What do we talk of marks and brands, whether on the bodice of her gown, or the flesh of her forehead?" cried another female, the ugliest as well as the most pitiless of these self-constituted judges. "This woman has brought shame upon us all, and ought to die. Is there not law for it? Truly there is, both in the Scripture and the statute-book.[9] Then let the magistrates, who have made it of no effect, thank themselves if their own wives and daughters go astray!"

"Mercy on us, goodwife," exclaimed a man in the crowd, "is there no virtue in woman, save what springs from a wholesome fear of the gallows? That is the hardest word yet! Hush, now, gossips; for the lock is turning in the prison-door, and here comes Mistress Prynne herself."

The door of the jail being flung open from within, there appeared, in the first place, like a black shadow emerging into the sunshine, the grim and grisly presence of the town-beadle,[10] with a sword by his side and his staff of office in his hand. This personage prefigured and represented in his aspect the whole dismal severity of the Puritanic code of law, which it was his business to administer in its final and closest application to the offender. Stretching forth the official staff in his left hand, he laid his right upon the shoulder of a young woman, whom he thus drew forward; until, on the threshold of the prison-door, she repelled him, by an action marked with natural dignity and force of character, and stepped into the open air, as if by her own free-will. She bore in her arms a child, a baby of some three months old, who winked and turned aside its little face from the too vivid

---

[9] Heeding such biblical injunctions as "Thou shalt not commit adultery" (Exod. 20.14) and "The adulterer and the adulteress shall surely be put to death" (Lev. 20.10), Puritans condemned adultery as both a crime and a sin, imposing punishments that ranged from public humiliation to execution.

[10] Constable.

light of day; because its existence, heretofore, had brought it acquainted only with the gray twilight of a dungeon, or other darksome apartment of the prison.

When the young woman—the mother of this child—stood fully revealed before the crowd, it seemed to be her first impulse to clasp the infant closely to her bosom; not so much by an impulse of motherly affection, as that she might thereby conceal a certain token, which was wrought or fastened into her dress. In a moment, however, wisely judging that one token of her shame would but poorly serve to hide another, she took the baby on her arm, and, with a burning blush, and yet a haughty smile, and a glance that would not be abashed, looked around at her townspeople and neighbours. On the breast of her gown, in fine red cloth, surrounded with an elaborate embroidery and fantastic flourishes of gold thread, appeared the letter A. It was so artistically done, and with so much fertility and gorgeous luxuriance of fancy, that it had all the effect of a last and fitting decoration to the apparel which she wore; and which was of a splendor in accordance with the taste of the age, but greatly beyond what was allowed by the sumptuary regulations of the colony.

The young woman was tall, with a figure of perfect elegance, on a large scale. She had dark and abundant hair, so glossy that it threw off the sunshine with a gleam, and a face which, besides being beautiful from regularity of feature and richness of complexion, had the impressiveness belonging to a marked brow and deep black eyes. She was lady-like, too, after the manner of the feminine gentility of those days; characterized by a certain state and dignity, rather than by the delicate, evanescent, and indescribable grace, which is now recognized as its indication. And never had Hester Prynne appeared more lady-like, in the antique interpretation of the term, than as she issued from the prison. Those who had before known her, and had expected to behold her dimmed and obscured by a disastrous cloud, were astonished, and even startled, to perceive how her beauty shone out, and made a halo of the misfortune and ignominy in which she was enveloped. It may be true, that, to a sensitive observer, there was something exquisitely painful in it. Her attire, which, indeed, she had wrought for the occasion, in prison, and had modelled much after her own fancy, seemed to express the attitude of her spirit, the desperate recklessness of her mood, by its wild and picturesque peculiarity. But the point which drew all eyes, and, as it were, transfigured the wearer,—so that both men and women, who had been familiarly acquainted with Hester Prynne, were now impressed as if they beheld her for the first time,—was that Scarlet Letter, so fantastically embroidered and illuminated upon her bosom. It had the effect of a spell, taking her out of the ordinary relations with humanity, and inclosing her in a sphere by herself.

"She hath good skill at her needle, that's certain," remarked one of the female spectators; "but did ever a woman, before this brazen hussy, contrive such a way of showing it! Why, gossips, what is it but to laugh in the faces of our godly magistrates, and make a pride out of what they, worthy gentlemen, meant for a punishment?"

"It were well," muttered the most iron-visaged of the old dames, "if we stripped Madam Hester's rich gown off her dainty shoulders; and as for the red letter, which she hath stitched so curiously, I'll bestow a rag of mine own rheumatic flannel, to make a fitter one!"

"O, peace, neighbours, peace!" whispered their youngest companion. "Do not let her hear you! Not a stitch in that embroidered letter, but she has felt it in her heart."

The grim beadle now made a gesture with his staff.

"Make way, good people, make way, in the King's name," cried he. "Open a passage; and, I promise ye, Mistress Prynne shall be set where man, woman, and child may have a fair sight of her brave apparel, from this time till an hour past meridian. A blessing on the righteous Colony of the Massachusetts, where iniquity is dragged out into the sunshine! Come along, Madam Hester, and show your scarlet letter in the market-place!"

A lane was forthwith opened through the crowd of spectators. Preceded by the beadle, and attended by an irregular procession of stern-browed men and unkindly-visaged women, Hester Prynne set forth towards the place appointed for her punishment. A crowd of eager and curious schoolboys, understanding little of the matter in hand, except that it gave them a half-holiday, ran before her progress, turning their heads continually to stare into her face, and at the winking baby in her arms, and at the ignominious letter on her breast. It was no great distance, in those days, from the prison-door to the market-place. Measured by the prisoner's experience, however, it might be reckoned a journey of some length; for, haughty as her demeanour was, she perchance underwent an agony from every foot-step of those that thronged to see her, as if her heart had been flung into the street for them all to spurn and trample upon. In our nature, however, there is a provision, alike marvellous and merciful, that the sufferer should never know the intensity of what he endures by its present torture, but chiefly by the pang that rankles after it. With almost a serene deportment, therefore, Hester Prynne passed through this portion of her ordeal, and came to a sort of scaffold, at the western extremity of the market-place. It stood nearly beneath the eaves of Boston's earliest church, and appeared to be a fixture there.

In fact, this scaffold constituted a portion of a penal machine, which now, for two or three generations past, has been merely historical and traditionary among us, but was held, in the old time, to be as effectual an agent in the promotion of good citizenship as ever was the guillotine among the terrorists of France.[11] It was, in short, the platform of the pillory; and above it rose the framework of that instrument of discipline, so fashioned as to confine the human head in its tight grasp, and thus hold it up to the public gaze. The very ideal of ignominy was embodied and made manifest in this contrivance of wood and iron. There can be no outrage, methinks, against our common nature, —whatever be the delinquencies of the individual, —no outrage more flagrant than to forbid the culprit to hide his face for shame; as it was the essence of this punishment to do. In Hester Prynne's instance, however, as not unfrequently in other cases, her sentence bore, that she should stand a certain time upon the platform, but without undergoing that gripe about the neck and confinement of the head, the proneness to which was the most devilish characteristic of this ugly engine. Knowing well her part, she ascended a flight of wooden steps, and was thus displayed to the surrounding multitude, at about the height of a man's shoulders above the street. Displayed as punishment

Had there been a Papist among the crowd of Puritans, he might have seen in this beautiful woman, so picturesque in her attire and mien, and with the infant at her bosom, an object to remind him of the image of Divine Maternity, which so many illustrious painters have vied with one another to represent; something which should remind him, indeed, but only by contrast, of that sacred image of sinless motherhood, whose infant was to redeem the world. Here, there was the taint of deepest sin in the most sacred quality of human life, working such effect, that the world was only the darker for this woman's beauty, and the more lost for the infant that she had borne.

The scene was not without a mixture of awe, such as must always invest the spectacle of guilt and shame in a fellow-creature, before society shall have grown corrupt enough to smile, instead of shuddering, at it. The witnesses of Hester Prynne's disgrace had not yet passed beyond their simplicity. They were stern enough to look upon her death, had that been the sentence, without a murmur at its severity, but had none of the heartlessness of another social state, which would find only a theme for jest in an exhibition like the present. Even had there been a disposition to turn the matter into ridicule, it must have been repressed and overpowered by the solemn presence of men no less dignified than the Governor, and several of his counsellors, a judge, a general, and the ministers of the town; all of

---

[11] The Decapitated Surveyor, implicitly identifying with his heroine, is comparing the scaffold to the guillotine, an instrument for beheading developed during the Reign of Terror in France (1793–94).

whom sat or stood in a balcony of the meeting-house, looking down upon the platform. When such personages could constitute a part of the spectacle, without risking the majesty or reverence of rank and office, it was safely to be inferred that the infliction of a legal sentence would have an earnest and effectual meaning. Accordingly, the crowd was sombre and grave. The unhappy culprit sustained herself as best a woman might, under the heavy weight of a thousand unrelenting eyes, all fastened upon her, and concentrated at her bosom. It was almost intolerable to be borne. Of an impulsive and passionate nature, she had fortified herself to encounter the stings and venomous stabs of public contumely, wreaking itself in every variety of insult; but there was a quality so much more terrible in the solemn mood of the popular mind, that she longed rather to behold all those rigid countenances contorted with scornful merriment, and herself the object. Had a roar of laughter burst from the multitude—each man, each woman, each little shrill-voiced child, contributing their individual parts—Hester Prynne might have repaid them all with a bitter and disdainful smile. But, under the leaden infliction which it was her doom to endure, she felt, at moments, as if she must needs shriek out with the full power of her lungs, and cast herself from the scaffold down upon the ground, or else go mad at once.

Yet there were intervals when the whole scene, in which she was the most conspicuous object, seemed to vanish from her eyes, or, at least, glimmered indistinctly before them, like a mass of imperfectly shaped and spectral images. Her mind, and especially her memory, was preternaturally active, and kept bringing up other scenes than this roughly hewn street of a little town, on the edge of the Western wilderness; other faces than were lowering upon her from beneath the brims of those steeple-crowned hats. Reminiscences, the most trifling and immaterial, passages of infancy and school-days, sports, childish quarrels, and the little domestic traits of her maiden years, came swarming back upon her, intermingled with recollections of whatever was gravest in her subsequent life; one picture precisely as vivid as another; as if all were of similar importance, or all alike a play. Possibly, it was an instinctive device of her spirit, to relieve itself, by the exhibition of these phantasmagoric forms, from the cruel weight and hardness of the reality.

Be that as it might, the scaffold of the pillory was a point of view that revealed to Hester Prynne the entire track along which she had been treading, since her happy infancy. Standing on that miserable eminence, she saw again her native village, in Old England, and her paternal home; a decayed house of gray stone, with a poverty-stricken aspect, but retaining a half-obliterated shield of arms over the portal, in token of antique gentility. She saw her father's face, with its bald brow, and reverend white beard, that

Standing on the Miserable Eminence by Mary Hallock Foote, engraved by
A. V. S. Anthony. Originally appeared in the 1877 Osgood and Company edition
of the novel.

flowed over the old-fashioned Elizabethan ruff; her mother's, too, with the look of heedful and anxious love which it always wore in her remembrance, and which, even since her death, had so often laid the impediment of a gentle remonstrance in her daughter's pathway. She saw her own face, glowing with girlish beauty, and illuminating all the interior of the dusky mirror in which she had been wont to gaze at it. There she beheld another countenance, of a man well stricken in years, a pale, thin, scholar-like visage, with eyes dim and bleared by the lamp-light that had served them to pore over many ponderous books. Yet those same bleared optics had a strange, penetrating power, when it was their owner's purpose to read the human soul. This figure of the study and the cloister, as Hester Prynne's womanly fancy failed not to recall, was slightly deformed, with the left shoulder a trifle higher than the right. Next rose before her, in memory's picture-gallery, the intricate and narrow thoroughfares, the tall, gray houses, the huge cathedrals, and the public edifices, ancient in date and quaint in architecture, of a Continental city;[12] where a new life had awaited her, still in connection with the misshapen scholar; a new life, but feeding itself on time-worn materials, like a tuft of green moss on a crumbling wall. Lastly, in lieu of these shifting scenes, came back the rude market-place of the Puritan settlement, with all the townspeople assembled and levelling their stern regards at Hester Prynne,—yes, at herself,—who stood on the scaffold of the pillory, an infant on her arm, and the letter A, in scarlet, fantastically embroidered with gold thread, upon her bosom!

Could it be true? She clutched the child so fiercely to her breast, that it sent forth a cry; she turned her eyes down-ward at the scarlet letter, and even touched it with her finger, to assure herself that the infant and the shame were real. Yes!—these were her realities,—all else had vanished!

III

The Recognition

From this intense consciousness of being the object of severe and universal observation, the wearer of the scarlet letter was at length relieved by discerning, on the outskirts of the crowd, a figure which irresistibly took possession of her thoughts. An Indian, in his native garb, was standing there; but the red men were not so infrequent visitors of the English settlements, that one of them would have attracted any notice from Hester Prynne, at

---

[12] Amsterdam, where English Puritans and Separatists assembled before sailing to America.

such a time; much less would he have excluded all other objects and ideas from her mind. By the Indian's side, and evidently sustaining a companionship with him, stood a white man, clad in a strange disarray of civilized and savage costume.

He was small in stature, with a furrowed visage, which, as yet, could hardly be termed aged. There was a remarkable intelligence in his features, as of a person who had so cultivated his mental part that it could not fail to mould the physical to itself, and become manifest by unmistakable tokens. Although, by a seemingly careless arrangement of his heterogeneous garb, he had endeavoured to conceal or abate the peculiarity, it was sufficiently evident to Hester Prynne, that one of this man's shoulders rose higher than the other. Again, at the first instant of perceiving that thin visage, and the slight deformity of the figure, she pressed her infant to her bosom, with so convulsive a force that the poor babe uttered another cry of pain. But the mother did not seem to hear it.

At his arrival in the market-place, and some time before she saw him, the stranger had bent his eyes on Hester Prynne. It was carelessly, at first, like a man chiefly accustomed to look inward, and to whom external matters are of little value and import, unless they bear relation to something within his mind. Very soon, however, his look became keen and penetrative. A writhing horror twisted itself across his features, like a snake gliding swiftly over them, and making one little pause, with all its wreathed intervolutions in open sight. His face darkened with some powerful emotion, which, nevertheless, he so instantaneously controlled by an effort of his will, that, save at a single moment, its expression might have passed for calmness. After a brief space, the convulsion grew almost imperceptible, and finally subsided into the depths of his nature. When he found the eyes of Hester Prynne fastened on his own, and saw that she appeared to recognize him, he slowly and calmly raised his finger, made a gesture with it in the air, and laid it on his lips.

Then, touching the shoulder of a townsman who stood next to him, he addressed him in a formal and courteous manner.

"I pray you, good Sir," said he, "who is this woman? —and wherefore is she here set up to public shame?"

"You must needs be a stranger in this region, friend," answered the townsman, looking curiously at the questioner and his savage companion; "else you would surely have heard of Mistress Hester Prynne, and her evil doings. She hath raised a great scandal, I promise you, in godly Master Dimmesdale's church."

"You say truly," replied the other, "I am a stranger, and have been a wanderer, sorely against my will. I have met with grievous mishaps by sea and land, and have been long held in bonds among the heathen-folk, to the southward; and am now brought hither by this Indian, to be redeemed out of my captivity. Will it please you, therefore, to tell me of Hester Prynne's,—have I her name rightly?—of this woman's offences, and what has brought her to yonder scaffold?"

"Truly, friend, and methinks it must gladden your heart, after your troubles and sojourn in the wilderness," said the townsman, "to find yourself, at length, in a land where iniquity is searched out, and punished in the sight of rulers and people; as here in our godly New England. Yonder woman, Sir, you must know, was the wife of a certain learned man, English by birth, but who had long dwelt in Amsterdam, whence, some good time agone, he was minded to cross over and cast in his lot with us of the Massachusetts. To this purpose, he sent his wife before him, remaining himself to look after some necessary affairs. Marry, good Sir, in some two years, or less, that the woman has been a dweller here in Boston, no tidings have come of this learned gentleman, Master Prynne; and his young wife, look you, being left to her own misguidance—"

"Ah!—aha!—I conceive you," said the stranger, with a bitter smile. "So learned a man as you speak of should have learned this too in his books. And who, by your favor, Sir, may be the father of yonder babe—it is some three or four months old, I should judge—which Mistress Prynne is holding in her arms?"

"Of a truth, friend, that matter remaineth a riddle; and the Daniel who shall expound it is yet a-wanting,"[13] answered the townsman. "Madam Hester absolutely refuseth to speak, and the magistrates have laid their heads together in vain. Peradventure the guilty one stands looking on at this sad spectacle, unknown of man, and forgetting that God sees him."

"The learned man," observed the stranger, with another smile, "should come himself to look into the mystery."

"It behooves him well, if he be still in life," responded the townsman. "Now, good Sir, our Massachusetts magistracy, bethinking themselves that this woman is youthful and fair, and doubtless was strongly tempted to her fall;—and that, moreover, as is most likely, her husband may be at the bottom of the sea;—they have not been bold to put in force the extremity of our righteous law against her. The penalty thereof is death. But, in their great mercy and tenderness of heart, they have doomed Mistress Prynne to stand only a space of three hours on the platform of the pillory, and then and thereafter, for the remainder of her natural life, to wear a mark of shame upon her bosom."

---

[13] The Hebrew prophet who interpreted the words on Belshazzar's wall that prophesied his defeat (Dan. 5).

"A wise sentence!" remarked the stranger, gravely bowing his head. "Thus she will be a living sermon against sin, until the ignominious letter be engraved upon her tombstone. It irks me, nevertheless, that the partner of her iniquity should not, at least, stand on the scaffold by her side. But he will be known! —he will be known! —he will be known!"

He bowed courteously to the communicative townsman, and, whispering a few words to his Indian attendant, they both made their way through the crowd.

While this passed, Hester Prynne had been standing on her pedestal, still with a fixed gaze towards the stranger; so fixed a gaze, that, at moments of intense absorption, all other objects in the visible world seemed to vanish, leaving only him and her. Such an interview, perhaps, would have been more terrible than even to meet him as she now did, with the hot, midday sun burning down upon her face, and lighting up its shame; with the scarlet token of infamy on her breast; with the sin-born infant in her arms; with a whole people, drawn forth as to a festival, staring at the features that should have been seen only in the quiet gleam of the fireside, in the happy shadow of a home, or beneath a matronly veil, at church. Dreadful as it was, she was conscious of a shelter in the presence of these thousand witnesses. It was better to stand thus, with so many betwixt him and her, than to greet him, face to face, they two alone. She fled for refuge, as it were, to the public exposure, and dreaded the moment when its protection should be withdrawn from her. Involved in these thoughts, she scarcely heard a voice behind her, until it had repeated her name more than once, in a loud and solemn tone, audible to the whole multitude.

"Hearken unto me, Hester Prynne!" said the voice.

It has already been noticed, that directly over the platform on which Hester Prynne stood was a kind of balcony, or open gallery, appended to the meeting-house. It was the place whence proclamations were wont to be made, amidst an assemblage of the magistracy, with all the ceremonial that attended such public observances in those days. Here, to witness the scene which we are describing, sat Governor Bellingham[14] himself, with four sergeants about his chair, bearing halberds, as a guard of honor. He wore a dark feather in his hat, a border of embroidery on his cloak, and a black velvet tunic beneath; a gentleman advanced in years, and with a hard experience written in his wrinkles. He was not ill fitted to be the head and representative of a community, which owed its origin and progress, and its present state of development, not to the impulses of youth, but to the stern

---

[14] Richard Bellingham (1592–1672), Governor of Massachusetts in 1641, 1654, and from 1665 to 1672.

and tempered energies of manhood, and the sombre sagacity of age; accomplishing so much, precisely because it imagined and hoped so little. The other eminent characters, by whom the chief ruler was surrounded, were distinguished by a dignity of mien, belonging to a period when the forms of authority were felt to possess the sacredness of divine institutions. They were, doubtless, good men, just, and sage. But, out of the whole human family, it would not have been easy to select the same number of wise and virtuous persons, who should be less capable of sitting in judgment on an erring woman's heart, and disentangling its mesh of good and evil, than the sages of rigid aspect towards whom Hester Prynne now turned her face. She seemed conscious, indeed, that whatever sympathy she might expect lay in the larger and warmer heart of the multitude; for, as she lifted her eyes towards the balcony, the unhappy woman grew pale and trembled.

The voice which had called her attention was that of the reverend and famous John Wilson,[15] the eldest clergyman of Boston, a great scholar, like most of his contemporaries in the profession, and withal a man of kind and genial spirit. This last attribute, however, had been less carefully developed than his intellectual gifts, and was, in truth, rather a matter of shame than self-congratulation with him. There he stood, with a border of grizzled locks beneath his skull-cap; while his gray eyes, accustomed to the shaded light of his study, were winking, like those of Hester's infant, in the unadulterated sunshine. He looked like the darkly engraved portraits which we see prefixed to old volumes of sermons; and had no more right than one of those portraits would have, to step forth, as he now did, and meddle with a question of human guilt, passion, and anguish.

"Hester Prynne," said the clergyman, "I have striven with my young brother here, under whose preaching of the word you have been privileged to sit," — here Mr. Wilson laid his hand on the shoulder of a pale young man beside him, — "I have sought, I say, to persuade this godly youth, that he should deal with you, here in the face of Heaven, and before these wise and upright rulers, and in hearing of all the people, as touching the vileness and blackness of your sin. Knowing your natural temper better than I, he could the better judge what arguments to use, whether of tenderness or terror, such as might prevail over your hardness and obstinacy; insomuch that you should no longer hide the name of him who tempted you to this grievous fall. But he opposes to me (with a young man's oversoftness, albeit wise beyond his years) that it were wronging the very nature of woman to force her to lay open her heart's secrets in such broad daylight, and in presence

---

[15] John Wilson (1591–1667), a Puritan minister who emigrated to Massachusetts in 1630.

of so great a multitude. Truly, as I sought to convince him, the shame lay in the commission of the sin, and not in the showing of it forth. What say you to it, once again, brother Dimmesdale? Must it be thou or I that shall deal with this poor sinner's soul?"

There was a murmur among the dignified and reverend occupants of the balcony; and Governor Bellingham gave expression to its purport, speaking in an authoritative voice, although tempered with respect towards the youthful clergyman whom he addressed.

"Good Master Dimmesdale," said he, "the responsibility of this woman's soul lies greatly with you. It behooves you, therefore, to exhort her to repentance, and to confession, as a proof and consequence thereof."

The directness of his appeal drew the eyes of the whole crowd upon the Reverend Mr. Dimmesdale; a young clergyman, who had come from one of the great English universities, bringing all the learning of the age into our wild forest-land. His eloquence and religious fervor had already given the earnest of high eminence in his profession. He was a person of very striking aspect, with a white, lofty, and impending brow, large, brown, melancholy eyes, and a mouth which, unless when he forcibly compressed it, was apt to be tremulous, expressing both nervous sensibility and a vast power of self-restraint. Notwithstanding his high native gifts and scholar-like attainments, there was an air about this young minister, — an apprehensive, a startled, a half-frightened look, — as of a being who felt himself quite astray and at a loss in the pathway of human existence, and could only be at ease in some seclusion of his own. Therefore, so far as his duties would permit, he trode in the shadowy by-paths, and thus kept himself simple and child-like; coming forth, when occasion was, with a freshness, and fragrance, and dewy purity of thought, which, as many people said, affected them like the speech of an angel.

Such was the young man whom the Reverend Mr. Wilson and the Governor had introduced so openly to the public notice, bidding him speak, in the hearing of all men, to that mystery of a woman's soul, so sacred even in its pollution. The trying nature of his position drove the blood from his cheek, and made his lips tremulous.

"Speak to the woman, my brother," said Mr. Wilson. "It is of moment to her soul, and therefore, as the worshipful Governor says, momentous to thine own, in whose charge hers is. Exhort her to confess the truth!"

The Reverend Mr. Dimmesdale bent his head, in silent prayer, as it seemed, and then came forward.

"Hester Prynne," said he, leaning over the balcony, and looking down stedfastly into her eyes, "thou hearest what this good man says, and seest the accountability under which I labor. If thou feelest it to be for thy soul's peace, and that thy earthly punishment will thereby be more effectual to salvation, I charge thee to speak out the name of thy fellow-sinner and fellow-sufferer! Be not silent from any mistaken pity and tenderness for him; for, believe me, Hester, though he were to step down from a high place, and stand there beside thee, on thy pedestal of shame, yet better were it so, than to hide a guilty heart through life. What can thy silence do for him, except it tempt him—yea, compel him, as it were—to add hypocrisy to sin? Heaven hath granted thee an open ignominy, that thereby thou mayest work out an open triumph over the evil within thee, and the sorrow without. Take heed how thou deniest to him—who, perchance, hath not the courage to grasp it for himself—the bitter, but wholesome, cup that is now presented to thy lips!"

The young pastor's voice was tremulously sweet, rich, deep, and broken. The feeling that it so evidently manifested, rather than the direct purport of the words, caused it to vibrate within all hearts, and brought the listeners into one accord of sympathy. Even the poor baby, at Hester's bosom, was affected by the same influence; for it directed its hitherto vacant gaze towards Mr. Dimmesdale, and held up its little arms, with a half pleased, half plaintive murmur. So powerful seemed the minister's appeal, that the people could not believe but that Hester Prynne would speak out the guilty name; or else that the guilty one himself, in whatever high or lowly place he stood, would be drawn forth by an inward and inevitable necessity, and compelled to ascend the scaffold.

Hester shook her head.

"Woman, transgress not beyond the limits of Heaven's mercy!" cried the Reverend Mr. Wilson, more harshly than before. "That little babe hath been gifted with a voice, to second and confirm the counsel which thou hast heard. Speak out the name! That, and thy repentance, may avail to take the scarlet letter off thy breast."

"Never!" replied Hester Prynne, looking, not at Mr. Wilson, but into the deep and troubled eyes of the younger clergyman. "It is too deeply branded. Ye cannot take it off. And would that I might endure his agony, as well as mine!"

"Speak, woman!" said another voice, coldly and sternly, proceeding from the crowd about the scaffold. "Speak; and give your child a father!"

"I will not speak!" answered Hester, turning pale as death, but responding to this voice, which she too surely recognized. "And my child must seek a heavenly Father; she shall never know an earthly one!"

"She will not speak!" murmured Mr. Dimmesdale, who, leaning over the balcony, with his hand upon his heart, had awaited the result of his appeal. He now drew back, with a long respiration. "Wondrous strength and generosity of a woman's heart! She will not speak!"

Discerning the impracticable state of the poor culprit's mind, the elder clergyman, who had carefully prepared himself for the occasion, addressed to the multitude a discourse on sin, in all its branches, but with continual reference to the ignominious letter. So forcibly did he dwell upon this symbol, for the hour or more during which his periods were rolling over the people's heads, that it assumed new terrors in their imagination, and seemed to derive its scarlet hue from the flames of the infernal pit. Hester Prynne, meanwhile, kept her place upon the pedestal of shame, with glazed eyes, and an air of weary indifference. She had borne, that morning, all that nature could endure; and as her temperament was not of the order that escapes from too intense suffering by a swoon, her spirit could only shelter itself beneath a stony crust of insensibility, while the faculties of animal life remained entire. In this state, the voice of the preacher thundered remorselessly, but unavailingly, upon her ears. The infant, during the latter portion of her ordeal, pierced the air with its wailings and screams; she strove to hush it, mechanically, but seemed scarcely to sympathize with its trouble. With the same hard demeanour, she was led back to prison, and vanished from the public gaze within its iron-clamped portal. It was whispered, by those who peered after her, that the scarlet letter threw a lurid gleam along the dark passage-way of the interior.

IV
The Interview

After her return to the prison, Hester Prynne was found to be in a state of nervous excitement that demanded constant watchfulness, lest she should perpetrate violence on herself, or do some half-frenzied mischief to the poor babe. As night approached, it proving impossible to quell her insubordination by rebuke or threats of punishment, Master Brackett, the jailer, thought fit to introduce a physician. He described him as a man of skill in all Christian modes of physical science, and likewise familiar with whatever the savage people could teach, in respect to medicinal herbs and roots that grew in the forest. To say the truth, there was much need of professional assistance, not merely for Hester herself, but still more urgently for the child; who, drawing its sustenance from the maternal bosom, seemed to have drank in with it all the turmoil, the anguish, and despair, which pervaded the mother's system. It now writhed in convulsions of pain, and was a forcible type, in its little frame, of the moral agony which Hester Prynne had borne throughout the day.

Closely following the jailer into the dismal apartment, appeared that individual, of singular aspect, whose presence in the crowd had been of such

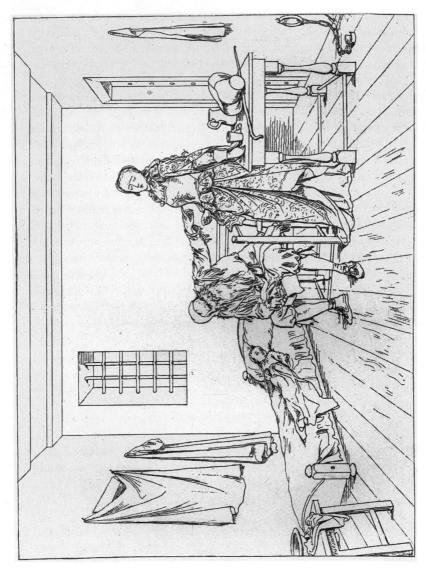

The Interview by F. O. C. Darley. Originally appeared in the 1879 Houghton Mifflin edition of the novel.

deep interest to the wearer of the scarlet letter. He was lodged in the prison, not as suspected of any offence, but as the most convenient and suitable mode of disposing of him, until the magistrates should have conferred with the Indian sagamores respecting his ransom. His name was announced as Roger Chillingworth. The jailer, after ushering him into the room, remained a moment, marvelling at the comparative quiet that followed his entrance; for Hester Prynne had immediately become as still as death, although the child continued to moan.

"Prithee, friend, leave me alone with my patient," said the practitioner. "Trust me, good jailer, you shall briefly have peace in your house; and, I promise you, Mistress Prynne shall hereafter be more amenable to just authority than you may have found her heretofore."

"Nay, if your worship can accomplish that," answered Master Brackett, "I shall own you for a man of skill indeed! Verily, the woman hath been like a possessed one; and there lacks little, that I should take in hand to drive Satan out of her with stripes."

The stranger had entered the room with the characteristic quietude of the profession to which he announced himself as belonging. Nor did his demeanour change, when the withdrawal of the prison-keeper left him face to face with the woman, whose absorbed notice of him, in the crowd, had intimated so close a relation between himself and her. His first care was given to the child; whose cries, indeed, as she lay writhing on the trundle-bed, made it of peremptory necessity to postpone all other business to the task of soothing her. He examined the infant carefully, and then proceeded to unclasp a leathern case, which he took from beneath his dress. It appeared to contain certain medical preparations, one of which he mingled with a cup of water.

"My old studies in alchemy," [16] observed he, "and my sojourn, for above a year past, among a people well versed in the kindly properties of simples, have made a better physician of me than many that claim the medical degree. Here, woman! The child is yours, — she is none of mine, — neither will she recognize my voice or aspect as a father's. Administer this draught, therefore, with thine own hand."

Hester repelled the offered medicine, at the same time gazing with strongly marked apprehension into his face.

"Wouldst thou avenge thyself on the innocent babe?" whispered she.

"Foolish woman!" responded the physician, half coldly, half soothingly.

---

[16] The main goal of alchemists was to transmute base metals into gold, but because they also sought a panacea (cure-all) and an elixir to prolong life indefinitely, they often served as doctors and administered simples (medicinal herbs).

"What should ail me to harm this misbegotten and miserable babe? The medicine is potent for good; and were it my child, —yea, mine own, as well as thine! —I could do no better for it."

As she still hesitated, being, in fact, in no reasonable state of mind, he took the infant in his arms, and himself administered the draught. It soon proved its efficacy, and redeemed the leech's pledge.[17] The moans of the little patient subsided; its convulsive tossings gradually ceased; and in a few moments, as is the custom of young children after relief from pain, it sank into a profound and dewy slumber. The physician, as he had a fair right to be termed, next bestowed his attention on the mother. With calm and intent scrutiny, he felt her pulse, looked into her eyes, —a gaze that made her heart shrink and shudder, because so familiar, and yet so strange and cold, —and, finally, satisfied with his investigation, proceeded to mingle another draught.

"I know not Lethe nor Nepenthe," remarked he; "but I have learned many new secrets in the wilderness, and here is one of them, —a recipe that an Indian taught me, in requital of some lessons of my own, that were as old as Paracelsus.[18] Drink it! It may be less soothing than a sinless conscience. That I cannot give thee. But it will calm the swell and heaving of thy passion, like oil thrown on the waves of a tempestuous sea."

He presented the cup to Hester, who received it with a slow, earnest look into his face; not precisely a look of fear, yet full of doubt and questioning, as to what his purposes might be. She looked also at her slumbering child.

"I have thought of death," she said, — "have wished for it, —would even have prayed for it, were it fit that such as I should pray for any thing. Yet, if death be in this cup, I bid thee think again, ere thou beholdest me quaff it. See! It is even now at my lips."

"Drink, then," replied he, still with the same cold composure. "Dost thou know me so little, Hester Prynne? Are my purposes wont to be so shallow? Even if I imagine a scheme of vengeance, what could I do better for my object than to let thee live, —than to give thee medicines against all harm and peril of life, —so that this burning shame may still blaze upon thy bosom?" —As he spoke, he laid his long forefinger on the scarlet letter, which forthwith seemed to scorch into Hester's breast, as if it had been red-

---

[17] A term for a doctor, since physicians often prescribed bloodletting by the application of leeches to the patient's body.

[18] Drinking from the underworld river Lethe induced oblivion, according to Greek mythology, and ancient Greeks believed that the drug nepenthe eased pain and sorrow. Paracelsus (1499–1541) was a Swiss alchemist reputed to be a great master of medicine.

hot. He noticed her involuntary gesture, and smiled.—"Live, therefore, and bear about thy doom with thee, in the eyes of men and women,—in the eyes of him whom thou didst call thy husband,—in the eyes of yonder child! And, that thou mayest live, take off this draught."

Without further expostulation or delay, Hester Prynne drained the cup, and, at the motion of the man of skill, seated herself on the bed where the child was sleeping; while he drew the only chair which the room afforded, and took his own seat beside her. She could not but tremble at these preparations; for she felt that—having now done all that humanity, or principle, or, if so it were, a refined cruelty, impelled him to do, for the relief of physical suffering—he was next to treat with her as the man whom she had most deeply and irreparably injured.

"Hester," said he, "I ask not wherefore, nor how, thou hast fallen into the pit, or say rather, thou hast ascended to the pedestal of infamy, on which I found thee. The reason is not far to seek. It was my folly, and thy weakness. I,—a man of thought,—the book-worm of great libraries,—a man already in decay, having given my best years to feed the hungry dream of knowledge,—what had I to do with youth and beauty like thine own! Misshapen from my birth-hour, how could I delude myself with the idea that intellectual gifts might veil physical deformity in a young girl's fantasy! Men call me wise. If sages were ever wise in their own behoof, I might have foreseen all this. I might have known that, as I came out of the vast and dismal forest, and entered this settlement of Christian men, the very first object to meet my eyes would be thyself, Hester Prynne, standing up, a statue of ignominy, before the people. Nay, from the moment when we came down the old church-steps together, a married pair, I might have beheld the bale-fire of that scarlet letter blazing at the end of our path!"

"Thou knowest," said Hester,—for, depressed as she was, she could not endure this last quiet stab at the token of her shame,—"thou knowest that I was frank with thee. I felt no love, nor feigned any."

"True!" replied he. "It was my folly! I have said it. But, up to that epoch of my life, I had lived in vain. The world had been so cheerless! My heart was a habitation large enough for many guests, but lonely and chill, and without a household fire. I longed to kindle one! It seemed not so wild a dream,—old as I was, and sombre as I was, and misshapen as I was,—that the simple bliss, which is scattered far and wide, for all mankind to gather up, might yet be mine. And so, Hester, I drew thee into my heart, into its innermost chamber, and sought to warm thee by the warmth which thy presence made there!"

"I have greatly wronged thee," murmured Hester.

"We have wronged each other," answered he. "Mine was the first wrong, when I betrayed thy budding youth into a false and unnatural relation with my decay. Therefore, as a man who has not thought and philosophized in vain, I seek no vengeance, plot no evil against thee. Between thee and me, the scale hangs fairly balanced. But, Hester, the man lives who has wronged us both! Who is he?"

"Ask me not!" replied Hester Prynne, looking firmly into his face. "That thou shalt never know!"

"Never, sayest thou?" rejoined he, with a smile of dark and self-relying intelligence. "Never know him! Believe me, Hester, there are few things, — whether in the outward world, or, to a certain depth, in the invisible sphere of thought, — few things are hidden from the man, who devotes himself earnestly and unreservedly to the solution of a mystery. Thou mayest cover up the secret from the prying multitude. Thou mayest conceal it, too, from the ministers and magistrates, even as thou didst this day, when they sought to wrench the name out of thy heart, and give thee a partner on thy pedestal. But, as for me, I come to the inquest with other senses than they possess. I shall seek this man, as I have sought truth in books; as I have sought gold in alchemy. There is a sympathy that will make me conscious of him. I shall see him tremble. I shall feel myself shudder, suddenly and unawares. Sooner or later, he must needs be mine!"

The eyes of the wrinkled scholar glowed so intensely upon her, that Hester Prynne clasped her hands over her heart, dreading lest he should read the secret there at once.

"Thou wilt not reveal his name? Not the less he is mine," resumed he, with a look of confidence, as if destiny were at one with him. "He bears no letter of infamy wrought into his garment, as thou dost; but I shall read it on his heart. Yet fear not for him! Think not that I shall interfere with Heaven's own method of retribution, or, to my own loss, betray him to the gripe of human law. Neither do thou imagine that I shall contrive aught against his life; no, nor against his fame, if, as I judge, he be a man of fair repute. Let him live! Let him hide himself in outward honor, if he may! Not the less he shall be mine!"

"Thy acts are like mercy," said Hester, bewildered and appalled. "But thy words interpret thee as a terror!"

"One thing, thou that wast my wife, I would enjoin upon thee," continued the scholar. "Thou hast kept the secret of thy paramour. Keep, likewise, mine! There are none in this land that know me. Breathe not, to any human soul, that thou didst ever call me husband! Here, on this wild outskirt of the earth, I shall pitch my tent; for, elsewhere a wanderer, and isolated from human interests, I find here a woman, a man, a child, amongst whom and myself there exist the closest ligaments. No matter whether of love or hate; no matter whether of right or wrong! Thou and thine, Hester Prynne, belong to me. My home is where thou art, and where he is. But betray me not!" *Doesn't want anything to do w/her*

"Wherefore dost thou desire it?" inquired Hester, shrinking, she hardly knew why, from this secret bond. "Why not announce thyself openly, and cast me off at once?"

"It may be," he replied, "because I will not encounter the dishonor that besmirches the husband of a faithless woman. It may be for other reasons. Enough, it is my purpose to live and die unknown. Let, therefore, thy husband be to the world as one already dead, and of whom no tidings shall ever come. Recognize me not, by word, by sign, by look! Breathe not the secret, above all, to the man thou wottest of. Shouldst thou fail me in this, beware! His fame, his position, his life, will be in my hands. Beware!"

"I will keep thy secret, as I have his," said Hester.

"Swear it!" rejoined he.

And she took the oath.

"And now, Mistress Prynne," said old Roger Chillingworth, as he was hereafter to be named, "I leave thee alone; alone with thy infant, and the scarlet letter! How is it, Hester? Doth thy sentence bind thee to wear the token in thy sleep? Art thou not afraid of nightmares and hideous dreams?"

"Why dost thou smile so at me?" inquired Hester, troubled at the expression of his eyes. "Art thou like the Black Man [19] that haunts the forest round about us? Hast thou enticed me into a bond that will prove the ruin of my soul?"

"Not thy soul," he answered, with another smile. "No, not thine!"

V

Hester at Her Needle

Hester Prynne's term of confinement was now at an end. Her prison-door was thrown open, and she came forth into the sunshine, which, falling on all alike, seemed, to her sick and morbid heart, as if meant for no other purpose than to reveal the scarlet letter on her breast. Perhaps there was a more real torture in her first unattended footsteps from the threshold of the prison, than even in the procession and spectacle that have been described, where she was made the common infamy, at which all mankind

---

[19] A folklore term for the Devil.

was summoned to point its finger. Then, she was supported by an unnatural tension of the nerves, and by all the combative energy of her character, which enabled her to convert the scene into a kind of lurid triumph. It was, moreover, a separate and insulated event, to occur but once in her lifetime, and to meet which, therefore, reckless of economy, she might call up the vital strength that would have sufficed for many quiet years. The very law that condemned her—a giant of stern features, but with vigor to support, as well as to annihilate, in his iron arm—had held her up, through the terrible ordeal of her ignominy. But now, with this unattended walk from her prison-door, began the daily custom, and she must either sustain and carry it forward by the ordinary resources of her nature, or sink beneath it. She could no longer borrow from the future, to help her through the present grief. To-morrow would bring its own trial with it; so would the next day, and so would the next; each its own trial, and yet the very same that was now so unutterably grievous to be borne. The days of the far-off future would toil onward, still with the same burden for her to take up, and bear along with her, but never to fling down; for the accumulating days, and added years, would pile up their misery upon the heap of shame. Throughout them all, giving up her individuality, she would become the general symbol at which the preacher and moralist might point, and in which they might vivify an embody their images of women's frailty and sinful passion. Thus the young and pure would be taught to look at her, with the scarlet letter flaming on her breast,—at her, the child of honorable parents,—at her, the mother of a babe, that would hereafter be a woman,—at her, who had once been innocent,—as the figure, the body, the reality of sin. And over her grave, the infamy that she must carry thither would be her only monument.

It may seem marvellous, that, with the world before her,—kept by no restrictive clause of her condemnation within the limits of the Puritan settlement, so remote and so obscure,—free to return to her birthplace, or to any other European land, and there hide her character and identity under a new exterior, as completely as if emerging into another state of being,—and having also the passes of the dark, inscrutable forest open to her, where the wildness of her nature might assimilate itself with a people whose customs and life were alien from the law that had condemned her,— it may seem marvellous, that this woman should still call that place her home, where, and where only, she must needs be the type of shame. But there is a fatality, a feeling so irresistible and inevitable that it has the force of doom, which almost invariably compels human beings to linger around and haunt, ghost-like, the spot where some great and marked event has given the color to their lifetime; and still the more irresistibly, the darker the tinge that saddens it. Her sin, her ignominy, were the roots which she had struck into the soil. It was as if a new birth, with stronger assimilations than the first, had converted the forest-land, still so uncongenial to every other pilgrim and wanderer, into Hester Prynne's wild and dreary, but life-long home. All other scenes of earth — even that village of rural England, where happy infancy and stainless maidenhood seemed yet to be in her mother's keeping, like garments put off long ago — were foreign to her, in comparison. The chain that bound her here was of iron links, and galling to her inmost soul, but never could be broken.

It might be, too, — doubtless it was so, although she hid the secret from herself, and grew pale whenever it struggled out of her heart, like a serpent from its hole, — it might be that another feeling kept her within the scene and pathway that had been so fatal. There dwelt, there trod the feet of one with whom she deemed herself connected in a union, that, unrecognized on earth, would bring them together before the bar of final judgment, and make that their marriage-altar, for a joint futurity of endless retribution. Over and over again, the temper of souls had thrust this idea upon Hester's contemplation, and laughed at the passionate and desperate joy with which she seized, and then strove to cast it from her. She barely looked the idea in the face, and hastened to bar it in its dungeon. What she compelled herself to believe, — what, finally, she reasoned upon, as her motive for continuing a resident of New England, — was half a truth, and half a self-delusion. Here, she said to herself, had been the scene of her guilt, and here should be the scene of her earthly punishment; and so, perchance, the tor- ✳ ture of her daily shame would at length purge her soul, and work out another purity than that which she had lost; more saint-like, because the result of martyrdom.

Hester Prynne, therefore, did not flee. On the outskirts of the town, within the verge of the peninsula, but not in close vicinity to any other habitation, there was a small thatched cottage. It had been built by an earlier settler, and abandoned, because the soil about it was too sterile for cultivation, while its comparative remoteness put it out of the sphere of that social activity which already marked the habits of the emigrants. It stood on the shore, looking across a basin of the sea at the forest-covered hills, towards the west. A clump of scrubby trees, such as alone grew on the peninsula, did not so much conceal the cottage from view, as seem to denote that here was some object which would fain have been, or at least ought to be, concealed. In this little, lonesome dwelling, with some slender means that she possessed, and by the license of the magistrates, who still kept an inquisitorial watch over her, Hester established herself, with her infant child. A mystic shadow of suspicion immediately attached itself to the spot.

Children, too young to comprehend wherefore this woman should be shut out from the sphere of human charities, would creep nigh enough to behold her plying her needle at the cottage-window, or standing in the doorway, or laboring in her little garden, or coming forth along the pathway that led townward; and, discerning the scarlet letter on her breast, would scamper off, with a strange, contagious fear.

Lonely as was Hester's situation, and without a friend on earth who dared to show himself, she, however, incurred no risk of want. She possessed an art that sufficed, even in a land that afforded comparatively little scope for its exercise, to supply food for her thriving infant and herself. It was the art—then, as now, almost the only one within a woman's grasp—of needle-work. She bore on her breast, in the curiously embroidered letter, a specimen of her delicate and imaginative skill, of which the dames of a court might gladly have availed themselves, to add the richer and more spiritual adornment of human ingenuity to their fabrics of silk and gold. Here, indeed, in the sable simplicity that generally characterized the Puritanic modes of dress, there might be an infrequent call for the finer productions of her handiwork. Yet the taste of the age, demanding whatever was elaborate in compositions of this kind, did not fail to extend its influence over our stern progenitors, who had cast behind them so many fashions which it might seem harder to dispense with. Public ceremonies, such as ordinations, the installations of magistrates, and all that could give majesty to the forms in which a new government manifested itself to the people, were, as a matter of policy, marked by a stately and well-conducted ceremonial, and a sombre, but yet a studied magnificence. Deep ruffs, painfully wrought bands, and gorgeously embroidered gloves, were all deemed necessary to the official state of men assuming the reins of power; and were readily allowed to individuals dignified by rank or wealth, even while sumptuary laws forbade these and similar extravagances to the plebeian order. In the array of funerals, too,—whether for the apparel of the dead body, or to typify, by manifold emblematic devices of sable cloth and snowy lawn,[20] the sorrow of the survivors,—there was a frequent and characteristic demand for such labor as Hester Prynne could supply. Baby-linen—for babies then wore robes of state—afforded still another possibility of toil and emolument.

By degrees, nor very slowly, her handiwork became what would now be termed the fashion. Whether from commiseration for a woman of so miserable a destiny; or from the morbid curiosity that gives a fictitious value even to common or worthless things; or by whatever other intangible cir-

---

[20] Black or dark cloth, and fine white linen or cotton.

cumstance was then, as now, sufficient to bestow, on some persons, what others might seek in vain; or because Hester really filled a gap which must otherwise have remained vacant; it is certain that she had ready and fairly requited employment for as many hours as she saw fit to occupy with her needle. Vanity, it may be, chose to mortify itself, by putting on, for ceremonials of pomp and state, the garments that had been wrought by her sinful hands. Her needle-work was seen on the ruff of the Governor; military men wore it on their scarfs, and the minister on his band; it decked the baby's little cap; it was shut up, to be mildewed and moulder away, in the coffins of the dead. But it is not recorded that, in a single instance, her skill was called in aid to embroider the white veil which was to cover the pure blushes of a bride. The exception indicated the ever relentless vigor with which society frowned upon her sin.

Hester sought not to acquire any thing beyond a subsistence, of the plainest and most ascetic description, for herself, and a simple abundance for her child. Her own dress was of the coarsest materials and the most sombre hue; with only that one ornament,—the scarlet letter,—which it was her doom to wear. The child's attire, on the other hand, was distinguished by a fanciful, or, we might rather say, a fantastic ingenuity, which served, indeed, to heighten the airy charm that early began to develop itself in the little girl, but which appeared to have also a deeper meaning. We may speak further of it hereafter. Except for that small expenditure in the decoration of her infant, Hester bestowed all her superfluous means in charity, on wretches less miserable than herself, and who not unfrequently insulted the hand that fed them. Much of the time, which she might readily have applied to the better efforts of her art, she employed in making coarse garments for the poor. It is probable that there was an idea of penance in this mode of occupation, and that she offered up a real sacrifice of enjoyment, in devoting so many hours to such rude handiwork. She had in her nature a rich, voluptuous, Oriental characteristic—a taste for the gorgeously beautiful, which, save in the exquisite productions of her needle, found nothing else, in all the possibilities of her life, to exercise itself upon. Women derive a pleasure, incomprehensible to the other sex, from the delicate toil of the needle. To Hester Prynne it might have been a mode of expressing, and therefore soothing, the passion of her life. Like all other joys, she rejected it as sin. This morbid meddling of conscience with an immaterial matter betokened, it is to be feared, no genuine and stedfast penitence, but something doubtful, something that might be deeply wrong, beneath.

In this manner, Hester Prynne came to have a part to perform in the world. With her native energy of character, and rare capacity, it could not entirely cast her off, although it had set a mark upon her, more intolerable to a woman's heart than that which branded the brow of Cain.[21] In all her intercourse with society, however, there was nothing that made her feel as if she belonged to it. Every gesture, every word, and even the silence of those with whom she came in contact, implied, and often expressed, that she was banished, and as much alone as if she inhabited another sphere, or communicated with the common nature by other organs and senses than the rest of human kind. She stood apart from mortal interests, yet close beside them, like a ghost that revisits the familiar fireside, and can no longer make itself seen or felt; no more smile with the household joy, nor mourn with the kindred sorrow; or, should it succeed in manifesting its forbidden sympathy, awakening only terror and horrible repugnance. These emotions, in fact, and its bitterest scorn besides, seemed to be the sole portion that she retained in the universal heart. It was not an age of delicacy; and her position, although she understood it well, and was in little danger of forgetting it, was often brought before her vivid self-perception, like a new anguish, by the rudest touch upon the tenderest spot. The poor, as we have already said, whom she sought out to be the objects of her bounty, often reviled the hand that was stretched forth to succor them. Dames of elevated rank, likewise, whose doors she entered in the way of her occupation, were accustomed to distil drops of bitterness into her heart; sometimes through that alchemy of quiet malice, by which women can concoct a subtile poison from ordinary trifles; and sometimes, also, by a coarser expression, that fell upon the sufferer's defenceless breast like a rough blow upon an ulcerated wound. Hester had schooled herself long and well; she never responded to these attacks, save by a flush of crimson that rose irrepressibly over her pale cheek, and again subsided into the depths of her bosom. She was patient,—a martyr, indeed,—but she forbore to pray for her enemies; lest, in spite of her forgiving aspirations, the words of the blessing should stubbornly twist themselves into a curse.

Continually, and in a thousand other ways, did she feel the innumerable throbs of anguish that had been so cunningly contrived for her by the undying, the ever-active sentence of the Puritan tribunal. Clergymen paused in the street to address words of exhortation, that brought a crowd, with its mingled grin and frown, around the poor, sinful woman. If she entered a church, trusting to share the Sabbath smile of the Universal Father, it was often her mishap to find herself the text of the discourse. She grew to have a dread of children; for they had imbibed from their parents a vague idea of something horrible in this dreary woman, gliding silently

---

[21] "And the Lord set a mark upon Cain, lest any finding him should kill him" (Genesis 4.15).

through the town, with never any companion but one only child. Therefore, first allowing her to pass, they pursued her at a distance with shrill
cries, and the utterance of a word that had no distinct purport to their own
minds, but was none the less terrible to her, as proceeding from lips that
babbled it unconsciously. It seemed to argue so wide a diffusion of her
shame, that all nature knew of it; it could have caused her no deeper pang,
had the leaves of the trees whispered the dark story among themselves, —
had the summer breeze murmured about it, — had the wintry blast shrieked
it aloud! Another peculiar torture was felt in the gaze of a new eye. When
strangers looked curiously at the scarlet letter, — and none ever failed to do
so, — they branded it afresh into Hester's soul; so that, oftentimes, she
could scarcely refrain, yet always did refrain, from covering the symbol
with her hand. But then, again, an accustomed eye had likewise its own
anguish to inflict. Its cool stare of familiarity was intolerable. From first to
last, in short, Hester Prynne had always this dreadful agony in feeling a
human eye upon the token; the spot never grew callous; it seemed, on the
contrary, to grow more sensitive with daily torture.

But sometimes, once in many days, or perchance in many months, she
felt an eye — a human eye — upon the ignominious brand, that seemed to
give a momentary relief, as if half of her agony were shared. The next instant, back it all rushed again, with still a deeper throb of pain; for, in that
brief interval, she had sinned anew. Had Hester sinned alone?

Her imagination was somewhat affected, and, had she been of a softer
moral and intellectual fibre, would have been still more so, by the strange
and solitary anguish of her life. Walking to and fro, with those lonely footsteps, in the little world with which she was outwardly connected, it now
and then appeared to Hester, — if altogether fancy, it was nevertheless
too potent to be resisted, — she felt or fancied, then, that the scarlet letter
had endowed her with a new sense. She shuddered to believe, yet could not
help believing, that it gave her a sympathetic knowledge of the hidden sin
in other hearts. She was terror-stricken by the revelations that were thus
made. What were they? Could they be other than the insidious whispers of
the bad angel,[22] who would fain have persuaded the struggling woman, as
yet only half his victim, that the outward guise of purity was but a lie, and
that, if truth were everywhere to be shown, a scarlet letter would blaze forth
on many a bosom besides Hester Prynne's? Or, must she receive those intimations — so obscure, yet so distinct — as truth? In all her miserable experience, there was nothing else so awful and so loathsome as this sense. It
perplexed, as well as shocked her, by the irreverent inopportuneness of the

---

[22] Satan.

occasions that brought it into vivid action. Sometimes, the red infamy upon her breast would give a sympathetic throb, as she passed near a venerable minister or magistrate, the model of piety and justice, to whom that age of antique reverence looked up, as to a mortal man in fellowship with angels. "What evil thing is at hand?" would Hester say to herself. Lifting her reluctant eyes, there would be nothing human within the scope of view, save the form of this earthly saint! Again, a mystic sisterhood would contumaciously assert itself, as she met the sanctified frown of some matron, who, according to the rumor of all tongues, had kept cold snow within her bosom throughout life. That unsunned snow in the matron's bosom, and the burning shame on Hester Prynne's—what had the two in common? Or, once more, the electric thrill would give her warning,—"Behold, Hester, here is a companion!"—and, looking up, she would detect the eyes of a young maiden glancing at the scarlet letter, shyly and aside, and quickly averted, with a faint, chill crimson in her cheeks; as if her purity were somewhat sullied by that momentary glance. O Fiend, whose talisman was that fatal symbol, wouldst thou leave nothing, whether in youth or age, for this poor sinner to revere?—Such loss of faith is ever one of the saddest results of sin. Be it accepted as a proof that all was not corrupt in this poor victim of her own frailty, and man's hard law, that Hester Prynne yet struggled to believe that no fellow-mortal was guilty like herself.

The vulgar, who, in those dreary old times, were always contributing a grotesque horror to what interested their imaginations, had a story about the scarlet letter which we might readily work up into a terrific legend. They averred, that the symbol was not mere scarlet cloth, tinged in an earthly dye-pot, but was red-hot with infernal fire, and could be seen glowing all alight, whenever Hester Prynne walked abroad in the night-time. And we must needs say, it seared Hester's bosom so deeply, that perhaps there was more truth in the rumor than our modern incredulity may be inclined to admit.

V I
Pearl

We have as yet hardly spoken of the infant; that little creature, whose innocent life had sprung, by the inscrutable decree of Providence, a lovely and immortal flower, out of the rank luxuriance of a guilty passion. How strange it seemed to the sad woman, as she watched the growth, and the beauty that became every day more brilliant, and the intelligence that threw its quivering sunshine over the tiny features of this child! Her Pearl!—For so had Hester called her; not as a name expressive of her aspect, which had nothing of the calm, white, unimpassioned lustre that would be indicated by the comparison. But she named the infant "Pearl," as being of great price,—purchased with all she had,—her mother's only treasure.[23] How strange, indeed! Man had marked this woman's sin by a scarlet letter, which had such potent and disastrous efficacy that no human sympathy could reach her, save it were sinful like herself. God, as a direct consequence of the sin which man thus punished, had given her a lovely child, whose place was on that same dishonored bosom, to connect her parent for ever with the race and descent of mortals, and to be finally a blessed soul in heaven! Yet these thoughts affected Hester Prynne less with hope than apprehension. She knew that her deed had been evil; she could have no faith, therefore, that its result would be for good. Day after day, she looked fearfully into the child's expanding nature; ever dreading to detect some dark and wild peculiarity, that should correspond with the guiltiness to which she owed her being.

Certainly, there was no physical defect. By its perfect shape, its vigor, and its natural dexterity in the use of all its untried limbs, the infant was worthy to have been brought forth in Eden; worthy to have been left there, to be the plaything of the angels, after the world's first parents were driven out. The child had a native grace, which does not invariably coexist with faultless beauty; its attire, however simple, always impressed the beholder as if it were the very garb that precisely became it best. But little Pearl was not clad in rustic weeds. Her mother, with a morbid purpose that may be better understood hereafter, had bought the richest tissues that could be procured, and allowed her imaginative faculty its full play in the arrangement and decoration of the dresses which the child wore, before the public eye. So magnificent was the small figure, when thus arrayed, and such was the splendor of Pearl's own proper beauty, shining through the gorgeous robes which might have extinguished a paler loveliness, that there was an absolute circle of radiance around her, on the darksome cottage-floor. And yet a russet gown, torn and soiled with the child's rude play, made a picture of her just as perfect. Pearl's aspect was imbued with a spell of infinite variety; in this one child there were many children, comprehending the full scope between the wild-flower prettiness of a peasant-baby, and the pomp, in little, of an infant princess. Throughout all, however, there was a trait of passion, a certain depth of hue, which she never lost; and if, in any of her changes, she had grown fainter or paler, she would have ceased to be herself;—it would have been no longer Pearl!

---

[23] "The kingdom of heaven is like unto a merchant man, seeking goodly pearls: Who, when he had found one pearl of great price, went out and sold all he had, and bought it" (Matthew 13.45–46).

This outward mutability indicated, and did not more than fairly express, the various properties of her inner life. Her nature appeared to possess depth, too, as well as variety; but—or else Hester's fears deceived her— it lacked reference and adaptation to the world into which she was born. The child could not be made amenable to rules. In giving her existence, a great law had been broken; and the result was a being, whose elements were perhaps beautiful and brilliant, but all in disorder; or with an order peculiar to themselves, amidst which the point of variety and arrangement was difficult or impossible to be discovered. Hester could only account for the child's character—and even then, most vaguely and imperfectly—by recalling what she herself had been, during that momentous period while Pearl was imbibing her soul from the spiritual world, and her bodily frame from its material of earth. The mother's impassioned state had been the medium through which were transmitted to the unborn infant the rays of its moral life; and, however white and clear originally, they had taken the deep stains of crimson and gold, the fiery lustre, the black shadow, and the untempered light, of the intervening substance. Above all, the warfare of Hester's spirit, at that epoch, was perpetuated in Pearl. She could recognize her wild, desperate, defiant mood, the flightiness of her temper, and even some of the very cloud-shapes of gloom and despondency that had brooded in her heart. They were now illuminated by the morning radiance of a young child's disposition, but, later in the day of earthly existence, might be prolific of the storm and whirlwind.

The discipline of the family, in those days, was of a far more rigid kind than now. The frown, the harsh rebuke, the frequent application of the rod, enjoined by Scriptural authority,[24] were used, not merely in the way of punishment for actual offences, but as a wholesome regimen for the growth and promotion of all childish virtues. Hester Prynne, nevertheless, the lonely mother of this one child, ran little risk of erring on the side of undue severity. Mindful, however, of her own errors and misfortunes, she early sought to impose a tender, but strict, control over the infant immortality that was committed to her charge. But the task was beyond her skill. After testing both smiles and frowns, and proving that neither mode of treatment possessed any calculable influence, Hester was ultimately compelled to stand aside, and permit the child to be swayed by her own impulses. Physical compulsion or restraint was effectual, of course, while it lasted. As to any other kind of discipline, whether addressed to her mind or heart, little Pearl might or might not be within its reach, in accordance

---

24 "He that spareth his rod hateth his son: but he that loveth him chasteneth him betimes" (Proverbs 13.24).

with the caprice that ruled the moment. Her mother, while Pearl was yet an infant, grew acquainted with a certain peculiar look, that warned her when it would be labor thrown away to insist, persuade, or plead. It was a look so intelligent, yet inexplicable, so perverse, sometimes so malicious, but generally accompanied by a wild flow of spirits, that Hester could not help questioning, at such moments, whether Pearl was a human child. She seemed rather an airy sprite, which, after playing its fantastic sports for a little while upon the cottage-floor, would flit away with a mocking smile. Whenever that look appeared in her wild, bright, deeply black eyes, it invested her with a strange remoteness and intangibility; it was as if she were hovering in the air and might vanish, like a glimmering light that comes we know not whence, and goes we know not whither. Beholding it, Hester was constrained to rush towards the child, — to pursue the little elf in the flight which she invariably began, — to snatch her to her bosom, with a close pressure and earnest kisses, — not so much from overflowing love, as to assure herself that Pearl was flesh and blood, and not utterly delusive. But Pearl's laugh, when she was caught, though full of merriment and music, made her mother more doubtful than before.

Heart-smitten at this bewildering and baffling spell, that so often came between herself and her sole treasure, whom she had bought so dear, and who was all her world, Hester sometimes burst into passionate tears. Then, perhaps, — for there was no foreseeing how it might affect her, — Pearl would frown, and clench her little fist, and harden her small features into a stern, unsympathizing look of discontent. Not seldom, she would laugh anew, and louder than before, like a thing incapable and unintelligent of human sorrow. Or — but this more rarely happened — she would be convulsed with a rage of grief, and sob out her love for her mother, in broken words, and seem intent on proving that she had a heart, by breaking it. Yet Hester was hardly safe in confiding herself to that gusty tenderness; it passed, as suddenly as it came. Brooding over all these matters, the mother felt like one who has evoked a spirit, but, by some irregularity in the process of conjuration, has failed to win the master-word that should control this new and incomprehensible intelligence. Her only real comfort was when the child lay in the placidity of sleep. Then she was sure of her, and tasted hours of quiet, sad, delicious happiness; until — perhaps with that perverse expression glimmering from beneath her opening lids — little Pearl awoke!

How soon — with what strange rapidity, indeed! — did Pearl arrive at an age that was capable of social intercourse, beyond the mother's ever-ready smile and nonsense-words! And then what a happiness would it have been, could Hester Prynne have heard her clear, bird-like voice mingling with the uproar of other childish voices, and have distinguished and unravelled her own darling's tones, amid all the entangled outcry of a group of sportive children! But this could never be. Pearl was a born outcast of the infantile world. An imp of evil, emblem and product of sin, she had no right among christened infants. Nothing was more remarkable than the instinct, as it seemed, with which the child comprehended her loneliness; the destiny that had drawn an inviolable circle round about her; the whole peculiarity, in short, of her position in respect to other children. Never, since her release from prison, had Hester met the public gaze without her. In all her walks about the town, Pearl, too, was there; first as the babe in arms, and afterwards as the little girl, small companion of her mother, holding a forefinger with her whole grasp, and tripping along at the rate of three or four footsteps to one of Hester's. She saw the children of the settlement, on the grassy margin of the street, or at the domestic thresholds, disporting themselves in such grim-fashion as the Puritanic nurture would permit; playing at going to church, perchance; or at scourging Quakers; or taking scalps in a sham-fight with the Indians; or scaring one another with freaks of imitative witchcraft. Pearl saw, and gazed intently, but never sought to make acquaintance. If spoken to, she would not speak again. If the children gathered about her, as they sometimes did, Pearl would grow positively terrible in her puny wrath, snatching up stones to fling at them, with shrill, incoherent exclamations that made her mother tremble, because they had so much the sound of a witch's anathemas in some unknown tongue.

The truth was, that the little Puritans, being of the most intolerant brood that ever lived, had got a vague idea of something outlandish, unearthly, or at variance with ordinary fashions, in the mother and child; and therefore scorned them in their hearts, and not unfrequently reviled them with their tongues. Pearl felt the sentiment, and requited it with the bitterest hatred that can be supposed to rankle in a childish bosom. These outbreaks of a fierce temper had a kind of value, and even comfort, for her mother; because there was at least an intelligible earnestness in the mood, instead of the fitful caprice that so often thwarted her in the child's manifestations. It appalled her, nevertheless, to discern here, again, a shadowy reflection of the evil that had existed in herself. All this enmity and passion had Pearl inherited, by inalienable right, out of Hester's heart. Mother and daughter stood together in the same circle of seclusion from human society; and in the nature of the child seemed to be perpetuated those unquiet elements that had distracted Hester Prynne before Pearl's birth, but had since begun to be soothed away by the softening influences of maternity.

At home, within and around her mother's cottage, Pearl wanted not a wide and various circle of acquaintance. The spell of life went forth from her ever creative spirit, and communicated itself to a thousand objects, as a torch kindles a flame wherever it may be applied. The unlikeliest materi-

Pearl by F. O. C. Darley. Originally appeared in the 1879 Houghton Mifflin edition of the novel.

als, a stick, a bunch of rags, a flower, were the puppets of Pearl's witchcraft, and, without undergoing any outward change, became spiritually adapted to whatever drama occupied the stage of her inner world. Her one baby-voice served a multitude of imaginary personages, old and young, to talk withal. The pine-trees, aged, black, and solemn, and flinging groans and other melancholy utterances on the breeze, needed little transformation to figure as Puritan elders; the ugliest weeds of the garden were their children, whom Pearl smote down and uprooted, most unmercifully. It was wonderful, the vast variety of forms into which she threw her intellect, with no continuity, indeed, but darting up and dancing, always in a state of preternatural activity, — soon sinking down, as if exhausted by so rapid and feverish a tide of life, — and succeeded by other shapes of a similar wild energy. It was like nothing so much as the phantasmagoric play of the northern lights. In the mere exercise of the fancy, however, and the sportiveness of a growing mind, there might be little more than was observable in other children of bright faculties; except as Pearl, in the dearth of human playmates, was thrown more upon the visionary throng which she created. The singularity lay in the hostile feelings with which the child regarded all these offspring of her own heart and mind. She never created a friend, but seemed always to be sowing broadcast the dragon's teeth, whence sprung a harvest of armed enemies, against whom she rushed to battle.[25] It was inexpressibly sad — then what depth of sorrow to a mother, who felt in her own heart the cause! — to observe, in one so young, this constant recognition of an adverse world, and so fierce a training of the energies that were to make good her cause, in the contest that must ensue.

Gazing at Pearl, Hester Prynne often dropped her work upon her knees, and cried out, with an agony which she would fain have hidden, but which made utterance for itself, betwixt speech and a groan, — "O Father in Heaven, — if Thou art still my Father, — what is this being which I have brought into the world!" And Pearl, overhearing the ejaculation, or aware, through some more subtle channel, of those throbs of anguish, would turn her vivid and beautiful little face upon her mother, smile with sprite-like intelligence, and resume her play.

One peculiarity of the child's deportment remains yet to be told. The very first thing which she had noticed, in her life, was — what? — not the mother's smile, responding to it, as other babies do, by that faint, embryo smile of the little mouth, remembered so doubtfully afterwards, and with such fond discussion whether it were indeed a smile. By no means! But that

[25] The Greek mythological hero Cadmus killed a dragon and planted its teeth, which grew into armed warriors.

first object of which Pearl seemed to become aware was—shall we say it?— the scarlet letter on Hester's bosom! One day, as her mother stooped over the cradle, the infant's eyes had been caught by the glimmering of the gold embroidery about the letter; and, putting up her little hand, she grasped at it, smiling, not doubtfully, but with a decided gleam that gave her face the look of a much older child. Then, gasping for breath, did Hester Prynne clutch the fatal token, instinctively endeavouring to tear it away; so infinite was the torture inflicted by the intelligent touch of Pearl's baby-hand. Again, as if her mother's agonized gesture were meant only to make sport for her, did little Pearl look into her eyes, and smile! From that epoch, except when the child was asleep, Hester had never felt a moment's safety; not a moment's calm enjoyment of her. Weeks, it is true, would sometimes elapse, during which Pearl's gaze might never once be fixed upon the scarlet letter; but then, again, it would come at unawares, like the stroke of sudden death, and always with that peculiar smile, and odd expression of the eyes.

Once, this freakish, elfish cast came into the child's eyes, while Hester was looking at her own image in them, as mothers are fond of doing; and, suddenly,—for women in solitude, and with troubled hearts, are pestered with unaccountable delusions,—she fancied that she beheld, not her own miniature portrait, but another face in the small black mirror of Pearl's eye. It was a face, fiend-like, full of smiling malice, yet bearing the semblance of features that she had known full well, though seldom with a smile, and never with malice, in them. It was as if an evil spirit possessed the child, and had just then peeped forth in mockery. Many a time afterwards had Hester been tortured, though less vividly, by the same illusion.

In the afternoon of a certain summer's day, after Pearl grew big enough to run about, she amused herself with gathering handfuls of wild-flowers, and flinging them, one by one, at her mother's bosom; dancing up and down, like a little elf, whenever she hit the scarlet letter. Hester's first motion had been to cover her bosom with her clasped hands. But, whether from pride or resignation, or a feeling that her penance might best be wrought out by this unutterable pain, she resisted the impulse, and sat erect, pale as death, looking sadly into little Pearl's wild eyes. Still came the battery of flowers, almost invariably hitting the mark, and covering her mother's breast with hurts for which she could find no balm in this world, nor knew how to seek it in another. At last, her shot being all expended, the child stood still and gazed at Hester, with that little, laughing image of a fiend peeping out—or, whether it peeped or no, her mother so imagined it—from the unsearchable abyss of her black eyes.

"Child, what art thou?" cried the mother.

"Oh, I am your little Pearl!" answered the child.

But, while she said it, Pearl laughed and began to dance up and down, with the humorsome gesticulation of a little imp, whose next freak[26] might be to fly up the chimney.

"Art thou my child, in very truth?" asked Hester.

Nor did she put the question altogether idly, but, for the moment, with a portion of genuine earnestness; for, such was Pearl's wonderful intelligence, that her mother half doubted whether she were not acquainted with the secret spell of her existence, and might not now reveal herself.

"Yes; I am little Pearl!" repeated the child, continuing her antics.

"Thou art not my child! Thou art no Pearl of mine!" said the mother, half playfully; for it was often the case that a sportive impulse came over her, in the midst of her deepest suffering. "Tell me, then, what thou art, and who sent thee hither?"

"Tell me, mother!" said the child, seriously, coming up to Hester, and pressing herself close to her knees. "Do thou tell me!"

"Thy Heavenly Father sent thee!" answered Hester Prynne.

But she said it with a hesitation that did not escape the acuteness of the child. Whether moved only by her ordinary freakishness, or because an evil spirit prompted her, she put up her small forefinger, and touched the scarlet letter.

"He did not send me!" cried she, positively. "I have no Heavenly Father!"

"Hush, Pearl, hush! Thou must not talk so!" answered the mother, suppressing a groan. "He sent us all into this world. He sent even me, thy mother. Then, much more, thee! Or, if not, thou strange and elfish child, whence didst thou come?"

"Tell me! Tell me!" repeated Pearl, no longer seriously, but laughing, and capering about the floor. "It is thou that must tell me!"

But Hester could not resolve the query, being herself in a dismal labyrinth of doubt. She remembered—betwixt a smile and a shudder—the talk of the neighbouring townspeople; who, seeking vainly elsewhere for the child's paternity, and observing some of her odd attributes, had given out that poor little Pearl was a demon offspring; such as, ever since old Catholic times, had occasionally been seen on earth, through the agency of their mothers' sin and to promote some foul and wicked purpose. Luther,[27] according to the scandal of his monkish enemies, was a brat of that hellish breed; nor was Pearl the only child to whom this inauspicious origin was assigned, among the New England Puritans.

---

[26] Prank.
[27] Martin Luther (1483–1546), Protestant reformer.

VII
The Governor's Hall

Hester Prynne went, one day, to the mansion of Governor Bellingham, with a pair of gloves, which she had fringed and embroidered to his order, and which were to be worn on some great occasion of state; for, though the chances of a popular election had caused this former ruler to descend a step or two from the highest rank, he still held an honorable and influential place among the colonial magistracy.[28]

Another and far more important reason than the delivery of a pair of embroidered gloves impelled Hester, at this time, to seek an interview with a personage of so much power and activity in the affairs of the settlement. It had reached her ears, that there was a design on the part of some of the leading inhabitants, cherishing the more rigid order of principles in religion and government, to deprive her of her child. On the supposition that Pearl, as already hinted, was of demon origin, these good people not unreasonably argued that a Christian interest in the mother's soul required them to remove such a stumbling-block from her path. If the child, on the other hand, were really capable of moral and religious growth, and possessed the elements of ultimate salvation, then, surely, it would enjoy all the fairer prospect of these advantages by being transferred to wiser and better guardianship than Hester Prynne's. Among those who promoted the design, Governor Bellingham was said to be one of the most busy. It may appear singular, and, indeed, not a little ludicrous, that an affair of this kind, which, in later days, would have been referred to no higher jurisdiction than that of the selectmen of the town, should then have been a question publicly discussed, and on which statesmen of eminence took sides. At that epoch of pristine simplicity, however, matters of even slighter public interest, and of far less intrinsic weight than the welfare of Hester and her child, were strangely mixed up with the deliberations of legislators and acts of state. The period was hardly, if at all, earlier than that of our story, when a dispute concerning the right of property in a pig, not only caused a fierce and bitter contest in the legislative body of the colony, but resulted in an important modification of the framework itself of the legislature.[29]

Full of concern, therefore, —but so conscious of her own right, that it seemed scarcely an unequal match between the public, on the one side,

---

[28] Bellingham became a magistrate in 1642 after completing his first term as governor.
[29] The case of *Sherman v. Keayne* (1642 – 43) led to judicial reforms including division of the Massachusetts legislature into two houses.

and a lonely woman, backed by the sympathies of nature, on the other, — Hester Prynne set forth from her solitary cottage. Little Pearl, of course, was her companion. She was now of an age to run lightly along by her mother's side, and, constantly in motion from morn till sunset, could have accomplished a much longer journey than that before her. Often, nevertheless, more from caprice than necessity, she demanded to be taken up in arms, but was soon as imperious to be set down again, and frisked onward before Hester on the grassy pathway, with many a harmless trip and tumble. We have spoken of Pearl's rich and luxuriant beauty; a beauty that shone with deep and vivid tints; a bright complexion, eyes possessing intensity both of depth and glow, and hair already of a deep, glossy brown, and which, in after years, would be nearly akin to black. There was fire in her and throughout her; she seemed the unpremeditated offshoot of a passionate moment. Her mother, in contriving the child's garb, had allowed the gorgeous tendencies of her imagination their full play; arraying her in a crimson velvet tunic, of a peculiar cut, abundantly embroidered with fantasies and flourishes of gold thread. So much strength of coloring, which must have given a wan and pallid aspect to cheeks of a fainter bloom, was admirably adapted to Pearl's beauty, and made her the very brightest little jet of flame that ever danced upon the earth.

But it was a remarkable attribute of this garb, and, indeed, of the child's whole appearance, that it irresistibly and inevitably reminded the beholder of the token which Hester Prynne was doomed to wear upon her bosom. It was the scarlet letter in another form; the scarlet letter endowed with life! The mother herself—as if the red ignominy were so deeply scorched into her brain, that all her conceptions assumed its form—had carefully wrought out the similitude; lavishing many hours of morbid ingenuity, to create an analogy between the object of her affection, and the emblem of her guilt and torture. But, in truth, Pearl was the one, as well as the other; and only in consequence of that identity had Hester contrived so perfectly to represent the scarlet letter in her appearance.

As the two wayfarers came within the precincts of the town, the children of the Puritans looked up from their play, — or what passed for play with those sombre little urchins, — and spake gravely one to another: —

"Behold, verily, there is the woman of the scarlet letter; and, of a truth, moreover, there is the likeness of the scarlet letter running along by her side! Come, therefore, and let us fling mud at them!"

But Pearl, who was a dauntless child, after frowning, stamping her foot, and shaking her little hand with a variety of threatening gestures, suddenly made a rush at the knot of her enemies, and put them all to flight. She resembled, in her fierce pursuit of them, an infant pestilence, — the scarlet fever, or some such half-fledged angel of judgment, — whose mission was to punish the sins of the rising generation. She screamed and shouted, too, with a terrific volume of sound, which doubtless caused the hearts of the fugitives to quake within them. The victory accomplished, Pearl returned quietly to her mother, and looked up smiling into her face.

Without further adventure, they reached the dwelling of Governor Bellingham. This was a large wooden house, built in a fashion of which there are specimens still extant in the streets of our elder towns; now moss-grown, crumbling to decay, and melancholy at heart with the many sorrowful or joyful occurrences, remembered or forgotten, that have happened, and passed away, within their dusky chambers. Then, however, there was the freshness of the passing year on its exterior, and the cheerfulness, gleaming forth from the sunny windows, of a human habitation into which death had never entered. It had indeed a very cheery aspect; the walls being overspread with a kind of stucco, in which fragments of broken glass were plentifully intermixed; so that, when the sunshine fell aslantwise over the front of the edifice, it glittered and sparkled as if diamonds had been flung against it by the double handful. The brilliancy might have befitted Aladdin's palace,[30] rather than the mansion of a grave old Puritan ruler. It was further decorated with strange and seemingly cabalistic[31] figures and diagrams, suitable to the quaint taste of the age, which had been drawn in the stucco when newly laid on, and had now grown hard and durable, for the admiration of after times.

Pearl, looking at this bright wonder of a house, began to caper and dance, and imperatively required that the whole breadth of sunshine should be stripped off its front, and given her to play with.

"No, my little Pearl!" said her mother. "Thou must gather thine own sunshine. I have none to give thee!"

They approached the door; which was of an arched form, and flanked on each side by a narrow tower or projection of the edifice, in both of which were lattice-windows, with wooden shutters to close over them at need. Lifting the iron hammer that hung at the portal, Hester Prynne gave a summons, which was answered by one of the Governor's bond-servants; a free-born Englishman, but now a seven years' slave. During that term he was to be the property of his master, and as much a commodity of bargain and sale as an ox, or a joint-stool. The serf wore the blue coat, which was the customary garb of serving-men at that period, and long before, in the old hereditary halls of England.

---

[30] In the *Arabian Nights*, the palace of the boy whose magic lamp and ring empower him to summon genies who fulfill his wishes.
[31] Occult.

"Is the worshipful Governor Bellingham within?" inquired Hester.

"Yea, forsooth," replied the bond-servant, staring with wide-open eyes at the scarlet letter, which, being a new-comer in the country, he had never before seen. "Yea, his honorable worship is within. But he hath a godly minister or two with him, and likewise a leech. Ye may not see his worship now."

"Nevertheless, I will enter," answered Hester Prynne; and the bond-servant, perhaps judging from the decision of her air and the glittering symbol in her bosom, that she was a great lady in the land, offered no opposition.

So the mother and little Pearl were admitted into the hall of entrance. With many variations, suggested by the nature of his building-materials, diversity of climate, and a different mode of social life, Governor Bellingham had planned his new habitation after the residences of gentlemen of fair estate in his native land. Here, then, was a wide and reasonably lofty hall, extending through the whole depth of the house, and forming a medium of general communication, more or less directly, with all the other apartments. At one extremity, this spacious room was lighted by the windows of the two towers, which formed a small recess on either side of the portal. At the other end, though partly muffled by a curtain, it was more powerfully illuminated by one of those embowed hall-windows which we read of in old books, and which was provided with a deep and cushioned seat. Here, on the cushion, lay a folio tome, probably of the Chronicles of England,[32] or other such substantial literature; even as, in our own days, we scatter gilded volumes on the centre-table, to be turned over by the casual guest. The furniture of the hall consisted of some ponderous chairs, the backs of which were elaborately carved with wreaths of oaken flowers; and likewise a table in the same taste; the whole being of the Elizabethan age, or perhaps earlier, and heirlooms, transferred hither from the Governor's paternal home. On the table — in token that the sentiment of old English hospitality had not been left behind — stood a large pewter tankard, at the bottom of which, had Hester or Pearl peeped into it, they might have seen the frothy remnant of a recent draught of ale.

On the wall hung a row of portraits, representing the forefathers of the Bellingham lineage, some with armour on their breasts, and others with stately ruffs and robes of peace. All were characterized by the sternness and severity which old portraits so invariably put on; as if they were the ghosts, rather than the pictures, of departed worthies, and were gazing with harsh and intolerant criticism at the pursuits and enjoyments of living men.

---

[32] Raphael Holinshed's *Chronicles of England, Scotland, and Ireland* (1577).

At about the centre of the oaken panels, that lined the hall, was suspended a suit of mail, not, like the pictures, an ancestral relic, but of the most modern date; for it had been manufactured by a skillful armorer in London, the same year in which Governor Bellingham came over to New England. There was a steel head-piece, a cuirass, a gorget, and greaves, with a pair of gauntlets[33] and a sword hanging beneath; all, and especially the helmet and breastplate, so highly burnished as to glow with white radiance, and scatter an illumination everywhere about upon the floor. This bright panoply was not meant for mere idle show, but had been worn by the Governor on many a solemn muster and training field, and had glittered, moreover, at the head of a regiment in the Pequod war.[34] For, though bred a lawyer, and accustomed to speak of Bacon, Coke, Noye, and Finch,[35] as his professional associates, the exigencies of this new country had transformed Governor Bellingham into a soldier, as well as a statesman and ruler.

Little Pearl—who was as greatly pleased with the gleaming armour as she had been with the glittering frontispiece of the house—spent some time looking into the polished mirror of the breastplate.

"Mother," cried she, "I see you here. Look! Look!"

Hester looked, by way of humoring the child; and she saw that, owing to the peculiar effect of this convex mirror, the scarlet letter was represented in exaggerated and gigantic proportions, so as to be greatly the most prominent feature of her appearance. In truth, she seemed absolutely hidden behind it. Pearl pointed upward, also, at a similar picture in the head-piece; smiling at her mother, with the elfish intelligence that was so familiar an expression on her small physiognomy. That look of naughty merriment was likewise reflected in the mirror, with so much breadth and intensity of effect, that it made Hester Prynne feel as if it could not be the image of her own child, but of an imp who was seeking to mould itself into Pearl's shape.

"Come along, Pearl!" said she, drawing her away. "Come and look into this fair garden. It may be, we shall see flowers there; more beautiful ones than we find in the woods."

Pearl, accordingly, ran to the bow-window, at the farther end of the hall, and looked along the vista of a garden-walk, carpeted with closely shaven grass, and bordered with some rude and immature attempt at shrubbery.

---

[33] Armor for the chest, neck, and shins, respectively.
[34] The Pequots, an Algonquin Indian tribe in eastern Connecticut, were virtually annihilated by English colonists in 1637.
[35] Sir Francis Bacon (1561–1626), Sir Edward Coke (1552–1634), William Noye (1577–1634), and Sir John Finch (1584–1660) were legal authorities.

But the proprietor appeared already to have relinquished, as hopeless, the effort to perpetuate on this side of the Atlantic, in a hard soil and amid the close struggle for subsistence, the native English taste for ornamental gardening. Cabbages grew in plain sight; and a pumpkin vine, rooted at some distance, had run across the intervening space, and deposited one of its gigantic products directly beneath the hall-window; as if to warn the Governor that this great lump of vegetable gold was as rich an ornament as New England earth would offer him. There were a few rose-bushes, however, and a number of apple-trees, probably the descendants of those planted by the Reverend Mr. Blackstone, the first settler of the peninsula; that half mythological personage who rides through our early annals, seated on the back of a bull.[36]

Pearl, seeing the rose-bushes, began to cry for a red rose, and would not be pacified.

"Hush, child, hush!" said her mother earnestly. "Do not cry, dear little Pearl! I hear voices in the garden. The Governor is coming, and gentlemen along with him!"

In fact, adown the vista of the garden-avenue, a number of persons were seen approaching towards the house. Pearl, in utter scorn of her mother's attempt to quiet her, gave an eldritch[37] scream, and then became silent; not from any notion of obedience, but because the quick and mobile curiosity of her disposition was excited by the appearance of these new personages.

VIII
The Elf-Child and the Minister

Governor Bellingham, in a loose gown and easy cap,—such as elderly gentlemen love to indue themselves with, in their domestic privacy,— walked foremost, and appeared to be showing off his estate, and expatiating on his projected improvements. The wide circumference of an elaborate ruff, beneath his gray beard, in the antiquated fashion of King James's reign,[38] caused his head to look not a little like that of John the Baptist in a charger.[39] The impression made by his aspect, so rigid and severe, and

---

[36] William Blackstone (1595–1675), the nonconformist Anglican minister who settled in the Boston area in 1623 and left for Rhode Island in 1634 after disputes with the Puritans; the legend that he rode on a bull is reported in Caleb H. Snow's *History of Boston* (1825).
[37] Uncanny.
[38] James I (1566–1625), king of England from 1603 to 1625.
[39] At Salome's request and King Herod's command, John the Baptist was decapitated and his head presented on a charger (platter) (Matthew 14.6–11).

frost-bitten with more than autumnal age, was hardly in keeping with the appliances of worldly enjoyment wherewith he had evidently done his utmost to surround himself. But it is an error to suppose that our grave forefathers—though accustomed to speak and think of human existence as a state merely of trial and warfare, and though unfeignedly prepared to sacrifice goods and life at the behest of duty—made it a matter of conscience to reject such means of comfort or even luxury, as lay fairly within their grasp. This creed was never taught, for instance, by the venerable pastor, John Wilson, whose beard, white as a snow-drift, was seen over Governor Bellingham's shoulder; while its wearer suggested that pears and peaches might yet be naturalized in the New England climate, and that purple grapes might possibly be compelled to flourish, against the sunny garden-wall. The old clergyman, nurtured at the rich bosom of the English Church, had a long established and legitimate taste for all good and comfortable things; and however stern he might show himself in the pulpit, or in his public reproof of such transgressions as that of Hester Prynne, still, the genial benevolence of his private life had won him warmer affection than was accorded to any of his professional contemporaries.

Behind the Governor and Mr. Wilson came two other guests; one, the Reverend Arthur Dimmesdale, whom the reader may remember, as having taken a brief and reluctant part in the scene of Hester Prynne's disgrace; and, in close companionship with him, old Roger Chillingworth, a person of great skill in physic, who, for two or three years past, had been settled in the town. It was understood that this learned man was the physician as well as friend of the young minister, whose health had severely suffered, of late, by his too unreserved self-sacrifice to the labors and duties of the pastoral relation.

The Governor, in advance of his visitors, ascended one or two steps, and, throwing open the leaves of the great hall-window, found himself close to little Pearl. The shadow of the curtain fell on Hester Prynne, and partially concealed her.

"What have we here?" said Governor Bellingham, looking with surprise at the scarlet little figure before him. "I profess, I have never seen the like, since my days of vanity, in old King James's time, when I was wont to esteem it a high favor to be admitted to a court mask! There used to be a swarm of these small apparitions, in holiday-time; and we called them children of the Lord of Misrule.[40] But how gat such a guest into my hall?"

"Ay, indeed!" cried good old Mr. Wilson. "What little bird of scarlet plumage may this be? Methinks I have seen just such figures, when the sun

---

[40] Leader of the revels in traditional English festivities, including Christmas games.

has been shining through a richly painted window, and tracing out the golden and crimson images across the floor. But that was in the old land. Prithee, young one, who art thou, and what has ailed thy mother to bedizen thee in this strange fashion? Art thou a Christian child,—ha? Dost know thy catechism? Or art thou one of those naughty elfs or fairies, whom we thought to have left behind us, with other relics of Papistry, in merry old England?"

"I am mother's child," answered the scarlet vision, "and my name is Pearl!"

"Pearl?—Ruby, rather!—or Coral!—or Red Rose, at the very least, judging from thy hue!" responded the old minister, putting forth his hand in a vain attempt to pat little Pearl on the cheek. "But where is this mother of thine? Ah! I see," he added; and, turning to Governor Bellingham, whispered,—"This is the selfsame child of whom we have held speech together; and behold here the unhappy woman, Hester Prynne, her mother!"

"Sayest thou so?" cried the Governor. "Nay, we might have judged that such a child's mother must needs be a scarlet woman, and a worthy type of her of Babylon![41] But she comes at a good time; and we will look into this matter forthwith."

Governor Bellingham stepped through the window into the hall, followed by his three guests.

"Hester Prynne," said he, fixing his naturally stern regard on the wearer of the scarlet letter, "there hath been much question concerning thee, of late. The point hath been weightily discussed, whether we, that are of authority and influence, do well discharge our consciences by trusting an immortal soul, such as there is in yonder child, to the guidance of one who hath stumbled and fallen, amid the pitfalls of this world. Speak thou, the child's own mother! Were it not, thinkest thou, for thy little one's temporal and eternal welfare, that she be taken out of thy charge, and clad soberly, and disciplined strictly, and instructed in the truths of heaven and earth? What canst thou do for the child, in this kind?"

"I can teach my little Pearl what I have learned from this!" answered Hester Prynne, laying her finger on the red token.

"Woman, it is thy badge of shame!" replied the stern magistrate. "It is because of the stain which that letter indicates, that we would transfer thy child to other hands."

"Nevertheless," said the mother calmly, though growing more pale, "this badge hath taught me,—it daily teaches me,—it is teaching me at this

---

[41] The biblical "whore of Babylon" was arrayed in scarlet (Rev. 17.3–5).

moment, —lessons whereof my child may be the wiser and better, albeit they can profit nothing to myself." *Teach Pearl from her mistakes*

"We will judge warily," said Bellingham, "and look well what we are about to do. Good Master Wilson, I pray you, examine this Pearl, —since that is her name, —and see whether she hath had such Christian nurture as befits a child of her age."

The old minister seated himself in an arm-chair, and made an effort to draw Pearl betwixt his knees. But the child, unaccustomed to the touch or familiarity of any but her mother, escaped through the open window and stood on the upper step, looking like a wild, tropical bird, of rich plumage, ready to take flight into the upper air. Mr. Wilson, not a little astonished at this outbreak, —for he was a grandfatherly sort of personage, and usually a vast favorite with children, —essayed, however, to proceed with the examination.

"Pearl," said he, with great solemnity, "thou must take heed to instruction, that so, in due season, thou mayest wear in thy bosom the pearl of great price. Canst thou tell me, my child, who made thee?"

Now Pearl knew well enough who made her; for Hester Prynne, the daughter of a pious home, very soon after her talk with the child about her Heavenly Father, had begun to inform her of those truths which the human spirit, at whatever stage of immaturity, imbibes with such eager interest. Pearl, therefore, so large were the attainments of her three years' lifetime, could have borne a fair examination in the New England Primer,[42] or the first column of the Westminster Catechism,[43] although unacquainted with the outward form of either of those celebrated works. But that perversity, which all children have more or less of, and of which little Pearl had a tenfold portion, now, at the most inopportune moment, took thorough possession of her, and closed her lips, or impelled her to speak words amiss. After putting her finger in her mouth, with many ungracious refusals to answer good Mr. Wilson's question, the child finally announced that she had not been made at all, but had been plucked by her mother off the bush of wild roses, that grew by the prison-door.

This fantasy was probably suggested by the near proximity of the Governor's red roses, as Pearl stood outside of the window; together with her recollection of the prison rose-bush, which she had passed in coming hither.

---

[42] A moralistic children's text.

[43] The question-and-answer drill formulated by the Westminster Assembly (1645–47) to teach children Christian beliefs and obligations.

Old Roger Chillingworth, with a smile on his face, whispered something in the young clergyman's ear. Hester Prynne looked at the man of skill, and even then, with her fate hanging in the balance, was startled to perceive what a change had come over his features, —how much uglier they were, — how his dark complexion seemed to have grown duskier, and his figure more misshapen, —since the days when she had familiarly known him. She met his eyes for an instant, but was immediately constrained to give all her attention to the scene now going forward.

"This is awful!" cried the Governor, slowly recovering from the astonishment into which Pearl's response had thrown him. "Here is a child of three years old, and she cannot tell who made her! Without question, she is equally in the dark as to her soul, its present depravity, and future destiny! Methinks, gentlemen, we need inquire no further."

Hester caught hold of Pearl, and drew her forcibly into her arms, confronting the old Puritan magistrate with almost a fierce expression. Alone in the world, cast off by it, and with this sole treasure to keep her heart alive, she felt that she possessed indefeasible rights against the world, and was ready to defend them to the death.

"God gave me the child!" cried she. "He gave her, in requital of all things else, which ye had taken from me. She is my happiness!—she is my torture, none the less! Pearl keeps me here in life! Pearl punishes me too! See ye not, she is the scarlet letter, only capable of being loved, and so endowed with a million-fold the power of retribution for my sin? Ye shall not take her! I will die first!"

"My poor woman," said the not unkind old minister, "the child shall be well cared for!—far better than thou canst do it."

"God gave her into my keeping," repeated Hester Prynne, raising her voice almost to a shriek. "I will not give her up!"—And here, by a sudden impulse, she turned to the young clergyman, Mr. Dimmesdale, at whom, up to this moment, she had seemed hardly so much as once to direct her eyes.—"Speak thou for me!" cried she. "Thou wast my pastor, and hadst charge of my soul, and knowest me better than these men can. I will not lose the child! Speak for me! Thou knowest,—for thou hast sympathies which these men lack!—thou knowest what is in my heart, and what are a mother's rights, and how much the stronger they are, when that mother has but her child and the scarlet letter! Look thou to it! I will not lose the child! Look to it!"

At this wild and singular appeal, which indicated that Hester Prynne's situation had provoked her to little less than madness, the young minister at once came forward, pale, and holding his hand over his heart, as was his custom whenever his peculiarly nervous temperament was thrown into

"Look thou to it! I will not lose the child!" by Mary Hallock Foote, engraved by A. V. S. Anthony. Originally appeared in the 1877 Osgood and Company edition of the novel.

agitation. He looked now more careworn and emaciated than as we described him at the scene of Hester's public ignominy; and whether it were his failing health, or whatever the cause might be, his large dark eyes had a world of pain in their troubled and melancholy depth.

"There is truth in what she says," began the minister, with a voice sweet, tremulous, but powerful, insomuch that the hall reechoed, and the hollow armour rang with it, — "truth in what Hester says, and in the feeling which inspires her! God gave her the child, and gave her, too, an instinctive knowledge of its nature and requirements, — both seemingly so peculiar, — which no other mortal being can possess. And, moreover, is there not a quality of awful sacredness in the relation between this mother and this child?"

"Ay! — how is that, good Master Dimmesdale?" interrupted the Governor. "Make that plain, I pray you!"

"It must be even so," resumed the minister. "For, if we deem it otherwise, do we not thereby say that the Heavenly Father, the Creator of all flesh, hath lightly recognized a deed of sin, and made of no account the distinction between unhallowed lust and holy love? This child of its father's guilt and its mother's shame hath come from the hand of God, to work in many ways upon her heart, who pleads so earnestly, and with such bitterness of spirit, the right to keep her. It was meant for a blessing; for the one blessing of her life! It was meant, doubtless, as the mother herself hath told us, for a retribution too; a torture, to be felt at many an unthought of moment; a pang, a sting, an ever-recurring agony, in the midst of a troubled joy! Hath she not expressed this thought in the garb of the poor child, so forcibly reminding us of that red symbol which sears her bosom?"

"Well said, again!" cried good Mr. Wilson. "I feared the woman had no better thought than to make a mountebank of her child!"

"O, not so! — not so!" continued Mr. Dimmesdale. "She recognizes, believe me, the solemn miracle which God hath wrought, in the existence of that child. And may she feel, too, — what, methinks, is the very truth, — that this boon was meant, above all things else, to keep the mother's soul alive, and to preserve her from blacker depths of sin into which Satan might else have sought to plunge her! Therefore it is good for this poor, sinful woman that she hath an infant immortality, a being capable of eternal joy or sorrow, confided to her care, — to be trained up by her to righteousness, — to remind her, at every moment, of her fall, — but yet to teach her, as it were by the Creator's sacred pledge, that, if she bring the child to heaven, the child also will bring its parent thither! Herein is the sinful mother happier than the sinful father. For Hester Prynne's sake, then, and no less for the poor child's sake, let us leave them as Providence hath seen fit to place them!"

"You speak, my friend, with a strange earnestness," said old Roger Chillingworth, smiling at him.

"And there is weighty import in what my young brother hath spoken," added the Reverend Mr. Wilson. "What say you, worshipful Master Bellingham? Hath he not pleaded well for the poor woman?"

"Indeed hath he," answered the magistrate, "and hath adduced such arguments, that we will even leave the matter as it now stands; so long, at least, as there shall be no further scandal in the woman. Care must be had, nevertheless, to put the child to due and stated examination in the catechism at thy hands or Master Dimmesdale's. Moreover, at a proper season, the tithing-men [44] must take heed that she go both to school and to meeting."

The young minister, on ceasing to speak, had withdrawn a few steps from the group, and stood with his face partially concealed in the heavy folds of the window-curtain; while the shadow of his figure, which the sunlight cast upon the floor, was tremulous with the vehemence of his appeal. Pearl, that wild and flighty little elf, stole softly towards him, and taking his hand in the grasp of both her own, laid her cheek against it; a caress so tender, and withal so unobtrusive, that her mother, who was looking on, asked herself, — "Is that my Pearl?" Yet she knew that there was love in the child's heart, although it mostly revealed itself in passion, and hardly twice in her lifetime had been softened by such gentleness as now. The minister, — for, save the long-sought regards of woman, nothing is sweeter than these marks of childish preference, accorded spontaneously by a spiritual instinct, and therefore seeming to imply in us something truly worthy to be loved, — the minister looked round, laid his hand on the child's head, hesitated an instant, and then kissed her brow. Little Pearl's unwonted mood of sentiment lasted no longer; she laughed, and went capering down the hall, so airily, that old Mr. Wilson raised a question whether even her tiptoes touched the floor.

"The little baggage hath witchcraft in her, I profess," said he to Mr. Dimmesdale. "She needs no old woman's broomstick to fly withal!"

"A strange child!" remarked old Roger Chillingworth. "It is easy to see the mother's part in her. Would it be beyond a philosopher's research, think ye, gentlemen, to analyze that child's nature, and, from its make and mould, to give a shrewd guess at the father?"

"Nay; it would be sinful, in such a question, to follow the clew of profane philosophy," said Mr. Wilson. "Better to fast and pray upon it; and

---

[44] Officials who collected tithes (one-tenth of parishioners' incomes levied for church support) and served as parish peace officers.

still better, it may be, to leave the mystery as we find it, unless Providence reveal it of its own accord. Thereby, every good Christian man hath a title to show a father's kindness towards the poor, deserted babe."

The affair being so satisfactorily concluded, Hester Prynne, with Pearl, departed from the house. As they descended the steps, it is averred that the lattice of a chamber-window was thrown open, and forth into the sunny day was thrust the face of Mistress Hibbins, Governor Bellingham's bitter-tempered sister, and the same who, a few years later, was executed as a witch.

"Hist, hist!" said she, while her ill-omened physiognomy seemed to cast a shadow over the cheerful newness of the house.[45] "Wilt thou go with us to-night? There will be a merry company in the forest; and I wellnigh promised the Black Man that comely Hester Prynne should make one."

"Make my excuse to him, so please you!" answered Hester, with a triumphant smile. "I must tarry at home, and keep watch over my little Pearl. Had they taken her from me, I would willingly have gone with thee into the forest, and signed my name in the Black Man's book too, and that with mine own blood!"

"We shall have thee anon!" said the witch-lady, frowning, as she drew back her head.

But here—if we suppose this interview betwixt Mistress Hibbins and Hester Prynne to be authentic, and not a parable—was already an illustration of the young minister's argument against sundering the relation of a fallen mother to the offspring of her frailty. Even thus early had the child saved her from Satan's snare.

IX

The Leech

Under the appellation of Roger Chillingworth, the reader will remember, was hidden another name, which its former wearer had resolved should never more be spoken. It has been related, how, in the crowd that witnessed Hester Prynne's ignominious exposure, stood a man, elderly, travel-worn, who, just emerging from the perilous wilderness, beheld the woman, in whom he hoped to find embodied the warmth and cheerfulness of home, set up as a type of sin before the people. Her matronly fame was trodden

---

[45] Physiognomy, one of the pseudosciences popular in Hawthorne's day, judged character through facial features. Mistress Hibbens is inviting Hester to a Witches' Sabbath, an orgiastic midnight assembly of the Devil's devotees (as in Hawthorne's story "Young Goodman Brown").

under all men's feet. Infamy was babbling around her in the public market-place. For her kindred, should the tidings ever reach them, and for the companions of her unspotted life, there remained nothing but the contagion of her dishonor; which would not fail to be distributed in strict accordance and proportion with the intimacy and sacredness of their previous relationship. Then why—since the choice was with himself—should the individual, whose connection with the fallen woman had been the most intimate and sacred of them all, come forward to vindicate his claim to an inheritance so little desirable? He resolved not to be pilloried beside her on her pedestal of shame. Unknown to all but Hester Prynne, and possessing the lock and key of her silence, he chose to withdraw his name from the roll of mankind, and, as regarded his former ties and interests, to vanish out of life as completely as if he indeed lay at the bottom of the ocean, whither rumor had long ago consigned him. This purpose once effected, new interests would immediately spring up, and likewise a new purpose; dark, it is true, if not guilty, but of force enough to engage the full strength of his faculties.

In pursuance of this resolve, he took up his residence in the Puritan town, as Roger Chillingworth, without other introduction than the learning and intelligence of which he possessed more than a common measure. As his studies, at a previous period of his life, had made him extensively acquainted with the medical science of the day, it was as a physician that he presented himself, and as such was cordially received. Skilful men, of the medical and chirurgical profession, were of rare occurrence in the colony. They seldom, it would appear, partook of the religious zeal that brought other emigrants across the Atlantic. In their researches into the human frame, it may be that the higher and more subtile faculties of such men were materialized, and that they lost the spiritual view of existence amid the intricacies of that wondrous mechanism, which seemed to involve art enough to comprise all of life within itself. At all events, the health of the good town of Boston, so far as medicine had aught to do with it, had hitherto lain in the guardianship of an aged deacon and apothecary, whose piety and godly deportment were stronger testimonials in his favor, than any that he could have produced in the shape of a diploma. The only surgeon was one who combined the occasional exercise of that noble art with the daily and habitual flourish of a razor. To such a professional body Roger Chillingworth was a brilliant acquisition. He soon manifested his familiarity with the ponderous and imposing machinery of antique physic; in which every remedy contained a multitude of far-fetched and heterogeneous ingredients, as elaborately compounded as if the proposed result had been the Elixir of Life. In his Indian captivity, moreover, he had gained much knowledge of the properties of native herbs and roots; nor did he conceal from his patients, that these simple medicines, Nature's boon to the untutored savage, had quite as large a share of his own confidence as the European pharmacopoeia, which so many learned doctors had spent centuries in elaborating.

This learned stranger was exemplary, as regarded at least the outward forms of a religious life, and, early after his arrival, had chosen for his spiritual guide the Reverend Mr. Dimmesdale. The young divine, whose scholar-like renown still lived in Oxford, was considered by his more fervent admirers as little less than a heaven-ordained apostle, destined, should he live and labor for the ordinary term of life, to do as great deeds for the now feeble New England Church, as the early Fathers had achieved for the infancy of the Christian faith. About this period, however, the health of Mr. Dimmesdale had evidently begun to fail. By those best acquainted with his habits, the paleness of the young minister's cheek was accounted for by his too earnest devotion to study, his scrupulous fulfillment of parochial duty, and, more than all, by the fasts and vigils of which he made a frequent practice, in order to keep the grossness of this earthly state from clogging and obscuring his spiritual lamp. Some declared, that, if Mr. Dimmesdale were really going to die, it was cause enough, that the world was not worthy to be any longer trodden by his feet. He himself, on the other hand, with characteristic humility, avowed his belief, that, if Providence should see fit to remove him, it would be because of his own unworthiness to perform its humblest mission here on earth. With all this difference of opinion as to the cause of his decline, there could be no question of the fact. His form grew emaciated; his voice, though still rich and sweet, had a certain melancholy prophecy of decay in it; he was often observed, on any slight alarm or other sudden accident, to put his hand over his heart, with first a flush and then a paleness, indicative of pain.

Such was the young clergyman's condition, and so imminent the prospect that his dawning light would be extinguished, all untimely, when Roger Chillingworth made his advent to the town. His first entry on the scene, few people could tell whence, dropping down, as it were, out of the sky, or starting from the nether earth, had an aspect of mystery, which was easily heightened to the miraculous. He was now known to be a man of skill; it was observed that he gathered herbs, and the blossoms of wildflowers, and dug up roots and plucked off twigs from the forest-trees, like one acquainted with hidden virtues in what was valueless to common eyes. He was heard to speak of Sir Kenelm Digby; [46] and other famous men, —whose

---

[46] An English Catholic scientist and naval commander (1603–65) who conducted experiments in chemistry and the occult sciences.

scientific attainments were esteemed hardly less than supernatural, — as having been his correspondents or associates. Why, with such rank in the learned world, had he come hither? What could he, whose sphere was in great cities, be seeking in the wilderness? In answer to this query, a rumor gained ground, — and, however absurd, was entertained by some very sensible people, — that Heaven had wrought an absolute miracle, by transporting an eminent Doctor of Physic, from a German university, bodily through the air, and setting him down at the door of Mr. Dimmesdale's study! Individuals of wiser faith, indeed, who knew that Heaven promotes its purposes without aiming at the stage-effect of what is called miraculous interposition, were inclined to see a providential hand in Roger Chillingworth's so opportune arrival.

This idea was countenanced by the strong interest which the physician ever manifested in the young clergyman; he attached himself to him as a parishioner, and sought to win a friendly regard and confidence from his naturally reserved sensibility. He expressed great alarm at his pastor's state of health, but was anxious to attempt the cure, and, if early undertaken, seemed not despondent of a favorable result. The elders, the deacons, the motherly dames, and the young and fair maidens, of Mr. Dimmesdale's flock, were alike importunate that he should make trial of the physician's frankly offered skill. Mr. Dimmesdale gently repelled their entreaties.

"I need no medicine," said he.

But how could the young minister say so, when, with every successive Sabbath, his cheek was paler and thinner, and his voice more tremulous than before, — when it had now become a constant habit, rather than a casual gesture, to press his hand over his heart? Was he weary of his labors? Did he wish to die? These questions were solemnly propounded to Mr. Dimmesdale by the elder ministers of Boston and the deacons of his church, who, to use their own phrase, "dealt with him" on the sin of rejecting the aid which Providence so manifestly held out. He listened in silence, and finally promised to confer with the physician.

"Were it God's will," said the Reverend Mr. Dimmesdale, when, in fulfilment of this pledge, he requested old Roger Chillingworth's professional advice, "I could be well content, that my labors, and my sorrows, and my sins, and my pains, should shortly end with me, and what is earthly of them be buried in my grave, and the spiritual go with me to my eternal state, rather than that you should put your skill to the proof in my behalf."

"Ah," replied Roger Chillingworth, with that quietness which, whether imposed or natural, marked all his deportment, "it is thus that a young clergyman is apt to speak. Youthful men, not having taken a deep root, give up their hold of life so easily! And saintly men, who walk with God on earth, would fain be away, to walk with him on the golden pavements of the New Jerusalem."

"Nay," rejoined the young minister, putting his hand to his heart, with a flush of pain flitting over his brow, "were I worthier to walk there, I could be better content to toil here."

"Good men ever interpret themselves too meanly," said the physician.

In this manner, the mysterious old Roger Chillingworth became the medical adviser of the Reverend Mr. Dimmesdale. As not only the disease interested the physician, but he was strongly moved to look into the character and qualities of the patient, these two men, so different in age, came gradually to spend much time together. For the sake of the minister's health, and to enable the leech to gather plants with healing balm in them, they took long walks on the seashore, or in the forest; mingling various talk with the plash and murmur of the waves, and the solemn wind-anthem among the tree-tops. Often, likewise, one was the guest of the other, in his place of study and retirement. There was a fascination for the minister in the company of the man of science, in whom he recognized an intellectual cultivation of no moderate depth or scope; together with a range and freedom of ideas, that he would have vainly looked for among the members of his own profession. In truth, he was startled, if not shocked, to find this attribute in the physician. Mr. Dimmesdale was a true priest, a true religionist, with the reverential sentiment largely developed, and an order of mind that impelled itself powerfully along the track of a creed, and wore its passage continually deeper with the lapse of time. In no state of society would he have been what is called a man of liberal views; it would always be essential to his peace to feel the pressure of a faith about him, supporting, while it confined him within its iron framework. Not the less, however, though with a tremulous enjoyment, did he feel the occasional relief of looking at the universe through the medium of another kind of intellect than those with which he habitually held converse. It was as if a window were thrown open, admitting a freer atmosphere into the close and stifled study, where his life was wasting itself away, amid lamp-light, or obstructed daybeams, and the musty fragrance, be it sensual or moral, that exhales from books. But the air was too fresh and chill to be long breathed, with comfort. So the minister, and the physician with him, withdrew again within the limits of what their church defined as orthodox.

Thus Roger Chillingworth scrutinized his patient carefully, both as he saw him in his ordinary life, keeping an accustomed pathway in the range of thoughts familiar to him, and as he appeared when thrown amidst other moral scenery, the novelty of which might call out something new to the surface of his character. He deemed it essential, it would seem, to know the man, before attempting to do him good. Wherever there is a heart and an intellect, the diseases of the physical frame are tinged with the peculiarities of these. In Arthur Dimmesdale, thought and imagination were so active, and sensibility so intense, that the bodily infirmity would be likely to have its groundwork there. So Roger Chillingworth—the man of skill, the kind and friendly physician—strove to go deep into his patient's bosom, delving among his principles, prying into his recollections, and probing every thing with a cautious touch, like a treasure-seeker in a dark cavern. Few secrets can escape an investigator, who has opportunity and license to undertake such a quest, and skill to follow it up. A man burdened with a secret should especially avoid the intimacy of his physician. If the latter possess native sagacity, and a nameless something more,—let us call it intuition; if he show no intrusive egotism, nor disagreeably prominent characteristics of his own; if he have the power, which must be born with him, to bring his mind into such affinity with his patient's, that this last shall unawares have spoken what he imagines himself only to have thought; if such revelations be received without tumult, and acknowledged not so often by an uttered sympathy, as by silence, an inarticulate breath, and here and there a word, to indicate that all is understood; if, to these qualifications of a confidant he joined the advantages afforded by his recognized character as a physician;—then, at some inevitable moment, will the soul of the sufferer be dissolved, and flow forth in a dark, but transparent stream, bringing all its mysteries into the daylight.

Roger Chillingworth possessed all, or most, of the attributes above enumerated. Nevertheless, time went on; a kind of intimacy, as we have said, grew up between these two cultivated minds, which had as wide a field as the whole sphere of human thought and study, to meet upon; they discussed every topic of ethics and religion, of public affairs, and private character; they talked much, on both sides, of matters that seemed personal to themselves; and yet no secret, such as the physician fancied must exist there, ever stole out of the minister's consciousness into his companion's ear. The latter had his suspicions, indeed, that even the nature of Mr. Dimmesdale's bodily disease had never fairly been revealed to him. It was a strange reserve!

After a time, at a hint from Roger Chillingworth, the friends of Mr. Dimmesdale effected an arrangement by which the two were lodged in the same house; so that every ebb and flow of the minister's life-tide might pass under the eye of his anxious and attached physician. There was much joy throughout the town, when this greatly desirable object was attained. It was held to be the best possible measure for the young clergyman's welfare; unless, indeed, as often urged by such as felt authorized to do so, he had selected some one of the many blooming damsels, spiritually devoted to him, to become his devoted wife. This latter step, however, there was no present prospect that Arthur Dimmesdale would be prevailed upon to take; he rejected all suggestions of the kind, as if priestly celibacy were one of his articles of church-discipline. Doomed by his own choice, therefore, as Mr. Dimmesdale so evidently was, to eat his unsavory morsel always at another's board, and endure the life-long chill which must be his lot who seeks to warm himself only at another's fireside, it truly seemed that this sagacious, experienced, benevolent, old physician, with his concord of paternal and reverential love for the young pastor, was the very man, of all mankind, to be constantly within reach of his voice.

The new abode of the two friends was with a pious widow, of good social rank, who dwelt in a house covering pretty nearly the site on which the venerable structure of King's Chapel has since been built. It had the grave-yard, originally Isaac Johnson's home-field, on one side, and so was well adapted to call up serious reflections, suited to their respective employments, in both minister and man of physic. The motherly care of the good widow assigned to Mr. Dimmesdale a front apartment, with a sunny exposure, and heavy window-curtains to create a noontide shadow, when desirable. The walls were hung round with tapestry, said to be from the Gobelin looms,[47] and, at all events, representing the Scriptural story of David and Bathsheba, and Nathan the Prophet,[48] in colors still unfaded, but which made the fair woman of the scene almost as grimly picturesque as the woe-denouncing seer. Here, the pale clergyman piled up his library, rich with parchment-bound folios of the Fathers,[49] and the lore of Rabbis, and monkish erudition, of which the Protestant divines, even while they vilified and decried that class of writers, were yet constrained often to avail themselves. On the other side of the house, old Roger Chillingworth arranged his study and laboratory; not such as a modern man of science would reckon even tolerably complete, but provided with a distilling apparatus, and the means of compounding drugs and chemicals, which the practised alchemist knew well how to turn to purpose. With such commodiousness of situation, these two learned persons sat themselves down, each in his own domain, yet familiarly passing from one apartment to the other, and bestowing a mutual and not incurious inspection into one another's business.

And the Reverend Arthur Dimmesdale's best discerning friends, as we have intimated, very reasonably imagined that the hand of Providence had done all this, for the purpose—besought in so many public, and domestic,

---

[47] The Gobelin works in Paris began producing tapestries in 1601.
[48] For King David's lust for Bathsheba and Nathan's rebuke, see II Samuel 11–12.
[49] Early Christian writers.

and secret prayers—of restoring the young minister to health. But—it must now be said—another portion of the community had latterly begun to take its own view of the relation betwixt Mr. Dimmesdale and the mysterious old physician. When an uninstructed multitude attempts to see with its eyes, it is exceedingly apt to be deceived. When, however, it forms its judgment, as it usually does, on the intuitions of its great and warm heart, the conclusions thus attained are often so profound and so unerring, as to possess the character of truths supernaturally revealed. The people, in the case of which we speak, could justify its prejudice against Roger Chillingworth by no fact or argument worthy of serious refutation. There was an aged handicraftsman, it is true, who had been a citizen of London at the period of Sir Thomas Overbury's murder, now some thirty years agone; he testified to having seen the physician, under some other name, which the narrator of the story had now forgotten, in company with Doctor Forman, the famous old conjurer, who was implicated in the affair of Overbury.[50] Two or three individuals hinted, that the man of skill, during his Indian captivity, had enlarged his medical attainments by joining in the incantations of the savage priests; who were universally acknowledged to be powerful enchanters, often performing seemingly miraculous cures by their skill in the black art. A large number—and many of these were persons of such sober sense and practical observation, that their opinions would have been valuable, in other matters—affirmed that Roger Chillingworth's aspect had undergone a remarkable change while he had dwelt in town, and especially since his abode with Mr. Dimmesdale. At first, his expression had been calm, meditative, scholar-like. Now, there was something ugly and evil in his face, which they had not previously noticed, and which grew still the more obvious to sight, the oftener they looked upon him. According to the vulgar idea, the fire in his laboratory had been brought from the lower regions, and was fed with infernal fuel; and so, as might be expected, his visage was getting sooty with the smoke.

To sum up the matter, it grew to be a widely diffused opinion, that the Reverend Arthur Dimmesdale, like many other personages of especial sanctity, in all ages of the Christian world, was haunted either by Satan himself, or Satan's emissary, in the guise of old Roger Chillingworth. This diabolical agent had the Divine permission, for a season, to burrow into the clergyman's intimacy, and plot against his soul. No sensible man, it was confessed, could doubt on which side the victory would turn. The people

---

[50] Because Sir Thomas Overbury (1581–1613) opposed the marriage of his patron Viscount Rochester to the countess of Essex, she arranged to have him killed. The astrologer and alchemist Simon Forman (1552–1611) was one of the plotters.

looked, with an unshaken hope, to see the minister come forth out of the conflict, transfigured with the glory which he would unquestionably win. Meanwhile, nevertheless, it was sad to think of the perchance mortal agony through which he must struggle towards his triumph.

Alas, to judge from the gloom and terror in the depths of the poor minister's eyes, the battle was a sore one, and the victory any thing but secure!

X

The Leech and His Patient

Old Roger Chillingworth, throughout life, had been calm in temperament, kindly, though not of warm affections, but ever, and in all his relations with the world, a pure and upright man. He had begun an investigation, as he imagined, with the severe and equal integrity of a judge, desirous only of truth, even as if the question involved no more than the air-drawn lines and figures of a geometrical problem, instead of human passions, and wrongs inflicted on himself. But, as he proceeded, a terrible fascination, a kind of fierce, though still calm, necessity seized the old man within its gripe, and never set him free again, until he had done all its bidding. He now dug into the poor clergyman's heart, like a miner searching for gold; or, rather, like a sexton delving into a grave, possibly in quest of a jewel that had been buried on the dead man's bosom, but likely to find nothing save mortality and corruption. Alas for his own soul, if these were what he sought!

Sometimes, a light glimmered out of the physician's eyes, burning blue and ominous, like the reflection of a furnace, or, let us say, like one of those gleams of ghastly fire that darted from Bunyan's awful door-way[51] in the hill-side, and quivered on the pilgrim's face. The soil where this dark miner was working had perchance shown indications that encouraged him.

"This man," said he, at one such moment, to himself, "pure as they deem him, —all spiritual as he seems, —hath inherited a strong animal nature from his father or his mother. Let us dig a little farther in the direction of this vein!"

Then, after long search into the minister's dim interior, and turning over many precious materials, in the shape of high aspirations for the welfare of his race, warm love of souls, pure sentiments, natural piety, strengthened by thought and study, and illuminated by revelation, —all of

---

[51] In John Bunyan's *Pilgrim's Progress* (1678), Christian sees the fiery "by-way to hell" while striving toward the Celestial City.

which invaluable gold was perhaps no better than rubbish to the seeker, — he would turn back, discouraged, and begin his quest towards another point. He groped along as stealthily, with as cautious a tread, and as wary an outlook, as a thief entering a chamber where a man lies only half asleep, — or, it may be, broad awake, — with purpose to steal the very treasure which this man guards as the apple of his eye. In spite of his premeditated carefulness, the floor would now and then creak; his garments would rustle; the shadow of his presence, in a forbidden proximity, would be thrown across his victim. In other words, Mr. Dimmesdale, whose sensibility of nerve often produced the effect of spiritual intuition, would become vaguely aware that something inimical to his peace had thrust itself into relation with him. But old Roger Chillingworth, too, had perceptions that were almost intuitive; and when the minister threw his startled eyes towards him, there the physician sat; his kind, watchful, sympathizing, but never intrusive friend.

Yet Mr. Dimmesdale would perhaps have seen this individual's character more perfectly, if a certain morbidness, to which sick hearts are liable, had not rendered him suspicious of all mankind. Trusting no man as his friend, he could not recognize his enemy when the latter actually appeared. He therefore still kept up a familiar intercourse with him, daily receiving the old physician in his study; or visiting the laboratory, and, for recreation's sake, watching the processes by which weeds were converted into drugs of potency.

One day, leaning his forehead on his hand, and his elbow on the sill of the open window, that looked towards the grave-yard, he talked with Roger Chillingworth, while the old man was examining a bundle of unsightly plants.

"Where," asked he, with a look askance at them, — for it was the clergyman's peculiarity that he seldom, now-a-days, looked straightforth at any subject, whether human or inanimate, — "where, my kind doctor, did you gather those herbs, with such a dark, flabby leaf?"

"Even in the grave-yard, here at hand," answered the physician, continuing his employment. "They are new to me. I found them growing on a grave, which bore no tombstone, nor other memorial of the dead man, save these ugly weeds that have taken upon themselves to keep him in remembrance. They grew out of his heart, and typify, it may be, some hideous secret that was buried with him, and which he had done better to confess during his lifetime."

"Perchance," said Mr. Dimmesdale, "he earnestly desired it, but could not."

"And wherefore?" rejoined the physician. "Wherefore not; since all the powers of nature call so earnestly for the confession of sin, that these black

The Leech and His Patient by F. O. C. Darley. Originally appeared in the 1879 Houghton Mifflin edition of the novel.

weeds have sprung up out of a buried heart, to make manifest an unspoken crime?"

"That, good Sir, is but a fantasy of yours," replied the minister. "There can be, if I forbode aright, no power, short of the Divine mercy, to disclose, whether by uttered words, or by type or emblem, the secrets that may be buried with a human heart. The heart, making itself guilty of such secrets, must perforce hold them, until the day when all hidden things shall be revealed.[52] Nor have I so read or interpreted Holy Writ, as to understand that the disclosure of human thoughts and deeds, then to be made, is intended as a part of the retribution. That, surely, were a shallow view of it. No; these revelations, unless I greatly err, are meant merely to promote the intellectual satisfaction of all intelligent beings, who will stand waiting, on that day, to see the dark problem of this life made plain. A knowledge of men's hearts will be needful to the completest solution of that problem. And I conceive, moreover, that the hearts holding such miserable secrets as you speak of will yield them up, at that last day, not with reluctance, but with a joy unutterable."

"Then why not reveal them here?" asked Roger Chillingworth, glancing quietly aside at the minister. "Why should not the guilty ones sooner avail themselves of this unutterable solace?"

"They mostly do," said the clergyman, griping hard at his breast, as if afflicted with an importunate throb of pain. "Many, many a poor soul hath given its confidence to me, not only on the death-bed, but while strong in life, and fair in reputation. And ever, after such an outpouring, O, what a relief have I witnessed in those sinful brethren! even as in one who at last draws free air, after long stifling with his own polluted breath. How can it be otherwise? Why should a wretched man, guilty, we will say, of murder, prefer to keep the dead corpse buried in his own heart, rather than fling it forth at once, and let the universe take care of it!"

"Yet some men bury their secrets thus," observed the calm physician.

"True; there are such men," answered Mr. Dimmesdale. "But, not to suggest more obvious reasons, it may be that they are kept silent by the very constitution of their nature. Or,—can we not suppose it?—guilty as they may be, retaining, nevertheless, a zeal for God's glory and man's welfare, they shrink from displaying themselves black and filthy in the view of men; because, thenceforward, no good can be achieved by them; no evil of the past be redeemed by better service. So, to their own unutterable torment, they go about among their fellow-creatures, looking pure as new-fallen

---

[52] Judgment Day.

snow; while their hearts are all speckled and spotted with iniquity of which they cannot rid themselves."

"These men deceive themselves," said Roger Chillingworth, with somewhat more emphasis than usual, and making a slight gesture with his forefinger. "They fear to take up the shame that rightfully belongs to them. Their love for man, their zeal for God's service, — these holy impulses may or may not coexist in their hearts with the evil inmates to which their guilt has unbarred the door, and which must needs propagate a hellish breed within them. But, if they seek to glorify God, let them not lift heavenward their unclean hands! If they would serve their fellow-men, let them do it by making manifest the power and reality of conscience, in constraining them to penitential self-abasement! Wouldst thou have me to believe, O wise and pious friend, that a false show can be better — can be more for God's glory, or man's welfare — than God's own truth? Trust me, such men deceive themselves!"

"It may be so," said the young clergyman indifferently, as waiving a discussion that he considered irrelevant or unseasonable. He had a ready faculty, indeed, of escaping from any topic that agitated his too sensitive and nervous temperament. — "But, now, I would ask of my well-skilled physician, whether, in good sooth, he deems me to have profited by his kindly care of this weak frame of mine?"

Before Roger Chillingworth could answer, they heard the clear, wild laughter of a young child's voice, proceeding from the adjacent burial-ground. Looking instinctively from the open window, — for it was summertime, — the minister beheld Hester Prynne and little Pearl passing along the footpath that traversed the enclosure. Pearl looked as beautiful as the day, but was in one of those moods of perverse merriment which, whenever they occurred, seemed to remove her entirely out of the sphere of sympathy or human contact. She now skipped irreverently from one grave to another; until, coming to the broad, flat, armorial tombstone of a departed worthy, — perhaps of Isaac Johnson himself, — she began to dance upon it. In reply to her mother's command and entreaty that she would behave more decorously, little Pearl paused to gather the prickly burrs from a tall burdock, which grew beside the tomb. Taking a handful of these, she arranged them along the lines of the scarlet letter that decorated the maternal bosom, to which the burrs, as their nature was, tenaciously adhered. Hester did not pluck them off.

Roger Chillingworth had by this time approached the window, and smiled grimly down.

"There is no law, nor reverence for authority, no regard for human ordinances or opinions, right or wrong, mixed up with that child's composition," remarked he, as much to himself as to his companion. "I saw her, the other day, bespatter the Governor himself with water, at the cattle trough in Spring Lane. What, in Heaven's name, is she? Is the imp altogether evil? Hath she affections? Hath she any discoverable principle of being?"

"None,—save the freedom of a broken law," answered Mr. Dimmesdale, in a quiet way, as if he had been discussing the point within himself. "Whether capable of good, I know not."

The child probably overheard their voices; for, looking up to the window, with a bright, but naughty smile of mirth and intelligence, she threw one of the prickly burrs at the Reverend Mr. Dimmesdale. The sensitive clergyman shrunk, with nervous dread, from the light missile. Detecting his emotion, Pearl clapped her little hands in the most extravagant ecstasy. Hester Prynne, likewise, had involuntarily looked up; and all these four persons, old and young, regarded one another in silence, till the child laughed aloud, and shouted,—"Come away, mother! Come away, or yonder old Black Man will catch you! He hath got hold of the minister already. Come away, mother, or he will catch you! But he cannot catch little Pearl!"

So she drew her mother away, skipping, dancing, and frisking fantastically among the hillocks of the dead people, like a creature that had nothing in common with a bygone and buried generation, nor owned herself akin to it. It was as if she had been made afresh, out of new elements, and must perforce be permitted to live her own life, and be a law unto herself, without her eccentricities being reckoned to her for a crime.

"There goes a woman," resumed Roger Chillingworth, after a pause, "who, be her demerits what they may, hath none of that mystery of hidden sinfulness which you deem so grievous to be borne. Is Hester Prynne the less miserable, think you, for that scarlet letter on her breast?"

"I do verily believe it," answered the clergyman. "Nevertheless, I cannot answer for her. There was a look of pain in her face, which I would gladly have been spared the sight of. But still, methinks, it must needs be better for the sufferer to be free to show his pain, as this poor woman Hester is, than to cover it all up in his heart." *expressing feelings*

There was another pause; and the physician began anew to examine and arrange the plants which he had gathered.

"You inquired of me, a little time agone," said he, at length, "my judgment as touching your health."

"I did," answered the clergyman, "and would gladly learn it. Speak frankly, I pray you, be it for life or death."

"Freely, then, and plainly," said the physician, still busy with his plants, but keeping a wary eye on Mr. Dimmesdale, "the disorder is a strange one; not so much in itself, nor as outwardly manifested,—in so far, at least, as the symptoms have been laid open to my observation. Looking daily at you, my good Sir, and watching the tokens of your aspect, now for months gone by, I should deem you a man sore sick, it may be, yet not so sick but that an instructed and watchful physician might well hope to cure you. But—I know not what to say—the disease is what I seem to know, yet know it not."

"You speak in riddles, learned Sir," said the pale minister, glancing aside out of the window.

"Then, to speak more plainly," continued the physician, "and I crave pardon, Sir,—should it seem to require pardon,—for this needful plainness of my speech. Let me ask,—as your friend,—as one having charge, under Providence, of your life and physical well-being,—hath all the operation of this disorder been fairly laid open and recounted to me?"

"How can you question it?" asked the minister. "Surely, it were child's play to call in a physician, and then hide the sore!"

"You would tell me, then, that I know all?" said Roger Chillingworth, deliberately, and fixing an eye, bright with intense and concentrated intelligence, on the minister's face. "Be it so! But, again! He to whom only the outward and physical evil is laid open knoweth, oftentimes, but half the evil which he is called upon to cure. A bodily disease, which we look upon as whole and entire within itself, may, after all, be but a symptom of some ailment in the spiritual part. Your pardon, once again, good Sir, if my speech give the shadow of offence. You, Sir, of all men whom I have known, are he whose body is the closest conjoined, and imbued, and identified, so to speak, with the spirit whereof it is the instrument."

"Then I need ask no further," said the clergyman, somewhat hastily rising from his chair. "You deal not, I take it, in medicine for the soul!"

"Thus, a sickness," continued Roger Chillingworth, going on, in an unaltered tone, without heeding the interruption,—but standing up, and confronting the emaciated and white-cheeked minister with his low, dark, and misshapen figure,—"a sickness, a sore place, if we may so call it, in your spirit, hath immediately its appropriate manifestation in your bodily frame. Would you, therefore, that your physician heal the bodily evil? How may this be, unless you first lay open to him the wound or trouble in your soul?"

"No!—not to thee!—not to an earthly physician!" cried Mr. Dimmesdale, passionately, and turning his eyes, full and bright, and with a kind of fierceness, on old Roger Chillingworth. "Not to thee! But, if it be the soul's disease, then do I commit myself to the one Physician of the soul! He, if it stand with his good pleasure, can cure; or he can kill! Let him do with me as, in his justice and wisdom, he shall see good. But who art thou, that meddlest in this matter?—that dares thrust himself between the sufferer and his God?"

With a frantic gesture, he rushed out of the room.

"It is as well to have made this step," said Roger Chillingworth to himself, looking after the minister with a grave smile. "There is nothing lost. We shall be friends again anon. But see, now, how passion takes hold upon this man, and hurrieth him out of himself! As with one passion, so with another! He hath done a wild thing ere now, this pious Master Dimmesdale, in the hot passion of his heart!"

It proved not difficult to reestablish the intimacy of the two companions, on the same footing and in the same degree as heretofore. The young clergyman, after a few hours of privacy, was sensible that the disorder of his nerves had hurried him into an unseemly outbreak of temper, which there had been nothing in the physician's words to excuse or palliate. He marvelled, indeed, at the violence with which he had thrust back the kind old man, when merely proffering the advice which it was his duty to bestow, and which the minister himself had expressly sought. With these remorseful feelings, he lost no time in making the amplest apologies, and besought his friend still to continue the care, which, if not successful in restoring him to health, had, in all probability, been the means of prolonging his feeble existence to that hour. Roger Chillingworth readily assented, and went on with his medical supervision of the minister; doing his best for him, in all good faith, but always quitting the patient's apartment, at the close of a professional interview, with a mysterious and puzzled smile upon his lips. This expression was invisible in Mr. Dimmesdale's presence, but grew strongly evident as the physician crossed the threshold.

"A rare case!" he muttered. "I must needs look deeper into it. A strange sympathy betwixt soul and body! Were it only for the art's sake, I must search this matter to the bottom!"

It came to pass, not long after the scene above recorded, that the Reverend Mr. Dimmesdale, at noonday, and entirely unawares, fell into a deep, deep slumber, sitting in his chair, with a large black-letter volume open before him on the table. It must have been a work of vast ability in the somniferous school of literature. The profound depth of the minister's repose was the more remarkable; inasmuch as he was one of those persons whose sleep, ordinarily, is as light, as fitful, and as easily scared away, as a small bird hopping on a twig. To such an unwonted remoteness, however, had his spirit now withdrawn into itself, that he stirred not in his chair, when old Roger Chillingworth, without any extraordinary precaution, came into the room. The physician advanced directly in front of his patient, laid his hand upon his bosom, and thrust aside the vestment, that, hitherto, had always covered it even from the professional eye.

Then, indeed, Mr. Dimmesdale shuddered, and slightly stirred.

After a brief pause, the physician turned away.

But with what a wild look of wonder, joy, and horror! With what a ghastly rapture, as it were, too mighty to be expressed only by the eye and features, and therefore bursting forth through the whole ugliness of his figure, and making itself even riotously manifest by the extravagant gestures with which he threw up his arms towards the ceiling, and stamped his foot upon the floor! Had a man seen old Roger Chillingworth, at that moment of his ecstasy, he would have had no need to ask how Satan comports himself, when a precious human soul is lost to heaven, and won into his kingdom.

But what distinguished the physician's ecstasy from Satan's was the trait of wonder in it!

XI
The Interior of a Heart

After the incident last described, the intercourse between the clergyman and the physician, though externally the same, was really of another character than it had previously been. The intellect of Roger Chillingworth had now a sufficiently plain path before it. It was not, indeed, precisely that which he had laid out for himself to tread. Calm, gentle, passionless, as he appeared, there was yet, we fear, a quiet depth of malice, hitherto latent, but active now, in this unfortunate old man, which led him to imagine a more intimate revenge than any mortal had ever wreaked upon an enemy. To make himself the one trusted friend, to whom should be confided all the fear, the remorse, the agony, the ineffectual repentance, the backward rush of sinful thoughts, expelled in vain! All that guilty sorrow, hidden from the world, whose great heart would have pitied and forgiven, to be revealed to him, the Pitiless, to him, the Unforgiving! All that dark treasure to be lavished on the very man, to whom nothing else could so adequately pay the debt of vengeance!

The clergyman's shy and sensitive reserve had balked this scheme. Roger Chillingworth, however, was inclined to be hardly, if at all, less satisfied with the aspect of affairs, which Providence—using the avenger and his victim for its own purposes, and, perchance, pardoning, where it seemed most to punish—had substituted for his black devices. A revelation, he could almost say, had been granted to him. It mattered little, for his object, whether celestial, or from what other region. By its aid, in all the subsequent relations betwixt him and Mr. Dimmesdale, not merely the external presence, but the very inmost soul of the latter seemed to be brought out before his eyes, so that he could see and comprehend its every movement. He became, thenceforth, not a spectator only, but a chief actor, in the poor minister's interior world. He could play upon him as he chose. Would he arouse him with a throb of agony? The victim was for ever on the rack; it needed only to know the spring that controlled the engine;—and the physician knew it well! Would he startle him with sudden fear? As at the waving of a magician's wand, uprose a grisly phantom,—uprose a thousand phantoms,—in many shapes, of death, or more awful shame, all flocking roundabout the clergyman, and pointing with their fingers at his breast!

All this was accomplished with a subtlety so perfect, that the minister, though he had constantly a dim perception of some evil influence watching over him, could never gain a knowledge of its actual nature. True, he looked doubtfully, fearfully,—even, at times, with horror and the bitterness of hatred,—at the deformed figure of the old physician. His gestures, his gait, his grizzled beard, his slightest and most indifferent acts, the very fashion of his garments, were odious in the clergyman's sight; a token, implicitly to be relied on, of a deeper antipathy in the breast of the latter than he was willing to acknowledge to himself. For as it was impossible to assign a reason for such distrust and abhorrence, so Mr. Dimmesdale, conscious that the poison of one morbid spot was infecting his heart's entire substance, attributed all his presentiments to no other cause. He took himself to task for his bad sympathies in reference to Roger Chillingworth, disregarded the lesson that he should have drawn from them, and did his best to root them out. Unable to accomplish this, he nevertheless, as a matter of principle, continued his habits of social familiarity with the old man, and thus gave him constant opportunities for perfecting the purpose to which—poor, forlorn creature that he was, and more wretched than his victim—the avenger had devoted himself.

While thus suffering under bodily disease, and gnawed and tortured by some black trouble of the soul, and given over to the machinations of his deadliest enemy, the Reverend Mr. Dimmesdale had achieved a brilliant popularity in his sacred office. He won it, indeed, in great part, by his sorrows. His intellectual gifts, his moral perceptions, his power of experiencing and communicating emotion, were kept in a state of preternatural activity by the prick and anguish of his daily life. His fame, though still on its upward slope, already overshadowed the soberer reputations of his fellow-clergymen, eminent as several of them were. There were scholars among them, who had spent more years in acquiring abstruse lore, connected with the divine profession, than Mr. Dimmesdale had lived; and who might well, therefore, be more profoundly versed in such solid and valuable attainments than their youthful brother. There were men, too, of a sturdier texture of mind than his, and endowed with a far greater share of shrewd, hard, iron or granite understanding; which, duly mingled with a fair proportion of doctrinal ingredient, constitutes a highly respectable, efficacious, and unamiable variety of the clerical species. There were others, again, true saintly fathers, whose faculties had been elaborated by weary toil among their books, and by patient thought, and etherealized, moreover, by spiritual communications with the better world, into which their purity of life had almost introduced these holy personages, with their garments of mortality still clinging to them. All that they lacked was the gift that descended upon the chosen disciples, at Pentecost, in tongues of flame;[53] symbolizing, it would seem, not the power of speech in foreign and unknown languages, but that of addressing the whole human brotherhood in the heart's native language. These fathers, otherwise so apostolic, lacked Heaven's last and rarest attestation of their office, the Tongue of Flame. They would have vainly sought—had they ever dreamed of seeking—to express the highest truths through the humblest medium of familiar words and images. Their voices came down, afar and indistinctly, from the upper heights where they habitually dwelt.

Not improbably, it was to this latter class of men that Mr. Dimmesdale, by many of his traits of character, naturally belonged. To their high mountain-peaks of faith and sanctity he would have climbed, had not the tendency been thwarted by the burden, whatever it might be, of crime or anguish, beneath which it was his doom to totter. It kept him down, on a level with the lowest; him, the man of ethereal attributes, whose voice the angels might else have listened to and answered! But this very burden it was, that gave him sympathies so intimate with the sinful brotherhood of mankind; so that his heart vibrated in unison with theirs, and received their pain into itself, and sent its own throb of pain through a thousand other hearts, in gushes of sad, persuasive eloquence. Oftenest persuasive, but sometimes terrible! The people knew not the power that moved them thus. They deemed the young clergyman a miracle of holiness. They fancied him the mouthpiece of Heaven's messages of wisdom, and rebuke, and love. In their eyes, the very ground on which he trod was sanctified. The virgins of his church grew pale around him, victims of a passion so imbued with religious sentiment that they imagined it to be all religion, and brought it openly, in their white bosoms, as their most acceptable sacrifice before the altar. The aged members of his flock, beholding Mr. Dimmesdale's frame so feeble, while they were themselves so rugged in their infirmity, believed that he would go heavenward before them, and enjoined it upon their children, that their old bones should be buried close to their young pastor's

---

[53] On Pentecost, the Holy Ghost appeared to the Apostles as tongues of flame that enabled them to preach the Gospel in foreign languages (Acts 2.1–8).

holy grave. And, all this time, perchance, when poor Mr. Dimmesdale was thinking of his grave, he questioned with himself whether the grass would ever grow on it, because an accursed thing must there be buried!

It is inconceivable, the agony with which this public veneration tortured him! It was his genuine impulse to adore the truth, and to reckon all things shadowlike, and utterly devoid of weight or value, that had not its divine essence as the life within their life. Then, what was he? — a substance? — or the dimmest of all shadows? He longed to speak out, from his own pulpit, at the full height of his voice, and tell the people what he was. "I, whom you behold in these black garments of the priesthood, — I, who ascend the sacred desk, and turn my pale face heavenward, taking upon myself to hold communion, in your behalf, with the Most High Omniscience — I, in whose daily life you discern the sanctity of Enoch[54] — I, whose footsteps, as you suppose, leave a gleam along my earthly track, whereby the pilgrims that shall come after me may be guided to the regions of the blest, — I, who have laid the hand of baptism upon your children, — I, who have breathed the parting prayer over your dying friends, to whom the Amen sounded faintly from a world which they had quitted, — I, your pastor, whom you so reverence and trust, am utterly a pollution and a lie!"

More than once, Mr. Dimmesdale had gone into the pulpit, with a purpose never to come down its steps, until he should have spoken words like the above. More than once, he had cleared his throat, and drawn in the long, deep, and tremulous breath, which, when sent forth again, would come burdened with the black secret of his soul. More than once — nay, more than a hundred times — he had actually spoken! Spoken! But how? He had told his hearers that he was altogether vile, a viler companion of the vilest, the worst of sinners, an abomination, a thing of unimaginable iniquity; and that the only wonder was, that they did not see his wretched body shrivelled up before their eyes, by the burning wrath of the Almighty! Could there be plainer speech than this? Would not the people start up in their seats, by a simultaneous impulse, and tear him down out of the pulpit which he defiled? Not so, indeed! They heard it all, and did but reverence him the more. They little guessed what deadly purport lurked in those self-condemning words. "The godly youth!" said they among themselves. "The saint on earth! Alas, if he discern such sinfulness in his own white soul, what horrid spectacle would he behold in thine or mine!" The minister well knew — subtle, but remorseful hypocrite that he was! — the light in which his vague confession would be viewed. He had striven to put a cheat

---

[54] Enoch "walked with God" and ascended to Heaven without dying (Gen. 5.21–24).

upon himself by making the avowal of a guilty conscience, but had gained only one other sin, and a self-acknowledged shame, without the momentary relief of being self-deceived. He had spoken the very truth, and transformed it into the veriest falsehood. And yet, by the constitution of his nature, he loved the truth, and loathed the lie, as few men ever did. Therefore, above all things else, he loathed his miserable self!

His inward trouble drove him to practices, more in accordance with the old, corrupted faith of Rome, than with the better light of the church in which he had been born and bred. In Mr. Dimmesdale's secret closet, under lock and key, there was a bloody scourge.[55] Oftentimes, this Protestant and Puritan divine had plied it on his own shoulders; laughing bitterly at himself the while, and smiting so much the more pitilessly, because of that bitter laugh. It was his custom, too, as it has been that of many other pious Puritans, to fast, —not, however, like them, in order to purify the body and render it the fitter medium of celestial illumination, —but rigorously, and until his knees trembled beneath him, as an act of penance. He kept vigils, likewise, night after night, sometimes in utter darkness; sometimes with a glimmering lamp; and sometimes, viewing his own face in a looking-glass, by the most powerful light which he could throw upon it. He thus typified the constant introspection wherewith he tortured, but could not purify, himself. In these lengthened vigils, his brain often reeled, and visions seemed to flit before him; perhaps seen doubtfully, and by a faint light of their own, in the remote dimness of the chamber, or more vividly, and close beside him, within the looking-glass. Now it was a herd of diabolic shapes, that grinned and mocked at the pale minister, and beckoned him away with them; now a group of shining angels, who flew upward heavily, as sorrow-laden, but grew more ethereal as they rose. Now came the dead friends of his youth, and his white-bearded father, with a saint-like frown, and his mother, turning her face away as she passed by. Ghost of a mother, —thinnest fantasy of a mother, —methinks she might yet have thrown a pitying glance towards her son! And now, through the chamber which these spectral thoughts had made so ghastly, glided Hester Prynne, leading along little Pearl, in her scarlet garb, and pointing her forefinger, first, at the scarlet letter on her bosom, and then at the clergyman's own breast.

None of these visions ever quite deluded him. At any moment, by an effort of his will, he could discern substances through their misty lack of substance, and convince himself that they were not solid in their nature, like yonder table of carved oak, or that big, square, leathern-bound and brazen-

---

[55] Whip.

clasped volume of divinity. But, for all that, they were, in one sense, the truest and most substantial things which the poor minister now dealt with. It is the unspeakable misery of a life so false as his, that it steals the pith and substance out of whatever realities there are around us, and which were meant by Heaven to be the spirit's joy and nutriment. To the untrue man, the whole universe is false, — it is impalpable, — it shrinks to nothing within his grasp. And he himself, in so far as he shows himself in a false light, becomes a shadow, or indeed, ceases to exist. The only truth, that continued to give Mr. Dimmesdale a real existence on this earth, was the anguish in his inmost soul, and the undissembled expression of it in his aspect. Had he once found power to smile, and wear a face of gayety, there would have been no such man!

On one of those ugly nights, which we have faintly hinted at, but forborne to picture forth, the minister started from his chair. A new thought had struck him. There might be a moment's peace in it. Attiring himself with as much care as if it had been for public worship, and precisely in the same manner, he stole softly down the staircase, undid the door, and issued forth.

XII
The Minister's Vigil

Walking in the shadow of a dream, as it were, and perhaps actually under the influence of a species of somnambulism, Mr. Dimmesdale reached the spot, where, now so long since, Hester Prynne had lived through her first hour of public ignominy. The same platform or scaffold, black and weather-stained with the storm or sunshine of seven long years, and footworn, too, with the tread of many culprits who had since ascended it, remained standing beneath the balcony of the meeting-house. The minister went up the steps.

It was an obscure night of early May. An unvaried pall of cloud muffled the whole expanse of sky from zenith to horizon. If the same multitude which had stood as eyewitnesses while Hester Prynne sustained her punishment could now have been summoned forth, they would have discerned no face above the platform, nor hardly the outline of a human shape, in the dark gray of the midnight. But the town was all asleep. There was no peril of discovery. The minister might stand there, if it so pleased him, until morning should redden in the east, without other risk than that the dank and chill night-air would creep into his frame, and stiffen his joints with rheumatism, and clog his throat with catarrh and cough; thereby defrauding the expectant audience of to-morrow's prayer and sermon. No eye could see him, save that ever-wakeful one which had seen him in his closet, wielding the bloody scourge. Why, then, had he come hither? Was it but the mockery of penitence? A mockery, indeed, but in which his soul trifled with itself! A mockery at which angels blushed and wept, while fiends rejoiced, with jeering laughter! He had been driven hither by the impulse of that Remorse which dogged him everywhere, and whose own sister and closely linked companion was that Cowardice which invariably drew him back, with her tremulous gripe, just when the other impulse had hurried him to the verge of a disclosure. Poor, miserable man! what right had infirmity like his to burden itself with crime? Crime is for the iron-nerved, who have their choice either to endure it, or, if it press too hard, to exert their fierce and savage strength for a good purpose, and fling it off at once! This feeble and most sensitive of spirits could do neither, yet continually did one thing or another, which intertwined, in the same inextricable knot, the agony of heaven-defying guilt and vain repentance.

And thus, while standing on the scaffold, in this vain show of expiation, Mr. Dimmesdale was overcome with a great horror of mind, as if the universe were gazing at a scarlet token on his naked breast, right over his heart. On that spot, in very truth, there was, and there had long been, the gnawing and poisonous tooth of bodily pain. Without any effort of his will, or power to restrain himself, he shrieked aloud; an outcry that went pealing through the night, and was beaten back from one house to another, and reverberated from the hills in the background; as if a company of devils, detecting so much misery and terror in it, had made a plaything of the sound, and were bandying it to and fro.

"It is done!" muttered the minister, covering his face with his hands. "The whole town will awake, and hurry forth, and find me here!"

But it was not so. The shriek had perhaps sounded with a far greater power, to his own startled ears, than it actually possessed. The town did not awake; or, if it did, the drowsy slumberers mistook the cry either for something frightful in a dream, or for the noise of witches; whose voices, at that period, were often heard to pass over the settlements or lonely cottages, as they rode with Satan through the air. The clergyman, therefore, hearing no symptoms of disturbance, uncovered his eyes and looked about him. At one of the chamber-windows of Governor Bellingham's mansion, which stood at some distance, on the line of another street, he beheld the appearance of the old magistrate himself, with a lamp in his hand, a white night-cap on his head, and a long white gown enveloping his figure. He looked like a ghost, evoked unseasonably from the grave. The cry had evidently startled him. At another window of the same house, moreover, appeared old Mistress Hibbins, the Governor's sister, also with a lamp, which, even thus far off, revealed the expression of her sour and discontented face. She thrust forth her head from the lattice, and looked anxiously upward. Beyond the shadow of a doubt, this venerable witchlady had heard Mr. Dimmesdale's outcry, and interpreted it, with its multitudinous echoes and reverberations, as the clamor of the fiends and night-hags, with whom she was well known to make excursions into the forest.

Detecting the gleam of Governor Bellingham's lamp, the old lady quickly extinguished her own, and vanished. Possibly, she went up among the clouds. The minister saw nothing further of her motions. The magistrate, after a wary observation of the darkness — into which, nevertheless, he could see but little farther than he might into a millstone — retired from the window.

The minister grew comparatively calm. His eyes, however, were soon greeted by a little, glimmering light, which, at first a long way off, was approaching up the street. It threw a gleam of recognition on here a post, and there a garden-fence, and here a latticed windowpane, and there a pump, with its full trough of water, and here, again, an arched door of oak, with an iron knocker, and a rough log for the doorstep. The Reverend Mr. Dimmesdale noted all these minute particulars, even while firmly convinced that the doom of his existence was stealing onward, in the footsteps which he now heard; and that the gleam of the lantern would fall upon him, in a few moments more, and reveal his long-hidden secret. As the light drew nearer, he beheld, within its illuminated circle, his brother clergyman, — or, to speak more accurately, his professional father, as well as highly valued friend, — the Reverend Mr. Wilson; who, as Mr. Dimmesdale now conjectured, had been praying at the bedside of some dying man. And so he had. The good old minister came freshly from the death-chamber of Governor Winthrop,[56] who had passed from earth to heaven within that very hour. And now, surrounded, like the saint-like personages of olden times, with a radiant halo, that glorified him amid this gloomy night of sin, — as if the departed Governor had left him an inheritance of his glory, or as if he had caught upon himself the distant shine of the celestial city, while looking thitherward to see the triumphant pilgrim pass within its gates, — now, in short, good Father Wilson was moving homeward, aiding his footsteps with a lighted lantern! The glimmer of this luminary suggested the above conceits to Mr. Dimmesdale, who smiled, — nay, almost laughed at them, and then wondered if he were going mad.

---

[56] John Winthrop (1588–1649), a founder of the Bay Colony who served several terms as governor, actually died in March (not May).

As the Reverend Mr. Wilson passed beside the scaffold, closely muffling his Geneva cloak[57] about him with one arm, and holding the lantern before his breast with the other, the minister could hardly restrain himself from speaking.

"A good evening to you, venerable Father Wilson! Come up hither, I pray you, and pass a pleasant hour with me!"

Good heavens! Had Mr. Dimmesdale actually spoken? For one instant, he believed that these words had passed his lips. But they were uttered only within his imagination. The venerable Father Wilson continued to step slowly onward, looking carefully at the muddy pathway before his feet, and never once turning his head towards the guilty platform. When the light of the glimmering lantern had faded quite away, the minister discovered, by the faintness which came over him, that the last few moments had been a crisis of terrible anxiety; although his mind had made an involuntary effort to relieve itself by a kind of lurid playfulness.

Shortly afterwards, the like grisly sense of the humorous again stole in among the solemn phantoms of his thought. He felt his limbs growing stiff with the unaccustomed chilliness of the night, and doubted whether he should be able to descend the steps of the scaffold. Morning would break, and find him there. The neighbourhood would begin to rouse itself. The earliest riser, coming forth in the dim twilight, would perceive a vaguely defined figure aloft on the place of shame; and, half crazed betwixt alarm and curiosity, would go, knocking from door to door, summoning all the people to behold the ghost — as he needs must think it — of some defunct transgressor. A dusky tumult would flap its wings from one house to another. Then — the morning light still waxing stronger — old patriarchs would rise up in great haste, each in his flannel gown, and matronly dames, without pausing to put off their night-gear. The whole tribe of decorous personages, who had never heretofore been seen with a single hair of their heads awry, would start into public view, with the disorder of a nightmare in their aspects. Old Governor Bellingham would come grimly forth, with his King James's ruff fastened askew; and Mistress Hibbins, with some twigs of the forest clinging to her skirts, and looking sourer than ever, as having hardly got a wink of sleep after her night ride; and good Father Wilson, too, after spending half the night at a deathbed, and liking ill to be disturbed, thus early, out of his dreams about the glorified saints. Hither, likewise, would come the elders and deacons of Mr. Dimmesdale's church,

---

[57] A long black cloak customarily worn by Puritan ministers and the Calvinist clergymen of Geneva, Switzerland.

and the young virgins who so idolized their minister, and had made a shrine for him in their white bosoms; which, now, by the by, in their hurry and confusion, they would scantly have given themselves time to cover with their kerchiefs. All people, in a word, would come stumbling over their thresholds, and turning up their amazed and horror-stricken visages aound the scaffold. Whom would they discern there, with the red eastern light upon his brow? Whom, but the Reverend Arthur Dimmesdale, half frozen to death, overwhelmed with shame, and standing where Hester Prynne had stood!

Carried away by the grotesque horror of this picture, the minister, unawares, and to his own infinite alarm, burst into a great peal of laughter. It was immediately responded to by a light, airy, childish laugh, in which, with a thrill of the heart, — but he knew not whether of exquisite pain, or pleasure as acute, — he recognized the tones of little Pearl.

"Pearl! Little Pearl!" cried he, after a moment's pause; then, suppressing his voice, — "Hester! Hester Prynne! Are you there?"

"Yes, it is Hester Prynne!" she replied, in a tone of surprise; and the minister heard her footsteps approaching from the sidewalk, along which she had been passing. — "It is I, and my little Pearl."

"Whence come you, Hester?" asked the minister. "What sent you hither?"

"I have been watching at a death-bed," answered Hester Prynne; — "at Governor Winthrop's death-bed, and have taken his measure for a robe, and am now going homeward to my dwelling."

"Come up hither, Hester, thou and little Pearl," said the Reverend Mr. Dimmesdale. "Ye have both been here before, but I was not with you. Come up hither once again, and we will stand all three together!"

She silently ascended the steps, and stood on the platform, holding little Pearl by the hand. The minister felt for the child's other hand, and took it. The moment that he did so, there came what seemed a tumultuous rush of new life, other life than his own, pouring like a torrent into his heart, and hurrying through all his veins, as if the mother and the child were communicating their vital warmth to his half-torpid system. The three formed an electric chain.

"Minister!" whispered little Pearl.

"What wouldst thou say, child?" asked Mr. Dimmesdale.

"Wilt thou stand here with mother and me, to-morrow noontide?" inquired Pearl.

"Nay; not so, my little Pearl!" answered the minister; for, with the new energy of the moment, all the dread of public exposure, that had so long been the anguish of his life, had returned upon him; and he was already

trembling at the conjunction in which—with a strange joy, nevertheless—
he now found himself. "Not so, my child. I shall, indeed, stand with thy
mother and thee one other day, but not to-morrow!"

Pearl laughed, and attempted to pull away her hand. But the minister
held it fast.

"A moment longer, my child!" said he.

"But wilt thou promise," asked Pearl, "to take my hand, and mother's
hand, to-morrow noontide?"

"Not then, Pearl," said the minister, "but another time!"

"And what other time?" persisted the child.

"At the great judgment day!" whispered the minister,—and, strangely
enough, the sense that he was a professional teacher of the truth impelled
him to answer the child so. "Then, and there, before the judgment-seat, thy
mother, and thou, and I, must stand together! But the daylight of this
world shall not see our meeting!"

Pearl laughed again.

But, before Mr. Dimmesdale had done speaking, a light gleamed far and
wide over all the muffled sky. It was doubtless caused by one of those meteors, which the night-watcher may so often observe burning out to waste,
in the vacant regions of the atmosphere. So powerful was its radiance, that
it thoroughly illuminated the dense medium of cloud betwixt the sky and
earth. The great vault brightened, like the dome of an immense lamp. It
showed the familiar scene of the street, with the distinctness of midday, but
also with the awfulness that is always imparted to familiar objects by an
unaccustomed light. The wooden houses, with their jutting stories and
quaint gable-peaks; the doorsteps and thresholds, with the early grass
springing up about them; the garden-plots, black with freshly turned earth;
the wheel-track, little worn, and, even in the market-place, margined with
green on either side;—all were visible, but with a singularity of aspect that
seemed to give another moral interpretation to the things of this world
than they had ever borne before. And there stood the minister, with his
hand over his heart; and Hester Prynne, with the embroidered letter glimmering on her bosom; and little Pearl, herself a symbol, and the connecting link between those two. They stood in the noon of that strange and
solemn splendor, as if it were the light that is to reveal all secrets, and the
daybreak that shall unite all who belong to one another.

There was witchcraft in little Pearl's eyes; and her face, as she glanced
upward at the minister, wore that naughty smile which made its expression
frequently so elfish. She withdrew her hand from Mr. Dimmesdale's, and
pointed across the street. But he clasped both his hands over his breast, and
cast his eyes towards the zenith.

They Stood in the Noon of That Strange Splendor by Mary Hallock Foote, engraved by A.V. S. Anthony. Originally appeared in the 1877 Osgood and Company edition of the novel.

Nothing was more common, in those days, than to interpret all meteoric appearances, and other natural phenomena, that occurred with less regularity than the rise and set of sun and moon, as so many revelations from a supernatural source. Thus, a blazing spear, a sword of flame, a bow, or a sheaf of arrows, seen in the midnight sky, prefigured Indian warfare. Pestilence was known to have been foreboded by a shower of crimson light. We doubt whether any marked event, for good or evil, ever befell New England, from its settlement down to Revolutionary times, of which the inhabitants had not been previously warned by some spectacle of this nature. Not seldom, it had been seen by multitudes. Oftener, however, its credibility rested on the faith of some lonely eyewitness, who beheld the wonder through the colored, magnifying, and distorting medium of his imagination, and shaped it more distinctly in his afterthought. It was, indeed, a majestic idea, that the destiny of nations should be revealed, in these awful hieroglyphics, on the cope[58] of heaven. A scroll so wide might not be deemed too expansive for Providence to write a people's doom upon. The belief was a favorite one with our forefathers, as betokening that their infant commonwealth was under a celestial guardianship of peculiar intimacy and strictness. But what shall we say, when an individual discovers a revelation, addressed to himself alone, on the same vast sheet of record! In such a case, it could only be the symptom of a highly disordered mental state, when a man, rendered morbidly self-contemplative by long, intense, and secret pain, had extended his egotism over the whole expanse of nature, until the firmament itself should appear no more than a fitting page for his soul's history and fate.

We impute it, therefore, solely to the disease in his own eye and heart, that the minister, looking upward to the zenith, beheld there the appearance of an immense letter,—the letter A,—marked out in lines of dull red light. Not but the meteor may have shown itself at that point, burning duskily through a veil of cloud; but with no such shape as his guilty imagination gave it; or, at least, with so little definiteness, that another's guilt might have seen another symbol in it.

There was a singular circumstance that characterized Mr. Dimmesdale's psychological state, at this moment. All the time that he gazed upward to the zenith, he was, nevertheless, perfectly aware that little Pearl was pointing her finger towards old Roger Chillingworth, who stood at no great distance from the scaffold. The minister appeared to see him, with the same glance that discerned the miraculous letter. To his features, as to all other objects, the meteoric light imparted a new expression; or it might well be

---

[58] Canopy.

that the physician was not careful then, as at all other times, to hide the malevolence with which he looked upon his victim. Certainly, if the meteor kindled up the sky, and disclosed the earth, with an awfulness that admonished Hester Prynne and the clergyman of the day of judgment, then might Roger Chillingworth have passed with them for the arch-fiend, standing there, with a smile and scowl, to claim his own. So vivid was the expression, or so intense the minister's perception of it, that it seemed still to remain painted on the darkness, after the meteor had vanished, with an effect as if the street and all things else were at once annihilated.

"Who is that man, Hester?" gasped Mr. Dimmesdale, overcome with terror. "I shiver at him! Dost thou know the man? I hate him, Hester!"

She remembered her oath, and was silent.

"I tell thee, my soul shivers at him," muttered the minister again. "Who is he? Who is he? Canst thou do nothing for me? I have a nameless horror of the man."

"Minister," said little Pearl, "I can tell thee who he is!"

"Quickly, then, child!" said the minister, bending his ear close to her lips. "Quickly! — and as low as thou canst whisper."

Pearl mumbled something into his ear, that sounded, indeed, like human language, but was only such gibberish as children may be heard amusing themselves with, by the hour together. At all events, if it involved any secret information in regard to old Roger Chillingworth, it was in a tongue unknown to the erudite clergyman, and did but increase the bewilderment of his mind. The elfish child then laughed aloud.

"Dost thou mock me now?" said the minister.

"Thou wast not bold! — thou wast not true!" answered the child. "Thou wouldst not promise to take my hand, and mother's hand, to-morrow noontide!"

"Worthy Sir," said the physician, who had now advanced to the foot of the platform. "Pious Master Dimmesdale! can this be you? Well, well, indeed! We men of study, whose heads are in our books, have need to be straitly looked after! We dream in our waking moments, and walk in our sleep. Come, good Sir, and my dear friend, I pray you, let me lead you home!"

"How knewest thou that I was here?" asked the minister, fearfully.

"Verily, and in good faith," answered Roger Chillingworth, "I knew nothing of the matter. I had spent the better part of the night at the bedside of the worshipful Governor Winthrop, doing what my poor skill might to give him ease. He was going home to a better world, I, likewise, was on my way homeward, when this strange light shone out. Come with me, I beseech you, Reverend Sir; else you will be poorly able to do Sabbath duty tomorrow. Aha! see now, how they trouble the brain, — these books! — these books! You should study less, good Sir, and take a little pastime; or these night-whimseys will grow upon you!"

"I will go home with you," said Mr. Dimmesdale.

With a chill despondency, like one awaking, all nerveless, from an ugly dream, he yielded himself to the physician, and was led away.

The next day, however, being the Sabbath, he preached a discourse which was held to be the richest and most powerful, and the most replete with heavenly influences, that had ever proceeded from his lips. Souls, it is said, more souls than one, were brought to the truth by the efficacy of that sermon, and vowed within themselves to cherish a holy gratitude towards Mr. Dimmesdale throughout the long hereafter. But, as he came down the pulpit-steps, the gray-bearded sexton met him, holding up a black glove, which the minister recognized as his own.

"It was found," said the sexton, "this morning, on the scaffold, where evil-doers are set up to public shame. Satan dropped it there, I take it, intending a scurrilous jest against your reverence. But, indeed, he was blind and foolish, as he ever and always is. A pure hand needs no glove to cover it!"

"Thank you, my good friend," said the minister gravely, but startled at heart; for, so confused was his remembrance, that he had almost brought himself to look at the events of the past night as visionary. "Yes, it seems to be my glove indeed!"

"And, since Satan saw fit to steal it, your reverence must needs handle him without gloves, henceforward," remarked the old sexton, grimly smiling. "But did your reverence hear of the portent that was seen last night? A great red letter in the sky, — the letter A, — which we interpret to stand for Angel. For, as our good Governor Winthrop was made an angel this past night, it was doubtless held fit that there should be some notice thereof!"

"No," answered the minister. "I had not heard of it."

XIII
Another View of Hester

In her late singular interview with Mr. Dimmesdale, Hester Prynne was shocked at the condition to which she found the clergyman reduced. His nerve seemed absolutely destroyed. His moral force was abased into more than childish weakness. It grovelled helpless on the ground, even while his intellectual faculties retained their pristine strength, or had perhaps acquired a morbid energy, which disease only could have given them. With her knowledge of a train of circumstances hidden from all others, she could readily infer, that, besides the legitimate action of his own conscience, a terrible machinery had been brought to bear, and was still operating, on Mr. Dimmesdale's well-being and repose. Knowing what this poor, fallen man had once been, her whole soul was moved by the shuddering terror with which he had appealed to her,—the outcast woman,—for support against his instinctively discovered enemy. She decided, moreover, that he had a right to her utmost aid. Little accustomed, in her long seclusion from society, to measure her ideas of right and wrong by any standard external to herself, Hester saw—or seemed to see—that there lay a responsibility upon her, in reference to the clergyman, which she owed to no other, nor to the whole world besides. The links that united her to the rest of human kind—links of flowers, or silk, or gold, or whatever the material—had all been broken. Here was the iron link of mutual crime, which neither he nor she could break. Like all other ties, it brought along with it its obligations.

Hester Prynne did not now occupy precisely the same position in which we beheld her during the earlier periods of her ignominy. Years had come, and gone. Pearl was now seven years old. Her mother, with the scarlet letter on her breast, glittering in its fantastic embroidery, had long been a familiar object to the townspeople. As is apt to be the case when a person stands out in any prominence before the community, and, at the same time, interferes neither with public nor individual interests and convenience, a species of general regard had ultimately grown up in reference to Hester Prynne. It is to the credit of human nature, that, except where its selfishness is brought into play, it loves more readily than it hates. Hatred, by a gradual and quiet process, will even be transformed to love, unless the change be impeded by a continually new irritation of the original feeling of hostility. In this matter of Hester Prynne, there was neither irritation nor irksomeness. She never battled with the public, but submitted uncomplainingly to its worst usage; she made no claim upon it, in requital for what she suffered; she did not weigh upon its sympathies. Then, also, the blameless purity of her life, during all these years in which she had been set apart to infamy, was reckoned largely in her favor. With nothing now to lose, in the sight of mankind, and with no hope, and seemingly no wish, of gaining any thing, it could only be a genuine regard for virtue that had brought back the poor wanderer to its paths.

It was perceived, too, that, while Hester never put forward even the humblest title to share in the world's privileges,—farther than to breathe the common air, and earn daily bread for little Pearl and herself by the faithful labor of her hands,—she was quick to acknowledge her sisterhood with the race of man, whenever benefits were to be conferred. None so ready as she to give of her little substance to every demand of poverty; even though the bitter-hearted pauper threw back a gibe in requital of the food brought regularly to his door, or the garments wrought for him by the fingers that could have embroidered a monarch's robe. None so self-devoted as Hester, when pestilence stalked through the town. In all seasons of calamity, indeed, whether general or of individuals, the outcast of society at once found her place. She came, not as a guest, but as a rightful inmate, into the household that was darkened by trouble; as if its gloomy twilight were a medium in which she was entitled to hold intercourse with her fellow-creatures. There glimmered the embroidered letter, with comfort in its unearthly ray. Elsewhere the token of sin, it was the taper of the sick-chamber. It had even thrown its gleam, in the sufferer's hard extremity, across the verge of time. It had shown him where to set his foot, while the light of earth was fast becoming dim, and ere the light of futurity could reach him. In such emergencies, Hester's nature showed itself warm and rich; a well-spring of human tenderness, unfailing to every real demand, and inexhaustible by the largest. Her breast, with its badge of shame, was but the softer pillow for the head that needed one. She was self-ordained a Sister of Mercy; or, we may rather say, the world's heavy hand had so ordained her, when neither the world nor she looked forward to this result. The letter was the symbol of her calling. Such helpfulness was found in her,—so much power to do, and power to sympathize,—that many people refused to inerpret the scarlet A by its original signification. They said that it meant Able; so strong was Hester Prynne, with a woman's strength.

It was only the darkened house that could contain her. When sunshine came again, she was not there. Her shadow had faded across the threshold. The helpful inmate had departed, without one backward glance to gather up the meed of gratitude, if any were in the hearts of those whom she had served so zealously. Meeting them in the street, she never raised her head to receive their greeting. If they were resolute to accost her, she laid her finger on the scarlet letter, and passed on. This might be pride, but was so like humility, that it produced all the softening influence of the latter quality on the public mind. The public is despotic in its temper; it is capable of denying common justice, when too strenuously demanded as a right; but quite as frequently it awards more than justice, when the appeal is made, as despots love to have it made, entirely to its generosity. Interpreting Hester Prynne's deportment as an appeal of this nature, society was inclined to show its former victim a more benign countenance than she cared to be favored with, or, perchance, than she deserved.

The rulers, and the wise and learned men of the community, were longer in acknowledging the influence of Hester's good qualities than the people. The prejudices which they shared in common with the latter were fortified in themselves by an iron framework of reasoning, that made it a far tougher labor to expel them. Day by day, nevertheless, their sour and rigid wrinkles were relaxing into something which, in the due course of years, might grow to be an expression of almost benevolence. Thus it was with the men of rank, on whom their eminent position imposed the guardianship of the public morals. Individuals in private life, meanwhile, had quite forgiven Hester Prynne for her frailty; nay, more, they had begun to look upon the scarlet letter as the token, not of that one sin, for which she had borne so long and dreary a penance, but of her many good deeds since. "Do you see that woman with the embroidered badge?" they would say to strangers. "It is our Hester,—the town's own Hester,—who is so kind to the poor, so helpful to the sick, so comfortable to the afflicted!" Then, it is true, the propensity of human nature to tell the very worst of itself, when embodied in the person of another, would constrain them to whisper the black scandal of bygone years. It was none the less a fact, however, that, in the eyes of the very men who spoke thus, the scarlet letter had the effect of the cross on a nun's bosom. It imparted to the wearer a kind of sacredness, which enabled her to walk securely amid all peril. Had she fallen among thieves, it would have kept her safe. It was reported, and believed by many, that an Indian had drawn his arrow against the badge, and that the missile struck it, but fell harmless to the ground.

The effect of the symbol—or rather, of the position in respect to society that was indicated by it—on the mind of Hester Prynne herself, was powerful and peculiar. All the light and graceful foliage of her character had been withered up by this redhot brand, and had long ago fallen away, leaving a bare and harsh outline, which might have been repulsive, had she possessed friends or companions to be repelled by it. Even the attractiveness of her person had undergone a similar change. It might be partly owing to the studied austerity of her dress, and partly to the lack of demonstration in her manners. It was a sad transformation, too, that her rich and luxuriant hair had either been cut off, or was so completely hidden by a cap, that not a shining lock of it ever once gushed into the sunshine. It was due in part to all these causes, but still more to something else, that there seemed to be no longer any thing in Hester's face for Love to dwell upon; nothing in Hester's form, though majestic and statue-like, that Passion would ever dream of clasping in its embrace; nothing in Hester's bosom, to make it ever again the pillow of Affection. Some attribute had departed from her, the permanence of which had been essential to keep her a woman. Such is frequently the fate, and such the stern development, of the feminine character and person, when the woman has encountered, and lived through, an experience of peculiar severity. If she be all tenderness, she will die. If she survive, the tenderness will either be crushed out of her, or—and the outward semblance is the same—crushed so deeply into her heart that it can never show itself more. The latter is perhaps the truest theory. She who has once been woman, and ceased to be so, might at any moment become a woman again, if there were only the magic touch to effect the transfiguration. We shall see whether Hester Prynne were ever afterwards so touched, and so transfigured.

Much of the marble coldness of Hester's impression was to be attributed to the circumstance that her life had turned, in a great measure, from passion and feeling, to thought. Standing alone in the world,—alone, as to any dependence on society, and with little Pearl to be guided and protected,—alone, and hopeless of retrieving her position, even had she not scorned to consider it desirable,—she cast away the fragments of a broken chain. The world's law was no law for her mind. It was an age in which the human intellect, newly emancipated, had taken a more active and a wider range than for many centuries before. Men of the sword had overthrown nobles and kings. Men bolder than these had overthrown and rearranged—not actually, but within the sphere of theory, which was their most real abode—the whole system of ancient prejudice, wherewith was linked much of ancient principle. Hester Prynne imbibed this spirit. She assumed a freedom of speculation, then common enough on the other side of the Atlantic, but which our forefathers, had they known of it, would have held to be a deadlier crime than that stigmatized by the scarlet letter. In her lonesome cottage, by the sea-shore, thoughts visited her, such as dared to enter no other dwelling in New England; shadowy guests, that would have been as perilous as demons to their entertainer, could they have been seen so much as knocking at her door.

It is remarkable, that persons who speculate the most boldly often conform with the most perfect quietude to the external regulations of society. The thought suffices them, without investing itself in the flesh and blood of action. So it seemed to be with Hester. Yet, had little Pearl never come to her from the spiritual world, it might have been far otherwise. Then, she might have come down to us in history, hand in hand with Ann Hutchinson, as the foundress of a religious sect. She might, in one of her phases, have been a prophetess. She might, and not improbably would, have suffered death from the stern tribunals of the period, for attempting to undermine the foundations of the Puritan establishment. But, in the education of her child, the mother's enthusiasm of thought had something to wreak itself upon. Providence, in the person of this little girl, had assigned to Hester's charge the germ and blossom of womanhood, to be cherished and developed amid a host of difficulties. Every thing was against her. The world was hostile. The child's own nature had something wrong in it, which continually betokened that she had been born amiss, — the effluence of her mother's lawless passion, — and often impelled Hester to ask, in bitterness of heart, whether it were for ill or good that the poor little creature had been born at all.

Indeed, the same dark question often rose into her mind, with reference to the whole race of womanhood. Was existence worth accepting, even to the happiest among them? As concerned her own individual existence, she had long ago decided in the negative, and dismissed the point as settled. A tendency to speculation, though it may keep woman quiet, as it does man, yet makes her sad. She discerns, it may be, such a hopeless task before her. As a first step, the whole system of society is to be torn down, and built up anew. Then, the very nature of the opposite sex, or its long hereditary habit, which has become like nature, is to be essentially modified, before woman can be allowed to assume what seems a fair and suitable position. Finally, all other difficulties being obviated, woman cannot take advantage of these preliminary reforms, until she herself shall have undergone a still mightier change; in which, perhaps, the ethereal essence, wherein she has her truest life, will be found to have evaporated. A woman never overcomes these problems by any exercise of thought. They are not to be solved, or only in one way. If her heart chance to come uppermost, they vanish. Thus, Hester Prynne, whose heart had lost its regular and healthy throb, wandered without a clew in the dark labyrinth of mind; now turned aside by an insurmountable precipice; now starting back from a deep chasm. There was wild and ghastly scenery all around her, and a home and comfort nowhere. At times, a fearful doubt strove to possess her soul, whether it were not better to send Pearl at once to heaven, and go herself to such futurity as Eternal Justice should provide.

The scarlet letter had not done its office.

Now, however, her interview with the Reverend Mr. Dimmesdale, on the night of his vigil, had given her a new theme of reflection, and held up to her an object that appeared worthy of any exertion and sacrifice for its attainment. She had witnessed the intense misery beneath which the minister struggled, or, to speak more accurately, had ceased to struggle. She saw that he stood on the verge of lunacy, if he had not already stepped across it. It was impossible to doubt, that, whatever painful effacy there might be in the secret sting of remorse, a deadlier venom had been infused into it by the hand that proffered relief. A secret enemy had been continually by his side, under the semblance of a friend and helper, and had availed himself of the opportunities thus afforded for tampering with the delicate springs of Mr. Dimmesdale's nature. Hester could not but ask herself, whether there had not originally been a defect of truth, courage, and loyalty, on her own part, in allowing the minister to be thrown into a position where so much evil was to be foreboded, and nothing auspicious to be hoped. Her only justification lay in the fact, that she had been able to discern no method of rescuing him from a blacker ruin than had overwhelmed herself, except by acquiescing in Roger Chillingworth's scheme of disguise. Under that impulse, she had made her choice, and had chosen, as it now appeared, the more wretched alternative of the two. She determined to redeem her error, so far as it might yet be possible. Strengthened by years of hard and solemn trial, she felt herself no longer so inadequate to cope with Roger Chillingworth as on that night, abased by sin, and half maddened by the ignominy that was still new, when they had talked together in the prison-chamber. She had climbed her way, since then, to a higher point. The old man, on the other hand, had brought himself nearer to her level, or perhaps below it, by the revenge which he had stooped for.

In fine, Hester Prynne resolved to meet her former husband, and do what might be in her power for the rescue of the victim on whom he had so evidently set his gripe. The occasion was not long to seek. One afternoon, walking with Pearl in a retired part of the peninsula, she beheld the old physician, with a basket on one arm, and a staff in the other hand, stooping along the ground, in quest of roots and herbs to concoct his medicines withal.

XIV

Hester and the Physician

Hester bade little Pearl run down to the margin of the water, and play with the shells and tangled seaweed, until she should have talked awhile with yonder gatherer of herbs. So the child flew away like a bird, and, making bare her small white feet, went pattering along the moist margin of the sea. Here and there, she came to a full stop, and peeped curiously into a pool, left by the retiring tide as a mirror for Pearl to see her face in. Forth peeped at her, out of the pool, with dark, glistening curls around her head and an elf-smile in her eyes, the image of a little maid, whom Pearl, having no other playmate, invited to take her hand and run a race with her. But the visionary little maid, on her part, beckoned likewise, as if to say, — "This is a better place! Come thou into the pool!" And Pearl, stepping in, mid-leg deep, beheld her own white feet at the bottom; while, out of a still lower depth, came the gleam of a kind of fragmentary smile, floating to and fro in the agitated water.

Meanwhile, her mother had accosted the physician.

"I would speak a word with you," said she, — "a word that concerns us much."

"Aha! And is it Mistress Hester that has a word for old Roger Chilling-worth?" answered he, raising himself from his stooping posture. "With all my heart! Why, Mistress, I hear good things of you on all hands! No longer ago than yester-eve, a magistrate, a wise and godly man, was discoursing of your affairs, Mistress Hester, and whispered me that there had been question concerning you in the council. It was debated whether or no, with safety to the common weal, yonder scarlet letter might be taken off your bosom. On my life, Hester, I made my entreaty to the worshipful magistrate that it might be done forthwith!"

"It lies not in the pleasure of the magistrates to take off this badge," calmly replied Hester. "Were I worthy to be quit of it, it would fall away of its own nature, or be transformed into something that should speak a different purport."

"Nay, then, wear it, if it suit you better," rejoined he. "A woman must needs follow her own fancy, touching the adornment of her person. The letter is gayly embroidered, and shows right bravely on your bosom!"

All this while, Hester had been looking steadily at the old man, and was shocked, as well as wonder-smitten, to discern what a change had been wrought upon him within the past seven years. It was not so much that he had grown older; for though the traces of advancing life were visible, he bore his age well, and seemed to retain a wiry vigor and alertness. But the former aspect of an intellectual and studious man, calm and quiet, which was what she best remembered in him, had altogether vanished, and been succeeded by an eager, searching, almost fierce, yet carefully guarded look. It seemed to be his wish and purpose to mask this expression with a smile; but the latter played him false, and flickered over his visage so derisively, that the spectator could see his blackness all the better for it. Ever and anon, too, there came a glare of red light out of his eyes; as if the old man's soul were on fire, and kept on smouldering duskily within his breast, until, by some casual puff of passion, it was blown into a momentary flame. This he repressed as speedily as possible, and strove to look as if nothing of the kind had happened.

In a word, old Roger Chillingworth was a striking evidence of man's faculty of transforming himself into a devil, if he will only, for a reasonable space of time, undertake a devil's office. This unhappy person had effected such a transformation by devoting himself, for seven years, to the constant analysis of a heart full of torture, and deriving his enjoyment thence, and adding fuel to those fiery tortures which he analyzed and gloated over.

The scarlet letter burned on Hester Prynne's bosom. Here was another ruin, the responsibility of which came partly home to her.

"What see you in my face," asked the physician, "that you look at it so earnestly?"

"Something that would make me weep, if there were any tears bitter enough for it," answered she. "But let it pass! It is of yonder miserable man that I would speak."

"And what of him?" cried Roger Chillingworth eagerly, as if he loved the topic, and were glad of an opportunity to discuss it with the only person of whom he could make a confidant. "Not to hide the truth, Mistress Hester, my thoughts happen just now to be busy with the gentleman. So speak freely; and I will make answer."

"When we last spake together," said Hester, "now seven years ago, it was your pleasure to extort a promise of secrecy, as touching the former relation betwixt yourself and me. As the life and good fame of yonder man were in your hands, there seemed no choice to me, save to be silent, in accordance with your behest. Yet it was not without heavy misgivings that I thus bound myself; for, having cast off all duty towards other human beings, there remained a duty towards him; and something whispered me that I was betraying it, in pledging myself to keep your counsel. Since that day, no man is so near to him as you. You tread behind his every footstep. You are beside him, sleeping and waking. You search his thoughts. You burrow and rankle in his heart! Your clutch is on his life, and you cause him to die daily a living death; and still he knows you not. In permitting this, I have surely acted a false part by the only man to whom the power was left me to be true!"

"What choice had you?" asked Roger Chillingworth. "My finger, pointed at this man, would have hurled him from his pulpit into a dungeon, — thence, peradventure, to the gallows!"

"It had been better so!" said Hester Prynne.

"What evil have I done the man?" asked Roger Chillingworth again. "I tell thee, Hester Prynne, the richest fee that ever physician earned from monarch could not have bought such care as I have wasted on this miserable priest! But for my aid, his life would have burned away in torments, within the first two years after the perpetration of his crime and thine. For, Hester, his spirit lacked the strength that could have borne up, as thine has, beneath a burden like thy scarlet letter. O, I could reveal a goodly secret! But enough! What art can do, I have exhausted on him. That he now breathes, and creeps about on earth, is owing all to me!"

"Better he had died at once!" said Hester Prynne.

"Yea, woman, thou sayest truly!" cried old Roger Chillingworth, letting the lurid fire of his heart blaze out before her eyes. "Better had he died at once! Never did mortal suffer what this man has suffered. And all, all, in the sight of his worst enemy! He has been conscious of me. He has felt an influence dwelling always upon him like a curse. He knew, by some spiritual sense,—for the Creator never made another being so sensitive as this,—he knew that no friendly hand was pulling at his heart-strings, and that an eye was looking curiously into him, which sought only evil, and found it. But he knew not that the eye and hand were mine! With the superstition common to his brotherhood, he fancied himself given over to a fiend, to be tortured with frightful dreams, and desperate thoughts, the sting of remorse, and despair of pardon; as a foretaste of what awaits him beyond the grave. But it was the constant shadow of my presence!—the closest propinquity of the man whom he had most vilely wronged!—and who had grown to exist only by this perpetual poison of the direst revenge! Yea, indeed!—he did not err!—there was a fiend at his elbow! A mortal man, with once a human heart, has become a fiend for his especial torment!" Reasons 4) Dismobilles Jemer.

The unfortunate physician, while uttering these words, lifted his hands with a look of horror, as if he had beheld some frightful shape, which he could not recognize, usurping the place of his own image in a glass. It was one of those moments—which sometimes occur only at the interval of years—when a man's moral aspect is faithfully revealed to his mind's eye. Not improbably, he had never before viewed himself as he did now.

"Hast thou not tortured him enough?" said Hester, noticing the old man's look. "Has he not paid thee all?"

"No!—no!—He has but increased the debt!" answered the physician; and, as he proceeded, his manner lost its fiercer characteristics, and subsided into gloom. "Dost thou remember me, Hester, as I was nine years agone? Even then, I was in the autumn of my days, nor was it the early autumn. But all my life had been made up of earnest, studious, thoughtful, quiet years, bestowed faithfully for the increase of mine own knowledge, and faithfully, too though this latter object was but casual to the other,—faithfully for the advancement of human welfare. No life had been more peaceful and innocent than mine; few lives so rich with benefits conferred. Dost thou remember me? Was I not, though you might deem me cold, nevertheless a man thoughtful for others, craving little for himself,—kind, true, just, and of constant, if not warm affections? Was I not all this?"

"All this, and more," said Hester.

"And what am I now?" demanded he, looking into her face, and permitting the whole evil within him to be written on his features. "I have already told thee what I am! A fiend! Who made me so?"

"It was myself!" cried Hester, shuddering. "It was I, not less than he. Why hast thou not avenged thyself on me?"

"I have left thee to the scarlet letter," replied Roger Chillingworth. "If that have not avenged me, I can do no more!"

He laid his finger on it, with a smile.

"It has avenged thee!" answered Hester Prynne.

"I judged no less," said the physician. "And now, what wouldst thou with me touching this man?"

"I must reveal the secret," answered Hester, firmly. "He must discern thee in thy true character. What may be the result, I know not. But this long debt of confidence, due from me to him, whose bane and ruin I have been, shall at length be paid. So far as concerns the overthrow of preservation of his fair fame and his earthly state, and perchance his life, he is in thy hands. Nor do I,—whom the scarlet letter has disciplined to truth, though it be the truth of red-hot iron, entering into the soul,—nor do I perceive such advantage in his living any longer a life of ghastly emptiness, that I shall stoop to implore thy mercy. Do with him as thou wilt! There is no good for him,—no good for me,—no good for thee! There is no good for little Pearl! There is no path to guide us out of this dismal maze!"

"Woman, I could wellnigh pity thee!" said Roger Chillingworth, unable to restrain a thrill of admiration too; for there was a quality almost majestic in the despair which she expressed. "Thou hadst great elements. Peradventure, hadst thou met earlier with a better love than mine, this evil had not been. I pity thee, for the good that has been wasted in thy nature!"

"And I thee," answered Hester Prynne, "for the hatred that has transformed a wise and just man to a fiend! Wilt thou yet purge it out of thee, and be once more human? If not for his sake, then doubly for thine own! Forgive, and leave his further retribution to the Power that claims it! I said, but now, that there could be no good event for him, or thee, or me, who are here wandering together in this gloomy maze of evil, and stumbling, at every step, over the guilt wherewith we have strewn our path. It is not so! There might be good for thee, and thee alone, since thou hast been deeply wronged, and hast it at thy will to pardon. Wilt thou give up that only privilege? Wilt thou reject that priceless benefit?"

"Peace, Hester, peace!" replied the old man, with gloomy sternness. "It is not granted me to pardon. I have no such power as thou tellest me of. My old faith, long forgotten, comes back to me, and explains all that we do, and all we suffer. By thy first step awry, thou didst plant the germ of evil; but, since that moment, it has all been a dark necessity. Ye that have wronged me are not sinful, save in a kind of typical illusion; neither am I fiend-like, who have snatched a fiend's office from his hands. It is our fate. Let the black flower blossom as it may! Now go thy ways, and deal as thou wilt with yonder man."

He waved his hand, and betook himself again to his employment of gathering herbs.

XV
Hester and Pearl

So Roger Chillingworth—a deformed old figure, with a face that haunted men's memories longer than they liked—took leave of Hester Prynne, and went stooping away along the earth. He gathered here and there an herb, or grubbed up a root, and put it into the basket on his arm. His gray beard almost touched the ground, as he crept onward. Hester gazed after him a little while, looking with half-fantastic curiosity to see whether the tender grass of early spring would not be blighted beneath him, and show the wavering track of his footsteps, sere and brown, across its cheerful verdure. She wondered what sort of herbs they were, which the old man was so sedulous to gather. Would not the earth, quickened to an evil purpose by the sympathy of his eye, greet him with poisonous shrubs, of species hitherto unknown, that would start up under his fingers? Or might it suffice him, that every wholesome growth should be converted into something deleterious and malignant at his touch? Did the sun, which shone so brightly everywhere else, really fall upon him? Or was there, as it rather seemed, a circle of ominous shadow moving along with his deformity, whichever way he turned himself? And whither was he now going? Would he not suddenly sink into the earth, leaving a barren and blasted spot, where, in due course of time, would be seen deadly nightshade, dogwood, henbane,[59] and whatever else of vegetable wickedness the climate could produce, all flourishing with hideous luxuriance? Or would he spread bat's wings and flee away, looking so much the uglier, the higher he rose towards heaven?

"Be it sin or no," said Hester Prynne bitterly, as she still gazed after him, "I hate the man!"

She upbraided herself for the sentiment, but could not overcome or lessen it. Attempting to do so, she thought of those long-past days, in a distant land, when he used to emerge at eventide from the seclusion of his study, and sit down in the fire-light of their home, and in the light of her nuptial smile. He needed to bask himself in that smile, he said, in order that the chill of so many lonely hours among his books might be taken off the scholar's heart. Such scenes had once appeared not otherwise than happy, but now, as viewed through the dismal medium of her subsequent life, they classed themselves among her ugliest remembrances. She marvelled how such scenes could have been! She marvelled how she could ever have been

---

[59] The poisonous plants deadly nightshade (belladonna) and hellbane were associated with witchcraft; the dogwood was considered magical because of its medicinal bark.

wrought upon to marry him! She deemed it her crime most to be repented of, that she had ever endured, and reciprocated, the lukewarm grasp of his hand, and had suffered the smile of her lips and eyes to mingle and melt into his own. And it seemed a fouler offence committed by Roger Chillingworth, than any which had since been done him, that, in the time when her heart knew no better, he had persuaded her to fancy herself happy by his side.

"Yes, I hate him!" repeated Hester, more bitterly than before. "He betrayed me! He has done me worse wrong than I did him!"

Let men tremble to win the hand of woman, unless they win along with it the utmost passion of her heart! Else it may be their miserable fortune, as it was Roger Chillingworth's, when some mightier touch than their own may have awakened all her sensibilities, to be reproached ever for the calm content, the marble image of happiness, which they will have imposed upon her as the warm reality. But Hester ought long ago to have done with this injustice. What did it betoken? Had seven long years, under the torture of the scarlet letter, inflicted so much of misery, and wrought out no repentance?

The emotions of that brief space, while she stood gazing after the crooked figure of old Roger Chillingworth, threw a dark light on Hester's state of mind, revealing much that she might not otherwise have acknowledged to herself.

He being gone, she summoned back her child.

"Pearl! Little Pearl! Where are you?"

Pearl, whose activity of spirit never flagged, had been at no loss for amusement while her mother talked with the old gatherer of herbs. At first, as already told, she had flirted fancifully with her own image in a pool of water, beckoning the phantom forth, and — as it declined to venture — seeking a passage for herself into its sphere of impalpable earth and unattainable sky. Soon finding, however, that either she or the image was unreal, she turned elsewhere for better pastime. She made little boats out of birch-bark, and freighted them with snail-shells, and sent out more ventures on the mighty deep than any merchant in New England; but the larger part of them foundered near the shore. She seized a live horseshoe by the tail, and made prize of several five-fingers[60] and laid out a jelly-fish to melt in the warm sun. Then she took up the white foam, that streaked the line of the advancing tide, and threw it upon the breeze, scampering after it with winged footsteps, to catch the great snow-flakes ere they fell. Perceiving a flock of beach-birds, that fed and fluttered along the shore, the naughty child picked up her apron full of pebbles, and creeping from rock to rock after these small sea-fowl, displayed remarkable dexterity in pelting them.

---

[60] A horseshoe crab and starfish.

One little gray bird, with a white breast, Pearl was almost sure, had been hit by a pebble, and fluttered away with a broken wing. But then the elf-child sighed, and gave up her sport; because it grieved her to have done harm to a little being that was as wild as the seabreeze, or as wild as Pearl herself.

Her final employment was to gather sea-weed, of various kinds, and make herself a scarf, or mantle, and a headdress, and thus assume the aspect of a little mermaid. She inherited her mother's gift for devising drapery and costume. As the last touch to her mermaid's garb, Pearl took some eel-grass, and imitated, as best she could, on her own bosom, the decoration with which she was so familiar on her mother's. A letter,—the letter A,—but freshly green, instead of scarlet! The child bent her chin upon her breast, and contemplated this device with strange interest; even as if the one only thing for which she had been sent into the world was to make out its hidden import.

"I wonder if mother will ask me what it means!" thought Pearl.

Just then, she heard her mother's voice, and, flitting along as lightly as one of the little sea-birds, appeared before Hester Prynne, dancing, laughing, and pointing her finger to the ornament upon her bosom.

"My little Pearl," said Hester, after a moment's silence, "the green letter, and on thy childish bosom, has no purport. But dost thou know, my child, what this letter means which thy mother is doomed to wear?"

"Yes, mother," said the child. "It is the great letter A. Thou hast taught it me in the horn-book."[61]

Hester looked steadily into her little face; but, though there was that singular expression which she had so often remarked in her black eyes, she could not satisfy herself whether Pearl really attached any meaning to the symbol. She felt a morbid desire to ascertain the point.

"Dost thou know, child, wherefore thy mother wears this letter?"

"Truly do I!" answered Pearl, looking brightly into her mother's face. "It is for the same reason that the minister keeps his hand over his heart!"

"And what reason is that?" asked Hester, half smiling at the absurd incongruity of the child's observation; but, on second thoughts, turning pale. "What has the letter to do with any heart, save mine?"

"Nay, mother, I have told all I know," said Pearl, more seriously than she was wont to speak. "Ask yonder old man whom thou hast been talking with! It may be he can tell. But in good earnest now, mother dear, what does this scarlet letter mean?—and why dost thou wear it on thy bosom?—and why does the minister keep his hand over his heart?"

---

[61] An alphabet for children printed on a sheet of parchment, mounted on a paddle and covered by a transparent sheet of horn.

She took her mother's hand in both her own, and gazed into her eyes with an earnestness that was seldom seen in her wild and capricious character. The thought occurred to Hester, that the child might really be seeking to approach her with childlike confidence, and doing what she could, and as intelligently as she knew how, to establish a meeting-point of sympathy. It showed Pearl in an unwonted aspect. Heretofore, the mother, while loving her child with the intensity of a sole affection, had schooled herself to hope for little other return than the waywardness of an April breeze; which spends its time in airy sport, and has its gusts of inexplicable passion, and is petulant in its best of moods, and chills oftener than caresses you, when you take it to your bosom; in requital of which misdemeanours, it will sometimes, of its own vague purpose, kiss your cheek with a kind of doubtful tenderness, and play gently with your hair, and then begone about its other idle business, leaving a dreamy pleasure at your heart. And this, moreover, was a mother's estimate of the child's disposition. Any other observer might have seen few but unamiable traits, and have given them a far darker coloring. But now the idea came strongly into Hester's mind, that Pearl, with her remarkable precocity and acuteness, might already have approached the age when she could be made a friend, and intrusted with as much of her mother's sorrows as could be imparted, without irreverence either to the parent or the child. In the little chaos of Pearl's character, there might be seen emerging—and could have been, from the very first—the stedfast principles of an unflinching courage,—an uncontrollable will,—a sturdy pride, which might be disciplined into self-respect,—and a bitter scorn of many things which, when examined, might be found to have the taint of falsehood in them. She possessed affections, too, though hitherto acrid and disagreeable, as are the richest flavors of unripe fruit. With all these sterling attributes, thought Hester, the evil which she inherited from her mother must be great indeed, if a noble woman do not grow out of this elfish child.

Pearl's inevitable tendency to hover about the enigma of the scarlet letter seemed an innate quality of her being. From the earliest epoch of her conscious life, she had entered upon this as her appointed mission. Hester had often fancied that Providence had a design of justice and retribution, in endowing the child with this marked propensity; but never, until now, had she bethought herself to ask whether, linked with that design, there might not likewise be a purpose of mercy and beneficence. If little Pearl were entertained with faith and trust, as a spirit-messenger no less than an earthly child, might it not be her errand to soothe away the sorrow that lay cold in her mother's heart and converted it into a tomb?—and to help her to overcome the passion, once so wild, and even yet neither dead nor asleep, but only imprisoned within the same tomb-like heart?

Such were some of the thoughts that now stirred in Hester's mind, with as much vivacity of impression as if they had actually been whispered into her ear. And there was little Pearl, all this while, holding her mother's hand in both her own, and turning her face upward, while she put these searching questions, once, and again, and still a third time.

"What does the letter mean, mother? —and why dost thou wear it? — and why does the minister keep his hand over his heart?"

"What shall I say?" thought Hester to herself. —"No! If this be the price of the child's sympathy, I cannot pay it."

Then she spoke aloud.

"Silly Pearl," said she, "what questions are these? There are many things in this world that a child must not ask about. What know I of the minister's heart? And as for the scarlet letter, I wear it for the sake of its gold thread!"

In all the seven bygone years, Hester Prynne had never before been false to the symbol on her bosom. It may be that it was the talisman of a stern and severe, but yet a guardian spirit, who now forsook her; as recognizing this in spite of his strict watch over her heart, some new evil had crept into it, or some old one had never been expelled. As for little Pearl, the earnestness soon passed out of her face.

But the child did not see fit to let the matter drop. Two or three times, as her mother and she went homeward, and often at supper-time, and while Hester was putting her to bed, and once after she seemed to be fairly asleep, Pearl looked up, with mischief gleaming in her black eyes.

"Mother," said she, "what does the scarlet letter mean?"

And the next morning, the first indication the child gave of being awake was by popping up her head from the pillow, and making that other inquiry, which she had so unaccountably connected with her investigations about the scarlet letter: —

"Mother! —Mother! —Why does the minister keep his hand over his heart?"

"Hold thy tongue, naughty child!" answered her mother, with an asperity that she had never permitted to herself before. "Do not tease me; else I shall shut thee into the dark closet!"

XVI

A Forest Walk

Hester Prynne remained constant in her resolve to make known to Mr. Dimmesdale, at whatever risk of present pain or ulterior consequences, the true character of the man who had crept into his intimacy. For several days, however, she vainly sought an opportunity of addressing him in some of the meditative walks which she knew him to be in the habit of taking, along the shores of the peninsula, or on the wooded hills of the neighbouring country. There would have been no scandal, indeed, nor peril to the holy whiteness of the clergyman's good fame, had she visited him in his own study; where many a penitent, ere now, had confessed sins of perhaps as deep a dye as the one betokened by the scarlet letter. But, partly that she dreaded the secret or undisguised interference of old Roger Chillingworth, and partly that her conscious heart imputed suspicion where none could have been felt, and partly that both the minister and she would need the whole wide world to breathe in, while they talked together,—for all these reasons, Hester never thought of meeting him in any narrower privacy than beneath the open sky.

At last, while attending in a sick-chamber, whither the Reverend Mr. Dimmesdale had been summoned to make a prayer, she learnt that he had gone, the day before, to visit the Apostle Eliot,[62] among his Indian converts. He would probably return, by a certain hour, in the afternoon of the morrow. Betimes, therefore, the next day, Hester took little Pearl,— who was necessarily the companion of all her mother's expeditions, however inconvenient her presence,—and set forth.

The road, after the two wayfarers had crossed from the peninsula to the mainland, was no other than a footpath. It straggled onward into the mystery of the primeval forest. This hemmed it in so narrowly, and stood so black and dense on either side, and disclosed such imperfect glimpses of the sky above, that, to Hester's mind, it imaged not amiss the moral wilderness in which she had so long been wandering. The day was chill and sombre. Overhead was a gray expanse of cloud, slightly stirred, however, by a breeze; so that a gleam of flickering sunshine might now and then be seen at its solitary play along the path. This flitting cheerfulness was always at the farther extremity of some long vista through the forest. The sportive sunlight—feebly sportive, at best, in the predominant pensiveness of the day and scene—withdrew itself as they came nigh, and left the spots where it had danced the drearier, because they had hoped to find them bright.

"Mother," said little Pearl, "the sunshine does not love you. It runs away and hides itself, because it is afraid of something on your bosom. Now, see! There it is, playing, a good way off. Stand you here, and let me run and catch it. I am but a child. It will not flee from me; for I wear nothing on my bosom yet!"

---

[62] John Eliot (1604–90), the minister who emigrated to Massachusetts in 1631, preached to the Indians in their own language and translated the Bible for them.

"Nor ever will, my child, I hope," said Hester.

"And why not, mother?" asked Pearl, stopping short, just at the beginning of her race. "Will not it come of its own accord, when I am a woman grown?"

"Run away, child," answered her mother, "and catch the sunshine! It will soon be gone."

Pearl set forth, at a great pace, and, as Hester smiled to perceive, did actually catch the sunshine, and stood laughing in the midst of it, all brightened by its splendor, and scintillating with the vivacity excited by rapid motion. The light lingered about the lonely child, as if glad of such a playmate, until her mother had drawn almost nigh enough to step into the magic circle too.

"It will go now!" said Pearl, shaking her head.

"See!" answered Hester, smiling. "Now I can stretch out my hand, and grasp some of it."

As she attempted to do so, the sunshine vanished; or, to judge from the bright expression that was dancing on Pearl's features, her mother could have fancied that the child had absorbed it into herself, and would give it forth again, with a gleam about her path, as they should plunge into some gloomier shade. There was no other attribute that so much impressed her with a sense of new and untransmitted vigor in Pearl's nature, as this never-failing vivacity of spirits; she had not the disease of sadness, which almost all children, in these latter days, inherit, with the scrofula,[63] from the troubles of their ancestors. Perhaps this too was a disease, and but the reflex of the wild energy with which Hester had fought against her sorrows, before Pearl's birth. It was certainly a doubtful charm, imparting a hard, metallic lustre to the child's character. She wanted—what some people want throughout life—a grief that should deeply touch her, and thus humanize and make her capable of sympathy. But there was time enough yet for little Pearl!

"Come, my child!" said Hester, looking about her, from the spot where Pearl had stood still in the sunshine. "We will sit down a little way within the wood, and rest ouselves."

"I am not aweary, mother," replied the little girl. "But you may sit down, if you will tell me a story meanwhile."

"A story, child!" said Hester. "And about what?"

"O, a story about the Black Man!" answered Pearl, taking hold of her mother's gown, and looking up, half earnestly, half mischievously, into her face. "How he haunts this forest, and carries a book with him,—a big,

---

[63] Pretubercular disease of the lymph glands.

heavy book, with iron clasps; and how this ugly Black Man offers his book and an iron pen to every body that meets him here among the trees; and they are to write their names with their own blood. And then he sets his mark on their bosoms! Didst thou ever meet the Black Man, mother?"

"And who told you this story, Pearl?" asked her mother, recognizing a common superstition of the period.

"It was the old dame in the chimney-corner, at the house where you watched last night," said the child. "But she fancied me asleep while she was talking of it. She said that a thousand and a thousand people had met him here, and had written in his book, and have his mark on them. And that ugly-tempered lady, old Mistress Hibbins, was one. And, mother, the old dame said that this scarlet letter was the Black Man's mark on thee, and that it glows like a red flame when thou meetest him at midnight, here in the dark wood. Is it true, mother? And dost thou go to meet him in the night-time?"

"Didst thou ever awake, and find thy mother gone?" asked Hester.

"Not that I remember," said the child. "If thou fearest to leave me in our cottage, thou mightest take me along with thee. I would very gladly go! But, mother, tell me now! Is there such a Black Man? And didst thou ever meet him? And is this his mark?"

"Wilt thou let me be at peace, if I once tell thee?" asked her mother.

"Yes, if thou tellest me all," answered Pearl.

"Once in my life I met the Black Man!" said her mother. "This scarlet letter is his mark!"

Thus conversing, they entered sufficiently deep into the wood to secure themselves from the observation of any casual passenger along the forest-track. Here they sat down on a luxuriant heap of moss; which, at some epoch of the preceding century, had been a gigantic pine, with its roots and trunk in the darksome shade, and its head aloft in the upper atmosphere. It was a little dell where they had seated themselves, with a leaf-strewn bank rising gently on either side, and a brook flowing through the midst, over a bed of fallen and drowned leaves. The trees impending over it had flung down great branches, from time to time, which choked up the current, and compelled it to form eddies and black depths at some points; while, in its swifter and livelier passages, there appeared a channel-way of pebbles, and brown, sparkling sand. Letting the eyes follow along the course of the stream, they could catch the reflected light from its water, at some short distance within the forest, but soon lost all traces of it amid the bewilderment of tree-trunks and underbrush, and here and there a huge rock, covered over with gray lichens. All these giant trees and boulders of granite seemed intent on making a mystery of the course of this small brook; fearing, perhaps, that, with its never-ceasing loquacity, it should whisper tales out of the heart of the old forest whence it flowed, or mirror its revelations on the smooth surface of a pool. Continually, indeed, as it stole onward, the streamlet kept up a babble, kind, quiet, soothing, but melancholy, like the voice of a young child that was spending its infancy without playfulness, and knew not how to be merry among sad acquaintance and events of sombre hue.

"O brook! O foolish and tiresome little brook!" cried Pearl, after listening awhile to its talk. "Why art thou so sad? Pluck up a spirit, and do not be all the time sighing and murmuring!"

But the brook, in the course of its little lifetime among the forest-trees, had gone through so solemn an experience that it could not help talking about it, and seemed to have nothing else to say. Pearl resembled the brook, inasmuch as the current of her life gushed from a well-spring as mysterious, and had flowed through scenes shadowed as heavily with gloom. But, unlike the little stream, she danced and sparkled, and prattled airily along her course.

"What does this sad little brook say, mother?" inquired she.

"If thou hadst a sorrow of thine own, the brook might tell thee of it," answered her mother, "even as it is telling me of mine! But now, Pearl, I hear a footstep along the path, and the noise of one putting aside the branches. I would have thee betake thyself to play, and leave me to speak with him that comes yonder."

"Is it the Black Man?" asked Pearl.

"Wilt thou go and play, child?" repeated her mother. "But do not stray far into the wood. And take heed that thou come at my first call."

"Yes, mother," answered Pearl. "But, if it be the Black Man, wilt thou not let me stay a moment, and look at him, with his big book under his arm?"

"Go silly child!" said her mother, impatiently. "It is no Black Man! Thou canst see him now through the trees. It is the minister!"

"And so it is!" said the child. "And, mother, he has his hand over his heart! Is it because, when the minister wrote his name in the book, the Black Man set his mark in that place? But why does he not wear it outside his bosom, as thou dost, mother?"

"Go now, child, and thou shalt tease me as thou wilt another time!" cried Hester Prynne. "But do not stray far. Keep where thou canst hear the babble of the brook."

The child went singing away, following up the current of the brook, and striving to mingle a more lightsome cadence with its melancholy voice. But the little stream would not be comforted, and still kept telling its unintelligible secret of some very mournful mystery that had happened—or making a prophetic lamentation about something that was yet to happen—

within the verge of the dismal forest. So Pearl, who had enough of shadow in her own little life, chose to break off all acquaintance with this repining brook. She set herself, therefore, to gathering violets and wood-anemones, and some scarlet columbines that she found growing in the crevices of a high rock.

When her elf-child had departed, Hester Prynne made a step or two towards the track that led through the forest, but still remained under the deep shadow of the trees. She beheld the minister advancing along the path, entirely alone, and leaning on a staff which he had cut by the wayside. He looked haggard and feeble, and betrayed a nerveless despondency in his air, which had never so remarkably characterized him in his walks about the settlement, nor in any other situation where he deemed himself liable to notice. Here it was wofully visible, in this intense seclusion of the forest, which of itself would have been a heavy trial to the spirits. There was a listlessness in his gait; as if he saw no reason for taking one step farther, nor felt any desire to do so, but would have been glad, could he be glad of any thing, to fling himself down at the root of the nearest tree, and lie there passive for evermore. The leaves might bestrew him, and the soil gradually accumulate and form a little hillock over his frame, no matter whether there were life in it or no. Death was too definite an object to be wished for, or avoided.

To Hester's eye, the Reverend Mr. Dimmesdale exhibited no symptom of positive and vivacious suffering, except that, as little Pearl had remarked, he kept his hand over his heart.

XVII
The Pastor and His Parishioner

Slowly as the minister walked, he had almost gone by, before Hester Prynne could gather voice enough to attract his observation. At length, she succeeded.

"Arthur Dimmesdale!" she said, faintly at first; then louder, but hoarsely. "Arthur Dimmesdale!"

"Who speaks?" answered the minister.

Gathering himself quickly up, he stood more erect, like a man taken by surprise in a mood to which he was reluctant to have witnesses. Throwing his eyes anxiously in the direction of the voice, he indistinctly beheld a form under the trees, clad in garments so sombre, and so little relieved from the gray twilight into which the clouded sky and the heavy foliage had darkened the noontide, that he knew not whether it were a woman or a shadow. It may be, that his pathway through life was haunted thus, by a spectre that had stolen out from among his thoughts.

He made a step nigher, and discovered the scarlet letter.

"Hester! Hester Prynne!" said he. "Is it thou? Art thou in life?"

"Even so!" she answered. "In such life as has been mine these seven years past! And thou, Arthur Dimmesdale, dost thou yet live?"

It was no wonder that they thus questioned one another's actual and bodily existence, and even doubted of their own. So strangely did they meet, in the dim wood, that it was like the first encounter, in the world beyond the grave, of two spirits who had been intimately connected in their former life, but now stood coldly shuddering, in mutual dread; as not yet familiar with their state, nor wonted to the companionship of disembodied beings. Each a ghost, and awe-stricken at the other ghost. They were awe-stricken likewise at themselves; because the crisis flung back to them their consciousness, and revealed to each heart its history and experience, as life never does, except at such breathless epochs. The soul beheld its features in the mirror of the passing moment. It was with fear, and tremulously, and, as it were, by a slow, reluctant necessity, that Arthur Dimmesdale put forth his hand, chill as death, and touched the chill hand of Hester Prynne. The grasp, cold as it was, took away what was dreariest in the interview. They now felt themselves, at least, inhabitants of the same sphere.

Without a word more spoken,—neither he nor she assuming the guidance, but with an unexpressed consent,—they glided back into the shadow of the woods, whence Hester had emerged, and sat down on the heap of moss where she and Pearl had before been sitting. When they found voice to speak, it was, at first, only to utter remarks and inquiries such as any two acquaintance might have made, about the gloomy sky, the theatening storm, and, next, the health of each. Thus they went onward, not boldly, but step by step, into the themes that were brooding deepest in their hearts. So long estranged by fate and circumstances, they needed something slight and casual to run before, and throw open the doors of intercourse, so that their real thoughts might be led across the threshold.

After a while, the minister fixed his eyes on Hester Prynne's.

"Hester," said he, "hast thou found peace?"

She smiled drearily, looking down upon her bosom.

"Hast thou?" she asked.

"None!—nothing but despair!" he answered. "What else could I look for, being what I am, and leading such a life as mine? Were I an atheist,—a man devoid of conscience,—a wretch with coarse and brutal instincts,—I might have found peace, long ere now. Nay, I never should have lost it! But, as matters stand with my soul, whatever of good capacity there originally was in me, all of God's gifts that were the choicest have become the ministers of spiritual torment. Hester, I am most miserable!"

"The people reverence thee," said Hester. "And surely thou workest good among them! Doth this bring thee no comfort?"

"More misery, Hester!—only the more misery!" answered the clergyman, with a bitter smile. "As concerns the good which I may appear to do, I have no faith in it. It must needs be a delusion. What can a ruined soul, like mine, effect towards the redemption of other souls?—or a polluted soul, towards their purification? And as for the people's reverence, would that it were turned to scorn and hatred! Canst thou deem it, Hester, a consolation, that I must stand up in my pulpit, and meet so many eyes turned upward to my face, as if the light of heaven were beaming from it!—must see my flock hungry for the truth, and listening to my words as if a tongue of Pentecost were speaking!—and then look inward, and discern the black reality of what they idolize? I have laughed, in bitterness and agony of heart, at the contrast between what I seem and what I am! And Satan laughs at it!"

"You wrong yourself in this," said Hester, gently. "You have deeply and sorely repented. Your sin is left behind you, in the days long past. Your present life is not less holy, in very truth, than it seems in people's eyes. Is there no reality in the penitence thus sealed and witnessed by good works? And wherefore should it not bring you peace?"

"No, Hester, no!" replied the clergyman. "There is no substance in it! It is cold and dead, and can do nothing for me! Of penance I have had enough! Of penitence there has been none! Else, I should long ago have thrown off these garments of mock holiness, and have shown myself to mankind as they will see me at the judgment-seat. Happy are you, Hester, that wear the scarlet letter openly upon your bosom! Mine burns in secret! Thou little knowest what a relief it is, after the torment of a seven years' cheat, to look into an eye that recognizes me for what I am! Had I one friend,—or were it my worst enemy!—to whom, when sickened with the praises of all other men, I could daily betake myself, and be known as the vilest of all sinners, methinks my soul might keep itself alive thereby. Even thus much of truth would save me! But, now, it is all falsehood!—all emptiness!—all death!"

Hester Prynne looked into his face, but hesitated to speak. Yet, uttering his long-restrained emotions so vehemently as he did, his words here offered her the very point of circumstances in which to interpose what she came to say. She conquered her fears, and spoke.

"Such a friend as thou hast even now wished for," said she, "with whom to weep over thy sin, thou hast in me, the partner of it!"—Again she hesitated, but brought out the words with an effort.—"Thou hast long had such an enemy, and dwellest with him under the same roof!"

The minister started to his feet, gasping for breath, and clutching at his heart as if he would have torn it out of his bosom.

"Ha! What sayest thou?" cried he. "An enemy! And under mine own roof! What mean you?"

Hester Prynne was now fully sensible of the deep injury for which she was responsible to this unhappy man, in permitting him to lie for so many years, or, indeed, for a single moment, at the mercy of one, whose purposes could not be other than malevolent. The very contiguity of his enemy, beneath whatever mask the latter might conceal himself, was enough to disturb the magnetic sphere of a being so sensitive as Arthur Dimmesdale. There had been a period when Hester was less alive to this consideration; or, perhaps, in the misanthropy of her own trouble, she left the minister to bear what she might picture to herself as a more tolerable doom. But of late, since the night of his vigil, all her sympathies towards him had been both softened and invigorated. She now read his heart more accurately. She doubted not, that the continual presence of Roger Chillingworth,—the secret poison of his malignity, infecting all the air about him,—and his authorized interference, as a physician, with the minister's physical and spiritual infirmities,—that these bad opportunities had been turned to a cruel purpose. By means of them, the sufferer's conscience had been kept in an irritated state, the tendency of which was, not to cure by wholesome pain, but to disorganize and corrupt his spiritual being. Its result, on earth, could hardly fail to be insanity, and hereafter, that eternal alienation from the Good and True, of which madness is perhaps the earthly type.

Such was the ruin to which she had brought the man, once,—nay, why should we not speak it?—still so passionately loved! Hester felt that the sacrifice of the clergyman's good name, and death itself, as she had already told Roger Chillingworth, would have been infinitely preferable to the alternative which she had taken upon herself to choose. And now, rather than have had this grievous wrong to confess, she would gladly have lain down on the forest-leaves, and died there, at Arthur Dimmesdale's feet.

"O Arthur," cried she, "forgive me! In all things else, I have striven to be true! Truth was the one virtue which I might have held fast, and did hold fast through all extremity; save when thy good,—thy life,—thy fame,—were put in question! Then I consented to a deception. But a lie is never good, even though death threaten on the other side! Dost thou not see what I would say? That old man!—the physician!—he whom they call Roger Chillingworth!—he was my husband!"

The minister looked at her, for an instant, with all that violence of passion, which—intermixed, in more shapes than one, with his higher, purer, softer qualities—was, in fact, the portion of him which the Devil claimed, and through which he sought to win the rest. Never was there a blacker or a fiercer frown, than Hester now encountered. For the brief space that it lasted, it was a dark transfiguration. But his character had been so much enfeebled by suffering, that even its lower energies were incapable of more than a temporary struggle. He sank down on the ground, and buried his face in his hands.

"I might have known it!" murmured he. "I did know it! Was not the secret told me in the natural recoil of my heart, at the first sight of him, and as often as I have seen him since? Why did I not understand? O Hester Prynne, thou little, little knowest all the horror of this thing. And the shame! — the indelicacy! — the horrible ugliness of this exposure of a sick and guilty heart to the very eye that would gloat over it! Woman, woman, thou art accountable for this! I cannot forgive thee!"

"Thou shalt forgive me!" cried Hester, flinging herself on the fallen leaves beside him. "Let God punish! Thou shalt forgive!"

With sudden and desperate tenderness, she threw her arms around him, and pressed his head against her bosom; little caring though his cheek rested on the scarlet letter. He would have released himself, but strove in vain to do so. Hester would not set him free, lest he should look her sternly in the face. All the world had frowned on her, — for seven long years had it frowned upon this lonely woman, — and still she bore it all, nor ever once turned away her firm, sad eyes. Heaven, likewise, had frowned upon her, and she had not died. But the frown of this pale, weak, sinful, and sorrow-stricken man was what Hester could not bear, and live!

"Wilt thou yet forgive me?" she repeated, over and over again. "Wilt thou not frown? Wilt thou forgive?"

"I do forgive you, Hester," replied the minister, at length, with a deep utterance out of an abyss of sadness, but no anger. "I freely forgive you now. May God forgive us both! We are not, Hester, the worst sinners in the world. There is one worse than even the polluted priest! That old man's revenge has been blacker than my sin. He has violated, in cold blood, the sanctity of a human heart. Thou and I, Hester, never did so!"

"Never, never!" whispered she. "What we did had a consecration of its own. We felt it so! We said so to each other! Hast thou forgotten it?"

"Hush, Hester!" said Arthur Dimmesdale, rising from the ground. "No; I have not forgotten!"

They sat down again, side by side, and hand clasped in hand, on the mossy trunk of the fallen tree. Life had never brought them a gloomier hour; it was the point whither their pathway had so long been tending, and darkening ever, as it stole along — and yet it inclosed a charm that made them linger upon it, and claim another, and another, and, after all, another moment. The forest was obscure around them, and creaked with a blast

"Wilt thou yet forgive me?" by Mary Hallock Foote, engraved by A. V. S. Anthony. Originally appeared in the 1877 Osgood and Company edition of the novel.

that was passing through it. The boughs were tossing heavily about their heads; while one solemn old tree groaned dolefully to another, as if telling the sad story of the pair that sat beneath, or constrained to forebode evil to come.

And yet they lingered. How dreary looked the forest-track that led backward to the settlement, where Hester Prynne must take up again the burden of her ignominy, and the minister the hollow mockery of his good name! So they lingered an instant longer. No golden light had ever been so precious as the gloom of this dark forest. Here, seen only by his eyes, the scarlet letter need not burn into the bosom of the fallen woman! Here, seen only by her eyes, Arthur Dimmesdale, false to God and man, might be, for one moment, true!

He started at a thought that suddenly occurred to him.

"Hester," cried he, "here is a new horror! Roger Chillingworth knows your purpose to reveal his true character. Will he continue, then, to keep our secret? What will now be the course of his revenge?"

"There is a strange secrecy in his nature," replied Hester, thoughtfully; "and it has grown upon him by the hidden practices of his revenge. I deem it not likely that he will betray the secret. He will doubtless seek other means of satiating his dark passion."

"And I!—how am I to live longer, breathing the same air with this deadly enemy?" exclaimed Arthur Dimmesdale, shrinking within himself, and pressing his hand nervously against his heart,—a gesture that had grown involuntary with him. "Think for me, Hester! Thou art strong. Resolve for me!"

"Thou must dwell no longer with this man," said Hester, slowly and firmly. "Thy heart must be no longer under his evil eye!"

"It were far worse than death!" replied the minister. "But how to avoid it? What choice remains to me? Shall I lie down again on these withered leaves, where I cast myself when thou didst tell me what he was? Must I sink down there, and die at once?"

"Alas, what a ruin has befallen thee!" said Hester, with the tears gushing into her eyes. "Wilt thou die for very weakness? There is no other cause!"

"The judgment of God is on me," answered the conscience-stricken priest. "It is too mighty for me to struggle with!"

"Heaven would show mercy," rejoined Hester, "hadst thou but the strength to take advantage of it."

"Be thou strong for me!" answered he. "Advise me what to do."

"Is the world then so narrow?" exclaimed Hester Prynne, fixing her deep eyes on the minister's and instinctively exercising a magnetic power over a spirit so shattered and subdued, that it could hardly hold itself erect. "Doth the universe lie within the compass of yonder town, which only a little time ago was but a leaf-strewn desert, as lonely as this around us? Whither leads yonder forest-track? Backward to the settlement, thou sayest! Yes; but onward too! Deeper it goes, and deeper, into the wilderness, less plainly to be seen at every step; until, some few miles hence, the yellow leaves will show no vestige of the white man's tread. There thou art free! So brief a journey would bring thee from a world where thou hast been most wretched, to one where thou mayest still be happy! Is there not shade enough in all this boundless forest to hide thy heart from the gaze of Roger Chillingworth?"

"Yes, Hester; but only under the fallen leaves!" replied the minister, with a sad smile.

"Then there is the broad pathway of the sea!" continued Hester. "It brought thee hither. If thou so choose, it will bear thee back again. In our native land, whether in some remote rural village or in vast London, — or, surely, in Germany, in France, in pleasant Italy, — thou wouldst be beyond his power and knowledge! And what hast thou to do with all these iron men, and their opinions? They have kept thy better part in bondage too long already!"

"It cannot be!" answered the minister, listening as if he were called upon to realize a dream. "I am powerless to go. Wretched and sinful as I am, I have had no other thought than to drag on my earthly existence in the sphere where Providence hath placed me. Lost as my own soul is, I would still do what I may for other human souls! I dare not quit my post, though an unfaithful sentinel, whose sure reward is death and dishonor, when his dreary watch shall come to an end!"

"Thou art crushed under this seven years' weight of misery," replied Hester, fervently resolved to buoy him up with her own energy. "But thou shalt leave it all behind thee! It shall not cumber thy steps, as thou treadest along the forest-path; neither shalt thou freight the ship with it, if thou prefer to cross the sea. Leave this wreck and ruin here where it hath happened! Meddle no more with it! Begin all anew! Hast thou exhausted possibility in the failure of this one trial? Not so! The future is yet full of trial and success. There is happiness to be enjoyed! There is good to be done! Exchange this false life of thine for a true one. Be, if thy spirit summon thee to such a mission, the teacher and apostle of the red men. Or, — as is more thy nature, — be a scholar and a sage among the wisest and the most renowned of the cultivated world. Preach! Write! Act! Do any thing, save to lie down and die! Give up this name of Arthur Dimmesdale, and make thyself another, and a high one, such as thou canst wear without fear or shame. Why shouldst thou tarry so much as one other day in the torments that have so gnawed into thy life! — that have made thee feeble to will and to do! — that will leave thee powerless even to repent! Up, and away!"

"O Hester!" cried Arthur Dimmesdale, in whose eyes a fitful light, kindled by her enthusiasm, flashed up and died away, "thou tellest of running a race to a man whose knees are tottering beneath him! I must die here. There is not the strength or courage left me to venture into the wide, strange, difficult world, alone!"

It was the last expression of the despondency of a broken spirit. He lacked energy to grasp the better fortune that seemed within his reach.

He repeated the word.

"Alone, Hester!"

"Thou shalt not go alone!" answered she, in a deep whisper.

Then, all was spoken!

XVIII

A Flood of Sunshine

Arthur Dimmesdale gazed into Hester's face with a look in which hope and joy shone out, indeed, but with fear betwixt them, and a kind of horror at her boldness, who had spoken what he vaguely hinted at, but dared not speak.

But Hester Prynne, with a mind of native courage and activity, and for so long a period not merely estranged, but outlawed, from society, had habituated herself to such latitude of speculation as was altogether foreign to the clergyman. She had wandered, without rule or guidance, in a moral wilderness; as vast, as intricate and shadowy, as the untamed forest, amid the gloom of which they were now holding a colloquy that was to decide their fate. Her intellect and heart had their home, as it were, in desert places, where she roamed as freely as the wild Indian in his woods. For years past she had looked from this estranged point of view at human institutions, and whatever priests or legislators had established; criticizing all with hardly more reverence than the Indian would feel for the clerical band, the judicial robe, the pillory, the gallows, the fireside, or the church. The tendency of her fate and fortunes had been to set her free. The scarlet letter was her passport into regions where other women dared not tread. Shame, Despair, Solitude! These had been her teachers,—stern and wild ones,—and they had made her strong, but taught her much amiss.

The minister, on the other hand, had never gone through an experience calculated to lead him beyond the scope of generally received laws; although, in a single instance, he had so fearfully transgressed one of the most sacred of them. But this had been a sin of passion, not of principle, nor even purpose. Since that wretched epoch, he had watched, with morbid zeal and minuteness, not his acts—for those it was easy to arrange,—

but each breath of emotion, and his every thought. At the head of the social system, as the clergymen of that day stood, he was only the more trammelled by its regulations, its principles, and even its prejudices. As a priest, the framework of his order inevitably hemmed him in. As a man who had once sinned, but who kept his conscience all alive and painfully sensitive by the fretting of an unhealed wound, he might have been supposed safer within the line of virtue, than if he had never sinned at all.

Thus, we seem to see that, as regarded Hester Prynne, the whole seven years of outlaw and ignominy had been little other than a preparation for this very hour. But Arthur Dimmesdale! Were such a man once more to fall, what plea could be urged in extenuation of his crime? None; unless it avail him somewhat, that he was broken down by long and exquisite suffering; that his mind was darkened and confused by the very remorse which harrowed it; that, between fleeing as an avowed criminal, and remaining as a hypocrite, conscience might find it hard to strike the balance; that it was human to avoid the peril of death and infamy, and the inscrutable machinations of an enemy; that, finally, to this poor pilgrim, on his dreary and desert path, faint, sick, miserable, there appeared a glimpse of human affection and sympathy, a new life, and a true one, in exchange for the heavy doom which he was now expiating. And be the stern and sad truth spoken, that the breach which guilt has once made into the human soul is never, in this mortal state, repaired. It may be watched and guarded; so that the enemy shall not force his way again into the citadel, and might even, in his subsequent assaults, select some other avenue, in preference to that where he had formerly succeeded. But there is still the ruined wall, and, near it, the stealthy tread of the foe that would win over again his unforgotten triumph.

The struggle, if there were one, need not be described. Let it suffice, that the clergyman resolved to flee, and not alone.

"If, in all these past seven years," thought he, "I could recall one instant of peace or hope, I would yet endure, for the sake of that earnest of Heaven's mercy. But now, — since I am irrevocably doomed, — wherefore should I not snatch the solace allowed to the condemned culprit before his execution? Or, if this be the path to a better life, as Hester would persuade me, I surely give up no fairer prospect by pursuing it! Neither can I any longer live without her companionship; so powerful is she to sustain, — so tender to soothe! O Thou to whom I dare not lift mine eyes, wilt Thou yet pardon me!"

"Thou wilt go!" said Hester calmly, as he met her glance.

The decision once made, a glow of strange enjoyment threw its flickering brightness over the trouble of his breast. It was the exhilarating effect — upon a prisoner just escaped from the dungeon of his own heart — of breathing the wild, free atmosphere of an unredeemed, unchristianized, lawless region. His spirit rose, as it were, with a bound, and attained a nearer prospect of the sky, than throughout all the misery which had kept him grovelling on the earth. Of a deeply religious temperament, there was inevitably a tinge of the devotional in his mood.

"Do I feel joy again?" cried he, wondering at himself. "Methought the germ of it was dead in me! O Hester, thou art my better angel! I seem to have flung myself—sick, sin-stained, and sorrow-blackened—down upon these forest-leaves, and to have risen up all made anew, and with new powers to glorify Him that hath been merciful! This is already the better life! Why did we not find it sooner?"

"Let us not look back," answered Hester Prynne. "The past is gone! Wherefore should we linger upon it now? See! With this symbol, I undo it all, and make it as it had never been!"

So speaking, she undid the clasp that fastened the scarlet letter, and, taking it from her bosom, threw it to a distance among the withered leaves. The mystic token alighted on the hither verge of the stream. With a hand's breadth farther flight it would have fallen into the water, and have given the little brook another woe to carry onward, besides the unintelligible tale which it still kept murmuring about. But there lay the embroidered letter, glittering like a lost jewel, which some ill-fated wanderer might pick up, and thenceforth be haunted by strange phantoms of guilt, sinkings of the heart, and unaccountable misfortune.

The stigma gone, Hester heaved a long, deep sigh, in which the burden of shame and anguish departed from her spirit. O exquisite relief! She had not known the weight, until she felt the freedom! By another impulse, she took off the formal cap that confined her hair; and down it fell upon her shoulders, dark and rich, with at once a shadow and a light in its abundance, and imparting the charm of softness to her features. There played around her mouth, and beamed out of her eyes, a radiant and tender smile, that seemed gushing from the very heart of womanhood. A crimson flush was glowing on her cheek, that had been long so pale. Her sex, her youth, and the whole richness of her beauty, came back from what men call the irrevocable past, and clustered themselves, with her maiden hope, and a happiness before unknown, within the magic circle of this hour. And, as if the gloom of the earth and sky had been but the effluence of these two mortal hearts, it vanished with their sorrow. All at once, as with a sudden smile of heaven, forth burst the sunshine, pouring a very flood into the obscure forest, gladdening each green leaf, transmuting the yellow fallen ones to gold, and gleaming adown the gray trunks of the solemn trees. The objects that had made a shadow hitherto, embodied the brightness now. The course of the little brook might be traced by its merry gleam afar into the wood's heart of mystery, which had become a mystery of joy.

Such was the sympathy of Nature — that wild, heathen Nature of the forest, never subjugated by human law, nor illumined by higher truth — with the bliss of these two spirits! Love, whether newly born, or aroused from a deathlike slumber, must always create a sunshine, filling the heart so full of radiance, that it overflows upon the outward world. Had the forest still kept its gloom, it would have been bright in Hester's eyes, and bright in Arthur Dimmesdale's!

Hester looked at him with the thrill of another joy.

"Thou must know Pearl!" said she. "Our little Pearl! Thou hast seen her, — yes, I know it! — but thou wilt see her now with other eyes. She is a strange child! I hardly comprehend her! But thou wilt love her dearly, as I do, and wilt advise me how to deal with her."

"Dost thou think the child will be glad to know me?" asked the minister, somewhat uneasily. "I have long shrunk from children, because they often show a distrust, — a backwardness to be familiar with me. I have even been afraid of little Pearl!"

"Ah, that was sad!" answered the mother. "But she will love thee dearly, and thou her. She is not far off. I will call her! Pearl! Pearl!"

"I see the child," observed the minister. "Yonder she is, standing in a streak of sunshine, a good way off, on the other side of the brook. So thou thinkest the child will love me?"

Hester smiled, and again called to Pearl, who was visible, at some distance, as the minister had described her, like a bright-apparelled vision, in a sunbeam, which fell down upon her through an arch of boughs. The ray quivered to and fro, making her figure dim or distinct, — now like a real child, now like a child's spirit, — as the splendor went and came again. She heard her mother's voice, and approached slowly through the forest.

Pearl had not found the hour pass wearisomely, while her mother sat talking with the clergyman. The great black forest — stern as it showed itself to those who brought the guilt and troubles of the world into its bosom — became the playmate of the lonely infant, as well as it knew how. Sombre as it was, it put on the kindest of its moods to welcome her. It offered her the partridgeberries, the growth of the preceding autumn, but ripening only in the spring, and now red as drops of blood upon the withered leaves. These Pearl gathered, and was pleased with their wild flavor. The small denizens of the wilderness hardly took pains to move out of her path. A partridge, indeed, with a brood of ten behind her, ran forward threateningly, but soon repented of her fierceness, and clucked to her young ones not to be afraid. A pigeon, alone on a low branch, allowed Pearl to come beneath, and uttered a sound as much of greeting as alarm. A squirrel, from the lofty depths of his domestic tree, chattered either in anger or merriment, — for a squirrel is such a choleric and humorous little personage that it is hard to distinguish between his moods, — so he chattered at the child, and flung down a nut upon her head. It was last year's nut, and already gnawed by his sharp tooth. A fox, startled from his sleep by her light footstep on the leaves, looked inquisitively at Pearl, as doubting whether it were better to steal off, or renew his nap on the same spot. A wolf, it is said, — but here the tale has surely lapsed into the improbable, — came up, and smelt of Pearl's robe, and offered his savage head to be patted by her hand. The truth seems to be, however, that the mother-forest, and these wild things which it nourished, all recognized a kindred wildness in the human child.

And she was gentler here than in the grassy-margined streets of the settlement, or in her mother's cottage. The flowers appeared to know it; and one and another whispered, as she passed, "Adorn thyself with me, thou beautiful child, adorn thyself with me!" — and, to please them, Pearl gathered the violets, and anemones, and columbines, and some twigs of the freshest green, which the old trees held down before her eyes. With these she decorated her hair, and her young waist, and became a nymph-child, or an infant dryad, or whatever else was in closest sympathy with the antique wood. In such guise had Pearl adorned herself, when she heard her mother's voice, and came slowly back.

Slowly; for she saw the clergyman!

XIX
The Child at the Brook-Side

"Thou wilt love her dearly," repeated Hester Prynne, as she and the minister sat watching little Pearl. "Dost thou not think her beautiful? And see with what natural skill she has made those simple flowers adorn her! Had she gathered pearls, and diamonds, and rubies, in the wood, they could not have become her better. She is a splendid child! But I know whose brow she has!"

"Dost thou know, Hester," said Arthur Dimmesdale, with an unquiet smile, "that this dear child, tripping about always at thy side, hast caused me many an alarm? Methought — O Hester, what a thought is that, and how terrible to dread it! — that my own features were partly repeated in her face, and so strikingly that the world might see them! But she is mostly thine!"

"No, no! Not mostly!" answered the mother with a tender smile. "A little longer, and thou needest not to be afraid to trace whose child she is.

But how strangely beautiful she looks, with those wild flowers in her hair! It is as if one of the fairies, whom we left in our dear old England, had decked her out to meet us."

It was with a feeling which neither of them had ever before experienced, that they sat and watched Pearl's slow advance. In her was visible the tie that united them. She had been offered to the world, these seven years past, as the living hieroglyphic, in which was revealed the secret they so darkly sought to hide,—all written in this symbol,—all plainly manifest,—had there been a prophet or magician skilled to read the character of flame! And Pearl was the oneness of their being. Be the foregone evil what it might, how could they doubt that their earthly lives and future destinies were conjoined, when they beheld at once the material union, and the spiritual idea, in whom they met, and were to dwell immortally together? Thoughts like these—and perhaps other thoughts, which they did not acknowledge or define—threw an awe about the child, as she came onward.

"Let her see nothing strange—no passion nor eagerness—in thy way of accosting her," whispered Hester. "Our Pearl is a fitful and fantastic little elf, sometimes. Especially, she is seldom tolerant of emotion, when she does not fully comprehend the why and wherefore. But the child hath strong affections! She loves me, and will love thee!"

"Thou canst not think," said the minister, glancing aside at Hester Prynne, "how my heart dreads this interview, and yearns for it! But, in truth, as I already told thee, children are not readily won to be familiar with me. They will not climb my knee, nor prattle in my ear, nor answer to my smile; but stand apart, and eye me strangely. Even little babes, when I take them in my arms, weep bitterly. Yet Pearl, twice in her little lifetime, hath been kind to me! The first time,—thou knowest it well! The last was when thou ledst her with thee to the house of yonder stern old Governor."

"And thou didst plead so bravely in her behalf and mine!" answered the mother. "I remember it; and so shall little Pearl. Fear nothing! She may be strange and shy at first, but will soon learn to love thee!"

By this time Pearl had reached the margin of the brook, and stood on the farther side, gazing silently at Hester and the clergyman, who still sat together on the mossy tree-trunk, waiting to receive her. Just where she had paused the brook chanced to form a pool, so smooth and quiet that it reflected a perfect image of her little figure, with all the brilliant picturesqueness of her beauty, in its adornment of flowers and wreathed foliage, but more refined and spiritualized than the reality. This image, so nearly identical with the living Pearl, seemed to communicate somewhat of its own shadowy and intangible quality to the child herself. It was strange, the way in which Pearl stood, looking so stedfastly at them through the dim medium of the forest-gloom; herself, meanwhile, all glorified with a ray of sunshine, that was attracted thitherward as by a certain sympathy. In the brook beneath stood another child,—another and the same,—with likewise its ray of golden light. Hester felt herself, in some indistinct and tantalizing manner, estranged from Pearl; as if the child, in her lonely ramble through the forest, had strayed out of the sphere in which she and her mother dwelt together, and was now vainly seeking to return to it.

There was both truth and error in the impression; the child and mother were estranged, but through Hester's fault, not Pearl's. Since the latter rambled from her side, another inmate had been admitted within the circle of the mother's feelings, and so modified the aspect of them all, that Pearl, the returning wanderer, could not find her wonted place, and hardly knew where she was.

"I have a strange fancy," observed the sensitive minister, "that this brook is the boundary between two worlds, and that thou canst never meet thy Pearl again. Or is she an elfish spirit, who, as the legends of our childhood taught us, is forbidden to cross a running stream? Pray hasten her; for this delay has already imparted a tremor to my nerves."

"Come, dearest child!" said Hester encouragingly, and stretching out both her arms. "How slow thou art! When hast thou been so sluggish before now? Here is a friend of mine, who must be thy friend also. Thou wilt have twice as much love, henceforward, as thy mother alone could give thee! Leap across the brook and come to us. Thou canst leap like a young deer!"

Pearl, without responding in any manner to these honeysweet expressions, remained on the other side of the brook. Now she fixed her bright, wild eyes on her mother, now on the minister, and now included them both in the same glance; as if to detect and explain to herself the relation which they bore to one another. For some unaccountable reason, as Arthur Dimmesdale felt the child's eyes upon himself, his hand—with that gesture so habitual as to have become involuntary—stole over his heart. At length, assuming a singular air of authority, Pearl stretched out her hand, with the small forefinger extended, and pointing evidently towards her mother's breast. And beneath, in the mirror of the brook, there was the flower-girdled and sunny image of little Pearl, pointing her small forefinger too.

"Thou strange child, why dost thou not come to me?" exclaimed Hester.

Pearl still pointed with her forefinger; and a frown gathered on her brow; the more impressive from the childish, the almost baby-like aspect of the features that conveyed it. As her mother still kept beckoning to her, and arraying her face in a holiday suit of unaccustomed smiles, the child stamped her foot with a yet more imperious look and gesture. In the brook, again, was the fantastic beauty of the image, with its reflected frown, its pointed finger, and imperious gesture, giving emphasis to the aspect of little Pearl.

"Hasten, Pearl; or I shall be angry with thee!" cried Hester Prynne, who, however inured to such behaviour on the elf-child's part at other seasons, was naturally anxious for a more seemly deportment now. "Leap across the brook, naughty child, and run hither! Else I must come to thee!"

But Pearl, not a whit startled at her mother's threats, any more than mollified by her entreaties, now suddenly burst into a fit of passion, gesticulating violently, and throwing her small figure into the most extravagant contortions. She accompanied this wild outbreak with piercing shrieks, which the woods reverberated on all sides; so that, alone as she was in her childish and unreasonable wrath, it seemed as if a hidden multitude were lending her their sympathy and encouragement. Seen in the brook, once more, was the shadowy wrath of Pearl's image, crowned and girdled with flowers, but stamping its foot, wildly gesticulating, and, in the midst of all, still pointing its small forefinger at Hester's bosom!

"I see what ails the child," whispered Hester to the clergyman, and turning pale in spite of a strong effort to conceal her trouble and annoyance. "Children will not abide any, the slightest, change in the accustomed aspect of things that are daily before their eyes. Pearl misses something which she has always seen me wear!"

"I pray you," answered the minister, "if thou hast any means of pacifying the child, do it forthwith! Save it were the cankered wrath of an old witch, like Mistress Hibbins," added he, attempting to smile, "I know nothing that I would not sooner encounter than this passion in a child. In Pearl's young beauty, as in the wrinkled witch, it has a preternatural effect. Pacify her, if thou lovest me!"

Hester turned again towards Pearl, with a crimson blush upon her cheek, a conscious glance aside at the clergyman, and then a heavy sigh; while, even before she had time to speak, the blush yielded to a deadly pallor.

"Pearl," said she, sadly, "look down at thy feet! There! —before thee! — on the hither side of the brook!"

The child turned her eyes to the point indicated; and there lay the scarlet letter, so close upon the margin of the stream, that the gold embroidery was reflected in it.

"Bring it hither!" said Hester.

"Come thou and take it up!" answered Pearl.

"Was ever such a child!" observed Hester aside to the minister. "O, I have much to tell thee about her. But, in very truth, she is right as regards this hateful token. I must bear its torture yet a little longer, — only a few

The Child at the Brook-Side by F. O. C. Darley. Originally appeared in the 1879 Houghton Mifflin edition of the novel.

days longer, — until we shall have left this region, and look back hither as to a land which we have dreamed of. The forest cannot hide it! The mid-ocean shall take it from my hand, and swallow it up for ever!"

With these words, she advanced to the margin of the brook, took up the scarlet letter, and fastened it again into her bosom. Hopefully, but a moment ago, as Hester had spoken of drowning it in the deep sea, there was a sense of inevitable doom upon her, as she thus received back this deadly symbol from the hand of fate. She had flung it into infinite space! — she had drawn an hour's free breath! — and here again was the scarlet misery, glittering on the old spot! So it ever is, whether thus typified or no, that an evil deed invests itself with the character of doom. Hester next gathered up the heavy tresses of her hair, and confined them beneath her cap. As if there were a withering spell in the sad letter, her beauty, the warmth and richness of her womanhood, departed, like fading sunshine; and a gray shadow seemed to fall across her.

When the dreary change was wrought, she extended her hand to Pearl.

"Dost thou know thy mother now, child?" asked she, reproachfully, but with a subdued tone. "Wilt thou come across the brook, and own thy mother, now that she has her shame upon her, — now that she is sad?"

"Yes; now I will!" answered the child, bounding across the brook, and clasping Hester in her arms. "Now thou art my mother indeed! And I am thy little Pearl!"

In a mood of tenderness that was not usual with her, she drew down her mother's head, and kissed her brow and both her cheeks. But then — by a kind of necessity that always impelled this child to alloy whatever comfort she might chance to give with a throb of anguish — Pearl put up her mouth, and kissed the scarlet letter too!

"That was not kind!" said Hester. "When thou hast shown me a little love, thou mockest me!"

"Why doth the minister sit yonder?" asked Pearl.

"He waits to welcome thee," replied her mother. "Come thou, and entreat his blessing! He loves thee, my little Pearl, and loves thy mother too. Wilt thou not love him? Come! he longs to greet thee!"

"Doth he love us?" said Pearl, looking up with acute intelligence into her mother's face. "Will he go back with us, hand in hand, we three together, into the town?"

"Not now, dear child," answered Hester. "But in days to come he will walk hand in hand with us. We will have a home and fireside of our own; and thou shalt sit upon his knee; and he will teach thee many things, and love thee dearly. Thou wilt love him; wilt thou not?"

"And will he always keep his hand over his heart?" inquired Pearl.

"Foolish child, what a question is that!" exclaimed her mother. "Come and ask his blessing!"

But, whether influenced by the jealousy that seems instinctive with every petted child towards a dangerous rival, or from whatever caprice of her freakish nature, Pearl would show no favor to the clergyman. It was only by an exertion of force that her mother brought her up to him, hanging back, and manifesting her reluctance by odd grimaces; of which, ever since her babyhood, she had possessed a singular variety, and could transform her mobile physiognomy into a series of different aspects, with a new mischief in them, each and all. The minister—painfully embarrassed, but hoping that a kiss might prove a talisman to admit him into the child's kindlier regards—bent forward, and impressed one on her brow. Hereupon, Pearl broke away from her mother, and, running to the brook, stooped over it, and bathed her forehead, until the unwelcome kiss was quite washed off, and diffused through a long lapse of the gliding water. She then remained apart, silently watching Hester and the clergyman; while they talked together, and made such arrangements as were suggested by their new position, and the purposes soon to be fulfilled.

And now this fateful interview had come to a close. The dell was to be left a solitude among its dark, old trees, which, with their multitudinous tongues, would whisper long of what had passed there, and no mortal be the wiser. And the melancholy brook would add this other tale to the mystery with which its little heart was already overburdened, and whereof it still kept up a murmuring babble, with not a whit more cheerfulness of tone than for ages heretofore.

XX
The Minister in a Maze

As the minister departed, in advance of Hester Prynne and little Pearl, he threw a backward glance; half expecting that he should discover only some faintly traced features or outline of the mother and the child, slowly fading into the twilight of the woods. So great a vicissitude in his life could not at once be received as real. But there was Hester, clad in her gray robe, still standing beside the tree-trunk, which some blast had overthrown a long antiquity ago, and which time had ever since been covering with moss, so that these two fated ones, with earth's heaviest burden on them, might there sit down together, and find a single hour's rest and solace. And there was Pearl, too, lightly dancing from the margin of the brook,—now that the intrusive third person was gone,—and taking her old place by her mother's side. So the minister had not fallen asleep, and dreamed!

In order to free his mind from this indistinctness and duplicity of impression, which vexed it with a strange disquietude, he recalled and more thoroughly defined the plans which Hester and himself had sketched for their departure. It had been determined between them, that the Old World, with its crowds and cities, offered them a more eligible shelter and concealment than the wilds of New England, or all America, with its alternatives of an Indian wigwam, or the few settlements of Europeans, scattered thinly along the seaboard. Not to speak of the clergyman's health, so inadequate to sustain the hardships of a forest life, his native gifts, his culture, and his entire development would secure him a home only in the midst of civilization and refinement; the higher the state, the more delicately adapted to it the man. In furtherance of this choice, it so happened that a ship lay in the harbour; one of those questionable cruisers, frequent at that day, which, without being absolutely outlaws of the deep, yet roamed over its surface with a remarkable irresponsibility of character. This vessel had recently arrived from the Spanish Main, and, within three days' time, would sail for Bristol. Hester Prynne—whose vocation, as a self-enlisted Sister of Charity, had brought her acquainted with the captain and crew—could take upon herself to secure the passage of two individuals and a child, with all the secrecy which circumstances rendered more than desirable.

The minister had inquired of Hester, with no little interest, the precise time at which the vessel might be expected to depart. It would probably be on the fourth day from the present. "That is most fortunate!" he had then said to himself. Now, why the Reverend Mr. Dimmesdale considered it so very fortunate, we hesitate to reveal. Nevertheless,—to hold nothing back from the reader,—it was because, on the third day from the present, he was to preach the Election Sermon,[64] and, as such an occasion formed an honorable epoch in the life of a New England clergyman, he could not have chanced upon a more suitable mode and time of terminating his professional career. "At least, they shall say of me," thought this exemplary man, "that I leave no public duty unperformed, nor ill performed!" Sad, indeed, that an introspection so profound and acute as this poor minister's should be so miserably deceived! We have had, and may still have, worse things to tell of him; but none, we apprehend, so pitiably weak; no evidence, at once so slight and irrefragable, of a subtle disease, that had long since begun to eat into the real substance of his character. No man, for any considerable period, can wear one face to himself, and another to the multitude, without finally getting bewildered as to which may be the true.

---

[64] A special sermon preached by an eminent minister to solemnize the inauguration of a newly elected colonial governor (here, John Endicott).

The excitement of Mr. Dimmesdale's feelings, as he returned from his interview with Hester, lent him unaccustomed physical energy, and hurried him town-ward at a rapid pace. The pathway among the woods seemed wilder, more uncouth with its rude natural obstacles, and less trodden by the foot of man, than he remembered it on his outward journey. But he leaped across the plashy places, thrust himself through the clinging underbrush, climbed the ascent, plunged into the hollow, and overcame, in short, all the difficulties of the track, with an unweariable activity that astonished him. He could not but recall how feebly, and with what frequent pauses for breath, he had toiled over the same ground only two days before. As he drew near the town, he took an impression of change from the series of familiar objects that presented themselves. It seemed not yesterday, not one, nor two, but many days, or even years ago, since he had quitted them. There, indeed, was each former trace of the street, as he remembered it, and all the peculiarities of the houses, with the due multitude of gable-peaks, and a weathercock at every point where his memory suggested one. Not the less, however, came this importunately obtrusive sense of change. The same was true as regarded the acquaintances whom he met, and all the well-known shapes of human life, about the little town. They looked neither older nor younger, now; the beards of the aged were no whiter, nor could the creeping babe of yesterday walk on his feet to-day; it was impossible to describe in what respect they differed from the individuals on whom he had so recently bestowed a parting glance; and yet the minister's deepest sense seemed to inform him of their mutability. A similar impression struck him most remarkably, as he passed under the walls of his own church. The edifice had so very strange, and yet so familiar, an aspect that Mr. Dimmesdale's mind vibrated between two ideas either that he had seen it only in a dream hitherto, or that he was merely dreaming about it now.

This phenomenon, in the various shapes which it assumed, indicated no external change, but so sudden and important a change in the spectator of the familiar scene that the intervening space of a single day had operated on his consciousness like the lapse of years. The minister's own will, and Hester's will, and the fate that grew between them, had wrought this transformation. It was the same town as heretofore; but the same minister returned not from the forest. He might have said to the friends who greeted him, — "I am not the man for whom you take me! I left him yonder in the forest, withdrawn into a secret dell, by a mossy tree-trunk, and near a melancholy brook! Go, seek your minister, and see if his emaciated figure, his thin cheek, his white, heavy, pain-wrinkled brow, be not flung down there like a cast-off garment!" His friends, no doubt, will still have insisted with him, — "Thou art thyself the man!" — but the error would have been their own, not his.

Before Mr. Dimmesdale reached home, his inner man gave him other evidences of a revolution in the sphere of thought and feeling. In truth, nothing short of a total change of dynasty and moral code, in that interior kingdom, was adequate to account for the impulses now communicated to the unfortunate and startled minister. At every step he was incited to do some strange, wild, wicked thing or other, with a sense that it would be at once involuntary and intentional; in spite of himself, yet growing out of a profounder self than that which opposed the impulse. For instance, he met one of his own deacons. The good old man addressed him with the paternal affection and patriarchal privilege, which his venerable age, his upright and holy character, and his station in the Church, entitled him to use; and, conjoined with this, the deep, almost worshiping respect, which the minister's professional and private claims alike demanded. Never was there a more beautiful example of how the majesty of age and wisdom may comport with the obeisance and respect enjoined upon it, as from a lower social rank and inferior order of endowment, towards a higher. Now, during a conversation of some two or three moments between the Reverend Mr. Dimmesdale and this excellent and hoary-bearded deacon, it was only by the most careful self control that the former could refrain from uttering certain blasphemous suggestions that rose into his mind, respecting the communion-supper. He absolutely trembled and turned pale as ashes, lest his tongue should wag itself, in utterance of these horrible matters, and plead his own consent for so doing, without his having fairly given it. And, even with this terror in his heart, he could hardly avoid laughing to imagine how the sanctified old patriarchal deacon would have been petrified by his minister's impiety!

Again, another incident of the same nature. Hurrying along the street, the Reverend Mr. Dimmesdale encountered the eldest female member of his church; a most pious and exemplary old dame; poor, widowed, lonely, and with a heart as full of reminiscences about her dead husband and children, and her dead friends of long ago, as a burial-ground is full of storied grave-stones. Yet all this, which would else have been such heavy sorrow, was made almost a solemn joy to her devout old soul by religious consolations and the truths of Scripture, wherewith she had fed herself continually for more than thirty years. And, since Mr. Dimmesdale had taken her in charge, the good grandam's chief earthly comfort—which, unless it had been likewise a heavenly comfort, could have been none at all—was to meet her pastor, whether casually, or of set purpose, and be refreshed with a word of warm, fragrant, heaven-breathing Gospel truth from his beloved lips into her dulled, but rapturously attentive ear. But, on this occasion, up to the moment of putting his lips to the old woman's ear, Mr. Dimmesdale, as the great enemy of souls would have it, could recall no text of Scripture, nor aught else, except a brief, pithy, and, as it then appeared to him, unanswerable argument against the immortality of the human soul. The instilment thereof into her mind would probably have caused this aged sister to drop down dead, at once, as by the effect of an intensely poisonous infusion. What he really did whisper, the minister could never afterwards recollect. There was, perhaps, a fortunate disorder in his utterance, which failed to impart any distinct idea to the good widow's comprehension, or which Providence interpreted after a method of its own. Assuredly, as the minister looked back, he beheld an expression of divine gratitude and ecstasy that seemed like the shine of the celestial city on her face, so wrinkled and ashy pale.

Again, a third instance. After parting from the old church-member, he met the youngest sister of them all. It was a maiden newly won — and won by the Reverend Mr. Dimmesdale's own sermon, on the Sabbath after his vigil — to barter the transitory pleasures of the world for the heavenly hope, that was to assume brighter substance as life grew dark around her, and which would gild the utter gloom with final glory. She was fair and pure as a lily that had bloomed in Paradise. The minister knew well that he was himself enshrined within the stainless sanctity of her heart, which hung its snowy curtains about his image, imparting to religion the warmth of love, and to love a religious purity. Satan, that afternoon, had surely led the poor young girl away from her mother's side, and thrown her into the pathway of this sorely tempted, or — shall we not rather say? — this lost and desperate man. As she drew nigh, the arch-fiend whispered him to condense into small compass and drop into her tender bosom a germ of evil that would be sure to blossom darkly soon, and bear black fruit betimes. Such was his sense of power over this virgin soul, trusting him as she did, that the minister felt potent to blight all the field of innocence with but one wicked look, and develop all its opposite with but a word. So — with a mightier struggle than he had yet sustained — he held his Geneva cloak before his face, and hurried onward, making no sign of recognition, and leaving the young sister to digest his rudeness as she might. She ransacked her conscience, — which was full of harmless little matters, like her pocket or her work-bag, — and took herself to task, poor thing, for a thousand imaginary faults; and went about her household duties with swollen eyelids the next morning.

Before the minister had time to celebrate his victory over this last temptation, he was conscious of another impulse, more ludicrous, and almost as horrible. It was, — we blush to tell it, — it was to stop short in the road, and teach some very wicked words to a knot of little Puritan children who were playing there, and had but just begun to talk. Denying himself this freak, as unworthy of his cloth, he met a drunken seaman, one of the ship's crew from the Spanish Main. And, here, since he had so valiantly forborne all other wickedness, poor Mr. Dimmesdale longed, at least, to shake hands with the tarry blackguard, and recreate himself with a few improper jests, such as dissolute sailors so abound with, and a volley of good, round, solid, satisfactory, and heaven-defying oaths! It was not so much a better principle, as partly his natural good taste, and still more his buckramed habit of clerical decorum, that carried him safely through the latter crisis.

"What is it that haunts and tempts me thus?" cried the minister to himself, at length, pausing in the street, and striking his hand against his forehead. "Am I mad? or am I given over utterly to the fiend? Did I make a contract with him in the forest, and sign it with my blood? And does he now summon me to its fulfilment, by suggesting the performance of every wickedness which his most foul imagination can conceive?"

At the moment when the Reverend Mr. Dimmesdale thus communed with himself, and struck his forehead with his hand, old Mistress Hibbins, the reputed witch-lady, is said to have been passing by. She made a very grand appearance; having on a high head-dress, a rich gown of velvet, and a ruff done up with the famous yellow starch, of which Ann Turner,[65] her especial friend, had taught her the secret, before this last good lady had been hanged for Sir Thomas Overbury's murder. Whether the witch had read the minister's thoughts, or no, she came to a full stop, looked shrewdly into his face, smiled craftily, and—though little given to converse with clergymen—began a conversation.

"So, reverend Sir, you have made a visit into the forest," observed the witch-lady, nodding her high head-dress at him. "The next time, I pray you to allow me only a fair warning, and I shall be proud to bear you company. Without taking overmuch upon myself, my good word will go far towards gaining any strange gentleman a fair reception from yonder potentate you wot of!"

"I profess, madam," answered the clergyman with a grave obeisance, such as the lady's rank demanded, and his own good-breeding made imperative, — "I profess, on my conscience and character, that I am utterly bewildered as touching the purport of your words! I went not into the forest to seek a potentate; neither do I, at any future time, design a visit thither, with a view to gaining the favor of such personage. My one sufficient object was to greet that pious friend of mine, the Apostle Eliot, and rejoice with him over the many precious souls he hath won from heathendom!"

"Ha, ha, ha!" cackled the old witch-lady, still nodding her high head-dress at the minister. "Well, well, we must needs talk thus in the daytime!

---

[65] One of the conspirators executed for the murder of Sir Thomas Overbury. See note 50.

You carry it off like an old hand! But at midnight, and in the forest, we shall have other talk together!"

She passed on with her aged stateliness, but often turning back her head and smiling at him, like one willing to recognize a secret intimacy of connection.

"Have I then sold myself," thought the minister, "to the fiend whom, if men say true, this yellow-starched and velveted old hag has chosen for her prince and master!"

The wretched minister! He had made a bargain very like it! Tempted by a dream of happiness, he had yielded himself with deliberate choice, as he had never done before, to what he knew was deadly sin. And the infectious poison of that sin had been thus rapidly diffused throughout his moral system. It had stupefied all blessed impulses, and awakened into vivid life the whole brotherhood of bad ones. Scorn, bitterness, unprovoked malignity, gratuitous desire of ill, ridicule of whatever was good and holy, all awoke, to tempt, even while they frightened him. And his encounter with old Mistress Hibbins, if it were a real incident, did but show his sympathy and fellowship with wicked mortals and the world of perverted spirits.

He had by this time reached his dwelling, on the edge of the burial-ground, and, hastening up the stairs, took refuge in his study. The minister was glad to have reached this shelter, without first betraying himself to the world by any of those strange and wicked eccentricities to which he had been continually impelled while passing through the streets. He entered the accustomed room, and looked around him on its books, its windows, its fireplace, and the tapestried comfort of the walls, with the same perception of strangeness that had haunted him throughout his walk from the forest-dell into the town, and thitherward. Here he had studied and written; here, gone through fast and vigil, and come forth half alive; here, striven to pray; here, borne a hundred thousand agonies! There was the Bible, in its rich old Hebrew, with Moses and the Prophets speaking to him, and God's voice through all! There, on the table, with the inky pen beside it, was an unfinished sermon, with a sentence broken in the midst, where his thoughts had ceased to gush out upon the page two days before. He knew that it was himself, the thin and white-cheeked minister, who had done and suffered these things, and written thus far into the Election Sermon! But he seemed to stand apart, and eye this former self with scornful, pitying, but half-envious curiosity. That self was gone! Another man had returned out of the forest; a wiser one; with a knowledge of hidden mysteries which the simplicity of the former never could have reached. A bitter kind of knowledge that!

While occupied with these reflections, a knock came at the door of the study, and the minister said, "Come in!"—not wholly devoid of an idea that he might behold an evil spirit. And so he did! It was old Roger Chillingworth that entered. The minister stood, white and speechless, with one hand on the Hebrew Scriptures, and the other spread upon his breast.

"Welcome home, reverend Sir!" said the physician. "And how found you that godly man, the Apostle Eliot? But methinks, dear Sir, you look pale; as if the travel through the wilderness had been too sore for you. Will not my aid be requisite to put you in heart and strength to preach your Election Sermon?"

"Nay, I think not so," rejoined the Reverend Mr. Dimmesdale. "My journey, and the sight of the holy Apostle yonder, and the free air which I have breathed, have done me good, after so long confinement in my study. I think to need no more of your drugs, my kind physician, good though they be, and administered by a friendly hand."

All this time, Roger Chillingworth was looking at the minister with the grave and intent regard of a physician towards his patient. But, in spite of this outward show, the latter was almost convinced of the old man's knowledge, or, at least, his confident suspicion, with respect to his own interview with Hester Prynne. The physician knew then, that, in the minister's regard, he was no longer a trusted friend, but his bitterest enemy. So much being known, it would appear natural that a part of it should be expressed. It is singular, however, how long a time often passes before words embody things; and with what security two persons, who choose to avoid a certain subject, may approach its very verge, and retire without disturbing it. Thus, the minister felt no apprehension that Roger Chillingworth would touch, in express words, upon the real position which they sustained towards one another. Yet did the physician, in his dark way, creep frightfully near the secret.

"Were it not better," said he, "that you use my poor skill to-night? Verily, dear Sir, we must take pains to make you strong and vigorous for this occasion of the Election discourse. The people look for great things from you; apprehending that another year may come about, and find their pastor gone."

"Yea, to another world," replied the minister, with pious resignation. "Heaven grant it be a better one; for, in good sooth, I hardly think to tarry with my flock through the flitting seasons of another year! But, touching your medicine, kind Sir, in my present frame of body I need it not."

"I joy to hear it," answered the physician. "It may be that my remedies, so long administered in vain, begin now to take due effect. Happy man were I, and well deserving of New England's gratitude, could I achieve this cure!"

"I thank you from my heart, most watchful friend," said the Reverend Mr. Dimmesdale, with a solemn smile. "I thank you, and can but requite your good deeds with my prayers."

"A good man's prayers are golden recompense!" rejoined old Roger Chillingworth, as he took his leave. "Yea, they are the current gold coin of the New Jerusalem, with the King's own mint-mark on them!"

Left alone, the minister summoned a servant of the house, and requested food, which, being set before him, he ate with ravenous appetite. Then, flinging the already written pages of the Election Sermon into the fire, he forthwith began another, which he wrote with such an impulsive flow of thought and emotion, that he fancied himself inspired; and only wondered that Heaven should see fit to transmit the grand and solemn music of its oracles through so foul an organ-pipe as he. However, leaving that mystery to solve itself, or go unsolved for ever, he drove his task onward, with earnest haste and ecstasy. Thus the night fled away, as if it were a winged steed, and he careering on it; morning came, and peeped blushing through the curtains; and at last sunrise threw a golden beam into the study, and laid it right across the minister's bedazzled eyes. There he was, with the pen still between his fingers, and a vast, immeasurable tract of written space behind him!

XXI
The New England Holiday

Betimes in the morning of the day on which the new Governor was to receive his office at the hands of the people, Hester Prynne and little Pearl came into the market-place. It was already thronged with the craftsmen and other plebeian inhabitants of the town, in considerable numbers; among whom, likewise, were many rough figures, whose attire of deerskins marked them as belonging to some of the forest settlements, which surrounded the little metropolis of the colony.

On this public holiday, as on all other occasions, for seven years past, Hester was clad in a garment of coarse gray cloth. Not more by its hue than by some indescribable peculiarity in its fashion, it had the effect of making her fade personally out of sight and outline; while, again, the scarlet letter brought her back from this twilight indistinctness, and revealed her under the moral aspect of its own illumination. Her face, so long familiar to the townspeople, showed the marble quietude which they were accustomed to behold there. It was like a mask; or rather, like the frozen calmness of a dead woman's features; owing this dreary resemblance to the fact that Hester was actually dead, in respect to any claim of sympathy, and had departed out of the world with which she still seemed to mingle.

It might be, on this one day, that there was an expression unseen before, nor, indeed, vivid enough to be detected now; unless some preternaturally gifted observer should have first read the heart, and have afterwards sought a corresponding development in the countenance and mien. Such a spiritual seer might have conceived, that, after sustaining the gaze of the multitude through seven miserable years as a necessity, a penance, and something which it was a stern religion to endure, she now, for one last time more, encountered it freely and voluntarily, in order to convert what had so long been agony into a kind of triumph. "Look your last on the scarlet letter and its wearer!"—the people's victim and life-long bondslave, as they fancied her, might say to them. "Yet a little while, and she will be beyond your reach! A few hours longer, and the deep, mysterious ocean will quench and hide for ever the symbol which ye have caused to burn upon her bosom!" Nor were it an inconsistency too improbable to be assigned to human nature, should we suppose a feeling of regret in Hester's mind, at the moment when she was about to win her freedom from the pain which had been thus deeply incorporated with her being. Might there not be an irresistible desire to quaff a last, long, breathless draught of the cup of wormwood and aloes, with which nearly all her years of womanhood had been perpetually flavored? The wine of life, henceforth to be presented to her lips, must be indeed rich, delicious, and exhilarating, in its chased and golden beaker; or else leave an inevitable and weary languor, after the lees of bitterness wherewith she had been drugged, as with a cordial of intensest potency.

Pearl was decked out with airy gayety. It would have been impossible to guess that this bright and sunny apparition owed its existence to the shape of gloomy gray; or that a fancy, at once so gorgeous and so delicate as must have been requisite to contrive the child's apparel, was the same that had achieved a task perhaps more difficult, in imparting so distinct a peculiarity to Hester's simple robe. The dress, so proper was it to little Pearl, seemed an effluence, or inevitable development and outward manifestation of her character, no more to be separated from her than the many-hued brilliancy from a butterfly's wing, or the painted glory from the leaf of a bright flower. As with these, so with the child; her garb was all of one idea with her nature. On this eventful day, moreover, there was a certain singular inquietude and excitement in her mood, resembling nothing so much as the shimmer of a diamond, that sparkles and flashes with the varied throbbings of the breast on which it is displayed. Children have always a sympathy in the agitations of those connected with them; always, especially, a sense of any trouble or impending revolution, of whatever kind, in domestic circumstances; and therefore Pearl, who was the gem on her mother's unquiet bosom, betrayed, by the very dance of her spirits, the emotions which none could detect in the marble passiveness of Hester's brow.

This effervescence made her flit with a bird-like movement, rather than walk by her mother's side. She broke continually into shouts of a wild, inarticulate, and sometimes piercing music. When they reached the market-place, she became still more restless, on perceiving the stir and bustle that enlivened the spot; for it was usually more like the broad and lonesome green before a village meetinghouse, than the centre of a town's business.

"Why, what is this, mother?" cried she. "Wherefore have all the people left their work to-day? Is it a play-day for the whole world? See, there is the blacksmith! He has washed his sooty face, and put on his Sabbath-day clothes, and looks as if he would gladly be merry, if any kind body would only teach him how! And there is Master Brackett, the old jailer, nodding and smiling at me. Why does he do so, mother?"

"He remembers thee a little babe, my child," answered Hester.

"He should not nod and smile at me, for all that,—the black, grim, ugly-eyed old man!" said Pearl. "He may nod at thee if he will; for thou art clad in gray, and wearest the scarlet letter. But, see, mother, how many faces of strange people, and Indians among them, and sailors! What have they all come to do here in the market-place?"

"They wait to see the procession pass," said Hester. "For the Governor and the magistrates are to go by, and the ministers, and all the great people and good people, with the music, and the soldiers marching before them."

"And will the minister be there?" asked Pearl. "And will he hold out both his hands to me, as when thou ledst me to him from the brook-side?"

"He will be there, child," answered her mother. "But he will not greet thee to-day; nor must thou greet him."

"What a strange, sad man is he!" said the child, as if speaking partly to herself. "In the dark night-time, he calls us to him, and holds thy hand and mine, as when we stood with him on the scaffold yonder! And in the deep forest, where only the old trees can hear, and the strip of sky see it, he talks with thee, sitting on a heap of moss! And he kisses my forehead, too, so that the little brook would hardly wash it off! But here in the sunny day, and among all the people, he knows us not; nor must we know him! A strange, sad man is he, with his hand always over his heart!"

"Be quiet, Pearl! Thou understandest not these things," said her mother. "Think not now of the minister, but look about thee, and see how cheery is every body's face to-day. The children have come from their schools, and the grown people from their workshops and their fields, on purpose to be happy. For, to-day, a new man is beginning to rule over them; and so—as has been the custom of mankind ever since a nation was first gathered—they make merry and rejoice; as if a good and golden year were at length to pass over the poor old world!"

It was as Hester said, in regard to the unwonted jollity that brightened the faces of the people. Into this festal season of the year—as it already was, and continued to be during the greater part of two centuries—the Puritans compressed whatever mirth and public joy they deemed allowable to human infirmity; thereby so far dispelling the customary cloud, that, for the space of a single holiday, they appeared scarcely more grave than most other communities at a period of general affliction.

But we perhaps exaggerate the gray or sable tinge, which undoubtedly characterized the mood and manners of the age. The persons now in the market-place of Boston had not been born to an inheritance of Puritanic gloom. They were native Englishmen, whose fathers had lived in the sunny richness of the Elizabethan epoch; a time when the life of England, viewed as one great mass, would appear to have been as stately, magnificent, and joyous, as the world has ever witnessed. Had they followed their hereditary taste, the New England settlers would have illustrated all events of public importance by bonfires, banquets, pageantries, and processions. Nor would it have been impracticable, in the observance of majestic ceremonies, to combine mirthful recreation with solemnity, and give, as it were, a grotesque and brilliant embroidery to the great robe of state, which a nation, at such festivals, puts on. There was some shadow of an attempt of this kind in the mode of celebrating the day on which the political year of the colony commenced. The dim reflection of a remembered splendor, a colorless and manifold diluted repetition of what they had beheld in proud old London — we will not say at a royal coronation, but at a Lord Mayor's show — might be traced in the customs which our forefathers instituted, with reference to the annual installation of magistrates. The fathers and founders of the commonwealth — the statesman, the priest, and the soldier — deemed it a duty then to assume the outward state and majesty, which, in accordance with antique style, was looked upon as the proper garb of public or social eminence. All came forth, to move in procession before the people's eye, and thus impart a needed dignity to the simple framework of a government so newly constructed.

Then, too, the people were countenanced, if not encouraged, in relaxing the severe and close application to their various modes of rugged industry, which, at all other times, seemed of the same piece and material with their religion. Here, it is true, were none of the appliances which popular merriment would so readily have found in the England of Elizabeth's time, or that of James; — no rude shows of a theatrical kind; no minstrel with his harp and legendary ballad, nor gleeman, with an ape dancing to his music; no juggler, with his tricks of mimic witchcraft; no Merry Andrew,[66] to stir up the multitude with jests, perhaps hundreds of years old, but still effective, by their appeals to the very broadest sources of

---

[66] Clown.

mirthful sympathy. All such professors of the several branches of jocularity would have been sternly repressed, not only by the rigid discipline of law, but by the general sentiment which gives law its vitality. Not the less, however, the great, honest face of the people smiled, grimly, perhaps, but widely too. Nor were sports wanting, such as the colonists had witnessed, and shared in, long ago, at the country fairs and on the village-greens of England; and which it was thought well to keep alive on this new soil, for the sake of the courage and manliness that were essential in them. Wrestling-matches, in the differing fashions of Cornwall and Devonshire, were seen here and there about the market-place; in one corner, there was a friendly bout at quarterstaff;[67] and—what attracted most interest of all—on the platform of the pillory, already so noted in our pages, two masters of defence were commencing an exhibition with the buckler[68] and broadsword. But, much to the disappointment of the crowd, this latter business was broken off by the interposition of the town beadle, who had no idea of permitting the majesty of the law to be violated by such an abuse of one of its consecrated places.

It may not be too much to affirm, on the whole (the people being then in the first stages of joyless deportment, and the offspring of sires who had known how to be merry, in their day) that they would compare favorably, in point of holiday keeping, with their descendants, even at so long an interval as ourselves. Their immediate posterity, the generation next to the early emigrants, wore the blackest shade of Puritanism, and so darkened the national visage with it, that all the subsequent years have not sufficed to clear it up. We have yet to learn again the forgotten art of gayety.

The picture of human life in the market-place, though its general tint was the sad gray, brown, or black of the English emigrants, was yet enlivened by some diversity of hue. A party of Indians—in their savage finery of curiously embroidered deer-skin robes, wampum-belts, red and yellow ochre, and feathers, and armed with the bow and arrow and stone headed spear—stood apart, with countenances of inflexible gravity, beyond what even the Puritan aspect could attain. Nor, wild as were these painted barbarians, were they the wildest feature of the scene. This distinction could more justly be claimed by some mariners,—a part of the crew of the vessel from the Spanish Main,—who had come ashore to see the humors of Election Day. They were rough-looking desperadoes, with sun-blackened faces, and an immensity of beard; their wide, short trousers were confined about the waist by belts, often clasped with a rough plate of gold, and sustaining

---

[67] An iron-tipped wooden staff six to eight feet long.
[68] A small, round shield.

always a long knife, and, in some instances, a sword. From beneath their broad-brimmed hats of palm-leaf, gleamed eyes which, even in good nature and merriment, had a kind of animal ferocity. They transgressed, without fear or scruple, the rules of behaviour that were binding on all others; smoking tobacco under the beadle's very nose, although each whiff would have cost a townsman a shilling; and quaffing, at their pleasure, draughts of wine or aqua-vitae from pocket-flasks, which they freely tendered to the gaping crowd around them. It remarkably characterized the incomplete morality of the age, rigid as we call it, that a license was allowed the seafaring class, not merely for their freaks on shore, but for far more desperate deeds on their proper element. The sailor of that day would go near to be arraigned as a pirate in our own. There could be little doubt, for instance, that this very ship's crew, though no unfavorable specimens of the nautical brotherhood, had been guilty, as we should phrase it, of depredations on the Spanish commerce, such as would have perilled all their necks in a modern court of justice.

But the sea, in those old times, heaved, swelled, and foamed very much at its own will, or subject only to the tempestuous wind, with hardly any attempts at regulation by human law. The buccaneer on the wave might relinquish his calling, and become at once, if he chose, a man of probity and piety on land; nor, even in the full career of his reckless life, was he regarded as a personage with whom it was disreputable to traffic, or casually associate. Thus, the Puritan elders, in their black cloaks, starched bands, and steeple-crowned hats, smiled not unbenignantly at the clamor and rude deportment of these jolly seafaring men; and it excited neither surprise nor animadversion when so reputable a citizen as old Roger Chillingworth, the physician, was seen to enter the market-place, in close and familiar talk with the commander of the questionable vessel.

The latter was by far the most showy and gallant figure, so far as apparel went, anywhere to be seen among the multitude. He wore a profusion of ribbons on his garment, and gold lace on his hat, which was also encircled by a gold chain, and surmounted with a feather. There was a sword at his side, and a sword-cut on his forehead, which, by the arrangement of his hair, he seemed anxious rather to display than hide. A landsman could hardly have worn this garb and shown this face, and worn and shown them both with such a galliard air, without undergoing stern question before a magistrate, and probably incurring fine or imprisonment, or perhaps an exhibition in the stocks. As regarded the shipmaster, however, all was looked upon as pertaining to the character, as to a fish his glistening scales.

After parting from the physician, the commander of the Bristol ship strolled idly through the marketplace; until, happening to approach the spot where Hester Prynne was standing, he appeared to recognize, and did not hesitate to address her. As was usually the case wherever Hester stood, a small, vacant area—a sort of magic circle—had formed itself about her, into which, though the people were elbowing one another at a little distance, none ventured, or felt disposed to intrude. It was a forcible type of the moral solitude in which the scarlet letter enveloped its fated wearer; partly by her own reserve, and partly by the instinctive, though no longer so unkindly, withdrawal of her fellow-creatures. Now, if never before, it answered a good purpose, by enabling Hester and the seaman to speak together without risk of being overheard; and so changed was Hester Prynne's repute before the public, that the matron in town most eminent for rigid morality could not have held such intercourse with less result of scandal than herself.

"So, mistress," said the mariner. "I must bid the steward make ready one more berth than you bargained for! No fear of scurvy or ship-fever, this voyage! What with the ship's surgeon and this other doctor, our only danger will be from drug or pill; more by token, as there is a lot of apothecary's stuff aboard, which I traded for with a Spanish vessel."

"What mean you?" inquired Hester, startled more than she permitted to appear. "Have you another passenger?"

"Why, know you not," cried the shipmaster, "that this physician here—Chillingworth, he calls himself—is minded to try my cabin-fare with you? Ay, ay, you must have known it; for he tells me he is of your party, and a close friend to the gentleman you spoke of,—he that is in peril from these sour old Puritan rulers!"

"They know each other well, indeed," replied Hester, with a mien of calmness, though in the utmost consternation. "They have long dwelt together."

Nothing further passed between the mariner and Hester Prynne. But, at that instant, she beheld old Roger Chillingworth himself, standing in the remotest corner of the market-place, and smiling on her; a smile which—across the wide and bustling square, and through all the talk and laughter, and various thoughts, moods, and interests of the crowd—conveyed secret and fearful meaning.

XXII

The Procession

Before Hester Prynne could call together her thoughts, and consider what was practicable to be done in this new and startling aspect of affairs, the sound of military music was heard approaching along a contiguous street. It denoted the advance of the procession of magistrates and citizens, on its way towards the meeting-house; where, in compliance with a custom thus early established, and ever since observed, the Reverend Mr. Dimmesdale was to deliver an Election Sermon.

Soon the head of the procession showed itself, with a slow and stately march, turning a corner, and making its way across the market-place. First came the music. It comprised a variety of instruments, perhaps imperfectly adapted to one another, and played with no great skill, but yet attaining the great object for which the harmony of drum and clarion addresses itself to the multitude, — that of imparting a higher and more heroic air to the scene of life than passes before the eye. Little Pearl at first clapped her hands, but then lost, for an instant, the restless agitation that had kept her in a continual effervescence throughout the morning; she gazed silently, and seemed to be borne upward, like a floating sea-bird, on the long heaves and swells of sound. But she was brought back to her former mood by the shimmer of the sunshine on the weapons and bright armour of the military company, which followed after the music, and formed the honorary escort of the procession. This body of soldiery — which still sustains a corporate existence, and marches down from past ages with an ancient and honorable fame — was composed of no mercenary materials. Its ranks were filled with gentlemen, who felt the stirrings of martial impulse, and sought to establish a kind of College of Arms,[69] where, as in an association of Knights Templars,[70] they might learn the science, and, so far as peaceful exercise would teach them, the practices of war. The high estimation then placed upon the military character might be seen in the lofty port of each individual member of the company. Some of them, indeed, by their services in the Low Countries and on other fields of European warfare, had fairly won their title to assume the name and pomp of soldiership. The entire array, moreover, clad in burnished steel, and with plumage nodding over their bright morions, had a brilliancy of effect which no modern display can aspire to equal.

And yet the men of civil eminence, who came immediately behind the military escort, were better worth a thoughtful observer's eye. Even in outward demeanour they showed a stamp of majesty that made the warrior's haughty stride look vulgar, if not absurd. It was an age when what we call talent had far less consideration than now, but the massive materials which produce stability and dignity of character a great deal more. The people possessed, by hereditary right, the quality of reverence; which, in their descendants, if it survive at all, exists in smaller proportion, and with a vastly

---

[69] An English corporation whose duties include recording genealogies and coats of arms.
[70] An order of knights established in the twelfth century to safeguard pilgrims to Jerusalem.

diminished force in the selection and estimate of public men. The change may be for good or ill, and is partly, perhaps, for both. In that old day, the English settler on these rude shores, —having left king, nobles, and all degrees of awful rank behind, while still the faculty and necessity of reverence were strong in him, —bestowed it on the white hair and venerable brow of age; on long-tried integrity; on solid wisdom and sad-colored experience; on endowments of that grave and weighty order, which gives the idea of permanence, and comes under the general definition of respectability. These primitive statesmen, therefore, —Bradstreet, Endicott, Dudley, Bellingham,[71] and their compeers, —who were elevated to power by the early choice of the people, seem to have been not often brilliant, but distinguished by a ponderous sobriety, rather than activity of intellect. They had fortitude and self-reliance, and, in time of difficulty or peril, stood up for the welfare of the state like a line of cliffs against a tempestuous tide. The traits of character here indicated were well represented in the square cast of countenance and large physical development of the new colonial magistrates. So far as a demeanour of natural authority was concerned, the mother country need not have been ashamed to see these foremost men of an actual democracy adopted into the House of Peers, or made the Privy Council of the sovereign.

Next in order to the magistrates came the young and eminently distinguished divine, from whose lips the religious discourse of the anniversary was expected. His was the profession, at that era, in which intellectual ability displayed itself far more than in political life; for—leaving a higher motive out of the question—it offered inducements powerful enough, in the almost worshipping respect of the community, to win the most aspiring ambition into its service. Even political power—as in the case of Increase Mather[72]—was within the grasp of a successful priest.

It was the observation of those who beheld him now, that never, since Mr. Dimmesdale first set his foot on the New England shore, had he exhibited such energy as was seen in the gait and air with which he kept his pace in the procession. There was no feebleness of step, as at other times; his frame was not bent; nor did his hand rest ominously upon his heart. Yet, if the clergyman were rightly viewed, his strength seemed not of the body. It might be spiritual, and imparted to him by angelic ministrations.

---

[71] Simon Bradstreet (1603–97), John Endicott (1588–1665), Thomas Dudley (1576–1653), and Richard Bellingham served Massachusetts as governors and in other official capacities.
[72] Both Increase Mather (1639–1723) and his son Cotton Mather (1663–1728) were powerful Puritan ministers.

It might be the exhilaration of that potent cordial, which is distilled only in the furnace-glow of earnest and long-continued thought. Or, perchance, his sensitive temperament was invigorated by the loud and piercing music, that swelled heavenward, and uplifted him on its ascending wave. Nevertheless, so abstracted was his look, it might be questioned whether Mr. Dimmesdale even heard the music. There was his body, moving onward, and with an unaccustomed force. But where was his mind? Far and deep in its own region, busying itself, with preternatural activity, to marshal a procession of stately thoughts that were soon to issue thence; and so he saw nothing, heard nothing, knew nothing, of what was around him; but the spiritual element took up the feeble frame, and carried it along, unconscious of the burden, and converting it to spirit like itself. Men of uncommon intellect, who have grown morbid, possess this occasional power of mighty effort, into which they throw the life of many days, and then are lifeless for as many more.

Hester Prynne, gazing stedfastly at the clergyman, felt a dreary influence come over her, but wherefore or whence she knew not; unless that he seemed so remote from her own sphere, and utterly beyond her reach. One glance of recognition, she had imagined, must needs pass between them. She thought of the dim forest, with its little dell of solitude, and love, and anguish, and the mossy tree-trunk, where, sitting hand in hand, they had mingled their sad and passionate talk with the melancholy murmur of the brook. How deeply had they known each other then! And was this the man? She hardly knew him now! He, moving proudly past, enveloped, as it were, in the rich music, with the procession of majestic and venerable fathers; he, so unattainable in his worldly position, and still more so in that far vista of his unsympathizing thoughts, through which she now beheld him! Her spirit sank with the idea that all must have been a delusion, and that, vividly as she had dreamed it, there could be no real bond betwixt the clergyman and herself. And thus much of woman was there in Hester, that she could scarcely forgive him,—least of all now, when the heavy footstep of their approaching Fate might be heard, nearer, nearer, nearer!—for being able so completely to withdraw himself from their mutual world; while she groped darkly, and stretched forth her cold hands, and found him not.

Pearl either saw and responded to her mother's feelings, or herself felt the remoteness and intangibility that had fallen around the minister. While the procession passed, the child was uneasy, fluttering up and down, like a bird on the point of taking flight. When the whole had gone by, she looked up into Hester's face.

"Mother," said she, "was that the same minister that kissed me by the brook?"

"Hold thy peace, dear little Pearl!" whispered her mother. "We must not always talk in the market-place of what happens to us in the forest."

"I could not be sure that it was he; so strange he looked," continued the child. "Else I would have run to him, and bid him kiss me now, before all the people; even as he did yonder among the dark old trees. What would the minister have said, mother? Would he have clapped his hand over his heart, and scowled on me, and bid me begone?"

"What should he say, Pearl," answered Hester, "save that it was no time to kiss, and that kisses are not to be given in the market-place? Well for thee, foolish child, that thou didst not speak to him!"

Another shade of the same sentiment, in reference to Mr. Dimmesdale, was expressed by a person whose eccentricities—or insanity, as we should term it—led her to do what few of the townspeople would have ventured on; to begin a conversation with the wearer of the scarlet letter, in public. It was Mistress Hibbins, who, arrayed in great magnificence, with a triple ruff, a broidered stomacher, a gown of rich velvet, and a gold-headed cane, had come forth to see the procession. As this ancient lady had the renown (which subsequently cost her no less a price than her life) of being a principal actor in all the works of necromancy that were continually going forward, the crowd gave way before her, and seemed to fear the touch of her garment, as if it carried the plague among its gorgeous folds. Seen in conjunction with Hester Prynne,—kindly as so many now felt towards the latter,—the dread inspired by Mistress Hibbins was doubled, and caused a general movement from that part of the market-place in which the two women stood.

"Now, what mortal imagination could conceive it!" whispered the old lady confidentially to Hester. "Yonder divine man! That saint on earth, as the people uphold him to be, and as—I must needs say—he really looks! Who, now, that saw him pass in the procession, would think how little while it is since he went forth out of his study,—chewing a Hebrew text of Scripture in his mouth, I warrant,—to take an airing in the forest! Aha! we know what that means, Hester Prynne! But, truly, forsooth, I find it hard to believe him the same man. Many a church-member saw I, walking behind the music, that has danced in the same measure with me, when Somebody was fiddler, and it might be, an Indian powwow or a Lapland wizard changing hands with us! That is but a trifle, when a woman knows the world. But this minister! Couldst thou surely tell, Hester, whether he was the same man that encountered thee on the forest-path!"

"Madam, I know not of what you speak," answered Hester Prynne, feeling Mistress Hibbins to be of infirm mind; yet strangely startled and awe-stricken by the confidence with which she affirmed a personal connection between so many persons (herself among them) and the Evil One. "It is not for me to talk lightly of a learned and pious minister of the Word, like the Reverend Mr. Dimmesdale!"

"Fie, woman, fie!" cried the old lady, shaking her finger at Hester. "Dost thou think I have been to the forest so many times, and have yet no skill to judge who else has been there? Yea; though no leaf of the wild garlands, which they wore while they danced, be left in their hair! I know thee, Hester; for I behold the token. We may all see it in the sunshine; and it glows like a red flame in the dark. Thou wearest it openly; so there need be no question about that. But this minister! Let me tell thee in thine ear! When the Black Man sees one of his own servants, signed and sealed, so shy of owning to the bond as is the Reverend Mr. Dimmesdale, he hath a way of ordering matters so that the mark shall be disclosed in open daylight to the eyes of all the world! What is it that the minister seeks to hide, with his hand always over his heart? Ha, Hester Prynne!"

"What is it, good Mistress Hibbins?" eagerly asked little Pearl. "Hast thou seen it?"

"No matter, darling!" responded Mistress Hibbins, making Pearl a profound reverence. "Thou thyself wilt see it, one time or another. They say, child, thou art of the lineage of the Prince of the Air! Wilt thou ride with me, some fine night, to see thy father? Then thou shalt know wherefore the minister keeps his hand over his heart!"

Laughing so shrilly that all the market-place could hear her, the weird old gentlewoman took her departure.

By this time the preliminary prayer had been offered in the meetinghouse, and the accents of the Reverend Mr. Dimmesdale were heard commencing his discourse. An irresistible feeling kept Hester near the spot. As the sacred edifice was too much thronged to admit another auditor, she took up her position close beside the scaffold of the pillory. It was in sufficient proximity to bring the whole sermon to her ears, in the shape of an indistinct, but varied, murmur and flow of the minister's very peculiar voice.

This vocal organ was in itself a rich endowment; insomuch that a listener, comprehending nothing of the language in which the preacher spoke, might still have been swayed to and fro by the mere tone and cadence. Like all other music, it breathed passion and pathos, and emotions high or tender, in a tongue native to the human heart, wherever educated. Muffled as the sound was by its passage through the church-walls, Hester Prynne listened with such intentness, and sympathized so intimately, that the sermon had throughout a meaning for her, entirely apart from its indistinguishable words. These, perhaps, if more distinctly heard, might have been only a grosser medium, and have clogged the spiritual sense. Now she caught the low undertone, as of the wind sinking down to repose itself; then ascended with it, as it rose through progressive gradations of sweetness and power, until its volume seemed to envelop her with an atmosphere of awe and solemn grandeur. And yet, majestic as the voice sometimes became, there was for ever in it an essential character of plaintiveness. A loud or low expression of anguish,—the whisper, or the shriek, as it might be conceived, of suffering humanity, that touched a sensibility in every bosom! At times this deep strain of pathos was all that could be heard, and scarcely heard, sighing amid a desolate silence. But even when the minister's voice grew high and commanding,—when it gushed irrepressibly upward,—when it assumed its utmost breadth and power, so overfilling the church as to burst its way through the solid walls, and diffuse itself in the open air,—still, if the auditor listened intently, and for the purpose, he could detect the same cry of pain. What was it? The complaint of a human heart, sorrow-laden, perchance guilty, telling its secret, whether of guilt or sorrow, to the great heart of mankind; beseeching its sympathy or forgiveness,—at every moment,—in each accent,—and never in vain! It was this profound and continual undertone that gave the clergyman his most appropriate power.

During all this time Hester stood, statue-like, at the foot of the scaffold. If the minister's voice had not kept her there, there would nevertheless have been an inevitable magnetism in that spot, whence she dated the first hour of her life of ignominy. There was a sense within her,—too ill-defined to be made a thought, but weighing heavily on her mind,—that her whole orb of life, both before and after, was connected with this spot, as with the one point that gave it unity.

Little Pearl, meanwhile, had quitted her mother's side, and was playing at her own will about the market-place. She made the sombre crowd cheerful by her erratic and glistening ray; even as a bird of bright plumage illuminates a whole tree of dusky foliage by darting to and fro, half seen and half concealed, amid the twilight of the clustering leaves. She had an undulating, but, oftentimes, a sharp and irregular movement. It indicated the restless vivacity of her spirit, which to-day was doubly indefatigable in its tiptoe dance, because it was played upon and vibrated with her mother's disquietude. Whenever Pearl saw any thing to excite her ever active and wandering curiosity, she flew thitherward, and, as we might say, seized upon that man or thing as her own property, so far as she desired it; but without yielding the minutest degree of control over her motions in requital. The Puritans looked on, and, if they smiled, were none the less inclined to pronounce the child a demon offspring, from the indescribable charm of beauty and eccentricity that shone through her little figure, and sparkled with its activity. She ran and looked the wild Indian in the face; and he grew conscious of a nature wilder than his own. Thence, with native audacity, but still with a reserve as characteristic, she flew into the midst of a group of mariners, the swarthy-cheeked wild men of the ocean, as the Indians were of the land; and they gazed wonderingly and admiringly at Pearl, as if a flake of the sea-foam had taken the shape of a little maid, and were gifted with a soul of the sea-fire, that flashes beneath the prow in the nighttime.

One of these seafaring men—the shipmaster, indeed, who had spoken to Hester Prynne—was so smitten with Pearl's aspect, that he attempted to lay hands upon her, with purpose to snatch a kiss. Finding it as impossible to touch her as to catch a humming-bird in the air, he took from his hat the gold chain that was twisted about it, and threw it to the child. Pearl immediately twined it around her neck and waist, with such happy skill, that, once seen there, it became a part of her, and it was difficult to imagine her without it.

"Thy mother is yonder woman with the scarlet letter," said the seaman. "Wilt thou carry her a message from me?"

"If the message pleases me I will," answered Pearl.

"Then tell her," rejoined he, "that I spake again with the black-a-visaged, hump-shouldered old doctor, and he engages to bring his friend, the gentleman she wots of, aboard with him. So let thy mother take no thought, save for herself and thee. Wilt thou tell her this, thou witch-baby?"

"Mistress Hibbins says my father is the Prince of the Air!" cried Pearl, with her naughty smile. "If thou callest me that ill name, I shall tell him of thee; and he will chase thy ship with a tempest!"

Pursuing a zigzag course across the market-place, the child returned to her mother, and communicated what the mariner had said. Hester's strong, calm, stedfastly enduring spirit almost sank, at last, on beholding this dark and grim countenance of an inevitable doom, which—at the moment when a passage seemed to open for the minister and herself out of their labyrinth of misery—showed itself, with an unrelenting smile, right in the midst of their path.

With her mind harassed by the terrible perplexity in which the shipmaster's intelligence involved her, she was also subjected to another trial. There were many people present, from the country roundabout, who had often heard of the scarlet letter, and to whom it had been made terrific by a hundred false or exaggerated rumors, but who had never beheld it with their own bodily eyes. These, after exhausting other modes of amusement, now thronged about Hester Prynne with rude and boorish intrusiveness. Unscrupulous as it was, however, it could not bring them nearer than a circuit of several yards. At that distance they accordingly stood, fixed there by the centrifugal force of the repugnance which the mystic symbol inspired. The whole gang of sailors, likewise, observing the press of spectators, and learning the purport of the scarlet letter, came and thrust their sunburnt and desperado-looking faces into the ring. Even the Indians were affected by a sort of cold shadow of the white man's curiosity, and, gliding through the crowd, fastened their snake-like black eyes on Hester's bosom; conceiving, perhaps, that the wearer of this brilliantly embroidered badge must needs be a personage of high dignity among her people. Lastly, the inhabitants of the town (their own interest in this worn-out subject languidly reviving itself, by sympathy with what they saw others feel) lounged idly to the same quarter, and tormented Hester Prynne, perhaps more than all the rest, with their cool, well-acquainted gaze at her familiar shame. Hester saw and recognized the self-same faces of that group of matrons, who had awaited her forthcoming from the prison-door, seven years ago; all save one, the youngest and only compassionate among them, whose burial-robe she had since made. At the final hour, when she was so soon to fling aside the burning letter, it had strangely become the centre of more remark and excitement, and was thus made to sear her breast more painfully, than at any time since the first day she put it on.

While Hester stood in that magic circle of ignominy, where the cunning cruelty of her sentence seemed to have fixed her for ever, the admirable preacher was looking down from the sacred pulpit upon an audience, whose very inmost spirits had yielded to his control. The sainted minister in the church! The woman of the scarlet letter in the market-place! What imagination would have been irreverent enough to surmise that the same scorching stigma was on them both?

XXIII
The Revelation of the Scarlet Letter

The eloquent voice, on which the souls of the listening audience had been borne aloft, as on the swelling waves of the sea, at length came to a pause. There was a momentary silence, profound as what should follow the utterance of oracles. Then ensued a murmur and half-hushed tumult; as if the auditors, released from the high spell that had transported them into the region of another's mind, were returning into themselves, with all their awe and wonder still heavy on them. In a moment more, the crowd began to gush forth from the doors of the church. Now that there was an end, they needed other breath, more fit to support the gross and earthly life into which they relapsed, than that atmosphere which the preacher had converted into words of flame, and had burdened with the rich fragrance of his thought.

In the open air their rapture broke into speech. The street and the market-place absolutely babbled, from side to side, with applauses of the minister. His hearers could not rest until they had told one another of what each knew better than he could tell or hear. According to their united testimony, never had man spoken in so wise, so high, and so holy a spirit, as he that spake this day; nor had inspiration ever breathed through mortal lips more evidently than it did through his. Its influence could be seen, as it were, descending upon him, and possessing him, and continually lifting him out of the written discourse that lay before him, and filling him with ideas that must have been as marvellous to himself as to his audience. His subject, it appeared, had been the relation between the Deity and the communities of mankind, with a special reference to the New England which they were here planting in the wilderness. And, as he drew towards the close, a spirit as of prophecy had come upon him, constraining him to its purpose as mightily as the old prophets of Israel were constrained; only with this difference, that, whereas the Jewish seers had denounced judgments and ruin on their country, it was his mission to foretell a high and glorious destiny for the newly gathered people of the Lord. But, throughout it all, and through the whole discourse, there had been a certain deep, sad undertone of pathos, which could not be interpreted otherwise than as the natural regret of one soon to pass away. Yes; their minister whom they so loved—and who so loved them all, that he could not depart heavenward without a sigh—had the foreboding of untimely death upon him, and would soon leave them in their tears! This idea of his transitory stay on earth gave the last emphasis to the effect which the preacher had produced; it was as if an angel, in his passage to the skies, had shaken his bright wings over the people for an instant,—at once a shadow and a splendor,—and had shed down a shower of golden truths upon them.

Thus, there had come to the Reverend Mr. Dimmesdale—as to most men, in their various spheres, though seldom recognized until they see it far behind them—an epoch of life more brilliant and full of triumph than any previous one, or than any which could hereafter be. He stood, at this moment, on the very proudest eminence of superiority, to which the gifts of intellect, rich lore, prevailing eloquence, and a reputation of whitest sanctity, could exalt a clergyman in New England's earliest days, when the professional character was of itself a lofty pedestal. Such was the position which the minister occupied, as he bowed his head forward on the cushions of the pulpit, at the close of his Election Sermon. Meanwhile, Hester Prynne was standing beside the scaffold of the pillory, with the scarlet letter still burning on her breast!

Now was heard again the clangor of the music, and the measured tramp of the military escort, issuing from the church-door. The procession was to be marshalled thence to the town-hall, where a solemn banquet would complete the ceremonies of the day.

Once more, therefore, the train of venerable and majestic fathers was seen moving through a broad pathway of the people, who drew back reverently, on either side, as the Governor and magistrates, the old and wise men, the holy ministers, and all that were eminent and renowned, advanced into the midst of them. When they were fairly in the market-place, their presence was greeted by a shout. This—though doubtless it might acquire additional force and volume from the childlike loyalty which the age awarded to its rulers—was felt to be an irrepressible outburst of the enthusiasm kindled in the auditors by that high strain of eloquence which was yet reverberating in their ears. Each felt the impulse in himself, and, in the same breath, caught it from his neighbour. Within the church, it had hardly been kept down; beneath the sky, it pealed upward to the zenith. There were human beings enough, and enough of highly wrought and symphonious feeling, to produce that more impressive sound than the organ-tones of the blast, or the thunder, or the roar of the sea; even that mighty swell of many voices, blended into one great voice by the universal impulse which makes likewise one vast heart out of the many. Never, from the soil of New England, had gone up such a shout! Never, on New England soil, had stood the man so honored by his mortal brethren as the preacher!

How fared it with him then? Were there not the brilliant particles of a halo in the air about his head? So etherealized by spirit as he was, and so apotheosized by worshipping admirers, did his footsteps in the procession really tread upon the dust of earth?

As the ranks of military men and civil fathers moved onward, all eyes were turned towards the point where the minister was seen to approach among them. The shout died into a murmur, as one portion of the crowd after another obtained a glimpse of him. How feeble and pale he looked amid all his triumph! The energy—or say, rather, the inspiration which had held him up, until he should have delivered the sacred message that brought its own strength along with it from heaven—was withdrawn, now that it had so faithfully performed its office. The glow, which they had just before beheld burning on his cheek, was extinguished, like a flame that sinks down hopelessly among the late-decaying embers. It seemed hardly the face of a man alive, with such a deathlike hue; it was hardly a man with life in him, that tottered on his path so nervelessly, yet tottered, and did not fall!

One of his clerical brethren,—it was the venerable John Wilson,—observing the state in which Mr. Dimmesdale was left by the retiring wave of intellect and sensibility, stepped forward hastily to offer his support. The minister tremulously, but decidedly, repelled the old man's arm. He still walked onward, if that movement could be so described, which rather resembled the wavering effort of an infant, with its mother's arms in view, outstretched to tempt him forward. And now, almost imperceptible as were the latter steps of his progress, he had come opposite the well-remembered and weather-darkened scaffold, where, long since, with all that dreary lapse of time between, Hester Prynne had encountered the world's ignominious stare. There stood Hester, holding little Pearl by the hand! And there was the scarlet letter on her breast! The minister here made a pause; although the music still played the stately and rejoicing march to which the procession moved. It summoned him onward—onward to the festival!—but here he made a pause.

Bellingham, for the last few moments, had kept an anxious eye upon him. He now left his own place in the procession, and advanced to give assistance; judging from Mr. Dimmesdale's aspect that he must otherwise inevitably fall. But there was something in the latter's expression that warned back the magistrate, although a man not readily obeying the vague intimations that pass from one spirit to another. The crowd, meanwhile, looked on with awe and wonder. This earthly faintness was, in their view, only another phase of the minister's celestial strength; nor would it have seemed a miracle too high to be wrought for one so holy, had he ascended before their eyes, waxing dimmer and brighter, and fading at last into the light of heaven!

He turned towards the scaffold, and stretched forth his arms.

"Hester," said he, "come hither! Come, my little Pearl!"

It was a ghastly look with which he regarded them; but there was something at once tender and strangely triumphant in it. The child, with the bird-like motion which was one of her characteristics, flew to him, and clasped her arms about his knees. Hester Prynne—slowly, as if impelled by inevitable fate, and against her strongest will—likewise drew near, but paused before she reached him. At this instant old Roger Chillingworth thrust himself through the crowd,—or, perhaps, so dark, disturbed, and evil was his look, he rose up out of some nether region,—to snatch back his victim from what he sought to do! Be that as it might, the old man rushed forward and caught the minister by the arm.

"Madman, hold! What is your purpose?" whispered he. "Wave back that woman! Cast off this child! All shall be well! Do not blacken your fame, and perish in dishonor! I can yet save you! Would you bring infamy on your sacred profession?"

"Ha, tempter! Methinks thou art too late!" answered the minister, encountering his eye, fearfully, but firmly. "Thy power is not what it was! With God's help, I shall escape thee now!"

He again extended his hand to the woman of the scarlet letter.

"Hester Prynne," cried he, with a piercing earnestness, "in the name of Him, so terrible and so merciful, who gives me grace, at this last moment, to do what—for my own heavy sin and miserable agony—I withheld myself from doing seven years ago, come hither now, and twine thy strength about me! Thy strength, Hester; but let it be guided by the will which God hath granted me! This wretched and wronged old man is opposing it with all his might! — with all his own might and the fiend's! Come, Hester, come! Support me up yonder scaffold!"

The crowd was in a tumult. The men of rank and dignity, who stood more immediately around the clergyman, were so taken by surprise, and so perplexed as to the purport of what they saw, — unable to receive the explanation which most readily presented itself, or to imagine any other, — that they remained silent and inactive spectators of the judgment which Providence seemed about to work. They beheld the minister, leaning on Hester's shoulder and supported by her arm around him, approach the scaffold, and ascend its steps; while still the little hand of the sin-born child was clasped in his. Old Roger Chillingworth followed, as one intimately connected with the drama of guilt and sorrow in which they had all been actors, and well entitled, therefore, to be present at its closing scene.

"Hadst thou sought the whole earth over," said he, looking darkly at the clergyman, "there was no place so secret, — no high place nor lowly place, where thou couldst have escaped me, — save on this very scaffold!"

"Thanks be to Him who hath led me hither!" answered the minister.

Yet he trembled, and turned to Hester with an expression of doubt and anxiety in his eyes, not the less evidently betrayed, that there was a feeble smile upon his lips.

"Is not this better," murmured he, "than what we dreamed of in the forest?"

"I know not! I know not!" she hurriedly replied. "Better? Yea; so we may both die, and little Pearl die with us!"

"For thee and Pearl, be it as God shall order," said the minister; "and God is merciful! Let me now do the will which he hath made plain before my sight. For, Hester, I am a dying man. So let me make haste to take my shame upon me."

Partly supported by Hester Prynne, and holding one hand of little Pearl's, the Reverend Mr. Dimmesdale turned to the dignified and venerable rulers; to the holy ministers, who were his brethren; to the people, whose great heart was thoroughly appalled, yet overflowing with tearful sympathy, as knowing that some deep life-matter — which, if full of sin, was full of anguish and repentance likewise — was now to be laid open to them. The sun, but little past its meridian, shone down upon the clergyman, and gave a distinctness to his figure, as he stood out from all the earth to put in his plea of guilty at the bar of Eternal Justice.

"People of New England!" cried he, with a voice that rose over them, high, solemn, and majestic, — yet had always a tremor through it, and sometimes a shriek, struggling up out of a fathomless depth of remorse and woe, —

"ye, that have loved me!—ye, that have deemed me holy!—behold me here, the one sinner of the world! At last!—at last!—I stand upon the spot where, seven years since, I should have stood; here, with this woman, whose arm, more than the little strength wherewith I have crept hitherward, sustains me, at this dreadful moment, from grovelling down upon my face! Lo, the scarlet letter which Hester wears! Ye have all shuddered at it! Wherever her walk hath been,—wherever, so miserably burdened, she may have hoped to find repose,—it hath cast a lurid gleam of awe and horrible repugnance roundabout her. But there stood one in the midst of you, at whose brand of sin and infamy ye have not shuddered!"

It seemed, at this point, as if the minister must leave the remainder of his secret undisclosed. But he fought back the bodily weakness,—and, still more, the faintness of heart,—that was striving for the mastery with him. He threw off all assistance, and stepped passionately forward a pace before the woman and the child.

"It was on him!" he continued, with a kind of fierceness; so determined was he to speak out the whole. "God's eye beheld it! The angels were for ever pointing at it! The Devil knew it well, and fretted it continually with the touch of his burning finger! But he hid it cunningly from men, and walked among you with the mien of a spirit, mournful, because so pure in a sinful world!—and sad, because he missed his heavenly kindred! Now, at the death-hour, he stands up before you! He bids you look again at Hester's scarlet letter! He tells you, that, with all its mysterious horror, it is but the shadow of what he bears on his own breast, and that even this, his own red stigma, is no more than the type of what has seared his inmost heart! Stand any here that question God's judgment on a sinner? Behold! Behold a dreadful witness of it!"

With a convulsive motion he tore away the ministerial band from before his breast. It was revealed! But it were irreverent to describe that revelation. For an instant the gaze of the horror-stricken multitude was concentrated on the ghastly miracle; while the minister stood with a flush of triumph in his face, as one who, in the crisis of acutest pain, had won a victory. Then, down he sank upon the scaffold! Hester partly raised him, and supported his head against her bosom. Old Roger Chillingworth knelt down beside him, with a blank, dull countenance, out of which the life seemed to have departed.

"Thou hast escaped me!" he repeated more than once. "Thou hast escaped me!"

"May God forgive thee!" said the minister. "Thou, too, hast deeply sinned!"

He withdrew his dying eyes from the old man, and fixed them on the woman and the child.

The Revelation of the Scarlet Letter by F. O. C. Darley. Originally appeared in the 1879 Houghton Mifflin edition of the novel.

"My little Pearl," said he feebly, — and there was a sweet and gentle smile over his face, as of a spirit sinking into deep repose; nay, now that the burden was removed, it seemed almost as if he would be sportive with the child, — "dear little Pearl, wilt thou kiss me now? Thou wouldst not yonder, in the forest! But now thou wilt?"

Pearl kissed his lips. A spell was broken. The great scene of grief, in which the wild infant bore a part, had developed all her sympathies; and as her tears fell upon her father's cheek, they were the pledge that she would grow up amid human joy and sorrow, nor for ever do battle with the world, but be a woman in it. Towards her mother, too, Pearl's errand as a messenger of anguish was all fulfilled.

"Hester," said the clergyman, "farewell!"

"Shall we not meet again?" whispered she, bending her face down close to his. "Shall we not spend our immortal life together? Surely, surely, we have ransomed one another, with all this woe! Thou lookest far into eternity, with those bright dying eyes! Then tell me what thou seest?"

"Hush, Hester, hush!" said he, with tremulous solemnity. "The law we broke! — the sin here so awfully revealed! — let these alone be in thy thoughts! I fear! I fear! It may be, that, when we forgot our God, — when we violated our reverence each for the other's soul, — it was thenceforth vain to hope that we could meet hereafter, in an everlasting and pure reunion. God knows; and He is merciful! He hath proved his mercy, most of all, in my afflictions. By giving me this burning torture to bear upon my breast! By sending yonder dark and terrible old man, to keep the torture always at red-heat! By bringing me hither, to die this death of triumphant ignominy before the people! Had either of these agonies been wanting, I had been lost for ever! Praised be his name! His will be done! Farewell!"

That final word came forth with the minister's expiring breath. The multitude, silent till then, broke out in a strange, deep voice of awe and wonder, which could not as yet find utterance, save in this murmur that rolled so heavily after the departed spirit.

XXIV

Conclusion

After many days, when time sufficed for the people to arrange their thoughts in reference to the foregoing scene, there was more than one account of what had been witnessed on the scaffold.

Most of the spectators testified to having seen, on the breast of the unhappy minister, a scarlet letter — the very semblance of that worn by Hester Prynne — imprinted in the flesh. As regarded its origin, there were various explanations, all of which must necessarily have been conjectural. Some affirmed that the Reverend Mr. Dimmesdale, on the very day when Hester Prynne first wore her ignominious badge, had begun a course of penance,—which he afterwards, in so many futile methods, followed out,—by inflicting a hideous torture on himself. Others contended that the stigma had not been produced until a long time subsequent, when old Roger Chillingworth, being a potent necromancer, had caused it to appear, through the agency of magic and poisonous drugs. Others, again,—and those best able to appreciate the minister's peculiar sensibility, and the wonderful operation of his spirit upon the body,—whispered their belief, that the awful symbol was the effect of the ever active tooth of remorse, gnawing from the inmost heart outwardly, and at last manifesting Heaven's dreadful judgment by the visible presence of the letter. The reader may choose among these theories. We have thrown all the light we could acquire upon the portent, and would gladly, now that it has done its office, erase its deep print out of our own brain; where long meditation has fixed it in very undesirable distinctness.

It is singular, nevertheless, that certain persons, who were spectators of the whole scene, and professed never once to have removed their eyes from the Reverend Mr. Dimmesdale, denied that there was any mark whatever on his breast, more than on a new-born infant's. Neither, by their report, had his dying words acknowledged, nor even remotely implied, any, the slightest connection, on his part, with the guilt for which Hester Prynne had so long worn the scarlet letter. According to these highly respectable witnesses, the minister, conscious that he was dying,—conscious, also, that the reverence of the multitude placed him already among saints and angels,—had desired, by yielding up his breath in the arms of that fallen woman, to express to the world how utterly nugatory is the choicest of man's own righteousness. After exhausting life in his efforts for mankind's spiritual good, he had made the manner of his death a parable, in order to impress on his admirers the mighty and mournful lesson, that, in the view of Infinite Purity, we are sinners all alike. It was to teach them, that the holiest among us has but attained so far above his fellows as to discern more clearly the Mercy which looks down, and repudiate more utterly the phantom of human merit, which would look aspiringly upward. Without disputing a truth so momentous, we must be allowed to consider this version of Mr. Dimmesdale's story as only an instance of that stubborn fidelity with which a man's friends—and especially a clergyman's—will sometimes uphold his character; when proofs, clear as the mid-day sunshine on the scarlet letter, establish him a false and sin-stained creature of the dust.

The authority which we have chiefly followed—a manuscript of old date, drawn up from the verbal testimony of individuals, some of whom had known Hester Prynne, while others had heard the tale from contemporary witnesses — fully confirms the view taken in the foregoing pages. Among many morals which press upon us from the poor minister's miserable experience, we put only this into a sentence: — "Be true! Be true! Be true! Show freely to the world, if not your worst, yet some trait whereby the worst may be inferred!"

Nothing was more remarkable than the change which took place, almost immediately after Mr. Dimmesdale's death, in the appearance and demeanour of the old man known as Roger Chillingworth. All his strength and energy — all his vital and intellectual force — seemed at once to desert him; insomuch that he positively withered up, shrivelled away, and almost vanished from mortal sight, like an uprooted weed that lies wilting in the sun. This unhappy man had made the very principle of his life to consist in the pursuit and systematic exercise of revenge; and when, by its completest triumph and consummation, that evil principle was left with no further material to support it, — when, in short, there was no more devil's work on earth for him to do, it only remained for the unhumanized mortal to betake himself whither his Master would find him tasks enough, and pay him his wages duly. But, to all these shadowy beings, so long our near acquaintances, — as well Roger Chillingworth as his companions, — we would fain be merciful. It is a curious subject of observation and inquiry, whether hatred and love be not the same thing at bottom. Each, in its utmost development, supposes a high degree of intimacy and heart-knowledge; each renders one individual dependent for the food of his affections and spiritual life upon another; each leaves the passionate lover, or the no less passionate hater, forlorn and desolate by the withdrawal of his object. Philosophically considered, therefore, the two passions seem essentially the same, except that one happens to be seen in a celestial radiance, and the other in a dusky and lurid glow. In the spiritual world, the old physician and the minister — mutual victims as they have been — may, unawares, have found their earthly stock of hatred and antipathy transmuted into golden love.

Leaving this discussion apart, we have a matter of business to communicate to the reader. At old Roger Chillingworth's decease (which took place within the year), and by his last will and testament of which Governor Bellingham and the Reverend Mr. Wilson were executors, he bequeathed a very considerable amount of property, both here and in England, to little Pearl, the daughter of Hester Prynne.

So Pearl — the elf-child, — the demon offspring, as some people, up to that epoch, persisted in considering her — became the richest heiress of her day, in the New World. Not improbably, this circumstance wrought a very material change in the public estimation; and, had the mother and child remained here, little Pearl, at a marriageable period of life, might have mingled her wild blood with the lineage of the devoutest Puritan among them all. But, in no long time after the physician's death, the wearer of the scarlet letter disappeared, and Pearl along with her. For many years, though a vague report would now and then find its way across the sea, —like a shapeless piece of driftwood tost ashore, with the initials of a name upon it, —yet no tidings of them unquestionably authentic were received. The story of the scarlet letter grew into a legend. Its spell, however, was still potent, and kept the scaffold awful where the poor minister had died, and likewise the cottage by the sea-shore, where Hester Prynne had dwelt. Near this latter spot, one afternoon, some children were at play, when they beheld a tall woman, in a gray robe, approach the cottage-door. In all those years it had never once been opened; but either she unlocked it, or the decaying wood and iron yielded to her hand, or she glided shadow-like through these impediments, —and, at all events, went in.

On the threshold she paused, —turned partly round, —for, perchance, the idea of entering, all alone, and all so changed, the home of so intense a former life, was more dreary and desolate than even she could bear. But her hesitation was only for an instant, though long enough to display a scarlet letter on her breast.

And Hester Prynne had returned, and taken up her long-forsaken shame. But where was little Pearl? If still alive, she must now have been in the flush and bloom of early womanhood. None knew—nor ever learned, with the fullness of perfect certainty—whether the elf-child had gone thus untimely to a maiden grave; or whether her wild, rich nature had been softened and subdued, and made capable of a woman's gentle happiness. But, through the remainder of Hester's life, there were indications that the recluse of the scarlet letter was the object of love and interest with some inhabitant of another land. Letters came, with armorial seals upon them, though of bearings unknown to English heraldry. In the cottage there were articles of comfort and luxury, such as Hester never cared to use, but which only wealth could have purchased, and affection have imagined for her. There were trifles, too, little ornaments, beautiful tokens of a continual remembrance, that must have been wrought by delicate fingers, at the impulse of a fond heart. And, once, Hester was seen embroidering a baby-garment, with such a lavish richness of golden fancy as would have raised a public tumult, had any infant, thus apparelled, been shown to our sombre-hued community.

In fine, the gossips of that day believed, —and Mr. Surveyor Pue, who made investigations a century later, believed, —and one of his recent successors in office, moreover, faithfully believes, —that Pearl was not only alive, but married, and happy, and mindful of her mother; and that she would most joyfully have entertained that sad and lonely mother at her fireside.

But there was a more real life for Hester Prynne, here, in New England, than in that unknown region where Pearl had found a home. Here had been her sin; here, her sorrow; and here was yet to be her penitence. She had returned, therefore, and resumed,—of her own free will, for not the sternest magistrate of that iron period would have imposed it,—resumed the symbol of which we have related so dark a tale. Never afterwards did it quit her bosom. But, in the lapse of the toilsome, thoughtful, and self-devoted years that made up Hester's life, the scarlet letter ceased to be a stigma which attracted the world's scorn and bitterness, and became a type of something to be sorrowed over, and looked upon with awe, yet with reverence too. And, as Hester Prynne had no selfish ends, nor lived in any measure for her own profit and enjoyment, people brought all their sorrows and perplexities, and besought her counsel, as one who had herself gone through a mighty trouble. Women, more especially,—in the continually recurring trials of wounded, wasted, wronged, misplaced, or erring and sinful passion,—or with the dreary burden of a heart unyielded, because unvalued and unsought,—came to Hester's cottage, demanding why they were so wretched, and what the remedy! Hester comforted and counselled them, as best she might. She assured them, too, of her firm belief, that, at some brighter period, when the world should have grown ripe for it, in Heaven's own time, a new truth would be revealed, in order to establish the whole relation between man and woman on a surer ground of mutual happiness. Earlier in life, Hester had vainly imagined that she herself might be the destined prophetess, but had long since recognized the impossibility that any mission of divine and mysterious truth should be confided to a woman stained with sin, bowed down with shame, or even burdened with a lifelong sorrow. The angel and apostle of the coming revelation must be a woman, indeed, but lofty, pure, and beautiful; and wise, moreover, not through dusky grief, but the ethereal medium of joy; and showing how sacred love should make us happy, by the truest test of a life successful to such an end!

So said Hester Prynne, and glanced her sad eyes downward at the scarlet letter. And, after many, many years, a new grave was delved, near an old and sunken one, in that burial-ground beside which King's Chapel has since been built. It was near that old and sunken grave, yet with a space between, as if the dust of the two sleepers had no right to mingle. Yet one tombstone served for both. All around, there were monuments carved with armorial bearings; and on this simple slab of slate—as the curious investigator may still discern, and perplex himself with the purport—there appeared the semblance of an engraved escutcheon. It bore a device, a herald's wording of which might serve for a motto and brief description of our now concluded legend; so sombre is it, and relieved only by one ever-glowing point of light gloomier than the shadow:—

ON A FIELD, SABLE, THE LETTER A, GULES [73]

---

[73] In heraldic terms, a red letter *A* on a black, shield-shaped background.

Part Three

CRITICISM

EARLY CRITICISM

The four early reviews of *The Scarlet Letter* excerpted in this section suggest the range and emphases of its initial reception. They all evaluate the novel in terms of its contributions to the culture's moral welfare and praise Hawthorne's literary "genius."

The first two were by colleagues of Hawthorne's publisher James T. Fields who were also Hawthorne's friends and admirers: Evert Duyckinck, editor of the *New York Literary World*, and the influential Boston critic E. P. Whipple. Predictably, both offered high but discriminating praise. Duyckinck provocatively defined *The Scarlet Letter* as "a psychological romance," called the story "a drama in which thoughts are acts," succinctly praised its "artistic power," and declared that the moral of the tale was severe but "wholesome." Similarly, Whipple lauded the novel's "certainty of touch and expression," its profound underlying philosophy, its "tragic power," and its strong "moral purpose." He also acknowledged the humor of "The Custom-House," and (adopting Hawthorne's ironic tone) attributed the entire book to Hawthorne's ejection from political office.

The more conservative Boston critic Annie Abbott began her review by stressing the "magic power" of the novel's style but deplored the novel's "revolting" subject and criticized its two adulterers on moral grounds. Hester excites the reader's pity "only while we have hope for her soul"; and Dimmesdale's unrelieved suffering is inconsistent with "God's moral world." But Abbott was remarkably sympathetic to Pearl, a child of "perfect and vivid individuality."

Orestes Brownson shared Abbott's conviction that adultery was not a "fit" literary subject. He thought that the sufferings of Hawthorne's adulterers were not adequately horrifying, and that the Puritans' treatment of Hester was "more Christian than [Hawthorne's] ridicule of it." Yet, like most reviewers, Brownson praised the novel's "fearful power," its narrative ease, and the "wizard power" of Hawthorne's language.

[A Psychological Romance]

Evert A. Duyckinck

[. . .] *The Scarlet Letter* is a psychological romance. The hardiest Mrs. Mala-
prop would never venture to call it a novel. It is a tale of remorse, a study
of character in which the human heart is anatomized, carefully, elaborately,
and with striking poetic and dramatic power. Its incidents are simply these.
A woman in the early days of Boston becomes the subject of the discipline
of the court of those times, and is condemned to stand in the pillory and
wear henceforth, in token of her shame, the scarlet letter A attached to her
bosom. She carries her child with her to the pillory. Its other parent is unknown. At this opening scene her husband from whom she had been separated in Europe, preceding him by ship across the Atlantic, reappears from
the forest, whither he had been thrown by shipwreck on his arrival. He was
a man of a cold intellectual temperament, and devotes his life thereafter
to search for his wife's guilty partner and a fiendish revenge. The young
clergyman of the town, a man of a devout sensibility and warmth of heart,
is the victim, as this Mephistophelean old physician fixes himself by his
side to watch over him and protect his health, an object of great solicitude
to his parishioners, and, in reality, to detect his suspected secret and gloat
over his tortures. This slow, cool, devilish purpose, like the concoction of
some sublimated hell broth, is perfected gradually and inevitably. The wayward, elfish child, a concentration of guilt and passion, binds the interests
of the parties together, but throws little sunshine over the scene. These
are all the characters, with some casual introductions of the grim personages and manners of the period, unless we add the scarlet letter, which, in
Hawthorne's hands, skilled to these allegorical, typical semblances, becomes vitalized as the rest. It is the hero of the volume. The denouement is
the death of the clergyman on a day of public festivity, after a public confession in the arms of the pilloried, branded woman. But few as are these

---

From David B. Kesterson, ed. *Critical Essays on Hawthorne's* The Scarlet
Letter. Boston: Hall, 1988. (Originally published in *Literary World* [Mar.
1850].)

main incidents thus briefly told, the action of the story, or its passion, is "long, obscure, and infinite." It is a drama in which thoughts are acts. The material has been thoroughly fused in the writer's mind, and springs forth an entire, perfect creation. We know of no American tales except some of the early ones of Mr. Dana, which approach it in conscientious completeness. Nothing is slurred over, superfluous, or defective. The story is grouped in scenes simply arranged, but with artistic power, yet without any of those painful impressions which the use of the words, as it is the fashion to use them, "grouping" and "artistic" excite, suggesting artifice [. . .].

Mr. Hawthorne has, in fine, shown extraordinary power in this volume, great feeling and discrimination, a subtle knowledge of character in its secret springs and outer manifestations. He blends, too, a delicate fancy with this metaphysical insight. We would instance the chapter towards the close, entitled "The Minster in a Maze," where the effects of a diabolic temptation are curiously depicted, or "The Minister's Vigil," the night scene in the pillory. The atmosphere of the piece also is perfect. It has the mystic element, the weird forest influences of the old Puritan discipline and era. Yet there is no affrightment which belongs purely to history, which has not its echo even in the unlike and perversely common-place custom-house of Salem. Then for the moral. Though severe, it is wholesome, and is a sounder bit of Puritan divinity than we have been of late accustomed to hear from the degenerate successors of Cotton Mather. We hardly know another writer who has lived so much among the new school who would have handled this delicate subject without an infusion of George Sand. The spirit of his old Puritan ancestors, to whom he refers in the preface, lives in Nathaniel Hawthorne.

[A True Artist's Certainty of Touch and Expression]

Edwin Percy Whipple

In this beautiful and touching romance Hawthorne has produced something really worthy of the fine and deep genius which lies within him. [. . .] In *The Scarlet Letter* we have a complete work, evincing a true artist's

From David B. Kesterson, ed. *Critical Essays on Hawthorne's* The Scarlet Letter. Boston: Hall, 1988. (Originally published in *Graham's Magazine* [May 1850].)

certainty of touch and expression in the exhibition of characters and events, and a keen-sighted and far-sighted vision into the essence and purpose of spiritual laws. There is a profound philosophy underlying the story which will escape many of the readers whose attention is engrossed by the narrative.

The book is prefaced by some fifty pages of autobiographical matter, relating to the author, his native city of Salem, and the Custom House, from which he was ousted by the Whigs. These pages, instinct with the vital spirit of humor, show how rich and exhaustless a fountain of mirth Hawthorne has at his command. The whole representation has the dreamy yet distinct remoteness of the purely comic ideal. [. . .]

With regard to *The Scarlet Letter*, the readers of Hawthorne might have expected an exquisitely written story, expansive in sentiment, and suggestive in characterization, but they will hardly be prepared for a novel of so much tragic interest and tragic power, so deep in thought and so condensed in style, as is here presented to them. It evinces equal genius in the region of great passions and elusive emotions, and bears on every page the evidence of a mind thoroughly alive, watching patiently the movements of morbid hearts when stirred by strange experiences, and piercing, by its imaginative power, directly through all the externals to the core of things. [. . .]

If there be, however, a comparative lack of relief to the painful emotions which the novel excites, owing to the intensity with which the author concentrates attention on the working of dark passions, it must be confessed that the moral purpose of the book is made more definite by this very deficiency. The most abandoned libertine could not read the volume without being thrilled into something like virtuous resolution, and the roué would find that the deep-seeing eye of the novelist had mastered the whole philosophy of that guilt of which practical roués are but childish disciples. [. . .]

In common, we trust, with the rest of mankind, we regretted Hawthorne's dismissal from the Custom House, but if that event compels him to exert his genius in the production of such books as the present, we shall be inclined to class the Honorable Secretary of the Treasury among the great philanthropists. [. . .]

[The Magic Power of Hawthorne's Style]

Anne Abbott

No one who has taken up the Scarlet Letter will willingly lay it down till he has finished it; and he will do well not to pause, for he cannot resume the story where he left it. He should give himself up to the magic power of the style, without stopping to open wide the eyes of his good sense and judgment, and shake off the spell; or half the weird beauty will disappear like a "dissolving view." [. . .]

As for Roger Chillingworth, he seems to have so little in common with man, he is such a gnome-like phantasm, such an unnatural personification of an abstract idea, that we should be puzzled to assign him a place among angels, men, or devils. [. . .] Hester at first strongly excites our pity, for she suffers like an immortal being; and our interest in her continues only while we have hope for her soul, that its baptism of tears will reclaim it from the foul stain which has been cast upon it. We see her humble, meek, self-denying, charitable, and heartwrung with anxiety for the moral welfare of her wayward child. But anon her humility catches a new tint, and we find it pride; and so a vague unreality steals by degrees over all her most humanizing traits — we lose our confidence in all — and finally, like Undine, she disappoints us, and shows the dream-land origin and nature, when we were looking to behold a Christian.

There is rather more power, and better keeping, in the character of Dimmesdale. But here again we are cheated into a false regard and interest, partly perhaps by the associations thrown around him without the intention of the author, and possibly contrary to it, by our habitual respect for the sacred order, and by our faith in religion, where it has once been rooted in the heart. We are told repeatedly, that the Christian element yet pervades his character and guides his efforts; but it seems strangely wanting. "High aspirations for the welfare of his race, warm love of souls, pure sentiments, natural piety, strengthened by thought and study, and illuminated by revelation — all of which invaluable gold was little better than rubbish" to Roger Chillingworth, are little better than rubbish at all, for any use to be made of them in the story. Mere suffering, aimless and without effect for

---

From David B. Kesterson, ed. *Critical Essays on Hawthorne's* The Scarlet Letter. Boston: Hall, 1988. (Originally published in *North American Review* [July 1850].)

purification or blessing to the soul, we do not find in God's moral world. The sting that follows crime is most severe in the purest conscience and the tenderest heart, in mercy, not in vengeance, surely; and we can conceive of any cause constantly exerting itself without its appropriate effects, as soon as of a seven years' agony without penitence. [. . .]

But Little Pearl—gem of the purest water—what shall we say of her? That if perfect truth to childish and human nature can make her a mortal, she is so; and immortal, if the highest creations of genius have any claim to immortality. Let the author throw what light he will upon her, from his magical prism, she retains her perfect and vivid human individuality. When he would have us call her elvish and implike, we persist in seeing only a capricious, roguish, untamed child, such as many a mother has looked upon with awe, and a feeling of helpless incapacity to rule. Every motion, every feature, every word and tiny shout, every naughty scream and wild laugh, come to us as if our very senses were conscious of them. The child is a true child, the only genuine and consistent mortal in the book; and wherever she crosses the dark and gloomy track of the story, she refreshes our spirit with pure truth and radiant beauty, and brings to grateful remembrance the like ministry of gladsome childhood, in some of the saddest scenes of actual life. We feel at once that the author must have a "Little Pearl" of his own, whose portrait, consciously or unconsciously, his pen sketches out. Not that we would deny to Mr. Hawthorne the power to call up any shape, angel or goblin, and present it before his readers in a striking and vivid light. But there is something more than imagination in the picture of "Little Pearl." The heart takes a part in it, and puts in certain inimitable touches of nature here and there, such as fancy never dreamed of, and only a long and loving observation of the ways of childhood could suggest. . . .

We know of no writer who better understands and combines the elements of the picturesque in writing than Mr. Hawthorne. His style may be compared to a sheet of transparent water, reflecting from its surface blue skies, nodding woods, and the smallest spray or flower that peeps over its grassy margin; while in its clear yet mysterious depths we espy rarer and stranger things, which we must dive for, if we would examine. [. . .] One cannot but wonder, by the way, that the master of such a wizard power over language as Mr. Hawthorne manifests should not choose a less revolting subject than this of the Scarlet Letter, to which fine writing seems as inappropriate as fine embroidery. The ugliness of pollution and vice is no more relieved by it than the gloom of the prison is by the rose tree at its door. [. . .]

The law undertakes to avenge its own dignity, to use a popular phrase; that is, it regards the community as one great family, and constitutes itself the avenger of blood in its behalf. It is not punishment, but retaliation, which does not contemplate the reform of the offender as well as the prevention of crime; and where it wholly loses the remedial element, and cuts off the opportunity for repentance which God's mercy allows, it is worthy of a barbarous, not a Christian, social alliance. What sort of combination for mutual safety is it, too, when no man feels safe, because fortuitous circumstances, ingeniously bound into a chain, may so entangle Truth that she cannot bestir herself to rescue us from the doom which the judgment of twelve fallible men pronounces, and our protector, the law, executes upon us?

But we are losing sight of Mr. Hawthorne's book, and of the old Puritan settlers, as he portrays them with few, but clearly cut and expressive, lines. In these sketchy groupings, Governor Bellingham is the only prominent figure, with the Rev. John Wilson behind him, "his beard, white as a snow-drift, seen over the Governor's shoulder." [. . .]

With this portrait, we close our remarks on the book, which we should not have criticized at so great length, had we admired it less. [. . .]

[An Unfit Subject for Literature]

Orestes Brownson

Mr. Hawthorne is a writer endowed with a large share of genius, and in the species of literature he cultivates has no rival in this country, unless it be Washington Irving. [. . .] The work before us is the largest and most elaborate of the romances he has as yet published, and no one can read half a dozen pages of it without feeling that none but a man of true genius and a highly cultivated mind could have written it. It is a work of rare, we may say of fearful power, and to the great body of our countrymen who have no well defined religious belief, and no fixed principles of virtue, it will be deeply interesting and highly pleasing.

[. . .] The story is told with great naturalness, ease, grace, and delicacy, but it is a story that should not have been told. It is a story of crime, of an adulteress and her accomplice, a meek and gifted and highly popular

From David B. Kesterson, ed. *Critical Essays on Hawthorne's* The Scarlet Letter. Boston: Hall, 1988. (Originally published in *Brownson's Quarterly Review* [Oct. 1850].)

Puritan minister in our early colonial days—a purely imaginary story, though not altogether improbable. Crimes like the one imagined were not unknown even in the golden days of Puritanism, and are perhaps more common among the descendants of the Puritans than it is at all pleasant to believe; but they are not fit subjects for popular literature, and moral health is not promoted by leading the imagination to dwell on them. There is an unsound state of public morals when the novelist is permitted, without a scorching rebuke, to select such crimes, and invest them with all the fascinations of genius, and all the charms of a highly polished style. In a moral community such crimes are spoken of as rarely as possible, and when spoken of at all, it is always in terms which render them loathsome, and repel the imagination.

Nor is the conduct of the story better than the story itself. The author makes the guilty parties suffer, and suffer intensely, but he nowhere manages so as to make their sufferings excite the horror of his readers for their crime. The adulteress suffers not from remorse, but from regret, and from the disgrace to which her crime has exposed her, in her being condemned to wear emblazoned on her dress the Scarlet Letter which proclaims to all the deed she has committed. The minister, her accomplice, suffers also, horribly, and feels all his life after the same terrible letter branded on his heart, but not from the fact of the crime itself, but from the consciousness of not being what he seems to the world, from his having permitted the partner in his guilt to be disgraced, to be punished, without his having the manliness to avow his share in the guilt, and to bear his share of the punishment. Neither ever really repents of the criminal deed; nay, neither ever regards it as really criminal, and both seem to hold it to have been laudable, because they *loved* one another—as if the love itself were not illicit, and highly criminal. No man has the right to love another man's wife, and no married woman has the right to love any man but her husband. Mr. Hawthorne in the present case seeks to excuse Hester Prynne, a married woman, for loving the Puritan minister, on the ground that she had no love for her husband, and it is hard that a woman should not have some one to love; but this only aggravated her guilt, because she was not only forbidden to love the minister, but commanded to love her husband, whom she had vowed to love, honor, cherish, and obey. The modern doctrine that represents the affections as fatal, and wholly withdrawn from voluntary control, and then allows us to plead them in justification of neglect of duty and breach of the most positive precepts of both the natural and the revealed law, cannot be too severely reprobated. [. . .]

As a picture of the old Puritans, taken from the position of a moderate transcendentalist and liberal of the modern school, the work has its merits;

but as little as we sympathize with those stern old Popery-haters, we do not regard the picture as at all just. We should commend where the author condemns, and condemn where he commends. Their treatment of the adulteress was far more Christian than his ridicule of it. But enough of faultfinding, and as we have no praise, except what we have given, to offer, we here close this brief notice.

Ο ne hundred and fifty years after its publication, *The Scarlet Letter* still challenges its readers. The following critical commentaries, chronologically arranged, were selected from a wide array of seminal and provocative discussions—biographical, formalist, Marxist, feminist, Freudian, and "new historical," among others.

[Out of the Very Heart of New England]

Henry James

In his 1879 book on Hawthorne, the novelist Henry James recalled that *The Scarlet Letter* was immediately received as "the finest piece of imaginative writing yet put forth in this country," an "absolutely American" book that ranked with the best that Europe had produced. James's tribute testifies to his own indebtedness to Hawthorne. Although he found fault with the characters' "want of reality" and thought Hawthorne's symbolism was sometimes overdone, and though he thought that Hester soon became only "an accessory figure," James found in Hawthorne's novel "the inexhaustible charm and mystery of great works of art." [ED.]

———

[. . . T]he publication of *The Scarlet Letter* was in the United States a literary event of the first importance. The book was the finest piece of imagi-

———

From David B. Kesterson, ed. *Critical Essays on Hawthorne's* The Scarlet Letter. Boston: Hall, 1988. (Originally published in Henry James. *Hawthorne*. London: Macmillan, 1879.)

native writing yet put forth in the country. There was a consciousness of this in the welcome that was given it — a satisfaction in the idea of America having produced a novel that belonged to literature, and to the forefront of it. Something might at last be sent to Europe as exquisite in quality as anything that had been received, and the best of it was that the thing was absolutely American; it belonged to the soil, to the air; it came out of the very heart of New England.

It is beautiful, admirable, extraordinary; it has in the highest degree that merit which I have spoken of as the mark of Hawthorne's best things — an indefinable purity and lightness of conception, a quality which in a work of art affects one in the same way as the absence of grossness does in a human being. His fancy, as I just now said, had evidently brooded over the subject for a long time; the situation to be represented had disclosed itself to him in all its phases. When I say in all its phases, the sentence demands modification; for it is to be remembered that if Hawthorne laid his hand upon the well-worn theme, upon the familiar combination of the wife, the lover, and the husband, it was, after all, but to one period of the history of these three persons that he attached himself. The situation is the situation after the woman's fault has been committed, and the current of expiation and repentance has set in. In spite of the relation between Hester Prynne and Arthur Dimmesdale, no story of love was surely ever less of a "love-story." To Hawthorne's imagination the fact that these two persons had loved each other too well was of an interest comparatively vulgar; what appealed to him was the idea of their moral situation in the long years that were to follow. The story, indeed, is in a secondary degree that of Hester Prynne; she becomes, really, after the first scene, an accessory figure; it is not upon her the *dénoûment* depends. It is upon her guilty lover that the author projects most frequently the cold, thin rays of his fitfully-moving lantern, which makes here and there a little luminous circle, on the edge of which hovers the livid and sinister figure of between the lover and the husband — the tormented young Puritan minister, who carries the secret of his own lapse from pastoral purity locked up beneath an exterior that commends itself to the reverence of his flock, while he sees the softer partner of his guilt standing in the full glare of exposure and humbling herself to the misery of atonement — between this more wretched and pitiable culprit, to whom dishonour would come as a comfort and the pillory as a relief, and the older, keener, wiser man, who, to obtain satisfaction for the wrong he has suffered, devises the infernally ingenious plan of conjoining himself with his wronger, living with him, living upon him; and while he pretends to minister to his hidden ailment and to sympathise with his pain, revels in his unsuspected knowledge of these things, and stimulates them by malignant arts. The attitude of Roger Chillingworth, and the means he takes to compensate himself—these are the highly original elements in the situation that Hawthorne so ingeniously treats. None of his works are so impregnated with that after-sense of the old Puritan consciousness of life to which allusion has so often been made. [. . .]

The faults of the book are, to my sense, a want of reality and an abuse of the fanciful element—of a certain superficial symbolism. The people strike me not as characters, but as representatives, very picturesquely arranged, of a single state of mind; and the interest of the story lies, not in them, but in the situation, which is insistently kept before us, with little progression, though with a great deal, as I have said, of a certain stable variation; and to which they, out of their reality, contribute little that helps it to live and move.[. . .]

In *The Scarlet Letter* there is a great deal of symbolism; there is, I think, too much. It is overdone at times, and becomes mechanical; it ceases to be impressive, and grazes triviality. The idea of the mystic *A* which the young minister finds imprinted upon his breast and eating into his flesh, in sympathy with the embroidered badge that Hester is condemned to wear, appears to me to be a case in point. This suggestion should, I think, have been just made and dropped; to insist upon it and return to it, is to exaggerate the weak side of the subject. Hawthorne returns to it constantly, plays with it, and seems charmed by it; until at last the reader feels tempted to declare that his enjoyment of it is puerile. In the admirable scene, so superbly conceived and beautifully executed, in which Mr. Dimmesdale, in the stillness of the night, in the middle of the sleeping town, feels impelled to go and stand upon the scaffold where his mistress had formerly enacted her dreadful penance, and then, seeing Hester pass along the street, from watching at a sick-bed, with little Pearl at her side, calls them both to come and stand there beside him—in this masterly episode the effect is almost spoiled by the introduction of one of these superficial conceits. [. . .]

I had not meant, however, to expatiate upon his defects, which are of the slenderest and most venial kind. *The Scarlet Letter* has the beauty and harmony of all original and complete conceptions, and its weaker spots, whatever they are, are not of its essence; they are mere light flaws and inequalities of surface. One can often return to it; it supports familiarity, and has the inexhaustible charm and mystery of great works of art. [. . .]

[Integrity of Effect]

F. O. Matthiessen

In his enormously influential study of the period in which Hawthorne flourished, *The American Renaissance*, F. O. Matthiessen praised the "inseparability of elements" in *The Scarlet Letter* — a coherent plot whose symmetrical design is structured by the three scaffold scenes, lucidly discriminated characters whose interactions generate the plot, and symbols that fuse "external events and inner significance." The novel offers alternative interpretations of symbols and symbolic events (as in the case of the *A* that appears in the sky at the novel's center and what Dimmesdale "unbreasts" at the end) — Matthiessen calls these "multiple choice." If Hawthorne seems to dwell excessively on what Pearl "stands for," Matthiessen nevertheless finds her characterization "based on exact psychological notation." [ED.]

[. . .] [I]n *The Scarlet Letter* [. . .] Hawthorne had developed his most coherent plot. Its symmetrical design is built around the three scenes on the scaffold of the pillory. There Hester endures her public shaming in the opening chapter. There, midway through the book, the minister, who has been driven almost crazy by his guilt but has lacked the resolution to confess it, ascends one midnight for self-torture, and is joined by Hester, on her way home from watching at a deathbed, and there they are overseen by Chillingworth. There, also, at the end, just after his own knowledge of suffering has endowed his tongue with eloquence in his great election sermon, the exhausted and death-stricken Dimmesdale totters to confess his sin at last to the incredulous and only half-comprehending crowd, and to die in Hester's arms.

Moreover, Hawthorne has also managed here his utmost approach to the inseparability of elements that James insisted on when he said that "character, in any sense in which we can get at it, is action, and action is plot." Of his four romances, this one grows most organically out of the

From *American Renaissance: Art and Expression in the Age of Emerson and Whitman*. New York: Oxford UP, 1941. Reprinted by permission of Ohio State University Press. (All parenthetical references are to this New Riverside Edition.)

interactions between the characters, depends least on the backdrops of scenery that so often impede the action in *The Marble Faun*. Furthermore, his integrity of effect is due in part to the incisive contrasts among the human types he is presenting. The sin of Hester and the minister, a sin of passion not of principle, is not the worst in the world, as they are aware, even in the depths of their misery. She feels that what they did "had a consecration of its own" (224); he knows that at least they have never "violated, in cold blood, the sanctity of a human heart" (224). They are distinguished from the wronged husband in accordance with the theological doctrine that excessive love for things which should take only a secondary place in the affections, though leading to the sin of lust, is less grave than love distorted, love turned from God and from his creatures, into self-consuming envy and vengeful pride. The courses that these three run are also in natural accord with their characters as worked upon by circumstance. The physician's native power in reading the human soul, when unsupported by any moral sympathies, leaves him open to degradation, step by step, from a man into a fiend. Dimmesdale, in his indecisive waverings, filled as he is with penance but no penitence, remains in touch with reality only in proportion to his anguish. The slower, richer movement of Hester is harder to characterize in a sentence. Even Chillingworth, who had married her as a young girl in the knowledge that she responded with no love for his old and slightly deformed frame, even he, after all that has happened, can still almost pity her "for the good that has been wasted" in her nature (210). Her purgatorial course through the book is from desperate recklessness to a strong, placid acceptance of her suffering and retribution.

But beyond any interest in ordering of plot or in lucid discrimination between characters, Hawthorne's imaginative energy seems to have been called out to the full here by the continual correspondences that his theme allowed him to make between external events and inner significances. Once again his version of this transcendental habit took it straight back to the seventeenth century, and made it something more complex than the harmony between sunrise and a young poet's soul. In the realm of natural phenomena, Hawthorne examined the older world's common belief that great events were foreboded by supernatural omens, and remarked how "it was, indeed, a majestic idea, that the destiny of nations should be revealed, in these awful hieroglyphics, on the cope of heaven." But when Dimmesdale, in his vigil on the scaffold, beholds an immense dull red letter in the zenith, Hawthorne attributes it solely to his diseased imagination, which sees in everything his own morbid concerns. Hawthorne remarks that the strange light was "doubtless caused" by a meteor "burning out to waste"(288); and yet he also allows the sexton to ask the minister the next morning if he had heard of the portent, which had been interpreted to stand for Angel, since Governor Winthrop had died during the night (200).

Out of such variety of symbolical reference Hawthorne developed one of his most fertile resources, the device of multiple choice [. . .]. One main source of Hawthorne's method lay in these remarkable providences, which his imagination felt challenged to search for the amount of emblematic truth that might lie hidden among their superstitions. He spoke at one point in this story of how "individuals of wiser faith" in the colony, while recognizing God's Providence in human affairs, knew that it "promotes its purposes without aiming at the stage-effect of what is called miraculous interposition"(173). But he could not resist experimenting with this dramatic value, and his imagination had become so accustomed to the weirdly lighted world of Cotton Mather that even the fanciful possibilities of the growth of the stigma on Dimmesdale did not strike him as grotesque. But when the minister "unbreasts" his guilt at last, the literal correspondence of that metaphor to a scarlet letter in his flesh, in strict accord with medieval and Spenserian personifications, is apt to strike us as a mechanical delimitation of what would otherwise have freer symbolical range.

For Hawthorne its value consisted in the variety of explanations to which it gave rise. Some affirmed that the minister had begun a course of self-mortification on the very day on which Hester Prynne had first been compelled to wear her ignominious badge, and had thus inflicted this hideous scar. Others held that Roger Chillingworth, "being a potent necromancer, had caused it to appear, through the agency of magic and poisonous drugs" (268). Still others, "those best able to appreciate the minister's peculiar sensibility, and the wonderful operation of his spirit upon the body," whispered that "the awful symbol was the effect of the ever-active tooth of remorse," gnawing from his inmost heart outward (268). With that Hawthorne leaves his reader to choose among these theories. He does not literally accept his own allegory, and yet he finds it symbolically valid because of its psychological exactitude. His most telling stroke comes when he adds that certain spectators of the whole scene denied that there was any mark whatever on Dimmesdale's breast. These witnesses were among the most respectable in the community, including his fellow-ministers who were determined to defend his spotless character. These maintained also that his dying confession was to be taken only in its general significance, that he had desired, by yielding up his breath in the arms of that fallen woman, to express to the world how utterly nugatory is the choicest of man's own righteousness" (268). But for this interpretation, so revelatory of its influential proponents, Hawthorne leaves not one shred of evidence. [. . .]

Pearl [. . .] is worth dissecting as the purest type of Spenserian characterization, which starts with abstract qualities and hunts for their proper embodiment; worth murdering, most modern readers of fiction would hold, since the tedious reiteration of what she stands for betrays Hawthorne at his most barren.

When Hester returned to the prison after standing her time on the scaffold, the infant she had clasped so tightly to her breast suddenly writhed in convulsions of pain, "a forcible type, in its little frame, of the moral agony" that its mother had borne throughout the day (135). As the story advances, Hawthorne sees in this child "the freedom of a broken law" (183). In the perverseness of some of her antics, in the heartless mockery that can shine from her bright black eyes, she sometimes seems to her harassed mother almost a witch baby. But Hester clings to the hope that her girl has capacity for strong affection, which needs only to be awakened by sympathy; and when there is some talk by the authorities of taking the willful child's rearing into their own hands, Hester also clings to her possession of it as both her torture and happiness, her blessing and retribution, the one thing that has kept her soul alive in its hours of desperation.

Hawthorne's range of intention in this characterization comes out most fully in the scene where Hester and the minister have met in the woods, and are alone for the first time after so many years. Her resolution to save him from Chillingworth's spying by flight together back to England, now sweeps his undermined spirit before it. In their moment of reunion, the one moment of released passion in the book, the beauty that has been hidden behind the frozen mask of her isolation reasserts itself. She takes off the formal cap that has confined the dark radiance of her hair and lets it stream down on her shoulders; she impulsively unfastens the badge of her shame and throws it to the ground. At that moment the minister sees Pearl, who has been playing by the brook, returning along the other side of it. Picked out by a beam of sunlight, with some wild flowers in her hair, she reminds Hester of "one of the fairies, whom we left in our dear old England," a sad reflection on the rich folklore that had been banished by the Puritans along with the maypoles. But as the two parents stand watching their child for the first time together, the graver thought comes to them that she is "the living hieroglyphic" of all they have sought to hide, of their inseparably intertwined fate (233).

As Pearl sees her mother, she stops by a pool, and her reflected image seems to communicate to her something "of its own shadowy and intangible quality" (233). Confronted with this double vision, dissevered from her by the brook, Hester feels, "in some indistinct and tantalizing manner," suddenly estranged from the child, who now fixes her eyes on her mother's breast (234). She refuses Hester's bidding to come to her. Instead she points her finger, and stamps her foot, and becomes all at once a little demon of extravagant protest, all of whose wild gestures are redoubled at her feet. Hester understands what the matter is, that the child is outraged by the unaccustomed change in her appearance. So she wearily picks up the letter, which had fallen just short of the brook, and hides her luxuriant hair once more beneath her cap. At that Pearl is mollified and bounds across to them. During the weeks leading up to this scene, she had begun to show an increasing curiosity about the letter, and had tormented her mother with questions. Now she asks whether the minister will walk back with them, hand in hand, to the village, and when he declines, she flings away from his kiss, because he is not "bold" and "true" (237–38). The question is increasingly raised for the reader, just how much of the situation this strange child understands.

Thus, when the stiff layers of allegory have been peeled away, even Hawthorne's conception of Pearl is seen to be based on exact psychological notation. [. . .]

[Actively Seizing Upon History]

Charles Feidelson, Jr.

Charles Feidelson examines the way in which Puritan ideals, ideas, and actualities shape *The Scarlet Letter*'s characters yet are also shaped by them. He also considers the book "modern" in its rendering of the "alienated individualism" that Hawthorne himself had experienced. Connecting "The Custom-House" to the novel, Feidelson observes that within its chronological frame, the past endures and is experienced in the present, as when Hawthorne's fictive discovery of Hester's scarlet letter promotes self-discovery and then becomes central to his novel's plot and meaning. In Feidelson's view, the doctrinaire Puritans view Hester and her letter as emblematic of the polarized world they inhabit, but Pearl is "the very principle of freedom, the essence of her time." [ED.]

From Roy Harvey Pearce, ed. *Hawthorne Centenary Essays*. Columbus: Ohio State UP, 1964. (All parenthetical references are to this New Riverside Edition).

The Scarlet Letter is a moral tale in a Christian setting, but the imaginative method of the book is not distinctively moral or religious. It is distinctively historical, and historical in a rather complex way. The issues of the story and the experiences of individual characters are projected in the peculiar terms of a specific epoch; Hester Prynne, the people of Boston, Dimmesdale, Chillingworth, and Pearl are shaped by and give shape to the meaning of their time. Yet the epoch is not simply "Puritan." It is also more generally "modern," despite the provincial locale and the idiosyncratic culture through which it is rendered. In many respects, Puritan manners and morals here become a modern instance, a test case of life in the "new" (that is, post-medieval) world. And this modern life was Hawthorne's as well as the life of his characters. The author of *The Scarlet Letter* looks back through time, but he exists in historical continuity with the world he describes. The book is most profoundly historical because it is not only *about* but also *written out of* a felt historical situation.

We need not suppose that Hawthorne had any theoretical idea of "modernity" (he had few theories of any kind, and none of much interest). What he had was the nineteenth- and twentieth-century experience of radical solitude, which he sought to encompass by externalizing it, taking it as his imaginative subject. Possibly his twelve years in the lonely chamber at Salem, for which he could "assign no reasonable why and wherefore," were motivated less by a desire for privacy than by an impulse to dramatize his spiritual isolation. He could escape it only by publicly acknowledging and expressing it. In any case, this was a characteristic maneuver of his literary imagination—as he put it, to render in "the style of a man of society" what would otherwise be "the talk of a secluded man with his own mind and heart." Yet "to open an intercourse with the world" in this way was not enough if the world was really a non-world, a society of isolatoes, as his experience drove him to depict it. Nor could he simply assert in the face of his experience that a "magnetic chain of humanity" was always open to the loving heart. The only adequate ground he had for communication and for faith in human community was paradoxical: alienation as a historical datum. Hawthorne turned to American history, the history of alienation, as the basis of his communion. What isolatoes had in common, their magnetic chain, was precisely the spiritual history of their isolation. Hawthorne became the historian of the historically disinherited.

The Puritans conceived alienation as the cause and consequence of sin, and up to a point it is so represented in *The Scarlet Letter*. Hester's pride of self is the essential crime within her crime and the essential aberration within her later secret heterodoxy. Much the same might be said of Dimmesdale and Chillingworth. But if alienation is equivalent to sin in the perspective of Hawthorne's seventeenth-century Boston, and if Hawthorne himself never wholly abandons that perspective, he also pictures a Puritan society that positively fosters an alienated individualism. Hester Prynne, her lover, and her husband are as much sinned against as sinning in their social isolation; they have been thrown back upon themselves by an inorganic community, a culture that substitutes external law for immediate relations. And if this is so, if the Puritan mind itself is in one sense guilty of the crime it abhors, in a further sense the book does not deal with crime as such but with a moral predicament, a style of thought. Though Hawthorne often echoes the Puritan language of moral reprobation, and though he often turns round and condemns the Puritans themselves for lack of humanitarian sympathy, he is always fully aware of a historical context for these moral stances—a world view that molds the Puritan consciousness as well as his own.

These people have experienced a disintegration of God's world into God-and-nature, a collapse of the secular world into nature-and-man, a fragmentation of the human world into community-and-individual, and a division of the private world into body-and-mind. Obviously there is nothing novel about such disjunctions in the long history of Christian theology and morals; but in the universe of *The Scarlet Letter* they have taken on a primacy that is striking and new. This disjunctive structure has become a metaphysical presupposition, a reality to be assumed rather than an actuality to be deplored. Moral existence is no longer a pursuit of the Good; it is experience in the goods and evils of a dichotomous world. The official creed of Massachusetts Congregationalism is one configuration of that world—an attempt to find coherence by making the most of disjunction. Hester, Dimmesdale, and Chillingworth devise and suffer other versions of the modern consciousness, worlds of profounder terror and hope. The imagination of Hawthorne, partaking of the condition it projects in the book, moves through the pages in a speculative, inquisitive, experimental mood. Like his characters—but on a much larger scale, since his vision is more inclusive—Hawthorne seeks the center of a world where centers do not hold. [. . .]

[. . .] In *The Scarlet Letter*, people know themselves by means of revelatory "images" that inform mind and body, and they apprehend other human beings as powerful "shapes" impinging upon them. Nature is portentous, the everyday scene is starkly structured and a dream-figure like Mistress Hibbens walks the streets. While this atmospheric "significance" recalls the medieval allegorical universe, it disintegrates instead of supporting the substance of things. The voices of God and Devil are heard in human discourse, and "Providence" presides over the action; but the supernatural voices are the riddles of natural man, and the providential design is something to be discovered, not assumed. The immanent Word has become completely immanent; the only sacramental form is the empty vessel of the letter *A*, whose content alters and grows with time. Correspondingly, the images inherent in the social scene and private experience are fugitive and multivalent. The author collects alternative interpretations; his tone shifts; his opinions are contradictory; his knowledge of fact is often uncertain. Beneath the measured speech and ceremonial behavior of the Boston theocracy is a vast realm of the publicly unsaid and even unsayable — the esoteric community of Hester, Dimmesdale, and Chillingworth. The demands for utterance that punctuate *The Scarlet Letter* ("Speak out the name!" — "What does this . . . letter mean?" 134, 213) are unanswerable theoretically as well as practically, for outside the official consensus no one knows exactly what to call himself or how to construe the significance of the central symbol.

Yet Hester Prynne, who is officially cast down into the underground world of "secrets," comes closest to positive vision and speech, as she comes closest to the substance of fictional character. Deprived of a public voice and reduced to a gray shadow, Hester lives out the problematic situation that everyone in the book knowingly or unknowingly experiences. Deliberately living it out, she emerges on the other side of it. She converts disinheritance into freedom, isolation into individuality, excommunication into a personal presence that is actual and communicable. To do this without denying the negative burden of history — her own and that of her time — is her moral achievement. It is analogous to Hawthorne's aesthetic achievement in the book as a whole. He must undergo his story if he is to tell it at all; *The Scarlet Letter* is imposed upon him, much as the letter itself is imposed upon Hester. But his narration is active; and out of the negative world that he inherits he constructs an image of positive human enterprise.

In "The Custom-House: Introductory to *The Scarlet Letter*," Hawthorne has nothing explicit to say about such matters as the modern consciousness; indeed, the essay at first seems designed to have as little as possible to do with the story it introduces. But Hawthorne's stance here is wholly consonant with his method in *The Scarlet Letter*; his preface functions as a modest suggestion of the nature of his art.

Reality in "The Custom House" is history — history in various forms that play upon one another, deny and reinforce each other, until a dense historical world surrounds us. It is a history that moves in chronological sequence from past to present to future, but it also endures. It is unchanging and changing, active and decadent, predetermined and indeterminate, vacuous and full of meaning. Above all, it is both private and public — a reality experienced individually and socially. Though the scarlet letter is discovered at the climax of a personal narrative, it is a public emblem apparently signifying some "rank, honor, and dignity, in by-past times" (appropriately, the letter and its attendant documents are found amid the archives of the Customs, "materials of local history," 108, 105). Conversely, the symbol communicates its social meaning only to the inner sense of the lonely Hawthorne, not to his analytic and rational public mind, and the documents are "not official, but of a private nature," written by an eighteenth-century predecessor "in his private capacity." When Hawthorne places the letter against his breast, two dimensions of history come into contact. This is a moment of social revelation on the one hand and self-discovery on the other:

> ... It strangely interested me. My eyes fastened themselves upon the old scarlet letter, and would not be turned aside. Certainly, there was some deep meaning in it, most worthy of interpretation, and which, as it were, streamed forth from the mystic symbol, subtly communicating itself to my sensibilities, but evading the analysis of my mind.
> While thus perplexed, ... I happened to place it on my breast. It seemed to me ... that I experienced a sensation not altogether physical, yet almost so, as of burning heat; and as if the letter were not of red cloth, but red-hot iron. (108)

It is not primarily a moment of conscience, for Hawthorne carefully avoids any explicit reference to the theme of adultery or even to the idea of sin. As a single letter, the most indeterminate of all symbols, and first letter of the alphabet, the beginning of all communication, Hester's emblem represents a potential point of coherence within a manifold historical experience.

There is another Hawthorne in "The Custom-House," one who is not inclined to take such apocalyptic moments very seriously. He is an image largely projected by style — frank, good-humored, a man of feeling, but urbane, sharp-eyed, something of an ironist. This cultivated and self-assured gentleman is somewhat complacent; and he belongs to a stable, secure public world of ready categories and easy communication. We might call him the Cosmopolitan. As readers, we quickly identify ourselves with him; we are all gentlemen together. Salem the Custom House and its denizens, the Surveyor himself with his literary ambitions, are the objects of our sophisticated interest. We are capable of reflecting that Hester Prynne, though she may have been an angel on earth for some of her contemporaries, was probably a mere "intruder and ... nuisance" (108) for others. We accede to the game while our whimsical author spins his tale of mysterious documents and grandly offers to show them to us. This is the social situation that Hawthorne invokes at the very beginning of his essay, when he assures us that he will speak as a man in company addressing "a kind and apprehensive, though not the closest friend" (87). He is a strong exponent of propriety, ensconced in a conventional but comfortable mid-world where the private man and the social forms may come into easy relation. He neither would give unseemly publicity to intimate matters nor (since he will be only the "editor, or very little more," of The Scarlet Letter, 88) would he give intimacy to public matters. He would speak in such a way as not to violate "either the reader's rights or his own"(87).

In the part of his mind that always greatly distrusted whatever he had written, Hawthorne obviously wanted to relieve the "gloom" of his book by a jaunty preface. As the Cosmopolitan, he is untouched by the experiences through which he has passed. He views his "autobiographical impulse" (87) as a kind of harmless seizure, and at the end of his discourse he still speaks as from a secure position outside of time. He tells the story of a "well balanced" man (103) in an essentially secure comic world; though he is thrown out of office, no real harm can come to him. But this self-projection is essentially dramatic; and in the essay as a whole, the Cosmopolitan turns out to be the least important of Hawthorne's roles. He is relatively naïve and imperceptive; he maintains his balance by excluding some unpleasant truths.

Throughout the opening paragraphs we feel the presence of an uneasy person within the suave personage who confronts us. Though he arrives at a reassuring formula, we can see him casting about for "the truth" of the matter—his "true relation with his audience," his "true reason for assuming a personal relation with the public," his "true position as editor" (88) Within the gentlemanly consensus that he presupposes, there are factors that pull apart. He reveals them with startling clarity, if only to deny them. On the one hand, there is "the inmost Me behind its veil," the state of alienation when "thoughts are frozen and utterance benumbed" (87). On the other hand, there is a dream of total interrelation, "the one heart and mind of perfect sympathy; as if the printed book . . . were certain to find out the divided segment of the writer's own nature, and complete his circle of existence by bringing him into communion with it" (87). The secure Hawthorne who is content with a social self and a conventional society, who is so much at home in history that he can ignore its tensions, is haunted by an alter ego whose circle of existence" is painfully incomplete, for whom history is the vain pursuit of total communion by an isolated self.

This malaise is mainly represented through another self-protection, the Surveyor of the Customs, who mediates between the Cosmopolitan and the historical visionary brooding over the scarlet letter. True to his title, the Surveyor makes it his business to "watch and study," to measure his colleagues, himself, and the house they inhabit (98). He is at once a solitary man, a self-appointed surveyor whose public office is hardly more than a title, and a social man, very much a creature of the "customs" he surveys. Inquisitive but tentative, he wanders through the building or stands aside and observes his fellow officers. He enters into the narrative voice in much the same spirit of inquiry: careless of contradiction, he adopts various perspectives with equal feeling, as though to make an inventory of the possibilities of life. Like the Cosmopolitan, the Surveyor never disappears from view or lapses into silence; at the end of the essay, he is still addressing us. But only in the climactic moment of communion with the letter, when he is transformed, do we see a potential author of *The Scarlet Letter* or a ground on which he can take his stand.

The ground of the Custom House is shaky — not only because Salem has outlived its time, but also because time still moves on. There are two aspects of social history here, to which we are introduced by the long sentence that leads us up the wharf to a "spacious edifice of brick" and down "the track of . . . years" from the old days of bustling commerce to the present era of decay. The house, a stage for mere mock-activity, the "formalities of office" zealously pursued by the custom officials, is also Uncle Sam's going concern. Though Salem, in comparison with other ports, is fast asleep, there are still merchants here, "men of traffic" whose names Hawthorne tells over (117). There are days when "affairs move onward" (89) and a bustle disturbs the torpid old retainers. There is even a "man of business" among them (102). The house itself, as opposed to its functionaries, often represents a commercial and political life full of action and change. The past counts for nothing in Uncle Sam's work. His old records are thrown aside as "rubbish" (105), and the labor that went into them is wholly lost. What counts is the future. Uncle Sam changes his garments, from Whig to Democrat and back again, striking terror into the hearts of those who look for passivity and permanence. His emblem, the national eagle displayed over the entrance to the Custom House, signifies destruction as well as protection. It is the emblem of a "struggling world" that is wholly unstable and immediate, always building the future out of its own dissolution.

On the other hand, there is old and forever unfinished business in the Custom House, work that will never begin again. The building was "originally projected . . . with an idea of subsequent prosperity destined never to be realized" (105), and a large room on the second floor, still unpaneled and unplastered, testifies to an arrest of time. The occasional activities of the customs are always "for the time being" (89): they are present moments without a future, hollow re-enactments of the past. This quality of fixation characterizes the "permanent" officials as they sit in their row of old-fashioned chairs tilted against the wall. They live in a changeless present, keeping their "accustomed" places (95) and ritualistically repeating their old yarns. The Collector, the most experienced of them all, is the most static; he stands on his past as on a pedestal. His life, like theirs, was once full of changes and chances; it was futuristic, like the world of affairs that now surrounds them. But it became a *past* life precisely by stopping short in a permanent present, a "new lease of existence" that negates the movement of existence and even death. The past, as embodied in these old men, is time that has ceased to act and to evolve new content — time denatured. Therefore they retain none of the substance of their earlier lives and seem to have learned nothing at all from their long experience. The Inspector, who has spent all his adult years in the Custom House, is an utterly mindless animal, for without time man ceases to be; his memory is a parody of memory, a long vista of dinner tables ranged behind the dinner of the day.

Just as the futurism of Uncle Sam has nothing behind it and emerges from a dissolving present, so the past of the Custom House officers is history that has come to nothing in a static present. A problematic duality of traditionalism and futurism lies beneath the positive surface of the Custom House world, and there is a certain emptiness within the apparent substance of that world, whether it be backward-looking or forward-looking. This is a very different social milieu from the one projected through the style of the Cosmopolitan. The world of the Surveyor is not a sustaining medium, a rich present; it is vitiated by chronological time, which either comes to a dead halt or abdicates before the putative future.

The Surveyor is very much aware of his own chronology: once a writer at the Old Manse, he is now Surveyor of the Revenue whose "prophetic instinct" tells him that another "change of custom" is in store for him (103). Back of his sojourn in the Old Manse lie the temporal depths of Salem, his "native place" (91); beyond his eventual discharge from office lies the time at which he will be a writer again, six months later, and beyond that a further future when he will be "a citizen of somewhere else." His sympathies point in both directions; the intrinsic duality of the Custom House world reappears in him. He is an activist and a decadent, a futurist and a traditionalist.

As an exponent of healthy change, he delights in the Custom House as a place of new experience for himself. Though his return to Salem has brought him back to his own earliest past and to the past of his race, his position there is a decided change from his more recent life. He has been wholly converted from a writer to "a man of affairs" (104), and his name emblazoned on boxes of merchandise will go where no title page would ever carry it. In this perspective, his previous literary career becomes unreal — becomes, indeed, a traffic in "unrealities." For the futurist Surveyor, literature is not only an archaic activity, out of date in Uncle Sam's new world, but doubly insubstantial, since it is associated with his own outmoded self. It also pertains to the side of him that continues to dabble in the social past, foolishly trying, amid "the materiality of . . . daily life," to go back into another age and create "the semblance of a world out of airy matter" (112). Literature ceases to be suspect only when it ceases to be past-centered and embraces "the reality of the flitting hour." When the Surveyor bids us farewell, he speaks as the realistic author of "A Rill from the Town-Pump," and the flitting hour is carrying him on to other realities. The Custom House "lies like a dream behind me"; Salem is now "no portion of the real earth, but an overgrown village in cloud-land" (117); and he foresees the time when "the great-grandchildren of the present race" will conceive of him (quite properly) as a "scribbler of bygone days" (117) known only to the village antiquary.

What had brought him to the Custom House, however, was not a quest for new experience but a "strange, indolent, unjoyous attachment" (93) to his birthplace and to the old Salem behind the new one. He has a "home-feeling with the past" (91), a sense of more reality in it than in "the present phase of the town" or his own actual existence. The "earnest and energetic men" (92) who founded his family and helped establish Salem have greater moral validity, "both good and evil" (91), than the activists of the dissolving present. If his relation to them is profitless, it is because their reality annihilates his present life, just as the old active life of the custom officers has terminated in a rigid posture, an empty form. The traditionalist decays because he is fixed; with "oyster-like tenacity" he "clings to the spot where his successive generations have been imbedded" (93). He feels his past as a doom. And if he is a writer, his role is as much diminished in his own eyes by his ancestors' contempt as by the condescension of his readers' great-grandchildren. The old Puritans looking over his shoulder see the future (any change from their pattern) as necessarily decadent; and for them literature, which is wholly a thing of the future, is mere idleness. The backward-oriented mind of the Surveyor can only share their view of himself. As a degenerate "writer of story-books" (92), he takes a feeble vengeance upon them for their tyranny over him: his triviality is their punishment, and he even undertakes, "as their representative," to enter a jocular apology for their sins.

In sum, the chronological world is a trap. If the Surveyor welcomes the Custom House as a "change of diet" (103), he knows all the while that it is a stagnant place, thoroughly detrimental to manly character and to his literary powers. It will change him into permanence ("make me permanently other than I had been," 103). And if he chooses, with equal paradox, to regard the stagnation as a "transitory life" and look toward "a new change of custom" (103), what can he have in view? Merely an opportunity to "recall whatever was valuable in the past"—in the aesthetic life that his futurism always belittles. Not surprisingly, a literary and intellectual torpor overcomes him. Though he mainly blames it on the inactive, dependent, static life of the customs, which destroys his sense of actuality, his impotence is equally a result of the surrounding practical activity, "actual circumstance" (112), in which his traditionalism can see nothing of value. The two aspects of his world meet only to negate each other; the personal existence of the Surveyor is canceled out by the negative world he surveys.

Superficially at home in the Custom House, the Surveyor is truly in the alienated condition that the Cosmopolitan mentions and blithely passes over: his "thoughts are frozen and utterance benumbed." [. . .] Providence, in the guise of a change of administration, saves him from his impasse. [. . .] With his head cut off and his sensibility thereby simplified, he sits down to prepare the "Posthumous Papers of a Decapitated Surveyor." He looks back only with tolerant amusement; parodies the backward-looking documents of Surveyor Pue, whose own "mental part" had survived the centuries; and deplores the "stern and sombre aspect" of *The Scarlet Letter*, in which there are unfortunate traces of his personal "turmoil" in the past.

Yet he notes the odd fact that he was very happy while writing *The Scarlet Letter*. The author of that book, who is quite another person, lurks within the Surveyor of the Customs, just as the latter haunts the Cosmopolitan. [. . .] And he is as solitary as the Surveyor, finally, is sociable. It is in a "deserted chamber of the Custom-House" that his mind returns to its "old track" (109) and he receives his charge from the ghost of Mr. Pue. Traditionalist and solitary, he is thoroughly immersed in the chronological condition. But he does not succumb to chronological determinism, the past that always threatens to come upon him as a doom and fixate him in an empty present. He turns it about, conceives it as an enduring past contained in and latently possessed by the present, as the scarlet letter is "present" beneath the dead records and illusory contemporary world of the Custom House. Nor does he accept the barren role of alienated imagination, reduced to a sluggish "fancy" by the senseless archives of the customs. He converts his solitude into self-pursuit, an active state, which is identical with pursuit of the "deep meaning" of the scarlet letter (108).

He had earlier felt a similar sense of duration in contemplating the statuesque Collector. Viewed with "affection," the old general seemed to lose his fixity and become the living vessel of a still-living past. Yet in this case, the would-be Author could only arrive at loose generalizations; he could not find his way through the ruins of time to the "real life" (101) that he supposed to exist within the old man's memory. The scarlet letter is a different case because it not only gives Hawthorne a token of duration but also includes him, alienated as he is, in the enduring reality it radiates. Coming to him in solitude, it is relevant to the meaning of his solitude; and he, poring over it, is saved from solitude. He is in communion; he belongs in the succession of Hester Prynne, who first wore the letter, and of Surveyor Pue, on whose mind it was so deeply branded. In a roundabout way he has found "the divided segment of . . . [his] own nature," completed his "circle of existence" (87).

If he is redeemed, he is also invested with a mission. Leaving behind his colleagues "seated . . . at the receipt of custom," he has been summoned "like Matthew . . . for apostolic errands." His mission is not to preach but to act—to appropriate the universe of discourse now open to him and thereby to "interpret" the reality of consciousness that "stream[s] forth from the mystic symbol." In *The Scarlet Letter*, the *A* will hang over the entire story, as in its greatest scene a portentous *A* hangs over and illuminates the persons of the drama: Hester, Pearl, and Dimmesdale on the scaffold, Chillingworth below them, and the surrounding town of Boston. Each of these five figures—for the Puritan town is an agent, not a mere setting—will acquire meaning from the universal center but reconstruct the meaning in a particular way. Thus the sphere of the book (which is full of references to "spheres" and "circles") will be progressively redefined as the emblematic letter is approached and shines out from one side or another. In this large sense, *The Scarlet Letter* will be the icon of a creative mind at work, not merely suffering or resting in its inheritance but actively seizing upon the history that made it. [. . .]

The book begins with a vignette of the people of Boston—a single sentence set off in a paragraph by itself: "A throng of bearded men, in sad-colored garments and gray, steeple-crowned hats, intermixed with women, some wearing hoods, and others bareheaded, was assembled in front of a wooden edifice, the door of which was heavily timbered with oak, and studded with iron spikes" (119). Just as Hawthorne gazes at the symbolic letter, seeking the meaning in it, they stand "with their eyes intently fastened on the iron-clamped oaken door," out of which Hester Prynne will come with the letter on her bosom (120). In effect, the prison door is their avenue to the meaning of the symbol; and these colorless men and women, though they stand outside the prison, have all the demeanor of prisoners. Any Utopian colony, Hawthorne declares, will soon find it necessary "to allot a portion of the virgin soil as a cemetery, and another portion as the site of a prison" (119); but these people embrace the necessity. Though they are "founders of a new colony," they have based it upon the oldest facts of human experience—crime and death (119). Though they would cultivate "human virtue and happiness," they have no faith in any direct approach to this end. The jail and its companion-place, the burial ground, are their proper meeting houses; the scaffold, situated "nearly beneath the eaves of Boston's earliest church" (124), is the center of the society. Not once in the book is a church physically described or a scene actually staged within it. Their true religious exercise is the contemplation of Hester, their scapegoat and counterpart, set up before them on the scaffold. Even as they denounce her, they are fascinated by her as an emblem of the world they inhabit.

The ceremony in the market place is genuinely religious, not merely perverse, but it is oblique. The ministers do not urge Hester to seek divine support but only to suffer her punishment, repent her transgression, and name another sinner. If there were some "Papist among the crowd of Puritans," this woman taken in adultery might recall to his mind the contrasting "image of Divine Maternity" (125). But the Puritans invoke no such image to relieve the horror before them; on the contrary, their faith positively depends on discovering a "taint of deepest sin in the most sacred quality of human life" (125). They would honor a transcendent God who enters this world mainly as law-giver and executioner. His mercy appears through his justice, his love through his power. His incarnation is the impress of his abstract supernatural code, which primarily reveals the evils of flesh and the universality of sin. As administrators of the code, the ministers and magistrates on the balcony have no concrete human existence for themselves or others, and they have no perception of the concrete reality of Hester on the scaffold. "Sages of rigid aspect," standing in God's holy fire, they are blind to the "mesh of good and evil" before them (132). They see only the abstract Adulteress. As when Hester later views her image in Governor Bellingham's breastplate, she is "absolutely hidden behind" the "exaggerated and gigantic" abstraction that engrosses her accusers.

If they were merely self-righteous and sadistic, these Bostonians would be much less formidable. They are impressive because their doctrinaire moralism has a metaphysical basis: they purge their town in token of a universe where only God is really pure and only purity is of any account. Hawthorne does full justice to the moral seriousness, the strength of character, and the practical ability that their way of thinking could foster. He affirms that the Puritan society "accomplish[ed] so much, precisely because it imagined and hoped so little" (132). And in various ways his Puritans, though eccentric, are old-fashioned folk, not radical innovators. In comparison with the "heartlessness" of a later era of sophisticated moral tolerance, the punishment inflected on Hester, however cruel, is dignified by moral principle. In comparison with later democratic irreverence, the respectfulness and loyalty of the Massachusetts citizens to their leaders are still close to the feudal virtues. In comparison with their genteel descendants, the merciless harpies of the market place still have a moral as well as physical substance, "a boldness and rotundity" (121), that derives from the old England they have put behind them.

But in all fundamental respects Hawthorne's Puritans are both problematic and unprecedented. They are men responding to an extreme intellectual predicament by extreme measures, and their predicament is one with their disseverance from the old world. The pompous forms and dress of their great public occasions, like the aristocratic menage of Governor Bellingham, are nostalgic and imitative, not characteristic. The old order vaguely survives in their consciousness because they stand at the beginning of a new epoch, but it survives much as memories of King James' court flit through the mind of the Reverend Mr. Wilson. It is true that Europe sometimes figures in the book as "newer" than the Puritan colony: the "other side of the Atlantic" (204) is a place of intellectual and social emancipation, to which Dimmesdale and Hester might flee and to which Pearl betakes herself at the end. But Europe is a refuge because, whether old or new, feudal or modern, it signifies no struggle of consciousness, no necessity to reckon with the foundations of the new era. New England is the place where men must confront the founding questions of their time, which are set forth in the topography, the intellectual landscape, of *The Scarlet Letter*.

Above them stretches the heaven of supernatural revelation, where "any marked event, for good or evil," is prefigured in "awful hieroglyphics" (198). The physical heavens are also spiritual, a medium of the divine word. But no civilized society was ever so directly in contact with brute nature. The settlement is encircled by the teeming "Western wilderness" (126) on one side and the open sea on the other. Though the townsmen studiously abjure this "wild, heathen Nature . . . , never subjugated by human law, nor illumined by higher truth," it invades their prison-fortress. Savage Indians and even more savage sailors are a familiar sight in their streets. And physical nature is equivocal in relation to man. While it reduces him to "animal ferocity," it also sanctions "human nature," the life of feeling, and the virtues of the heart (251). The possibility of a humanistic naturalism lurks in the wild rosebush growing out of "the deep heart of Nature" beside the prison door (119). The possibility becomes actual in the person of Hester Prynne on the scaffold and later in her cottage on the outskirts of the town between the sea and the forest. What is more, Hester represents a positive individualism, alien to Puritan society but capable of creating a human community of its own. By her refusal to play out her appointed role on the scaffold, she becomes doubly an outcast from Boston; and yet, standing there in all her concrete individuality, she seems to claim a general truth, a concrete universality. [. . .] [T]he ferocity of the women in the market place is as lawless and as natural as the lust they denounce, and it complements the rigid natural law that dominates their men. For all of them, "civilized life" consists of putting nature into prison; but the prison itself, the "black flower" of their town, partakes of the subhuman nature they contemn and obsessively scrutinize. The black flower blossoms apace, as Chillingworth observes. Meanwhile, natural affection, the red flower, lives on, unwanted and disclaimed, in the heart of Mr. Wilson and in the potential "heart of the multitude." [. . .] Puritanism contains and secretly invites its opposite, as it contained Anne Hutchinson from whose footsteps the wild rose bush may have sprung.

In this sense, the Puritans of *The Scarlet Letter* are deeply involved in the dialectic of modern freedom. They themselves are creatures of the early modern era with which Hawthorne explicitly associates Hester — that moment when "the human intellect, newly emancipated, . . . [took] a more active and a wider range than for many centuries before" (204). In Europe, "men of the sword [have] overthrown nobles and kings," and "men bolder than these [have] overthrown and rearranged . . . the whole system of ancient prejudice, wherewith was linked much of ancient principle" (204). The mind of Hawthorne's Puritans is a negative version of this same libertarianism, which has cut loose the secular world from God, mankind from nature, and individual men from universal Man. In them, freedom appears as *deprivation*: a world removed from God and definable only in terms of that distance — a mankind at war with nature and able to create value out of it only by denying its intrinsic value, as God denies the value of man — and an individual alienated from humanity, who can rehabilitate himself only by self-annihilation before an external public law. [. . .]

Hester comes to dominate the landscape not only as a character in the eyes of the reader but also as an agent of transvaluation for her contemporaries. The natural affections of the "multitude," oriented toward her, escape from the abstract law of the ministers and magistrates. The final scene in the market place is very different in tonality from that of the first three chapters. There is variety, color, and movement in the picture; the darting figure of the antinomian Pearl weaves through the crowd. And yet we are reminded that "the blackest shade of Puritanism" (250) still lies in the future and that its effect will linger on for two centuries. The populace gathered for this New England holiday are intent on the sign of sin and once more condemn Hester to "moral solitude" (252). The climactic death of Dimmesdale in utter self-negation recalls the basic negativity of the Puritan vision which underlies the solemn procession of dignitaries and his own eloquent sermon on God's work in Massachusetts. For, given Hawthorne's historical method, he can have no intellectual right, and indeed no desire, to represent a complete and irreversible transformation of

Puritan orthodoxy. It is the Puritan mind that proposes his subject, postu-
lates the scarlet letter; he can move beyond this negative frame of reference
only by keeping it in view. If the letter were not potentially more than a
doom and a sign of doom, he could not turn back upon it and repossess it;
but if it did not continue to have power to burn, he would not be trying to
discover its meaning. [. . .]

The Puritan mind in *The Scarlet Letter* follows a logic of negative freedom.
The antithetical good and evil of Puritan morality reflect a universe that is
polarized into external relations on every level, so that good can be conceived only as an external order imposed by God on a fallen world, by man
on a fallen nature, and by society on a fallen individual. Hester Prynne
does not abandon that framework of thought but conceives and enacts a
dialectical relation between evil and good based on a dialectical conversion
of negative into positive freedom. She is creative in the face of destruction,
and she is constantly making an idea of creativity—of individual value,
organic community, and natural divinity—out of the tough negations of
Puritan doctrine. Dimmesdale is torn apart, rendered insubstantial, by this
dialectic, which gives substance to Hester even while it torments her. Unlike her, he experiences the ambiguity of freedom in a primarily negative
form; and at the end of his life he commits himself to the negative Puritan
rationale. Chillingworth, perverting both the Puritan vision and Hester's,
takes evil as his good and thereby ultimately destroys the meaning of such
terms as well as the meaning of liberation itself. His amoral world beyond
good and evil is also beyond freedom, whether negative or positive.

In one way or another all these persons lay claim to the child that Hester clutches to her when she first appears on the scene. The Puritan elders
would instruct Pearl "as to her soul, its present depravity, and future destiny" (166). As the child of sin, she is their human archetype. Dimmesdale,
pathetically treasuring the memory of her moments of affection for him,
sees her as his hope of life, but infected with the doubtfulness of his hope.
Looking at her with eyes accustomed to staring at himself, he cannot say
whether one whose only "discoverable principle of being" is "the freedom of a broken law" may yet be "capable of good" (183). Chillingworth,
pursuing his amoral drive for power, is struck by Pearl's indifference to
"human ordinances or opinions, right or wrong" (182); and he would use
her, the embodiment of an amoral letter, as material for another such exercise of experimental power as he practices upon Dimmesdale. But the
child evades them all, literally by skipping away and figuratively by eluding
their conceptions of her. She partly evades even Hester, for whom she is
identical with the moral dialectic within the embroidered letter. Pearl is not

completely seized by any of the claims made on her—and from the reader's standpoint, she can never be fully grasped as a fictional "character"—because she represents something latent in all who observe her but incapable of being completely objectified in a single human form.

Pearl is the very principle of freedom, the essence of her time. She dances among the graves "like a creature that [has] nothing in common with a bygone and buried generation, nor own[s] herself akin to it" (183). Since she seems to have been "made afresh, out of new elements," she "must perforce be permitted to live her own life, and be a law unto herself, without her eccentricities being reckoned to her for a crime" (183). In this sense, Pearl's freedom is not a moral principle; she is prior to moral categories (though not, like Chillingworth, "beyond" them). The only good she affirms is the "boldness" of her "truth." And her truth consists wholly in her multiplicity, the "infinite variety" of her possibilities, the "many children" she intrinsically is. Hester looks in vain for "the master-word that should control this new and incomprehensible intelligence" (151), for all the major terms of the book are applicable to it to some extent. Pearl is sheer energy, as Chillingworth perceives, and aware of her power; but her passionate, impulsive, capricious emotions are not primarily aggressive. She is by turns malicious and affectionate, as Hester and Dimmesdale discover, but never fully intimate in either way. Often she seems an entirely negative principle of "disorder," whose "freedom" is synonymous with the "broken law" that gave her birth (183). [. . .]

So extreme is Pearl's sense of absolute freedom that all the drama of Dimmesdale's final agony is needed to complete her transformation. In some sense, of course, she must already have entered the human world, the world of sorrow, in order to feel his loss at all. Her earlier affection for him, the man with his hand over his heart, like her obsession with Hester's letter, indicates her nascent awareness of suffering and her correlative "humanization." But in the final episode she flits about the market place in utter independence and joy as though to affirm her infinitude for the last time. She must be drawn down to earth by a principle as strong as her own. Dimmesdale's "great scene of grief . . . develop[s] all her sympathies," commits her to "human joy and sorrow" (267), because he has reached an extreme of negation that counterbalances her libertarian extreme. Just as the kiss he asks from her is his last concession to the world of human relations that he rejects in his dying speech, so her bestowal of the kiss is her first act within the human world to which he has drawn her. [. . .]

[. . .] As a "human child," she is a growing point of human experience, and she betokens a "oneness of . . . being" in the parents who created her (232, 233). This is her role, apparently assumed with some self-awareness, when she, Hester, and Dimmesdale form "an electric chain" (195). It is validated when the celestial "A" shines down upon this archetypal trio: Pearl, "herself a symbol," is the human counterpart of the divine signature in the sky. Though the noonday light that suffuses the scene is like that of Judgment Day, it is not a visitation by an angry God; if it gives a new "moral interpretation to the things of this world" (196), it does so by consecrating the emergent meaning of temporal life—in Dimmesdale, "with his hand over his heart"; in Hester, "with the embroidered letter glimmering on her bosom"; but especially in Pearl, "the connecting link between those two" (196). And in this role Pearl is an aesthetic, as well as a moral, exemplar. She represents not only a secular morality but also a secularized symbolism. She recalls us once more to the distinctive imaginative medium of her author—the liberated modern consciousness that often dissolves, like Pearl, into a "vast variety of forms" (154), but of which, again like Pearl, the imaginative structure of *The Scarlet Letter* is a "living hieroglyphic" (233).

The Ruined Wall

Frederick C. Crews

Explicating Hawthorne's metaphor of the soul's guilt-breached "ruined wall" in Freudian terms, Frederick Crews argues that Dimmesdale's guilt for yielding to a libidinous impulse leads to neurotic repression of the libido and to sublimations which culminate in his Election Sermon. His "morbid remorse"—the "destructive outlet" for his passion—is a punishment that is also a form of gratification which paradoxically renews his conscience's demand for self-punishment. More broadly, Crews argues that the tragic action of *The Scarlet Letter* springs from its characters' inner world of frustrated desires that they can "neither understand or control." [ED.]

Hester Prynne and Arthur Dimmesdale, in the protective gloom of the forest surrounding Boston, have had their fateful reunion. While little Pearl, sent discreetly out of hearing range, has been romping about in her

From *The Sins of the Fathers: Hawthorne's Psychological Themes*. New York: Oxford UP, 1966. (The author no longer believes in the cause of psychoanalytic criticism. See his explanatory Afterword in the 1989 UC Press edition. All parenthetical references are to this New Riverside Edition. [ED.])

unrestrained way, the martyred lovers have unburdened themselves. Hester has revealed the identity of Chillingworth and has succeeded in winning Dimmesdale's forgiveness for her previous secrecy. Dimmesdale has explained the agony of his seven years' torment. Self-pity and compassion have led unexpectedly to a revival of desire; "what we did," as Hester boldly remembers, "had a consecration of its own" (224), and Arthur Dimmesdale cannot deny it. In his state of helpless longing he allows himself to be swayed by Hester's insistence that the past can be forgotten, that deep in the wilderness or across the ocean, accompanied and sustained by Hester, he can free himself from the revengeful gaze of Roger Chillingworth.

Hester's argument is of course a superficial one; the ultimate source of Dimmesdale's anguish is not Chillingworth but his own remorse, and this cannot be left behind in Boston. The closing chapters of *The Scarlet Letter* demonstrate this clearly enough, but Hawthorne, with characteristic license, tells us at once that Hester is wrong. "And be the stern and sad truth spoken," he says,

> that the breach which guilt has once made into the human soul is never, in this mortal state, repaired. It may be watched and guarded; so that the enemy shall not force his way again into the citadel, and might even, in his subsequent assaults, select some other avenue, in preference to that where he had formerly succeeded. But there is still the ruined wall, and, near it, the stealthy tread of the foe that would win over again his unforgotten triumph. (229)

This metaphor is too striking to be passed over quickly. Like Melville's famous comparison of the unconscious mind to a subterranean captive king in Chapter XLI of *Moby-Dick*, it provides us with a theoretical understanding of behavior we might otherwise judge to be poorly motivated. Arthur Dimmesdale, like Ahab, is "gnawed within and scorched without, with the infixed, unrelenting fangs of some incurable idea," and Hawthorne's metaphor, inserted at a crucial moment in the plot, enables us to see the inner mechanism of Dimmesdale's torment.

At first, admittedly, we do not seem entitled to draw broad psychological conclusions from these few sentences. Indeed, we may even say that the metaphor reveals a fruitless confusion of terms. Does Hawthorne mean to describe the soul's precautions against the repetition of overt sin? Apparently not, since the "stealthy foe" is identified as *guilt* rather than as the forbidden urge to sin. But if the metaphor means what it says, how are we to reduce it to common sense? It is plainly inappropriate to see "guilt" as the original assailant of the citadel, for feelings of guilt arise only in *reaction against* condemned acts or thoughts. The metaphor would seem to be plausible only in different terms from those that Hawthorne selected.

We may resolve this confusion by appealing to Arthur Dimmesdale's literal situation. In committing adultery he has succumbed to an urge which, because of his ascetic beliefs, he had been unprepared to find in himself. Nor, given the high development of his conscience and the sincerity of his wish to be holy, could he have done otherwise than to have violently expelled and denied the sensual impulse, once gratified. It was at this point, we may say—the point at which one element of Dimmesdale's nature passed a sentence of exile on another—that the true psychological damage was done. The original foe of his tranquility *was* guilt, but guilt for his thoughtless surrender to passion. In this light we see that Hawthorne's metaphor has condensed two ideas that are intimately related. Dimmesdale's moral enemy is the forbidden impulse, while his psychological enemy is guilt; but there is no practical difference between the two, for they always appear together. We may understand Hawthorne's full meaning if we identify the potential invader of the citadel as a libidinal impulse, *now necessarily bearing a charge of guilt.*

This hypothesis helps us to understand the sophisticated view of Dimmesdale's psychology that Hawthorne's metaphor implies. Dimmesdale's conscience (the watchful guard) has been delegated to prevent repetition of the temptation's "unforgotten triumph." The deterrent weapon of conscience is its capacity to generate feelings of guilt, which are of course painful to the soul. Though the temptation retains all its strength (its demand for gratification), this is counterbalanced by its burden of guilt. To readmit the libidinal impulse through the guarded breach (to gratify it in the original way) would be to admit insupportable quantities of guilt. The soul thus keeps temptation at bay by meeting it with an equal and opposite force of condemnation.

But let us consider the most arresting feature of Hawthorne's metaphor. The banished impulse, thwarted in one direction, "might even, in his subsequent assaults, select some other avenue, in preference to that where he had formerly succeeded" (229). Indeed, the logic of Hawthorne's figure seems to assure success to the temptation in finding another means of entrance, since conscience is massing all its defenses at the breach. This devious invasion would evidently be less gratifying than the direct one, for we are told that the stealthy foe would stay in readiness to attack the breach again. Some entry, nevertheless, is preferable to none, especially when it can be effectuated with a minimum resistance on the part of conscience. Hawthorne has set up a strong likelihood that the libidinal impulse will change or disguise its true object, slip past the guard of conscience with relative ease, and take up a secret dwelling in the soul.

In seeking to explain what Hawthorne means by this "other avenue" of invasion, we must bear in mind the double reference of his metaphor. It describes the soul's means of combating both sin and guilt—that is, both *gratification* of the guilty impulse and *consciousness* of it. For Dimmesdale the greatest torment is to acknowledge that his libidinous wishes are really his, and not a temptation from the Devil. His mental energy is directed, not simply to avoiding sin, but to expelling it from consciousness—in a word, to repressing it. The "other avenue" is the means his libido chooses, given the fact of repression, to gratify itself surreptitiously. In psychoanalytic terms this is the avenue of compromise that issues in a neurotic symptom.

Hawthorne's metaphor of the beseiged citadel cuts beneath the theological and moral explanations in which Dimmesdale puts his faith, and shows us instead an inner world of unconscious compulsion. Guilt will continue to threaten the timid minister in spite of his resolution to escape it, and indeed (as the fusion of "temptation" and "guilt" in the metaphor implies) this resolution will only serve to upset the balance of power and enable guilt to conquer the soul once more. Hawthorne's metaphor demands that we see Dimmesdale not as a free moral agent but as a victim of feelings he can neither understand nor control. And the point can be extended to include Chillingworth and even Hester, whose minds have been likewise altered by the consequences of the unforgotten act, the permanent breach in the wall. If, as Chillingworth asserts, the awful course of events has been "a dark necessity" from the beginning (210), it is not because Hawthorne believes in Calvinistic predestination or wants to imitate Greek tragedy, but because all three of the central characters have been ruled by motives inaccessible to their conscious will.

The implications we have drawn, perhaps over-subtly, from Hawthorne's metaphor begin to take on substance as we examine Arthur Dimmesdale in the forest scene. His nervousness, his mental exhaustion, and his compulsive gesture of placing his hand on his heart reveal a state that we would now call neurotic inhibition. His lack of energy for any of the outward demands of life indicates how all-absorbing is his internal trouble, and the stigma on his chest, though a rather crass piece of symbolism on Hawthorne's part, must also be interpreted psychosomatically. Nor can we avoid observing that Dimmesdale shows the neurotic's reluctance to give up his symptoms. How else can we account for his obtuseness in not having recognized Chillingworth's character? "I might have known it!" he murmurs when Hester forces the revelation upon him. "I did know it! Was not the secret told me in the natural recoil of my heart, at the first sight of him, and as often as I have seen him since? Why did I not understand?" (224). The answer, hidden from Dimmesdale's surface reasoning, is that his relationship with Chillingworth, taken together with the change in mental economy that has accompanied it, has offered perverse satisfactions which he is even now powerless to renounce. Hester, whose will is relatively independent and strong, is the one who makes the decision to break with the past.

We can understand the nature of Dimmesdale's illness by defining the state of mind that has possessed him for seven years. It is of course his concealed act of adultery that lies at the bottom of his self-torment. But why does he lack the courage to make his humiliation public? Dimmesdale himself offers us the clue in a cry of agony: "Of penance I have had enough! Of penitence there has been none! Else, I should long ago have thrown off these garments of mock holiness, and have shown myself to mankind as they will see me at the judgment-seat" (222). The plain meaning of this outburst is that Dimmesdale has never surmounted the libidinal urge that produced his sin. His "penance," including self-flagellation and the more refined torment of submitting to Chillingworth's influence, has failed to purify him because it has been unaccompanied by the feeling of penitence, the resolution to sin no more. Indeed, I submit, Dimmesdale's penance has incorporated and embodied the very urge it has been punishing. If, as he says, he has kept his garments of mock holiness *because* he has not repented, he must mean that in some way or another the forbidden impulse has found gratification in the existing circumstances, in the existing state of his soul. And this state is one of morbid remorse. The stealthy foe has re-entered the citadel through the avenue of remorse.

This conclusion may seem less paradoxical if we bear in mind a distinction between remorse and true repentance. In both states the sinful act is condemned morally, but in strict repentance the soul abandons the sin and turns to holier thoughts. Remorse of Dimmesdale's type, on the other hand, is attached to a continual re-enacting of the sin in fantasy and hence a continual renewal of the need for self-punishment. Roger Chillingworth, the psychoanalyst *manqué*, understands the process perfectly: "the fear, the remorse, the agony, the ineffectual repentance, the backward rush of sinful thoughts, expelled in vain!" (186). As Hawthorne explains, Dimmesdale's cowardice is the "sister and closely linked companion" (192) of his remorse.

Thus Dimmesdale is helpless to reform himself at this stage because the passional side of his nature has found an outlet, albeit a self-destructive one, in his present miserable situation. The original sexual desire has been granted recognition *on the condition of being punished*, and the punishment itself is a form of gratification. Not only the overt masochism of fasts, vigils, and self-scourging (the last of these makes him laugh, by the way), but also Dimmesdale's emaciation and weariness attest to the spending of his energy against himself. It is important to recognize that this is the same energy previously devoted to passion for Hester. We do not exaggerate the facts of the romance in saying that the question of Dimmesdale's fate, for all its religious decoration, amounts essentially to the question of what use is to be made of his libido.

We are now prepared to understand the choice that the poor minister faces when Hester holds out the idea of escape. It is not a choice between a totally unattractive life and a happy one (not even Dimmesdale could feel hesitation in that case), but rather a choice of satisfactions, of avenues into the citadel. The seemingly worthless alternative of continuing to admit the morally condemned impulse by the way of remorse has the advantage, appreciated by all neurotics, of preserving the status quo. Still, the other course naturally seems more attractive. If only repression can be weakened—and this is just the task of Hester's rhetoric about freedom—Dimmesdale can hope to return to the previous "breach" of adultery.

In reality, however, these alternatives offer no chance for happiness or even survival. The masochistic course leads straight to death, while the other, which Dimmesdale allows Hester to choose for him, is by now so foreign to his withered, guilt-ridden nature that it can never be put into effect. The resolution to sin will, instead, necessarily redouble the opposing force of conscience, which will be stronger in proportion to the overtness of the libidinal threat. As the concluding chapters of The Scarlet Letter prove, the only possible result of Dimmesdale's attempt to impose, in Hawthorne's phrase, "a total change of dynasty and moral code, in that interior kingdom" (240), will be a counter-revolution so violent that it will slay Dimmesdale himself along with his upstart libido. We thus see that in the forest, while Hester is prating of escape, renewal, and success, Arthur Dimmesdale unknowingly faces a choice of two paths to suicide.

Now, this psychological impasse is sufficient in itself to refute the most "liberal" critics of The Scarlet Letter—those who take Hester's proposal of escape as Hawthorne's own advice. However much we may admire Hester and prefer her boldness to Dimmesdale's self-pity, we cannot agree that she understands human nature very deeply. Her shame, despair, and solitude "had made her strong," says Hawthorne, "but taught her much amiss" (228). What she principally ignores is the truth embodied in the metaphor of the ruined wall, that men are altered irreparably by their violations of conscience. Hester herself is only an apparent exception to this rule. She handles her guilt more successfully than Dimmesdale because, in the first place, her conscience is less highly developed than his; and secondly because, as he tells her, "Heaven hath granted thee an open ignominy, that thereby thou mayest work out an open triumph over the evil within thee, and the sorrow without" (134). Those who believe that Hawthorne is an advocate of free love, that adultery has no ill effects on a "normal" nature like Hester's, have failed to observe that Hester, too, undergoes self-inflicted punishment. Though permitted to leave, she has remained in Boston not simply because she wants to be near Arthur Dimmesdale, but because this has been the scene of her humiliation. "Her sin, her ignominy, were the roots which she had struck into the soil," says Hawthorne. "The chain that bound her here was of iron links, and galling to her inmost soul, but never could be broken" (143).

We need not dwell on this argument, for the liberal critics of *The Scarlet Letter* have been in retreat for many years. Their place has been taken by subtler readers who say that Hawthorne brings us from sin to redemption, from materialistic error to pure spiritual truth. The moral heart of the novel, in this view, is contained in Dimmesdale's Election Sermon, and Dimmesdale himself is pictured as Christ-like in his holy death. Hester, in comparison, degenerates spiritually after the first few chapters; the fact that her thoughts are still on earthly love while Dimmesdale is looking toward heaven is a serious mark against her.

This redemptive scheme, which rests on the uncriticized assumption that Hawthorne's point of view is identical with Dimmesdale's at the end, seems to me to misrepresent the "felt life" of *The Scarlet Letter* more drastically than the liberal reading. Both take for granted the erroneous belief that the novel consists essentially of the dramatization of a moral idea. The tale of human frailty and sorrow, as Hawthorne calls it in his opening chapter, is treated merely as the fictionalization of an article of faith. [. . .]

All parties can agree, in any case, that there is a terrible irony in Dimmesdale's exhilaration when he has resolved to flee with Hester. Being, as Hawthorne describes him, "a true religionist," to whom it would always remain essential "to feel the pressure of a faith about him, supporting, while it confined him within its iron framework" (174), he is ill-prepared to savor his new freedom for what it is. His joy is that of his victorious libido, of the "enemy" which is now presumably sacking the citadel, but this release is acknowledged by consciousness only after a significant bowdlerization:

> "Do I feel joy again?" cried he, wondering at himself. "Methought the germ of it was dead in me! O Hester, thou art my better angel! I seem to have flung myself—sick, sin-stained, and sorrow-blackened—down upon these forest leaves, and to have risen up all made anew, and with new powers to glorify Him that hath been merciful! This is already the better life! Why did we not find it sooner?" (230)

Hawthorne's portrayal of self-delusion and his compassion are nowhere so powerfully combined as in this passage. The Christian reference to the putting on of the New Man is grimly comic in the light of what has inspired it, but we feel no more urge to laugh at Dimmesdale than we do at Milton's Adam. If in his previous role he has been only, in Hawthorne's phrase, a "subtle, but remorseful hypocrite" (189), here he is striving pathetically to be sincere. His case becomes poignant as we imagine the revenge that his tyrannical conscience must soon take against these new promptings of the flesh. To say merely that Dimmesdale is in a state of theological error is to miss part of the irony; it is precisely his theological loyalty that necessitates his confusion. His sexual nature must be either denied with unconscious sophistry, as in this scene, or rooted out with heroic fanaticism, as in his public confession at the end.

On one point, however, Dimmesdale is not mistaken: he has been blessed with a new energy of body and will. The source of this energy is obviously his libido; he has become physically strong to the degree that he has ceased directing his passion against himself and has attached it to his thoughts of Hester. But as he now returns to town, bent upon renewing his hypocrisy for the four days until the Election Sermon has been given and the ship is to sail, we see that his "cure" has been very incomplete. "At every step he was incited to do some strange, wild, wicked thing or other, with a sense that it would be at once involuntary and intentional; in spite of himself, yet growing out of a profounder self than that which opposed the impulse" (241). The minister can scarcely keep from blaspheming to his young and old parishioners as he passes them in the street; he longs to shock a deacon and an old widow with arguments against Christianity, to poison the innocence of a naïve girl who worships him, to teach wicked words to a group of children, and to exchange bawdy jests with a drunken sailor. Here, plainly, is a return of the repressed, and in a form which Freud noted to be typical in severely holy persons. The fact that these impulses have reached the surface of Dimmesdale's mind attests to the weakening of repression in the forest scene, while their perverse and furtive character shows us that repression has not ceased altogether. Hawthorne's own explanation, that Dimmesdale's hidden vices have been awakened because "he had yielded himself *with deliberate choice,* as he had never done before, to what he *knew* was deadly sin" (244; my italics), gives conscience its proper role as a causative factor. Having left Hester's immediate influence behind in the forest, and having returned to the society where he is known for his purity, Dimmesdale already finds his "wicked" intentions constrained into the form of a verbal naughtiness which he cannot even bring himself to express.

Now Dimmesdale, presumably after a brief interview with the taunting Mistress Hibbins, arrives at his lodgings. Artfully spurning the attentions of Roger Chillingworth, he eats his supper "with ravenous appetite" (246) and sits down to write the Election Sermon. Without really knowing what words he is setting on paper, and wondering to himself how God could in-

spire such a sinner as himself, he works all night "with earnest haste and ecstasy" (246). The result is a sermon which, with the addition of sponta-
neous interpolations in the delivery, will impress its Puritan audience as an
epitome of holiness and pathos. Nothing less than the descent of the Holy
Ghost will be held sufficient to account for such a performance.

Yet insofar as the Election Sermon will consist of what Dimmesdale has
recorded in his siege of "automatic writing," we must doubt whether
Hawthorne shares the credulous view of the Puritans. Dimmesdale has
undergone no discernible change in attitude from the time of his eccentric
impulses in the street until the writing of the sermon. Though he works in
the room where he has fasted and prayed, and where he can see his old
Bible, he is not [. . .] sustained by these reminders of his faith. Quite the
contrary: he can scarcely believe that he has ever breathed such an atmosphere. "But he seemed to stand apart, and eye this former self with scornful, pitying, but half-envious curiosity. That self was gone! Another man
had returned out of the forest; a wiser one; with a knowledge of hidden
mysteries which the simplicity of the former never could have reached"
(244). In short, the Election Sermon is written by the same man who wants
to corrupt young girls in the street, and the same newly liberated sexuality
"inspires" him in both cases. If the written form of the Election Sermon *is*
a great Christian document, as we have no reason to doubt, this is attrib-
utable not to Dimmesdale's holiness but to his libido, which gives him creative strength and an intimate acquaintance with the reality of sin.

Thus Dimmesdale's sexual energy has temporarily found a new alternative to its battle with repression—namely, sublimation. In sublimation, we
are told, the libido is not repressed but redirected to aims that are acceptable to conscience. The writing of the Election Sermon is just such an aim,
and readers who are familiar with psychoanalysis will not be puzzled to
find that Dimmesdale has passed without hesitation from the greatest blasphemy to fervent religious rhetoric.

There is little doubt that Dimmesdale has somehow recovered his
piety in the three days that intervene between the writing of the sermon
and its delivery. Both Hester and Mistress Hibbins "find it hard to believe
him the same man" (256) who emerged from the forest. Though he is pre-
occupied with his imminent sermon as he marches past Hester, his energy
seems greater than ever and his nervous mannerism is absent. We could
say, if we liked, that at this point God's grace has already begun to sustain
Dimmesdale, but there is nothing in Hawthorne's description to warrant a
resort to supernatural explanations. It seems likely that Dimmesdale has
by now felt the full weight of his conscience's case against adultery, has already determined to confess his previous sin publicly, and so is no longer

suffering from repression. His libido is now free, not to attach itself to Hester, but to be sublimated into the passion of delivering his sermon and then expelled forever.

The ironies in Dimmesdale's situation as he leaves the church, having preached with magnificent power, are extremely subtle. His career, as Hawthorne tells us, has touched the proudest eminence that any clergyman could hope to attain, yet this eminence is due, among other things, to "a reputation of whitest sanctity" (261). Furthermore, Hester has been silently tormented by an inquisitive mob while Dimmesdale has been preaching, and we feel the injustice of the contrast. And yet Dimmesdale has already made the choice that will render him worthy of the praise he is now receiving. If his public hypocrisy has not yet been dissolved, his hypocrisy with himself is over. It would be small-minded not to recognize that Dimmesdale has, after all, achieved a point of heroic independence — an independence not only of his fawning congregation but also of Hester, who frankly resents it. If the Christian reading of *The Scarlet Letter* judges Hester too roughly on theological grounds, it is at least correct in seeing that she lacks the detachment to appreciate Dimmesdale's final act of courage. While she remains on the steady level of her womanly affections, Dimmesdale, who has previously stooped below his ordinary manhood, is now ready to act with the exalted fervor of a saint.

All the moral ambiguity of *The Scarlet Letter* makes itself felt in Dimmesdale's moment of confession. We may truly say that no one has a total view of what is happening. The citizens of Boston, for whom it would be an irreverent thought to connect their minister with Hester, turn to various rationalizations to avoid comprehending the scene. Hester is bewildered, and Pearl feels only a generalized sense of grief. But what about Arthur Dimmesdale? Is he really on his way to heaven as he proclaims God's mercy in his dying words?

> He hath proved his mercy, most of all, in my afflictions. By giving me this burning torture to bear upon my breast! By sending yonder dark and terrible old man, to keep the torture always at red-heat! By bringing me hither, to die this death of triumphant ignominy before the people! Had either of these agonies been wanting, I had been lost for ever! Praised be his name! His will be done! Farewell! (267)

This reasoning, which sounds so cruel to the ear of rational humanism, has the logic of Christian doctrine behind it; it rests on the paradox that a man must lose his life to save it. The question that the neo-orthodox interpreters of *The Scarlet Letter* invariably ignore, however, is whether Hawthorne has prepared us to understand this scene only in doctrinal terms. Has he abandoned his usual irony and lost himself in religious transport?

[. . .] Hawthorne offers us naturalistic explanations for everything that happens, and though he also puts forth opposite theories—Pearl is an elf-child, Mistress Hibbins is a witch, and so on—this mode of thinking is discredited by the simplicity of the people who employ it. We cannot conscientiously say that Chillingworth *is* a devil, for example, when Hawthorne takes such care to show us how his devilishness has proceeded from his physical deformity, his sense of inferiority and impotence, his sexual jealousy, and his perverted craving for knowledge. Hawthorne carries symbolism to the border of allegory but does not cross over. As for Dimmesdale's retrospective idea that God's mercy has been responsible for the whole chain of events, we cannot absolutely deny that this may be true; but we can remark that if it *is* true, Hawthorne has vitiated his otherwise brilliant study of motivation.

Nothing in Dimmesdale's behavior on the scaffold is incongruous with his psychology as we first examined it in the forest scene. [. . .] Dimmesdale has been heroic in choosing to eradicate his libidinal self with one stroke, but his heroism follows a sound principle of mental economy. Further repression, which is the only other alternative for his conscience-ridden nature, would only lead to a slower and more painful death through masochistic remorse. Nor can we help but see that his confession passes beyond a humble admission of sinfulness and touches the pathological. His stigma has become the central object in the universe: "God's eye beheld it! The angels were for ever pointing at it! The Devil knew it well, and fretted it continually with the touch of his burning finger!" (265). Dimmesdale is so obsessed with his own guilt that he negates the Christian dogma of original sin: "behold me here, the one sinner of the world!" (265). This strain of egoism in his "triumphant ignominy" does not subtract from his courage, but it casts doubt on his theory that all the preceding action has been staged by God for the purpose of saving his soul.

However much we may admire Dimmesdale's final asceticism, there are no grounds for taking it as Hawthorne's moral ideal. The last developments of plot in *The Scarlet Letter* approach the "mythic level" which redemption-minded critics love to discover, but the myth is wholly secular and worldly. Pearl, who has hitherto been a "messenger of anguish" to her mother, is emotionally transformed as she kisses Dimmesdale on the scaffold. "A spell was broken. The great scene of grief, in which the wild infant bore a part, had developed all her sympathies; and as her tears fell upon her father's cheek, they were the pledge that she would grow up amid human joy and sorrow, nor for ever do battle with the world, but be a woman in it" (267). Thanks to Chillingworth's bequest—for Chillingworth, too, finds that a spell is broken when Dimmesdale confesses, and he is capable of at least one generous act before he dies—Pearl is made "the richest heiress of her day, in the New World" (269). At last report she has become the wife of a European nobleman and is living very happily across the sea. This grandiose and perhaps slightly whimsical epilogue has one undeniable effect on the reader: it takes him as far as possible from the scene and spirit of Dimmesdale's farewell. Pearl's immense wealth, her noble title, her lavish and impractical gifts to Hester, and of course her successful escape from Boston all serve to disparage the Puritan sense of reality. From this distance we look back to Dimmesdale's egocentric confession, not as a moral example which Hawthorne would like us to follow, but as the last link in a chain of compulsion that has now been relaxed.

To counterbalance this impression we have the case of Hester, for whom the drama on the scaffold can never be completely over. After raising Pearl in a more generous atmosphere she voluntarily returns to Boston to resume, or rather to begin, her state of penitence. We must note, however, that this penitence seems to be devoid of theological content; Hester has returned because Boston and the scarlet letter offer her "a more real life" (271) than she could find elsewhere, even with Pearl. This simply confirms Hawthorne's emphasis on the irrevocability of guilty acts. And though Hester is now selfless and humble, it is not because she believes in Christian submissiveness but because all passion has been spent. To the women who seek her help "in the continually recurring trials of wounded, wasted, wronged, misplaced, or erring and sinful passion" (271), Hester does not disguise her conviction that women are pathetically misunderstood in her society. She assures her wretched friends that at some later period "a new truth would be revealed, in order to establish the whole relation between man and woman on a surer ground of mutual happiness" (271). Hawthorne may or may not believe the prediction, but it has a retrospective importance in *The Scarlet Letter*. Hawthorne's characters originally acted in ignorance of passion's strength and persistence, and so they became its slaves.

"It is a curious subject of observation and inquiry," says Hawthorne at the end,

> whether hatred and love be not the same thing at bottom. Each, in its utmost development, supposes a high degree of intimacy and heart-knowledge; each renders one individual dependent for the food of his affections and spiritual life upon another; each leaves the passionate lover, or the no less passionate hater, forlorn and desolate by the withdrawal of his object. (269)

These penetrating words remind us that the tragedy of *The Scarlet Letter* has chiefly sprung, not from Puritan society's imposition of false social ideals on the three main characters, but from their own inner world of frustrated desires. Hester, Dimmesdale, and Chillingworth have been ruled by feelings only half perceived, much less understood and regulated by consciousness; and these feelings, as Hawthorne's bold equation of love and hatred implies, successfully resist translation into terms of good and evil. Hawthorne does not leave us simply with the Sunday-school lesson that we should "be true" (269), but with a tale of passion through which we glimpse the ruined wall—the terrible certainty that, as Freud put it, the ego is not master in its own house. It is this intuition that enables Hawthorne to reach a tragic vision worthy of the name: to see to the bottom of his created characters, to understand the inner necessity of everything they do, and thus to pity and forgive them in the very act of laying bare their weaknesses.

Dark Light on the Letter

Hyatt H. Waggoner

According to Hyatt H. Waggoner, the "ultimate question" posed by *The Scarlet Letter* is whether the tragic conflicts it presents are inevitable. Noting that the rose that Hawthorne offers the reader in the first chapter to "symbolize some sweet moral blossom" does not reappear at the end, Waggoner argues that Hawthorne could find no plausible "happy ending" for his "tragic heroine."[ED.]

[. . .] Emerson and Hawthorne were contemporaries and for several years neighbors and something like friends in Concord, but the two men could hardly have been more unlike in temperament, in approaches to life, and in their final conclusions about it. It would be oversimplifying both men to say that Emerson saw only the light, Hawthorne only the darkness of life. However, it would not be misleading to find Emerson's chief thrust in his effort to illustrate "human power in every department" of life, and to try to persuade us that this power results from the fact that, as he said, when we achieve the proper angle of vision we learn that God IS; that he is in me; and that all things are shadows of him"; and, correspondingly, to find that Hawthorne's predominant concern in his fiction is with just those

From *The Presence of Hawthorne*. Baton Rouge: Louisiana State UP, 1979. (All parenthetical references are to this New Riverside Edition.)

experiences of guilt and limitation that Emerson thought it possible to transcend. "Sin" for Emerson was, as he once said, "the soul's mumps," a childhood disease to be outgrown. For Hawthorne, except during the early years of his marriage, sin seemed the only certainty besides death.

The ultimate question *The Scarlet Letter* poses to us is whether there is ever to be any escape from such tragic conflicts as those the novel presents. In Hester Prynne's story we find society in conflict with the individual's drive for self-realization, religious and moral codes in conflict with natural impulse, and, within individuals, duty in conflict with the desire for pleasure and happiness. For Hester there is no escape, only sublimation and self-control. For Dimmesdale there is only public confession of guilt and submission to a will he conceives as higher than his own. Are suffering and defeat then inevitably and always the law of life?

Fortunately for the lasting power the novel has over us, Hawthorne does not attempt here, as he later would in *The House of the Seven Gables*, to tell us overtly what he thinks, or hopes, the answer is. He lets his story, and the images he finds to tell it, speak for themselves, not distorting his picture to make it suggest the hope he personally entertained, as he so often did in his lesser works, not manipulating what he had imagined but being controlled by it. The one "moral" of his story he felt certain enough of to state for us is not a hopeful one: "Be true! Be true! Show freely to the world, if not your worst, yet some trait whereby the worst may be inferred!"

The complex image with which the tale concludes is as preponderantly dark, despite Hawthorne's wish that he might lighten it, as the images in the first chapter. The inscription on the stone that marks the double grave of Hester and her one-time lover is given us only as a medieval herald might have worded it, not in its Puritan starkness; but even when lifted and rendered legendary—distanced—by the heraldic language, it is dark enough. The words the herald might have written to be placed on the coat of arms of a noble family were, Hawthorne tells us, illuminated "only by one ever-glowing point of light gloomier than the shadow—ON A FIELD, SABLE, THE LETTER A, GULES" (272).

The darkness of this ending suggests that life is tragic but not that it is pointless, meaningless, absurd. In the course of the novel, the image of red ("gules," the heraldic term for the color red) has come to suggest both sin and guilt, and also the natural, the passionate, and the beautiful. It has been associated with the rose beside the jail, with Pearl's dress, and with its biblical and traditional uses, all of which point toward prohibited sexual activity. Blackness and darkness have been associated with both secrecy and death. But in the final double image there is no suggestion left of the "positive" (the "natural," the happy) implication of red, only the "negative"— the guilt and the death—and the darkness that began to be apparent in the story's opening sentences is now "relieved" only by a "point" of light that is too gloomy to "glow" [. . .]. A story in which the action has moved, metaphorically, between the points defined in the first chapter as the cemetery, the prison, and the rose, ends with one of its reference points, the rose, missing. Guilt and death, the prison and the cemetery, appear to be the last words that can be spoken about these lives.

There are of course other ways of reading Hawthorne's "romance," not counting the way of looking for its "latent" meaning—signs in it of Hawthorne's neurosis—hidden beneath the "manifest" content. (Only by radically changing the meaning of the word "meaning" can this way seem to be relevant to literary criticism.) We may, for instance, take more seriously than we have so far what was, as both external and internal evidence attest, Hawthorne's conscious effort to lighten the ending of his dark tale. For example, he allows Pearl to escape the environment (and the moral code?) that prevented her mother from finding fulfillment as a woman and a person. Pearl, after she grows up, lives in Europe, which for Hawthorne, as for Henry James later, ambiguously symbolizes freedom from Puritanic inhibitions.

Or again, we might try to find more light in the ending by seeing Dimmesdale's words and gestures as he approaches the scaffold and faces his death of "triumphant ignominy" (267) as Christ-like, and so suggesting not defeat but final triumph, not darkness but, ultimately, light. Hawthorne probably intended that we should notice Dimmesdale's gesture with his arms, his words of forgiveness of Chillingworth, and his way of embracing his fate.

Or we might remember what Hawthorne knew: that the language of heraldry not only distanced, it lifted, enhanced, and ennobled, the deeds of which it spoke in its own peculiar symbolism. Illegitimate birth, for example, ceased to be a disgrace when emblazoned on a feudal coat of arms. An earl descended from a bastard was still an earl: public acknowledgment of the family's "disgrace" on their shield "wiped out" the stigma.

Hawthorne's most obvious attempt to lighten his ending becomes clear when we consider his source for the words he places last in his book. Andrew Marvell's poem "The Unfortunate Lover" concludes with these lines,

This is the only *Banneret*
That ever love created yet:
Who though, by the malignant Starrs,
Forced to live in Storms and Warrs:

Yet dying leaves a perfume here,
And Musick within every Ear:
And he in Story only rules,
In a Field *Sable* a Lover *Gules*.

The discoverer of this undoubted "source" of Hawthorne's words at the end of his work[1] saw it as removing the tale to a greater distance from us — as though it were not already distant enough — and as supporting an interpretation that would lay "greater emphasis on aesthetic rather than moralistic intention" — whatever such a dichotomy would mean. But of course Hawthorne's use of Marvell to help him end his story testifies chiefly to his desire — his "hope," as he had put it in the final sentence of his first chapter — that he might find something somewhere in the story he was about to tell that would lighten or "relieve" what he called "the darkening close of a tale of human frailty and sorrow." (Note that he did *not* call it, as some of his interpreters have, a tale of "sin" and merited suffering.)

Marvell had said that love created a flag, to be flown proudly; that the lovers were victims of circumstances; and that yet the unhappy story affects us as perfume and music do: as wholly to be admired, not condemned. The use to which Hawthorne put Marvell's words in his ending reveals the extent to which, in a part of his mind at least, Hawthorne felt that his own doomed lovers were victims. The ending suggests how deeply, how much more deeply than he knew — or at least was able to admit to himself — Hawthorne sympathized with the adulterous lovers of his tale, how close he was to agreeing with the words he put in Hester's mouth, "What we did had a consecration of its own."

For most modern readers, Hawthorne's efforts to relieve the darkness of his ending do not — cannot — succeed. They did not for Hawthorne himself and his wife Sophia either, when they read the story aloud together after he had finished it, and wept. Pearl, after all, exists as an adult and achieves happiness outside the story. The parallels between Dimmesdale's words and actions in the last scaffold scene and Christ's at the time of his crucifixion do not work either — if indeed they really were intended to. They are likely either to go unnoticed by most readers today or to strike them as a mere contrivance on Hawthorne's part. Jesus after all did not wait until he was dying of "natural" causes, and with no other course open to him, to embrace his destiny. As for Marvell's lines, they do not so much effectively "lighten" the tale as reveal Hawthorne's desire that it should be lightened.

For Hawthorne, the focal point of his story, I suspect, was the fate of a young woman married to an old man. Scholars who have uncovered the "sources" of *The Scarlet Letter* in New England's history have found the passages in Hawthorne's favorite reading that probably suggested to him the penalty of having to wear the scarlet letter, the name "Hester" for his heroine, and much more. But the history of Mary Latham, married to an

---

[1] Robert L. Brant, "Hawthorne and Melville," *American Literature*, XXX (1958), 366.

old and (presumably) impotent man, a girl who committed adultery with "divers young men," was probably the story that ignited his imagination. It was very likely her story that prompted his notebook entry in 1844 or 1845, "The life of a woman, who, by the old colony law, was condemned always to wear the letter A, sewed on her garment, in token of her having committed adultery." What was such a person to do, in a society that demanded and enforced repression of sexual impulses except as they could be satisfied in marriage? What "happy" outcome for her *could* there be?

When he finally came to write his novel Hawthorne did everything he could do without committing himself to open approval of her defiance of Puritan morality to make us sympathize with Hester, who knowingly defied the Puritan code and who dreamed of a day in the future, beyond her time, when women would be considered as people, not property. In the beginning of his tale, Hawthorne gave Hester great beauty and vitality, and a halo; at the end, he knew he had made her a tragic heroine who had managed, by the strength of her courage and integrity, to find meaning and purpose in life despite her frustration.

He could think of no "happy ending" for her, no escape that could be made plausible. He did not think her "innocent," but he did consider her a victim. Her tale, when his wife read it to him, moved him more than any of his later novels would have the power to do. Could any escape from frustration be imagined? He thought perhaps it could—at least for those more fortunately placed than Hester and Dimmesdale—and quickly undertook to write a happier work, *The House of the Seven Gables,* which he would later describe as more "representative" of him. In a sense he would be right, but only half: the self it represented was more the ideal self-image, the man he wished to be, than the total man. It better suggested what he believed but less powerfully embodied what he felt.

Hawthorne's sensibility and outlook more closely and clearly foreshadow Robert Penn Warren's than do those of any other nineteenth-century American writer of fiction. His tensions between desire and belief, feeling and thought, have been Warren's. In theme, image, and situation, Hawthorne's fiction, especially his short tales, anticipates the fiction of Warren. The "Hawthorne tradition" in American fiction runs through Melville to James (despite James's effort to break free from it) to Faulkner to Warren. What this whole tradition leaves unclear is whether there is any—any conceivable, any possible—escape from the consequences of "human frailty," any emotion possible to conceive besides "sorrow."

For Hawthorne, when he wrote *The Scarlet Letter,* the cemetery and the prison of the opening chapter were undeniably evident in life. The rose, which he hoped might serve to "symbolize some sweet ["fulfilling"? "self-realizing"?] moral [fulfilling but not condemned, not "guilt-producing"?]

blossom [flowers, like Hester, are beautiful and, also like her, feel no guilt], that may be found along the track, or relieve the darkening close of a tale of human frailty and sorrow"—for Hawthorne, the rose could only be postulated and hoped for. In this novel at least, Hawthorne's most deeply felt, it could not be found.

Can it be found—and found to be authentic, not just professed or wished for—granted that as we look back through history it seems mostly not to have been found, except perhaps by the mystics and the saints? Can guilty, suffering, and dying man find fulfillment of his conflicting desires to satisfy himself and at the same time love and be loved by others? Can he find a way to be himself and yet live in community with others, to be true at once to "nature" and to "society"?

If he can, he must do so without denying the tragic truths Hawthorne's novel so beautifully embodies. *The Scarlet Letter* is Hawthorne's finest expression of his feeling of "the way life is." Emerson's effort to tell us how it *might* be for the enlightened was not Hawthorne's subject here. As he wrote to his publisher about what he was creating, "*The Scarlet Letter* is positively a hell-fired story, into which I find it almost impossible to throw any cheering light."[2] To most of us today, the story is likely to seem not so much "hell-fired" as true to ordinary experience as most people suffer it most of the time.

The Romances

Rita K. Gollin

Rita K. Gollin singles out the occasions in *The Scarlet Letter* when Hester and Dimmesdale engage in reveries that dramatize the causes and effects of their sin. Reverie for Hawthorne is a state of mind in which the moral imagination and external reality intersect, provoking profound truths. Gollin argues that Hester's single developed reverie provides her with a temporary respite from her noontime ordeal on the scaffold, reveals to her and the reader the entire "track"

From *Nathaniel Hawthorne and the Truth of Dreams*. Baton Rouge: Louisiana State UP, 1979. (All parenthetical references are to this New Riverside Edition.)

[2] The letter, which is not to Hawthorne's publisher but to his friend Horatio Bridge, appears on pages 38–39 in this volume. [ED.]

that led her there, and leads to self-knowledge. By contrast, the reverie preceding Dimmesdale's midnight ordeal on the scaffold is a "compendium" of his nightly self-punishment. [ED.]

[. . .] In *The Scarlet Letter* there are no dreams at all; but daydreams bring the reader into intimacy with the two main characters as they try to come to terms with the consequences of their sexual encounter. Hester's daydream takes place at the outset of the novel as she stands on the scaffold, her baby in her arms and the A on her breast. Dimmesdale's takes place midway in the novel, in his study, in a torrent of guilt that later drives him out to the same scaffold. Hester's daydream establishes her character, and Dimmesdale's explores his dilemma. Both are integral to the novel's central problem—the causes and (more important) the effects of sin on the two sinners. The reveries are deliberately initiated acts of introspection that implicitly explain their public behavior.

Daydreaming is psychologically necessary for them both, since each is essentially alone in the Puritan community. The narrator of [Hawthorne's] "Foot-prints on the Sea-shore" can go from daydreaming to a picnic, but easy social gratification is not available to Hester or Dimmesdale. With the single exception of the forest interlude, they can share intimate thoughts with no one.

Structurally, the two episodes of daydreaming are integral to two of the novel's three major scaffold scenes. The first introduces Hester as she takes inner refuge from her public shame; the second reveals Dimmesdale's inner mortification and leads to his midnight travesty of public shame on the scaffold. Only in the final scaffold scene when the hidden relationship is publicly revealed are we not granted privileged entry into the sinner's mind.

By placing Hester's reverie near the beginning of the novel, Hawthorne deftly establishes the expository background of her predicament while accomplishing another important task. The reader approaching Hester through her inner consciousness necessarily sympathizes with her. The occasion of her reverie is psychologically convincing: standing on the scaffold, weighted by grief while her punishment is still new, she has no other hope of relief. She is not temperamentally a habitual dreamer; but like the sufferers in "The Hall of Fantasy," she takes brief refuge from "the gloom and chilliness of actual life." At the same time, her recollections implicitly explain how she came to violate the Puritan code.

The discursive structure of the reverie expresses Hawthorne's understanding of how the mind drifts along its levels of consciousness, one idea drawing another in its wake, while a single strong emotion dominates the stream of association. As Hester moves from active perception to semipassive consciousness, the reader follows the inward spiral of her thoughts. From her stance on the scaffold, the marketplace sometimes seems blurred: "There were intervals when the whole scene . . . seemed to vanish from her eyes, or at least, glimmered indistinctly before them, like a mass of imperfectly shaped and spectral images" (126). The familiar word "glimmered" serves its usual purpose of suggesting the threshold stage when perceptions and imagined forms fleetingly intermingle: Hester's consciousness of the marketplace fades as her inner visions intensify.

The scaffold now becomes a neutral territory: she sees "other faces than were lowering upon her from beneath the brims of those steeple-crowned hats" (126) as spectral memories emerge in rapid sequence. "Reminiscences, the most trifling and immaterial, passages of infancy and school-days, sports, childish quarrels, and the little domestic traits of her maiden years, came swarming back upon her, intermingled with recollections of whatever was gravest in her subsequent life; one picture precisely as vivid as another; as if all were of similar importance, or all alike a play" (126). In keeping with the principles of association, the visual swarm is roughly ordered by chronology, but interpenetrated by recollections associated with her present gloom. Her will virtually in abeyance, she becomes the observer of thoughts that appear before her as a changing spectacle, a pageant emerging from "memory's picture-gallery" (128). Here Hawthorne speculates about the daydreamer's involuntary strategies of self-protection: "Possibly, it was an instinctive device of her spirit, to relieve itself, by the exhibition of these phantasmagoric forms, from the cruel weight and hardness of the reality" (126).

The chief narrative function of the "phantasmagoric forms," however, is to suggest the causes of her predicament, more than she consciously comprehends. The scaffold not only defines her physical separation as an emotional and moral isolation, but it provides "a point of view that revealed to Hester Prynne the entire track along which she had been treading, since her happy infancy."

Although she tries to take refuge in happy memories, like Robin in [Hawthorne's story] "My Kinsman, Major Molineux," sorrow immediately obtrudes. Thoughts of "happy infancy" lead to thoughts of the "poverty-stricken aspect" of her family home, with its "half-obliterated shield of arms" (implicitly suggesting why Chillingworth might have been welcomed as a suitor, 126). She recalls the faces of her loving parents and her dead mother's disturbing "look of heedful and anxious love." Next an even more detailed image implicitly explains her eventual moral vulnerability: she recalls her own "girlish beauty," her face "illuminating all the interior of the dusky mirror in which she had been wont to gaze at it." The mirror of Hester's imagination reflects a memory of a real mirror, revealing both her beauty and her vanity.

She then immediately envisions in the same mirror the misshapen individual who became her husband. This second reflected image is more detailed and disturbing than anything else in the daydream; it emphatically establishes Hester's narcissism and her physical distaste for Chillingworth. She recalls him as a pale and thin old man, with eyes "dim and bleared" by study, yet able to "read the human soul." The next sentence describes his physical deformity and Hester's awareness of it: her "womanly fancy failed not to recall" that one shoulder was higher than the other. The curious negative phrase "failed not to recall" emphasizes Hester's forthright nature: even in the refuge of memory, she does not avert her attention from unpleasantness. The mirror separates and frames Beauty and the Beast in a monstrous marriage portrait, suggesting why Chillingworth desired her and why she could not be happy with him.

Her last "shifting scene" is set in an ancient "Continental city," her "new life" there likened to "a tuft of green moss on a crumbling wall," thus pointing to the incongruity of her marriage and the sense of disjunction and futility that later made her vulnerable to sin. An emphatic inversion of subject and verb signals Hester's abrupt return from "memory's picture-gallery" to the present: "In lieu of these shifting scenes, came back the rude market-place of the Puritan settlement" (128). The hiatus between memory and perception invites sympathy and asserts that Hester knows where she is. Imagination offered only momentary escape.

This passage colors the reader's subsequent views of Hester. It is her only reverie, but Hawthorne later draws on imagery he usually reserved for dreams to define the two preoccupations of her inner life. The first is her passion for Dimmesdale. In a brief passage near the beginning, that passion is likened to a monster imprisoned within her (like the dream phantoms of "The Haunted Mind"). It emerges from time to time "like a serpent from its hole," and she must then struggle to reimprison it (143).

Her second preoccupation is with moral speculation, established in three passages which use almost identical words and images. In all three, Hester wanders through a labyrinthine wilderness, a terrain more dangerous and terrifying than the forest of [Hawthorne's] "Young Goodman Brown," and as in that tale, the metaphor has a literal equivalent. The first of these passages asserts that Hester's heart is not in harmony with her mind, envisaging her mind as a confusing and dangerous place: "Thus, Hester Prynne, whose heart had lost its regular and healthy throb, wandered without a clew in the dark labyrinth of mind; now turned aside by an insurmountable precipice; now starting back from a deep chasm. There

was wild and ghastly scenery all around her, and a home and comfort nowhere" (205). Her journey through this landscape links her to the heroines
of Gothic romance; but unlike them, Hester is no tremulous figure in flight.
She is a seeker, though with no specific goal; a challenger of the social order, though with no alternative program.

Next, in a brief passage, the metaphor of wilderness emerges in Hester's
own mind as she enters the real forest, suggesting how readily she assimi-
lates experience. The path she takes into the "primeval forest" where she
expects to encounter Dimmesdale offers "such imperfect glimpses of the
sky above, that, to Hester's mind, it imaged not amiss the moral wilderness
in which she had so long been wandering" (216). On the real path and the
metaphorical one, Hester has gone beyond the frontiers of civilization; and
as in Goodman Brown's forest or in the Valley of the Shadow, there is no
hope of celestial illumination.

The last and longest of these passages offers a retrospective summary
of Hester's inner life during her years of punishment, paradoxically establishing her strength of character despite her moral uncertainty. While
Dimmesdale had remained confined by the social order, "she had wandered, without rule or guidance, in a moral wilderness; as vast, as intricate
and shadowy, as the untamed forest. . . . Her intellect and heart had their
home, as it were, in desert places, where she roamed as freely as the wild Indian in his woods." In these gloomy regions "where other women dared
not tread," her teachers are "Shame, Despair, Solitude," familiar demons
of "The Haunted Mind." They taught her much "amiss," yet they strengthened her (228).

Hester is the only woman comparable to the central figure of the Oberon
tales or the major dream stories, alone in her dark mind. Like theirs, her
inner life becomes more absorbing than her outer experience, although
unlike the earlier dreamers and unlike Dimmesdale, she is never confused
about what is real. Her character develops as her initial reverie suggested it
would: she is a figure of fortitude. But at the end of the novel Hawthorne
suggests that she did not have to wander forever in a moral wilderness: near
the end of her life she "had no selfish ends," but gave comfort and counsel
to wretched women, assuring them she believed in a brighter future when
man and woman might join together "on a surer ground of mutual happiness" (271). The mirror of self had been put away.

Dimmesdale's long reverie in the middle of the novel is more an attempt
to recover than to discover self. Significantly, it is not a particular reverie
but an abstraction and compendium of all his reveries, a credible expression of his continual spiritual probing, self-torment, and irresolution.
Dimmesdale is no ordinary dreamer adrift in a sombre dream world, but a
man out of tune with himself. Chillingworth, an agent of malevolence, had

stirred up demons of thought to trouble the minister's mind; in Dimmesdale's reverie, spiritual aspiration and guilt struggle for mastery. Yet he learns nothing new: his reverie can only restate his problem, not resolve it. Because he is an "untrue man, the whole universe is false"; and he is too cowardly to become "true" (191).

The reader does not accompany him in and out of his reverie, as with Hester's; yet Hawthorne describes how Dimmesdale's usually begin, and how they end. His nightly vigils, "sometimes with a glimmering lamp; and sometimes, viewing his own face in a looking-glass, by the most powerful light which he could throw upon it," not only induce his reveries, but are emblematic of them: "He thus typified the constant introspection wherewith he tortured, but could not purify, himself " (190).

However abstracted, the reverie is psychologically credible. The glimmering lamp and the mirror create an atmosphere that invites dreams. Dimmesdale's brain "reeled, and visions seemed to flit before him; perhaps seen doubtfully, and by a faint light of their own, in the remote dimness of the chamber, or more vividly, and close beside him, within the looking-glass." Fantasies mingle with memories, and by an act of imaginative projection, he can see them "vividly" in the mirror. By contrast with the mirror Hester remembers, envisaging herself with Chillingworth, Dimmesdale looks not at but into himself with the aid of a real mirror which then seems to reflect his fantasies.

In the next stage, the images become more specific, arranged as in a morality play: "Now it was a herd of diabolic shapes, that grinned and mocked at the pale minister, and beckoned him away with them; now a group of shining angels, who flew upward heavily, as sorrow-laden, but grew more ethereal as they rose" (190). The chapter in which the reverie is set is called "The Interior of a Heart," but the word "mind" would be equally appropriate, since within that interior theater the vices and virtues engage in a struggle for Dimmesdale's soul. The moral conflict is appropriate to the mind of a conventional minister trying to come to terms with a sin he can neither publicly acknowledge nor expiate.

The rest of the paragraph is given to more realistic visions, figures of memory who pass in brief parade, notably his father "with a saint-like frown, and his mother, turning her face away as she passed by" (190), embodiments of his own self-loathing. Hawthorne as narrator invites pity for Dimmesdale with curious indirection, saying the fantasy mother "might yet have thrown a pitying glance towards her son!" But in his self-contempt, Dimmesdale cannot imagine such pity. In the final and most psychologically convincing sentence, Hester glides in with Pearl, pointing like the embodiment of Shame at her own scarlet letter and then at the minister's breast. With the compression of dreams, this composite image dramatizes the bond between the sinners, his obsession with his guilt, and his urge to confession.

The silent figures dominating the minister's guilty imagination seem to have real existence in his "ghastly" chamber, like the nightmare figures of "The Haunted Mind." They are also a direct link to the crucial scenes that soon follow, Dimmesdale's midnight vigil on the scaffold and the forest meeting with Hester. In both he is uncertain whether Hester and Pearl are real or imagined. Dimmesdale is like Dugald Stewart's man of disordered imagination whose thoughts are dominated by creatures of his mind.

At the conclusion of the passage, Hawthorne distances us from the reverie by speaking of "those ugly nights, which we have faintly hinted at, but forborne to picture forth," as if further specification would be indecorous (191). The dream images of [Hawthorne's stories] "The Haunted Mind" and "The Celestial Railroad" are equally abstract, but the first person narrators more fully involve the reader in their "heart-quake." In most of Hawthorne's fictional reveries, the protagonist reaches some unbearable knowledge; but Dimmesdale is only a passive witness to familiar images of distress. One night is much like another on this treadmill of self-abasement; Dimmesdale is too cowardly to move forward into an inner forest like Hester's. Yet these self-punishing vigils have more reality for Dimmesdale than his daily duties as minister.

His moral perturbation is best understood by comparing his tormented visions with those of Hester's noontime reverie. The visions of Hester's reverie emerge in continuous linear order, each adding onto the earlier ones; Dimmesdale's are disjunctive, dialectically ordered as a tug-of-war. Hester is informed and Dimmesdale threatened by their separate fantasies. She remains essentially an observer, but he is also the focus of the conflict he envisages, tormented by its imperatives for action. Hester's daydream confronts the initial cause of her guilt and leads her to accept the realities she must live by; Dimmesdale's articulates his continuing anxiety and shows his inability to reconcile his conscience with his public behavior. Hester moves toward knowledge of her heart; Dimmesdale is paralyzed by knowledge of his soul.

Dimmesdale's midnight vigil on the scaffold immediately follows his reverie. Without artifice or melodrama, the scene unfolds as a nightmare. The chapter opens with Dimmesdale no longer transfixed in his chamber but "walking in the shadow of a dream, as it were, and perhaps actually under the influence of a species of somnambulism" (191), without full control of his behavior. Chillingworth later reinforces the idea that Dimmesdale is neither fully awake nor fully asleep when he says that studious men dream even when awake, then walk in their sleep.

As he stands on the scaffold where Hester had stood seven years before, Dimmesdale's horror erupts in a shriek; then his mind makes another "involuntary effort to relieve itself" in a grimly humorous vision intermixed with "solemn phantoms" of thought. He imagines the townsfolk, "with the disorder of a nightmare in their aspects," discovering him in the morning, frozen on the scaffold in his posture of shame. He involuntarily responds to his own fantasy as Robin had responded to real mockery: with "a great peal of laughter" (195).

As with Robin, the laugh returns him from fantastic nightmare to the nightmare of his real distress. Instead of his fantasy, he sees Hester and Pearl, who join him on the scaffold. Now a strange red meteor appears, and its light agitates his imagination more powerfully than moonlight: the familiar street takes on "a singularity of aspect that seemed to give another moral interpretation to the things of this world than they had ever borne before" (196). His guilty imagination reads the meteor as a celestial accusation in the form of the scarlet A. Then he sees Chillingworth, whose malevolent expression remains "painted on the darkness" after the meteor vanishes. This is almost too horrifying to endure. When Chillingworth urges him to return home, Dimmesdale responds "like one awaking, all nerveless, from an ugly dream" (200).

Dimmesdale's continuing inability to distinguish what he imagines from what is real explains his vacillation about Hester's plan of escape when they meet in the forest. At first he thinks she is a spectre that stole out of his thoughts, and when she suggests that they escape from Boston, he reacts to her suggestion as an impotent dreamer: "'It cannot be!' answered the minister, listening as if he were called upon to realize a dream. 'I am powerless to go'" (227). Only when he accepts her plan can he escape "from the dungeon of his own heart"; but that escape is brief (229). Leaving the forest, he again wonders whether Hester is real; he must look back to reassure himself that he "had not fallen asleep, and dreamed!" (238).

His temporary acquiescence to Hester's plan generates even greater perplexity in the chapter called "The Minister in a Maze." As he looks at his own church, his perceptions are so strange that his "mind vibrated between two ideas; either that he had seen it only in a dream hitherto, or that he was merely dreaming about it now" (240). Up to this point, his inner visions had seemed as vivid as reality; now both the town and the townspeople seem as mutable as dreams. Hawthorne then explains this delusion: "Tempted by a dream of happiness, he had yielded himself with deliberate choice . . . to what he knew was deadly sin" (244). Only Dimmesdale's knowledge enables him to put the tempting dream behind him and seek salvation through confession on the scaffold.

Dimmesdale finally stands on the scaffold in public, leaning on Hester and holding Pearl's hand, "doubt and anxiety in his eyes" yet "a feeble smile upon his lips." His question to Hester conveys both his anxiety and his hope: "Is not this better . . . than what we dreamed of in the forest?" (264). The question is crucial, but it remains unanswered. Whether he found salvation also remains an open question, though waking from his dreamlike confusion does bring Dimmesdale to a height of spiritual exaltation before he dies. Through his death, however, Hawthorne suggests what he had already asserted through the dreamers of such minor fictions as "Sylph Etherege" and "Old Esther Dudley": man's inner and outer lives are continuous, and abandoning one destroys them both.

The Major Phase I
1850

Nina Baym

In her discussion of Hester's and Dimmesdale's relations to their Puritan community and to their own selves, Nina Baym stresses the minister's internalization of Puritan repressiveness and Hester's relative independence from it, as evident in her "development of a certain feminist ideology." In Baym's view, Chillingworth and Pearl are their alter egos, embodiments of their sin and their inner disharmony. But, Baym says, Hester's beautifully embroidered letter subverts the magistrates' intentions, and her return to Boston and her decision to continue wearing the letter are not an acknowledgment of guilt. In fact, Baym argues, Hester effects a "modest social change" by winning social acceptance. In her discussion of "The Custom-House" as an "autobiographical romance," Baym connects Hawthorne to his passionate heroine. [Ed.]

[. . .] [Hawthorne] designed "The Custom-House" for many purposes: to balance the mood and tone of *The Scarlet Letter,* which, he feared, was monotonous in its single effect; to increase the length of the volume in which

From *The Shape of Hawthorne's Career*. Ithaca: Cornell University Press, 1976. (All parenthetical references are to this New Riverside Edition.)

The Scarlet Letter would be published; to take revenge on the politicians who had caused his removal from the Custom House. But above all he wrote it as a commentary on, and a frame for, *The Scarlet Letter.* The essay tells the story of how Hawthorne came to write *The Scarlet Letter* and in so doing tells us a good deal about how to read it. If "The Custom-House" makes an introduction to *The Scarlet Letter,* so does *The Scarlet Letter* provide the conclusion for "The Custom-House."

In *The Scarlet Letter* Hawthorne defined the focus of all four of his completed long romances: the conflict between passionate, self-assertive, and self-expressive inner drives and the repressing counterforces that exist in society and are also internalized within the self. In this romance he also formulated some of the recurrent elements in his continuing exploration of this theme. In Hester he developed the first of a group of female representatives of the human creative and passionate forces, while in Dimmesdale he created the first of several guilt-prone males, torn between rebellious and conforming impulses. These two characters operate in *The Scarlet Letter* in a historical setting, which was not repeated in any of Hawthorne's later romances, but the historical setting is shaped according to thematic preoccupations that do recur. Nominally Puritan, the society in *The Scarlet Letter* in fact symbolizes one side of the conflict.

None of his many treatments of the Puritans depicted them in their own terms — that is, as a group bound together by a covenant among themselves and with God, to establish "a due form of government both civil and ecclesiastical," in accordance with "a special overruling providence." (The words are John Winthrop's, from "A Model of Christian Charity.") The historical first generation of Puritans made constant reference out from their every act to the divine purpose for which they acted and the greater will they were bound to serve. Hawthorne, however, always treated the Puritans within an entirely secular framework. His early works constantly balance their punitive intolerance against their strong sense of their own rights and their hardy endurance. "Main-street" manifested, for the first time, a discrimination between them and their descendants on the grounds of their pure religious faith, but his treatment did not operate *within* that faith. The formulation in *The Scarlet Letter* is different from both of these, but retains the same secularity.

In *The Scarlet Letter,* unlike Hawthorne's stories about Ann Hutchinson, the Quakers, Roger Williams, or the Salem witches, the Puritans are not punishing a heresy but an act that in its essence does not appear to quarrel with Puritan doctrine. What Hester and Dimmesdale have done is not a crime against belief but against the law. Many critics have maintained that, since the act violates one of the Ten Commandments, it is necessarily seen by Hawthorne as a crime against Divine Law. But in *The Scarlet Letter* he considers the act entirely as a social crime. Precisely because he does not take up the issue of whether the law broken is a divine law, the issues center on the relations of Hester and Dimmesdale to their community and to themselves as they accept or deny the judgment of the community on them. They differ from one another, not as beings more or less religious, more or less "saved," but as beings differently bound to the community and differently affected by it.

Such a thematic situation is created in *The Scarlet Letter* by the virtual absence of God from the text, and in this respect the romance is a very poor representation of the Puritan mental life as the Puritan himself would have experienced it. Divinity in this romance is a remote, vague, ceremonially invoked concept that functions chiefly to sanction and support the secular power of the Puritan rulers. And—another difference from Hawthorne's earlier formulation of Puritan psychology—these rulers are not transfigured by the zeal of a recovered faith burning like a lamp in their hearts. Remove the sense of communal purpose and service in behest of God, and a self-satisfied secular autocracy remains; this is what we find in *The Scarlet Letter*. The Puritans of this community are sagacious, practical, realistic; they are lovers of form and display; they even tend toward luxury—consider Hester's many opportunities for fancy embroidery, and the elegance of Governor Bellingham's residence.

The ruling group is composed of old males, aptly epitomized in the Governor, "a gentleman advanced in years, and with a hard experience written in his wrinkles. He was not ill fitted to be the head and representative of a community, which owed its origin and progress, and its present state of development, not to the impulses of youth, but to the stern and tempered energies of manhood, and the sombre sagacity of age; accomplishing so much, precisely because it imagined and hoped so little. This patriarchy surrounds itself with displays of power, and when Hawthorne writes that this was "a period when the forms of authority were felt to possess the sacredness of divine institutions" (132), he makes the point, crucial for his story, that the Puritans venerate authority, not because it is an instrument in God's service, but because they believe secular authority itself to be divine.

What Hawthorne says of this group at the beginning of the romance he repeats at the end. In the final scene we see them as men of "long-tried integrity," of "solid wisdom and sad-colored experience," with "endowments of that grave and weighty order, which gives the idea of permanence, and comes under the general definition of respectability" (254). The portrait is by no means wholly unfavorable (although respectable or authoritarian types will become increasingly unattractive in the subsequent romances) because Hawthorne feels, as he felt in *Grandfather's Chair*, that men of this type were required to establish a new nation: "They had fortitude and self-reliance, and, in time of difficulty or peril, stood up for the welfare of the state like a line of cliffs against a tempestuous tide" (254). But such men are totally unfit to "meddle with a question of human guilt, passion, and anguish" (132)—to meddle, that is, with the private, inner, imaginative life of the person. They are purely formal, purely public men; the society they devise accordingly recognizes no private life, and it is against this obtuseness that Hester and Dimmesdale must try to understand their own behavior and feelings.

A community that embodies the qualities of aging public males must necessarily repress those of the young and female. Dimmesdale is a brilliant young minister who, in order to maintain himself as a favorite among the oligarchs, has repressed himself—made himself prematurely old by resolutely clinging to childhood. He "trode in the shadowy by-paths, and thus kept himself simple and childlike; coming forth, when occasion was, with a freshness, and fragrance, and dewy purity of thought, which, as many people said, affected them like the speech of an angel" (133). In this dewy innocent we recognize faint traces of Hawthorne's earlier men of fancy, and like them Dimmesdale does not so much want power as approval. He is a dependent personality. But he is still a young man, and to forgo the engagement with life characteristic of youth he must continually hold himself back. His "sin" is an impulsive relaxation of self-restraint and a consequent assertion of his youthful energies against the restrictions established by the elders. He does a passionate, thoughtless, willful thing. Precipitated out of his protected security as much by fear as by guilt, he must now confront the conflicts of adulthood. It is not only that he has been initiated into sex; it is less the sexual than the mental and emotional that interests Hawthorne, the inner rather than the outer aspects of the experience. Dimmesdale must now recognize and deal with previously hidden, subversive, and disobedient parts of himself.

Hester begins from no such position of security as Dimmesdale, and her relative lack of protection is at once a disadvantage and a blessing. He is the darling insider while she is in many ways an outsider even before her deed exposes her to public disgrace. She has been sent to Massachusetts by her husband, there to await his arrival; her own will is not implicated in her residence in the community. She thus has nothing like Dimmesdale's tie to the group at the outset. If, as the unfolding of the romance demonstrates, she is a far more independent character than Dimmesdale, her independence may be partly the effect of her relative unimportance in and to society and her consequent paradoxical freedom within it. To judge by the development of a certain feminist ideology in Hester's thinking over the years, it would seem that Hawthorne intended to represent a basic difference in the status of men and women within a patriarchal structure. Since women are of less account than men—are not fully members of the society—they are coerced physically rather than psychologically. Forced to wear a symbol of shame in public, Hester is left alone behind that symbol to develop as she will.

[. . .] The original sexual encounter between Hester and Dimmesdale was an act neither of deliberate moral disobedience nor of conscious social rebellion. The characters had forgotten society and were thinking only of themselves. But seven years later when they meet again, they deliberately reject the judgment society has passed upon them. "What we did had a consecration of its own," Hester says, and "what hast thou to do with all these iron men, and their opinions?" (224, 227). Deciding to leave the community, they in effect deny its right to punish them. Hester is mainly responsible for this decision; seven years of solitude have made of her a rebel and a radical. The consequent catastrophe originates with Dimmesdale, whose fragile personality cannot sustain the posture of defiance once Hester's support has been removed and he is back in the community. He reverts—rather quickly—to the view that society has the right to judge and therefore that its judgment is right. His dying speech does not convince Hester. "Is not this better," he demands, "than what we dreamed of in the forest?" "I know not! I know not!" she replies (264). She undertakes alone the journey they had planned together and secures the fruit of her sin from the consequences of a Puritan judgment. Then, surprisingly, she returns.

But by returning, even though she takes up the scarlet letter and wears it until her death, she does not acknowledge her guilt. Rather, she admits that the shape of her life has been determined by the interaction between that letter, the social definition of her identity, and her private attempt to withstand that definition. Her life is neither the letter nor her resistance— neither the inner nor the outer—but the totality. But by again wearing the letter after her return—a gesture nobody would have required of her after so many years—and thus bringing the community to accept that letter on her terms rather than its own, Hester has in fact brought about a modest social change. Society expands to accept her with the letter—the private life carves out a small place for itself in the community's awareness. This is a small, but real, triumph for the heroine.

Hester and Dimmesdale work through their seven-year purgatory accompanied by alter egos, partly supernatural and parasitic beings related in several symbolic ways to their hosts: for Hester, Pearl; for Dimmesdale, Chillingworth. These subsidiary figures embody the sin that has been committed as it is felt and understood by each of the two actors; they are figures of the imagination made real. Since Hester and Dimmesdale imagine their act quite differently, the deed assumes a radically different shape in each one's inner life. Hester perceives her "sin" in the shape of the beautiful child, wild, unmanageable, and unpredictable, who has been created from it; Dimmesdale sees his in the form of the vengeful and embittered husband who has been offended by it.

Splintered off from the characters with whom they are associated, Pearl and Chillingworth indicate disharmony and disunity within Hester's and Dimmesdale's emotional lives, a direct result of the conflict between their sense of themselves and their awareness of how the community perceives them. Each character is alienated from a different part of his nature; crudely, Hester is tormented by her passions and Dimmesdale by his conscience. [. . .]

For the seven solitary years that she remains in the community, Hester tries to come to terms with its judgment. She actually wants to accept that judgment, for, if she can, she will see purpose and meaning in her suffering. But her attempts cannot shake her deepest conviction that she has not sinned — that is, that the social judgment is not a divine judgment:

> Man had marked this woman's sin by a scarlet letter, which had such potent and disastrous efficacy that no human sympathy could reach her, save it were sinful like herself. God, as a direct consequence of the sin which man thus punished, had given her a lovely child, whose place was on that same dishonored bosom, to connect her parent for ever with the race and descent of mortals, and to be finally a blessed soul in heaven! (149)

As an embodiment of Hester's sin, Pearl is a kind of variant of the scarlet letter. Hester perceives her as such, and dresses her to bring out the identity, "arraying her in a crimson velvet tunic, of a peculiar cut, abundantly embroidered with fantasies and flourishes of gold thread. . . . It was a remarkable attribute of this garb, and indeed, of the child's whole appearance, that it irresistibly and inevitably reminded the beholder of the token which Hester Prynne was doomed to wear upon her bosom. It was the scarlet letter in another form; the scarlet letter endowed with life!" (158). In dressing Pearl to look like the letter, Hester appears to be trying to accept the Puritan idea that Pearl is a creature of guilt. But her behavior is subversive and cunning, for she has already transformed the letter into a work of art with her gorgeous embroidery, and it is to this transfigured symbol that she matches Pearl.

Hester's art [. . .] is not pretty but splendid, and not cold but fiercely passionate, for it stems directly from the passionate self that engendered Pearl and is now denied all other expression: "She had in her nature a rich, voluptuous, Oriental characteristic — a taste for the gorgeously beautiful, which, save in the exquisite productions of her needle, found nothing else, in all the possibilities of her life, to exercise itself upon" (145). Now this expressive activity, which is fundamentally nonsocial, must be realized in shapes that are perceived and classified and judged by society. Hester's activity is permissible when it is employed in giving "majesty to the forms in which a new government manifested itself to the people," that is, by creating "deep ruffs, painfully wrought bands, and gorgeously embroidered gloves" (144). With these items her gift is brought into the service of authority. But when Hester employs this same activity on her own letter, it is quite another matter. By making the letter beautiful, Hester is denying its literal meaning and thereby subverting the intention of the magistrates who condemn her to wear it. Moreover, by applying this art to her own letter, she puts her gift to work in the service of her private thoughts and feelings rather than in support of public rituals. The Puritan women understand at once what she has done: "She hath good skill at her needle, that's certain . . . but did ever a woman, before this brazen hussy, contrive such a way of showing it! Why, gossips, what is it but to laugh in the faces of our godly magistrates, and make a pride out of what they, worthy gentlemen, meant for a punishment?" (124). [. . .] In the interplay between Pearl and the letter, Hawthorne and Hester both wrestle with the problem of bringing together the artist's "idea," which is nonsocial and even nonverbal, and the eventual product. At the most basic level the writer must use language, a social construct, for his expression. Thereby his product becomes social even if his idea is not. Pearl, the antisocial creature, must be transformed into the letter A. Ultimately, artistic conceptions that are expressive but perhaps not meaningful in a declarative sense must acquire meanings through the form in which they are expressed, meanings that may be irrelevant to and even at odds with the conception. The undecorated scarlet letter would certainly be a form false to Hester's conception of what she has done. Her recourse is to play with that form in order to loosen it, expand it, undercut it, and thereby make it capable of a sort of many-layered communication. Her artist's activity is directly contrasted to the operation of the Puritan mind, forever anxiously codifying the phenomena of its world into the rigid system of its alphabet.

If Pearl is Hester's imagination of her sin, she also symbolizes the sinful part of Hester's self—the wild, amoral, creative core. Hester is at odds with this part of herself (though she probably would not be if society had not judged as it did) and, until she comes to some sort of resolution, is a divided personality. Truly to assent to her punishment, Hester must come to judge her own nature, or that part of it, as society has judged it. She does try to feel guilty, and hopes that by behaving like a guilty person she will eventually create a sense of guilt within her. She tries to restrain and discipline the child according to society's judgments, but her passionate nature—pushed by ostracism into defiance—continues to assert itself. Pearl expresses all the resentment, pride, anger, and blasphemy that Hester feels but may not voice, and perhaps does not even admit to feeling. One recalls the famous catechism scene where Pearl, to Hester's mortification, proclaims that "she had not been made at all, but had been plucked by her mother off the bush of wild roses, that grew by the prison-door" (165). Pearl repudiates all patriarchs: God, the magistrates, her actual father. [. . .]

Hester's ultimately unshakable belief in the goodness of this wild and nonsocial core of her being, frightening though it may sometimes be, saves her from taking the readily available and far less imaginative route of witchcraft. This path, which leads straight from the governor's door in the person of his sister, Mistress Hibbens, is in fact a legitimate Puritan social institution. The witches are rebels, but their rebellion arises from accepting the Puritan world view and defining themselves as evil. Yes, they say, we are indeed terribly wicked creatures, and we rejoice in our badness. Because they view themselves as society views them, the witches indirectly validate the social structure. Hester's defiance is another thing entirely.

Alone, her emotions repressed, she does her needlework and thinks. She "assumed a freedom of speculation . . . which our forefathers, had they known of it, would have held to be a deadlier crime than that stigmatized by the scarlet letter" (204). [. . .] Naturally, her mind dwells much on her condition as a woman, especially because caring for a girl-child forces her to see her situation in more general terms: "Was existence worth accepting, even to the happiest among [women]?" Pursuing her thought, she is overwhelmed by the magnitude of the changes that must occur before woman's lot becomes generally tolerable. There is certainly no individual solution; there is only individual escape into happy love.[1] But love for Hester is the instrument of misery rather than an escape into bliss, for it is love that keeps her in Boston close to Dimmesdale all those long, sad years. And when she proposes to leave, it is not for herself but for him that she is concerned. The limitation imposed by love on freedom is an aspect of woman's (as distinct from the general human) condition, and this is partly why

---

[1] Some critics have taken Hawthorne's comment that these speculations vanish in a woman's mind "if her heart chance to come uppermost" as a patronizing antifeminist comment which undercuts the validity of Hester's thinking. But such an interpretation is too simple, for it is precisely Hawthorne's point that the existing system very rarely allows the heart to come uppermost. The fact that one woman in a thousand (let us say) is happy and therefore not a radical says nothing to the urgency of the need of the other nine hundred and ninety-nine.

Hester, returned to Boston, hopes for the revelation of a new truth that will "establish the whole relation between man and woman on a surer ground of mutual happiness" (271).

Hester, labeled guilty by society, gradually rejects the meaning of that label although she cannot reject the label itself. Dimmesdale, thought to be innocent, eventually displays himself in public as a guilty man. His character contrasts completely with Hester's, except in one crucial respect: both of them must ultimately, at whatever cost, be true to the imperatives of their own natures. No matter how she tries to assent to it, Hester cannot help but reject the judgment of the letter. Dimmesdale must finally stigmatize himself no matter how much a part of him longs to concur in the idea of his innocence. [. . .] Hester is naturally independent and romantic, Dimmesdale dependent and conservative, and these tendencies are reinforced by their different places in the social structure.

"Mr. Dimmesdale," Hawthorne writes, "was a true priest, a true religionist, with the reverential sentiment largely developed, and an order of mind that impelled itself powerfully along the track of a creed, and wore its passage continually deeper with the lapse of time. In no state of society would he have been what is called a man of liberal views; it would always be essential to his peace to feel the pressure of a faith about him, supporting, while it confined him within its iron framework" (174). Observe how, characteristically for Hawthorne, the particular content of a creed is seen as irrelevant to its essential purpose of satisfying the psychological needs of a certain kind of personality. In any society, Dimmesdale would have been a "religionist" because he is a reverent person — that is, he requires authority over him. Although he happens to be a Puritan, Dimmesdale's type is not confined to the Puritan community or bounded by the specific nature of Puritan doctrines. This is a psychological, and not an ethical or philosophical, portrait.

Because of his dependent nature, Dimmesdale is profoundly sincere in his wish to conform. He has apparently remained ignorant of his own passions until his encounter with Hester reveals them. But the passion has been there all the time. Hester must not be misread, as D. H. Lawrence so egregiously misread her, as a dark lady with an appetite for corrupting pure men. She occasions Dimmesdale's passion but does not create it. There are physical signs of struggle in Dimmesdale — his perpetual paleness, the tremor of his mouth denoting both "nervous sensibility and a vast power of self-restraint" (138). In fact, Hawthorne shows what the minister can never accept: the true source of his power over the people is not the spirituality to which he sincerely attributes his success but his denied and despised passionate nature.

Dimmesdale reaches his audience not by argument but by emotion. His instrument is the music of his voice: "This vocal organ was in itself a rich endowment; insomuch that a listener, comprehending nothing of the language in which the preacher spoke, might still have been swayed to and fro by the mere tone and cadence. Like all other music, it breathed passion and pathos, and emotions high or tender, in a tongue native to the human heart, wherever educated." It ranges from a "low undertone, as of the wind sinking down to repose itself," through "progressive gradations of sweetness and power" to a climax of "awe and solemn grandeur. And yet, majestic as the voice sometimes became, there was for ever in it an essential character of plaintiveness" (258). The voice bypasses language to become a direct expression of unmediated feeling.

After his encounter with Hester, Dimmesdale becomes a much more effective preacher, because his feelings have surfaced and cannot entirely be suppressed thereafter. Dimmesdale's congregation is no more aware than he of the source of his power: "They deemed the young clergymen a miracle of holiness. . . . The virgins of his church grew pale around him, victims of a passion so imbued with religious sentiment that they imagined it to be all religion, and brought it openly, in their white bosoms, as their most acceptable sacrifice before the altar" (188). The passionate man arouses passion in others. In spite of himself, Dimmesdale has become an artist. But an artist is not what he intended to be. He is bewildered and horrified by his success. A man like this, deeply committed to the furthering of the social aims of permanence and respectability, who yet finds himself possessed of this subversive power, is necessarily a psychologically ravaged human being. Before he knew Hester, his profession had provided him with a refuge. Afterward, the refuge becomes his prison. Unable to identify his "self" with the passionate core he regards as sinful, he is even less able to admit that this sinful core can produce great sermons. He is obsessed with a feeling of falseness. [. . .]

The guiltiness of his act, as it appears to him, is well expressed in the hideous figure of Chillingworth, who materializes out of thin air and, after establishing a superficial connection with Hester, moves on to his true mission of persecuting Dimmesdale. This monster becomes his constant companion and oppressor. If Pearl, to borrow a Freudian metaphor, may be seen as representing Hester's "id," so Chillingworth can be interpreted as Dimmesdale's "superego." That he is intended as a part of Dimmesdale's personality is made clear not only by the magical ways in which he appears on the scene and disappears from it, and his unrealistic fixation (for a cuckolded husband) on the guilty *man*, but also by the spatial disposition of the two together in a single dwelling, just as Hester and Pearl are housed together. Chillingworth is the watchful eye of the personality, linked with both intellect and conscience.

Fearing the punishment of society, and yet afraid of going unpunished, Dimmesdale has substituted an internal for a social punishment. The replacement of his kindly, benevolent mentor Reverend Wilson by this malevolent inner demon symbolizes the self-imposed punishment. Chillingworth's cruelty represents Hawthorne's idea that the internal judge, freed (exactly as Pearl at the other end of the spectrum is freed) from "reference and adaptation to the world into which it was born" (150), is unmitigatedly merciless. [. . .]

By virtue of his age and relation to Hester, Chillingworth invites a classical Freudian explanation for Dimmesdale's feelings of guilt. In a larger, more mythic framework, to characterize Chillingworth as a sort of father is to establish his connection to the patriarchal structure of the Puritan society. Dimmesdale feels guilty because he has offended the "fathers," the male gods of his universe. But he did not offend them by stealing one of their women, for they are all men without women and do not appear to covet Hester for themselves. His offense is to have repudiated their rule by acknowledging her dominion. In the forest [. . .] Hester fulfills the image of "Divine Maternity" that she suggested at the scaffold (125). Here is the pre-civilized nature goddess opposing western civilization, the impulsive heart defying the repressive letter of the law. Here, in brief, is a profoundly romantic mythology.

The protracted relationship with Chillingworth during the seven-year span of the romance represents Dimmesdale's strategy to keep from confessing. Nothing frightens him more than the idea of public exposure. He pacifies his inner thirst for punishment by self-castigation. Of course, he fails to confess partly because he cannot bear the thought of social ostracism. For a being who defines himself largely by the image he sees reflected back from the watching eyes around him, loss of social place implies loss of identity. It would be far more difficult for him than for Hester to survive a public disgrace. But confession would mean more than this. It would be a final capitulation to his sense of guilt. No matter how he persecutes himself, no matter what masochistic free rein he allows his overbearing conscience, he does not fully assent to his guilt until he admits it openly, because open admission has irreversible consequences.

[. . .] Chillingworth as a substitute for social judgment actually forestalls that judgment and protects Dimmesdale from an ultimate condemnation. Once he confesses, he has no psychological alternative but to die. Quite literally, Chillingworth the physician has kept him alive all these years, even if only to torment him.

Dimmesdale's resistance is roundabout and neurotic, but it keeps him functioning and is appropriate to his deep internal divisions. The aftermath of the forest scene breaks his will to resist, convincing him that he is as evil as he had feared. Leaving the forest, Dimmesdale is possessed by a flood of impulses, which, although amusingly puerile to the reader, are horrifying to him. He wants to teach obscene words to a group of little boys, blaspheme before a devout old woman, and solicit the sexual favors of a maiden in his congregation. At long last freeing his passionate self, he finds freedom expressed in a series of silly, wicked wishes. Lacking Hester's long evolution of thought and independence, the "free" Dimmesdale is no more than a naughty boy. In his own eyes he is a monster. He ceases, therefore, to resist social judgment. He turns his new burst of life into the writing of his greatest sermon, still not recognizing the source of his power, still bewildered that "Heaven should see fit to transmit the grand and solemn music of its oracles through so foul an organ-pipe as he" (246). He delivers the sermon to great approbation and, at the height of his triumph, confesses. By that confession, he executes himself.

The final scene on the scaffold seems to suggest that the public institutions of society and the private needs of the personality are irreconcilable. Dimmesdale, revealing his inner nature, has died. Hester, in order to express herself at last and to permit Pearl to develop freely, must leave the community. But her return to Boston and the consequent loosening of the community to accommodate her lighten the gloomy conclusion. A painfully slow process of social relaxation may, perhaps, be hoped for. The human heart may not need to be an outcast forever.

The Puritan community in *The Scarlet Letter* is a symbol of society in general. It is portrayed as a set of institutions unresponsive to personal needs and deliberately repressive of the private experience. Puritan institutions define the human being as all surface, all public. So far as the inner life is made public, it must be submitted to social definitions. Social institutions, however, may not be defined in the language of individual needs. The Puritan magistrates are not hypocrites. For them, the business of establishing and perpetuating a society demands the full energies of all the members of the community; there is no time for the indulgence of a private dimension of the personality. Self-expression is therefore a threat to the community.

Since the magistrates believe that self-expression is a threat, they make it a crime. Thereby, of course, they make it a threat as well. *The Scarlet Letter* asks whether this state of opposition between passion and authority is necessary; it expresses the hope that a society allowing greater individual expression might evolve, but it does not commit itself to a certain conclusion.

It makes clear, however, that in a society such as the romance describes, the relationship of the artist who speaks for passion to the social institutions that suppress it can only be one of estrangement, duplicity, or subversion. Dimmesdale's voice and Hester's letter enunciate and undermine the social creed. Disguised as a social document, the work of art secretly expresses the cry of the heart. Doing this, it covertly defies society in response to hidden but universal needs.

Two questions arise: what relation does the situation depicted in *The Scarlet Letter* bear to Hawthorne's idea of his own contemporary society? And what relation does the thematic design of the romance bear to his own function as an artist? Clearly, *The Scarlet Letter* is quite different from all of Hawthorne's earlier work, which had argued that the individual finds rich fulfillment when integrated into society, that society expresses the personality. Now although Hawthorne does not suggest in *The Scarlet Letter* that there is any joy in isolation, he does show that the individual pays a very high price to be a member of the group. The earlier fictions and sketches exhibited the imagination at work in the service of society; *The Scarlet Letter* makes it clear that imagination serves the self. The earlier works tended to define serving the self as obsession, egotism, or eccentricity; *The Scarlet Letter* asserts that the self has needs and claims that must be satisfied. The earlier works restricted the exercise of imagination to the surface of events, while *The Scarlet Letter* ties imagination to the life beneath appearances. Evidently, Hawthorne jettisoned the whole load of commonsense assumptions about imagination and art and replaced them with a romantic vision.

If the vision of *The Scarlet Letter* is romantic, then Hawthorne must be presenting his own role and function in an entirely new way. One wonders whether Hawthorne actually underwent some sort of conversion or simply adopted another in a long series of authorial stances designed to find favor with an audience. Clearly, a romantic view was more up-to-date than the late eighteenth-century ideology his works had been expressing. And Hawthorne was too great a realist ever to publish a work that he thought might actually harm his reputation. One might conclude that in *The Scarlet Letter* he was accommodating himself to the taste of the times. The conception of art, imagination, and the artist implicit in this romantic formulation is nevertheless intellectually and aesthetically far richer and more vigorous than the formulation he had abandoned; consequently, it might have given him the support and justification for his professional commitment that he had not found before. Since it propelled him into the most productive decade of his career and thrust him immediately into the forefront of living American authors, this romantic vision certainly was usable.

"The Custom-House" invites us to view it as a deeply held belief as well. The essay tells the story of a conversion to the idea of literature as self-expression, in defiance of external and introjected social demands. It suggests that the psychological survival of the "I" depended upon that conversion. A product, Hawthorne says, of the same "autobiographical impulse" that motivated "The Old Manse," "The Custom-House" takes up his story where the earlier essay left it. Ignoring what we know to have been the economic imperatives that took him back to Salem, Hawthorne projects a psychological story in the conventions of romance. Appropriately, then, we may label "The Custom-House" an autobiographical romance.

Hawthorne interprets his return to Salem and his employment at the Custom House as the answer to psychological longings that his life at the Manse failed to satisfy and in part created. After three years of living in a transcendental cloud land, it was time to return to solid earth. He needed to participate in the ongoing work of the world, to prove himself a contributing member of society. He had to confront what might be called the persisting influence of Salem on his artistic life. By "Salem" is meant the combined environmental and personal pressures that made him think writing an idle and sinful craft.

Hawthorne personifies Salem in his Puritan ancestry, whose imagined judgment on him as a writer survives all his attempts to overcome it: "What is he? . . . A writer of story-books! What kind of a business in life, — what mode of glorifying God, or being serviceable to mankind in his day and generation, — may that be? Why, the degenerate fellow might as well have been a fiddler!" (92). Hawthorne's attempts to resist these imagined strictures by castigating his ancestors in turn for their bitter persecuting spirit and hard severity (91) have no effect, because these Puritan ancestors, of course, represent a part of Hawthorne himself. "And yet, let them scorn me as they will, strong traits of their nature have intertwined themselves with mine" (92). There is nothing to do but accede to the pressures they exert and return to Salem.

So far as these ancestors (or that part of Hawthorne they represent) are concerned, the sojourn in the Custom House has a twofold benefit. To work there is to satisfy their demand that he be serviceable. And the Custom House may provide Hawthorne with materials for a literature to mediate between the requirement of service and his self's need for imaginative expression. [. . .]

Hawthorne makes no attempt to hide the fact that he did not choose to leave his position, but we are never meant to think that he enjoyed it. We know from the biographies that he stayed because he could not afford to go; in "The Custom-House," however, Hawthorne presents himself as remaining because he sincerely wants to do what the ancestors expect of him. Like Dimmesdale, he is trying to be socially acceptable. But [. . .] the Custom House thoroughly isolates him. Everybody there appears to exist in a state of suspended animation. All are old men, of torpid imaginations and emotionally atrophied. The work itself is trivial, monotonous, and dispiriting.

The Custom House building, Uncle Sam's institution, quickly becomes a metaphorical prison. Working for society instead of himself, the Custom House officer loses his manhood. [. . .] The ejected officer, left "to totter along the difficult footpath of life as best he may," is one who "forever afterwards looks wistfully about him in quest of support external to himself" (113), and sounds a good deal like Arthur Dimmesdale. The iron framework of the Puritan oligarchy has been replaced by a more benevolent but ultimately equally debilitating kind of paternalism.

Hawthorne represents his romance, *The Scarlet Letter*, as originating in the attempts of his imagination to make itself felt and keep itself alive in the deadly atmosphere of the Custom House. His withdrawal from the tedium of the first-floor routine into the cluttered chambers of the upper story signifies Hawthorne's withdrawal into his own mind, his escape into fantasy. But in these circumstances, fantasy is an escape to freedom rather than a retreat from life. It is an affirmative rather than a denying gesture. In one of his flights of fancy, Hawthorne comes upon a roll of parchment enclosed within "a certain affair of fine red cloth" wrought "with wonderful skill of needlework" and "intended, there could be no doubt, as an ornamental article of dress" (107–08). Examination proves it to be a fabric representation of the letter *A*.

[. . .] Impulsively, Hawthorne puts the letter to his breast and experiences "a sensation not altogether physical, yet almost so, as of burning heat; and as if the letter were not of red cloth, but red-hot iron" (108). In this electric moment, which many critics have recognized as central to both "The Custom-House" and *The Scarlet Letter*, Hawthorne senses with a mixture of fear and excitement that he has found his subject. The letter — a verbal sign, a symbol, and the channel of inspiration — becomes the type of Art.

Because in *The Scarlet Letter* the *A* signifies a social crime, Hawthorne suggests that the writing of his romance is in some sense an analogously guilty act. [. . .] For Hawthorne, the romance originated as expression of his own feelings of social defiance and discontent, as a reaction to the stifling position of surveyor in the Custom House at Salem. The decision to write the romance, or to try to write it, involves a transference of Hawthorne's allegiance from his Puritan conscience to his imagination, personified in "The Custom-House" by Surveyor Pue. Adopting this figure as his "official ancestor," Hawthorne accepts the former surveyor's charge that he publicize Hester's story.

Now Hawthorne discovers that to generate a fantasy is not the same thing as to give it body. As he attempts in his free hours to compose his tale, he becomes aware in a frighteningly new way of the terrible effect the Custom House is having on his imaginative faculties. And he realizes how profoundly he values these faculties. "My imagination was a tarnished mirror. . . . The characters of the narrative would not be warmed and rendered malleable, by any heat that I could kindle at my intellectual forge. . . . 'What have you to do with us?' [they] seemed to say. 'The little power you might once have possessed over the tribe of unrealities is gone! You have bartered it for a pittance of the public gold. Go, then, and earn your wages!'" (110). [. . .] Clearly, then, it is impossible for Hawthorne to continue to be a writer of romances while placating the inner Puritan. The unexpected fruits of the Custom House interlude are the authentication of just those theories he laid aside when he left Concord for Salem and the validation of a definition of happiness as living throughout the whole range of one's faculties and sensibilities (114) — in brief, living the fullest inner life.

Yet Hawthorne, in accepting Hester as his subject, does not return to the transcendentalists so much as go beyond them. She represents everything the transcendentalists believe and more besides, for in her Emerson's "Spirit" is transformed into Eros and thus allied to sex, passion, eroticism, flesh, and the earth. The Puritans seek to repress Spirit not only because of their dedication to permanence and form, but also because as shrewd men of hard experience they are aware of its sexual sources. Thus, the sin in *The Scarlet Letter* is sexual, and a sexual sin can symbolize Hawthorne's writing of romances. This is why Hawthorne epitomizes Puritan severity in a depiction of their persecution of women. In women they see the occasion of a dangerous passion. Their opposition to sex is not prudish but pragmatic. As he goes beyond transcendentalism in his rejection of the concept of an unearthly spiritualism, Hawthorne goes beyond most of his earlier work, but echoes some of the themes expressed in "The Birthmark," "Drowne's Wooden Image," and, ironically, "The Artist of the Beautiful." In *The Scarlet Letter* he also presents an advocate of unearthly spiritualism, Dimmesdale.

Hawthorne's servitude in the Custom House generated, as a reactive defense, the fantasy of the scarlet letter; his dismissal led to its creation. In both idea and execution, the romance is related to maladjustment between Hawthorne and his society. Miserable as Hawthorne had been in the Custom House, to be forced out of it represented an evident failure: "The moment when a man's head drops off is seldom or never, I am inclined to think, precisely the most agreeable of his life. . . . In view of my previous weariness of office, and vague thoughts of resignation, my fortune somewhat resembled that of a person who should entertain an idea of committing suicide, and, altogether beyond his hopes, meet with the good hap to be murdered" (125). Observe the ambivalence of the images. Hawthorne's thoughts of resigning from the Custom House are like thoughts of suicide. Why should this be, if the Custom House is so unpleasant? Obviously Hawthorne is torn.

Like Hester, he becomes a rebel because he is thrown out of society, by society: "Meanwhile, the press had taken up my affair, and kept me, for a week or two, careering through the public prints, in my decapitated state. . . . So much for my figurative self. The real human being, all this time, with his head safely on his shoulders, had brought himself to the comfortable conclusion, that everything was for the best; and, making an investment in ink, paper, and steel-pens, had opened his long-disused writing-desk, and was again a literary man" (126). Anxious for so long to "be of some importance in [my good townspeople's] eyes, and to win myself a pleasant memory in this abode and burial-place of so many of my forefathers" (117), Hawthorne has finally accepted his destiny. The Custom House self, the man of affairs and the world, the public servant, becomes a figurative self, and Hawthorne accepts the conjunction of the real being with the literary man. The autobiographical episode has a happy ending, for in composing *The Scarlet Letter* he found himself "happier, while straying through the gloom of these sunless fantasies, than at any time since he had quitted the Old Manse" (116). The direct attack of "The Custom-House" on some of the citizens of Salem adds a fillip of personal revenge to the theoretical rebellion that it dramatizes.

In the current state of biographical knowledge we cannot be sure to what degree the symbolic representation in "The Custom-House" corresponds to the facts. We do not know, for example, whether the germ of *The Scarlet Letter* actually occurred to Hawthorne in the Custom House or was conceived entirely in the months after his dismissal. Many readers have noted the foreshadowing appearance of a beautiful young woman with an embroidered *A* on her bosom in "Endicott and the Red Cross"; it is at least possible that the story had, in some form, been in his mind for years. We also do not know if Hawthorne really tried to write *The Scarlet Letter* before he was dismissed from the Custom House and, failing, actually became distracted and gloomy over the loss of his powers. But if, in fact, the story is not a symbolic representation of the truth, then it is all the more striking that Hawthorne should wish to represent *The Scarlet Letter* as a gesture of insubordination.

Even at his most defiant, Hawthorne could not entirely avoid the tone of self-deprecation. But in "The Custom-House" he almost appears to satirize his own formerly characteristic apologetic mode. "It was a folly," he writes, "with the materiality of this daily life pressing so intrusively upon me, to attempt to fling myself back into another age; or to insist on creating the semblance of a world out of airy matter, when, at every moment, the impalpable beauty of my soap-bubble was broken by the rude contact of some actual circumstance" (111). [. . .] But "The Custom-House" has shown that it was not folly, but absolute necessity, to turn into his own mind for sustenance. [. . .] Despite the apparent humility of his conclusion to this paragraph—"A better book than I shall ever write was there"—Hawthorne was never less humble.

This lack of humility is clearly evident in his preface to the second edition of *The Scarlet Letter*, dated March 30, 1850, some two weeks after his romance had been published. The book had already sold well enough to assure Hawthorne that he had, at last, a solid success. He acknowledges the furor caused by "The Custom House" with evident delight. He has learned the interesting lesson that to create a scandal is not necessarily to hurt sales. [. . .] And then, with relish, he pens his final sentence: "The author is constrained, therefore, to republish his introductory sketch without the change of a word" (85).

New and Old Tales
The Scarlet Letter

Richard H. Brodhead

Stressing the "strict economy" of Hawthorne's narrative art in *The Scarlet Letter*, Richard Brodhead discusses the interrelationships of objects, events, and characters' inner and outer lives throughout the novel as they generate meaning and invite interpretation. Contrasting Chillingworth's rigidified diabolism with Hester's more realistic "variegated selfhood," for example, Brodhead notes that the "different fictional modes in which they are realized" reflect "their own imaginative outlooks." And Brodhead regards Hawthorne's presenting of alternative possibilities—e.g., about what people saw

From *Hawthorne, Melville, and the Novel*. Chicago: U of Chicago P, 1976. Reprinted by permission. (All parenthetical references are to this New Riverside Edition.)

on Dimmesdale's chest—as a way of making readers weigh the alternatives of fact and significance, aware of their own "imaginative procedure." [ED.]

The Scarlet Letter is at the same time Hawthorne's debut in a new artistic medium and a kind of retrospective exhibit of his work. No other of his novels is so close to the preoccupations of his tales. His choice of chronological setting aligns the book with all his studies of the historical past, and in particular with his explorations of the energetic restrictiveness of the Puritans in tales like "The Maypole of Merry Mount" and "Endicott and the Red Cross." The dramas that Hawthorne enacts in this setting are also familiar ones. Dimmesdale's experience exhibits the self-destructive operations of concealed guilt and the obsession with sin portrayed in "Roger Malvin's Burial" and "Young Goodman Brown"; Roger Chillingworth's passionate intellectual curiosity looks back to Ethan Brand's, and he shares Brand's experience of willed violation of others and the unwilled dehumanization of the self. In composing *The Scarlet Letter* Hawthorne seems purposely to gather together the themes—historical, moral, psychological—that have given his work its distinct identity; then, by integrating them and projecting them onto a larger canvas, he manages to eclipse his earlier achievements exactly by fully realizing their subjects' interest and potential.

When *The Scarlet Letter* is approached through Hawthorne's tales its status as an almost self-conscious culmination of his artistic career is the first thing that is striking; the second is the confidence with which Hawthorne proceeds to execute his larger design. The rightness of the opening scene as a suggestive introduction to the novel's major concerns; the gradual but steady unfolding of its action, in which Hawthorne unobtrusively scores in part after part; the firm balance of continuing action and authorial exposition—all demonstrate his assured artistry as a novelist and serve to announce, in an understated way, his mastery of his new craft.

The first scene of *The Scarlet Letter* involves the punishment of the convicted adulteress, Hester Prynne, by public exposure on the scaffold in the Boston marketplace. The scene unfolds with a slow and deliberate pace. Before he allows Hester to appear, Hawthorne focuses our attention on the prison door, meditating on it in such a way as both to localize it in a specific time and place and to see in it a dark exigency, a "black flower of civilized society" (119). Then he allows the point of view to pass over to other observers of this scene, a group of Puritan women. In their comments—ranging from a legalistic, punitive desire to brand or execute the adulteress

to a softer voice that recognizes the anguish of the victim of punishment—
Hawthorne affords us a series of vantage points by which to frame our own
initial response to Hester. But in offering possible attitudes in this way the
women do not cease to be participants in a specific scene. They are part of
the audience before which Hester is to be exposed, and by surrounding
Hester's emergence with their reactions Hawthorne makes us see the experience of his main characters from the first as being bounded by, as well as
the affair of, a larger society. His own commentary emphasizes the nature
of the community the women represent. By placing them near the age of
"man-like Elizabeth" (121) and contrasting them with the paler women of
his own day he sees their coarseness of body and speech in relation to a
specific moment in a historical evolution. Their sentiments are understood
historically as well, as exemplifications of "the early severity of the Puritan
character" (120). In their concern with the rigid administration of punishment to a criminal and sinner they exhibit the special outlook of "a people
amongst whom religion and law were almost identical" (120). Through
them we recognize the values by which their society defines itself and also
the quality of private feeling that upholds those values, "the general sentiment which gives law its vitality" (250).

By choosing the punishment of Hester as his first scene Hawthorne is
able to reveal the Puritan community in what seems to him its most essential aspect, enacting its deepest social and religious values. The scene is typical of his handling of the Puritans in *The Scarlet Letter* in its focus on their
celebration of their community's own special nature and its bonds of authority. We see this again in the Election Day scene which balances this one
at the book's conclusion. In both cases he is unusually attentive to what he
calls "the forms of authority" (132), the ceremonious behavior through
which they act out their values. The comments of the chorus of women end
when the prison door opens and the town beadle emerges, "with a sword
by his side and his staff of office in his hand."

> This personage prefigured and represented in his aspect the whole dis-
> mal severity of the Puritanic code of law, which it was his business to ad-
> minister in its final and closest application to the offender. Stretching
> forth the official staff in his left hand, he laid his right upon the shoulder
> of a young woman, whom he thus drew forward. (122)

The action here has the stylization of a ritual. The beadle submerges his individual personality into his role as agent of justice, identified by appropriate emblems. He acts out that role in his ceremonious gesture, converting Hester's emergence into a carefully contrived visual allegory of civil and
spiritual righteousness: "A blessing on the righteous Colony of Massachusetts, where iniquity is dragged out into the sunshine!" (124).

But his ritual is disrupted. Hester pushes his staff aside and walks forward "as if by her own free-will" (122). This is Hester's first act, and its resonance is amplified by the next detail Hawthorne presents: "On the breast of her gown, in fine red cloth, surrounded with an elaborate embroidery and fantastic flourishes of gold thread, appeared the letter A" (123). The Puritan pageant casts Hester as Iniquity; the A they impose on her is the symbolic badge of her office, that of Adulteress. Their strict symbolism moves to rigidify experience into formal categories of virtue and sin, and they conceive of their symbols as having sanction for their meaning in divine principles of good and evil. As Hester rejects their pageant she also rejects the code on which it is based. She converts the spectacle of "iniquity dragged forth" into an act proceeding from her own free choice. She accepts the designation of adulteress, but on her own terms; her embroidery of the scarlet letter turns it into a more complex symbol, one that does justice to the inseparable conjunction of something guilty and something vital and fertile in her passionate nature. And while the art of the Puritans' A has the sanction of divine truth, her personalized letter is presented as an act of creative self-expression, a product of her own imagination that has its meaning in terms of her own knowledge of herself.

Hester's rejection or modification of the pageant prefigures the conflict between her and her society, but it also suggests a larger conflict in *The Scarlet Letter* of which this is only one version, a strife between two modes of experience and understanding: one that tends toward restriction, fixity, and orthodoxy, and one that tends toward a freer expression and recognition of the self's desires, needs, and powers. The moment marks, as well, a turning point in the scene from a social and historical perspective to an individual and psychological one. As Hester mounts the scaffold Hawthorne adopts her point of view, measuring the nature of the assembled crowd now by registering its presence to her consciousness. As he notes her urge to reckless defiance, her anguished shame, and her peculiar defenselessness against the solemnity of the occasion, he qualifies her initial assertion of freedom, enabling us to see the power the community holds over her emotional life. The freedom she does attain here comes through the reveries of her past life that intervene between her and the crowd's awful gaze. At the same time, her daydream finally destroys its own value as a means of escape; as she watches her life unfold she is led back inexorably to the present moment and the present scene.

In presenting Hester's reverie Hawthorne skillfully observes both her psyche's instinctive mechanism of self-protection and her own coming to an awareness that her position on the scaffold is the inevitable outcome of the whole course of her life. His observation here gives us our first glimpse of the exquisite shorthand by which he records the processes of consciousness throughout the novel. In addition to demonstrating his skill as a psychological analyst Hester's reverie also illustrates Hawthorne's more basic craft as a storyteller. *The Scarlet Letter* emphatically opens in the middle of an action, and through this vision he is able to sketch in, in two paragraphs, the past that has led up to this action. Further, Hester's momentary recollection of her husband, "a man well stricken in years, a pale, thin, scholarlike visage . . . with the left shoulder a trifle higher than the right" (128), serves to prepare us for the immediate future. Exactly as Hester's reverie comes to a close we look back out at the scene and recognize, at the edge of the crowd, the figure whom Hester has just seen.

As Hester recognizes her husband her relation to the crowd changes. Their gaze now becomes a "shelter" (131) from the intenser gaze of Chillingworth and from the more specific shame and guilt that she feels before him. The appearance of Chillingworth marks a subtle shift in the action of the scene. The dramatic conflict between Hester and the Puritans gives way to a more private drama involving the characters most intimately connected with the fact of adultery. Thus it is appropriate that in the next scenic transition, to the injunctions of the Puritan magistrates and ministers, what is ostensibly a cut back to the Puritans is actually the occasion for Hawthorne's first introduction of Dimmesdale. The role that Dimmesdale must play in this scene, again, implicitly suggests the whole ambiguity of the position of this "remorseful hypocrite" (189). In urging Hester to reveal the name of her child's father he speaks as the voice of community authority and righteousness. At the same time, the combination of his equivocation — "If thou feelest it to be for thy soul's peace" (133–34) — and his impassioned appeal that she ease her accomplice of the burden of his secrecy hints at his own part in the plot, reflecting his dread of being, as well as his desperate longing to be, revealed in his true position.

The characters who belong together are now assembled, placed in the suggestive grouping around the scaffold that they will form again in "The Minister's Vigil" and once again when the true relations that that grouping embodies are revealed in the book's final scene. And as it gathers together the characters of this private drama, so too this scene engenders the energies of that drama. Dimmesdale, poised with his hand upon his heart, is seen protecting his secret; Chillingworth's resolution — "He will be known!" (131) — already incarnates his fierce purpose to expose that secret.

A consideration of this much of *The Scarlet Letter* may be enough to demonstrate the remarkable skill of Hawthorne's narrative exposition. Everything that he tells us contributes to our understanding and visualization of this highly charged scene. And without ever going outside that scene in these chapters he manages to establish all the characters, motives, and thematic conflicts that will animate the rest of the book. These chapters serve as well as any others to reveal a persistent feature of Hawthorne's art of the novel, his strict economy.

If the first scene is typical of Hawthorne's artistry, it also exemplifies the sort of fictional world he creates in *The Scarlet Letter*. This world possesses, first, a dense social and historical reality. The feelings and forms of behavior of the Puritan characters are linked to the outlook of a particular group set in a particular moment in time. The prison and the scaffold, located in accordance with the actual topography of early Boston, are also understood as extensions of the Puritans' care for lawful authority and punishment. Hawthorne's concern for accuracy of historical detail is evident throughout the book, but his interest is never merely antiquarian; all his descriptions of physical settings work to exhibit the nature of the society that creates them. This is true even of his minute account of the architecture, furnishings, and garden of Governor Bellingham's hall in the seventh chapter, which seems at first like the one point in the book where he aims at a purely factual description of place. The overbearing defensive outer wall and Bellingham's suit of armor suggest once again the stern militance of the Puritans. The glass of ale on the table, the comfortable furnishings, and the evidences of a failed attempt to create an English garden show a kind of counterimpulse, an inclination toward a more pleasurable way of life out of which these men of iron try to re-create what they can of the more commodious civilization they have left behind. By the time he finishes his description of the hall Hawthorne has revealed, through the details of the scene, a complex image both of the Puritans' temperament and of the historical situation that gives rise to that temperament, their situation between Elizabethan England and America's hostile and barren strand.

In addition Hawthorne's world possesses a dense psychological reality. He endows his characters with their own individuating tempers and desires, then watches their peculiar consciousnesses responding to their situations and to one another. If he describes the interior of a house in "The Governor's Hall," much more often he turns to sift the contents of "the interior of a heart" (186). His brief account of Hester's feelings on the scaffold prepares the way for chapters like "Hester at Her Needle," "The Interior of a Heart," "Another View of Hester," and "The Minister in a Maze," chapters which have as their only actions Hawthorne's minute dissections of his characters' inner worlds—their responses to their daily positions before the community, their continuing desires, and the new forms that their desires take under the pressure of their circumstances.

The first chapters also illustrate how Hawthorne animates the social and psychological realities he creates and gives them the forward motion of an action. There are three levels of interaction here, the public one involving the Puritan community, the internal one of feeling, thought, and psychic struggle, and the private drama of interaction among the main characters. Hawthorne's subtle modulations among them prefigure the larger movements of his narrative, which alternates in the same way among communal scenes, introspections of characters seen in isolation, and dramatizations of their personal encounters. Each level generates its own conflicts, such that the initiative of the action can pass back and forth among them. Thus for example the public exposure of Hester rebounds on the nature of Chillingworth in such a way as to generate the jealous and revengeful passion to know that governs his action throughout the story; Dimmesdale's private obsession with penance leads him onto the scaffold at night, and Hester's recognition of his feebleness in their encounter here in turn generates her desire to make Chillingworth known to him and to propose their mutual escape.

The world Hawthorne creates in *The Scarlet Letter* is the final product of the inspiration that he dramatized in "The Custom-House," and the nature of this world enables us now to understand more precisely the relation of his inspiration to his process of fictional creation. The scarlet letter comes to him streaming with revelation. But this revelation is peculiarly inarticulate; the "deep meaning in it, most worthy of interpretation" communicates itself to his sensibilities, but it evades "the analysis of my mind" (108). Further, while the letter itself is full of fixating power, the story that accompanies it—the dingy roll of paper pertaining to Hester Prynne—is at this point lifeless and uninteresting to him. In the moonlit room he attempts to spread out his intuited revelation into imagined characters and scenes, to transfer the burning heat of the symbol into a warmth that will animate the participants in his story.

The Scarlet Letter illustrates how Hawthorne does this. He converts the isolated symbol into a badge fashioned by a historical community. The A becomes the Puritans' A, the emblem through which they impose their judgment on a violator of their communal values. The letter thus brings the book's social and historical stratum into being, and by meditating on their use of the symbol Hawthorne can analyze the peculiar nature of the Puritans—their devotion to law and religion, their addiction to formalized behavior, the imaginative outlook inherent in their orthodox symbolism. At the same time the A is a badge for individuals, a token of their act of adultery and the passions that have led to that act, and a mark as well of the complex system of guilt and responsibility that ensues from that act. In this aspect the scarlet letter becomes the focal point of the characters' daily experience and the center of their attention. Chillingworth's vengeful inquiry reaches its first climax when he discovers the letter on Dimmesdale's chest. Dimmesdale's obsession with his guilt is most clearly revealed in his compulsive visions of the letter in the world outside his mind. Hawthorne presents Hester's life as an outcast by recording the variety of responses she feels as others look at her scarlet letter, and he measures her efforts at creative resistance by showing her various modifications of the letter into tentative expressions of a complex truth. He passes his own experience of fixation before the scarlet letter on to his characters; their need, like his own, is to find out or express the meaning of the symbol even as they live out that meaning, if they are to free themselves from its purely obsessive power. As he grounds the letter in his characters' experience and observes their motives and modes of passion before it, the symbol evolves into the dense web of psychological and dramatic relationships in his novel.

By composing a narrative in this way Hawthorne overcomes the tensions within his own creative vision. The symbol and the ingredients of a story come together in a seamless unity in which each manifestation of the letter illuminates an aspect of the characters' or the community's evolving experience. He overcomes, as well, the initial gap between what he calls his sensibilities and his conscious mind. By calling forth dramatic scenes and then analyzing the implications of their actions he achieves a synthesis in which imagining and understanding are continually changing into each other. And there is no sense of a gap here between what he calls the Actual and the Imaginary. He freely draws on both social history and psychic activity, creating his novel's world by engaging the two in a process of dynamic interchange.

[. . .] What makes the descriptive sketch in "The Governor's Hall" stand out from the rest of *The Scarlet Letter* is that it is the only point at which Hawthorne seems to be describing daily life simply for its own sake. But even here description gives way to significant action, to Hester's defense against the Puritans' desire to take Pearl, the product of her sin, away from her. [. . .] He himself notes the sort of tautness and single-mindedness his work possesses when, in a letter, he describes *The Scarlet Letter* as "keeping so close to its point . . . and diversified no otherwise than by turning different sides of the same dark idea to the reader's eye" [*Letters, 1843–1853* 307].

This phrase suggests another way of accounting for the singular intensity of *The Scarlet Letter*. It is not just that Hawthorne does not include an abundant record of variegated life, but that the details he does include are so intimately bound together as "sides of the same dark idea." Part of what works against a sense of openness and free life in the novel is its marshaling of its components into strong patterns of interrelation. Thus we see the scaffold as a physical object, and also as a social creation; but our sense of its meaning is also shaped by its appearance in Hawthorne's figurative language. He says of Dimmesdale: "it would always be essential to his peace to feel the pressure of a faith about him, supporting, while it confined him within its iron framework" (174). He uses a related image to describe

Hester's emotions on the scaffold: "The very law that condemned her—a giant of stern features, but with vigor to support, as well as to annihilate, in its iron arm—had held her up, through the terrible ordeal of her ignominy" (142). The framework that both supports and confines recalls the actual pillory on the scaffold, and the resonance between the object and these images suggests a complex relation between things and inner experience. It links the actual forms the Puritans construct as instruments of their law on the one hand to the individual psychic needs that make law strong and on the other to the individual psychic experience produced by the law's implementation. The sort of complex link between public and private that this cluster of images establishes is a recurrent feature of *The Scarlet Letter*. To choose another example, Hawthorne tells us in "The Prison-Door" that every community contains a prison and a graveyard. The novel begins outside an actual prison and ends in contemplation of an actual grave. But between these points we see them in other forms: the Dimmesdale who keeps the truth of his life secret is called a "prisoner" in the "dungeon of his own heart" (229); when Hester allows her continuing love for Dimmesdale to surface into her conscious mind she hastens "to bar it in its dungeon" (143). Both the town and the mind contain dungeons, and both the Puritans and the main characters are jailers; their private and psychic acts of repression repeat the public and social one. What makes Hawthorne's dramatization of the conflict between untamed desire and repressive restraint interesting is his sense that the self contains its own version of the parties to this conflict within itself. Some of the most moving passages of analysis in the whole novel are those in which he shows how his characters, under the burden of their situation, come to dehumanize themselves even more thoroughly than their oppressors do. His images of the dungeon are the means by which he shows the dynamic interaction between the external and the internal versions of this conflict.

The cross-linking of things and images that these two examples illustrate takes place constantly in *The Scarlet Letter*. The novel's world obeys a rigid law of conservation, such that whatever appears in its physical world is bound to reappear, before long, in the figurative language describing its mental world. This rule holds true for its obvious symbolic objects—the red rose and the black flower that appear in the first scene reappear as metaphors by which Pearl is linked to the wild vitality of nature and by which Chillingworth expresses his dark determinism. But it holds true as well for relatively less significant objects. Chillingworth's freethinking is as a "window . . . thrown open" (174) to Dimmesdale, and shortly after this is said the two men look out of an actual open window and see Hester and Pearl. Hester embroiders robes for occasions of state, and official ceremonies like the Election Day pageant are called the "brilliant embroidery to the great robe of state" (249). It is all but impossible to isolate an item in *The Scarlet Letter* that does not make both physical and metaphorical appearances.

The system of cross-reference that this kind of repetition establishes is obviously one of the major ways in which Hawthorne suggests and controls meaning in *The Scarlet Letter*. But what is more important for our discussion here is the effect that this system has on the texture of reality in the novel. It makes that texture an insistently patterned one; and the participation of each of the novel's details in such larger configurations of elements works against their functions as simply aspects of a representation of actual life. Further, it works against a clear distinction between mental and physical reality. The supportive framework and the area of repressive confinement float between the two, making themselves manifest now as parts of an actual scene, now as features of the mind. The forest in which Hester meets Dimmesdale is both a topographical fact and an image of "the moral wilderness in which she had been so long wandering" (216); the sunshine that brightens and fades in strict accordance with their emotions of joy and despair makes the forest appear both as a natural place and as an externalization of their mental states. [. . .] Our experience in the world of this novel is akin to Hawthorne's own in the moonlit room. Ordinary boundaries become fluid, such that things are both seen as things and felt as thoughts. Above all Hawthorne's world is governed by the moonlit room's sense of haunted interconnectedness. It is not enough to describe it as economical or compact; its fluid interrelatedness of parts and its supersaturation with significant patterns give it the quality of overdetermination that Freud ascribes to dreams.

This double sense of distinctness of individual outline and dreamlike interconnectedness is exactly the effect produced by the item that reappears most insistently in the book, the scarlet letter itself. Hester's A is almost always before us, and it has a curious power to replicate itself in a series of visual variants. It is reflected in suits of armor, pools, brooks, and eyes; it is repeated in Pearl's clothing and in her seaweed creations; it shines forth in the midnight sky; it burns itself onto Dimmesdale's chest. In each of its manifestations the letter has an analyzable meaning in terms of the characters' and the community's experience. But at the same time the various letters keep returning our attention to something prior to its specific embodiments, to the fact of the scarlet letter itself.

[. . .] Some of the details of Pearl's wild and wayward playfulness are taken from Hawthorne's notebook observations of his daughter Una, and this illustrates the sort of fidelity to life that he aims at in creating his elf-child. In both the notebook and the novel he is particularly interested in the succession of games by which the child both acts out her imaginative freedom and, unconsciously, prepares herself for a mature life. Some of the finest passages in *The Scarlet Letter* are those in which Hawthorne describes the imaginative counterworld Pearl establishes in her play, in an effort to gain control over her hostile and baffling environment—her savage uprooting of the weeds that represent the Puritan children to her, for instance, or her re-creation of the mysterious scarlet letter in seaweed. These serve as well to show forth the modification of her nature by her specific situation. Her alternate moods of hostility and affection, of perverse glee and anxious brooding over her origin and separateness, mark her as the child who has grown up in the shadow of her mother's isolation, rebelliousness, and despair.

Hawthorne thus presents Pearl as having a complex psychological nature with its own origins in her environment, but this is only one version of her character in the novel. At other points she is seen not just as Hester's child but as an externalization of her repressed character; thus in the Election Day scene Pearl acts out the impulses that her mother stifles in herself. Her "trait of passion" (149), her luxuriance of imagination, the natural wildness in her that refuses to comply with rules and restraints link her to the aspect of Hester that has found expression in her crime. These qualities are what lead Hester to identify Pearl with the scarlet letter; and to a surprising extent Hawthorne accepts the simile she creates as indicating a true identity: Pearl *is* the scarlet letter. She is, thus, the "emblem and product of sin" (152), a "living hieroglyphic" (233), now acting like a perverse or bewildered child, now serving an allegorical office of embodying the complex of traits that the letter stands for or reminding others of the power of the symbol when they try to ignore it. [. . .]

One of the most interesting moments of symbolic experience in *The Scarlet Letter,* and one that best shows how Hawthorne complicates our relation to his fiction, is found in "The Minister's Vigil." In this chapter Dimmesdale goes to the scaffold at midnight to do public penance for his sin. But even as he does so he is half-aware that his act, like the rest of his rituals of self-scrutiny and self-torture, is a "vain show of expiation" (192). By going through the forms of penitence without actually revealing his guilt Dimmesdale only succeeds in renewing his sin of concealment. Each renewal reinforces his imaginative allegiance to the law that condemns him—thus Hawthorne notes that his sin has the effect of binding him more tightly to the categories of Puritan orthodoxy—so that the fact of his own untruth becomes his only reality and his only identity. "The Minister's Vigil" provides an extreme close-up of the processes of Dimmesdale's mind. Its noting of his masochistic fantasies of exposure before the townspeople, of his involuntary and perverse attempts to betray himself by laughing and shrieking, and of his recoils of dread from the prospect of discovery gives us the book's richest realization of the compulsive fantasy life in which Dimmesdale's obsession with his guilt imprisons him. In the midst of these fantasies he gains for a moment an opportunity to escape from his unreal world. He stops Hester and Pearl as they pass through the marketplace, making them stand with him on the scaffold. As he joins hands with them he feels "a tumultuous rush of new life, other life than his own," an "electric chain" (195) of vital relatedness. But he refuses to embrace the possibility for release that this moment offers. When Pearl asks him when he will stand with them publicly he replies: "At the great judgment day!" (196). And exactly as he states his refusal a version of the judgment day takes place: the sky is illuminated as if by "the light that is to reveal all secrets" (196).

At this point Hawthorne does not trouble us unduly about the nature of this light, allowing us to accept, if we like, the plausible explanation that it is "doubtless caused by one of those meteors" (196). Doubtless. But to Dimmesdale the light looks like a scarlet A, and in the brief scene that concludes the chapter the sexton informs us that many of the townspeople saw the same thing. The scarlet letter makes, here, its most audacious appearance. And its appearance works here, as in "The Governor's Hall" and "The Child at the Brook-Side," to reverse the direction of our perception. We have been reading a psychological novel, observing the course of a character's perceptions and emotions; even when we watch Dimmesdale seeing the portent we are still considering the symbol in terms of a character's mental experience of it. But with the sexton's second sighting Hawthorne gives the symbol an independent reality and makes us observe the characters under its aspect as it announces itself as an imperious necessity. Under its aspect the relationships that the characters must live through in the book's dramatic plot are revealed, in an instantaneous vision, in their essential nature. Dimmesdale, Hester, and Pearl stand joined together in the place of punishment, and Chillingworth, looking like the "arch-fiend" (199), looks on. And above them, including them all in its light, is the scarlet letter.

Was it a vision, or a waking dream? Hawthorne does everything he can to make his letter in the sky unsettling for his readers, but correspondingly he does everything he can to afford us ways of coping with it. We might take it as a naturalistic fact, a somewhat oddly shaped and colored meteor. Or we might treat its apparent supernaturalism as really a psychic projection of Dimmesdale's guilty mind; by refusing to pass judgment on himself he compulsively sees that judgment as being passed on him by the world. Or we might join the Puritans, who unblinkingly accept the supernaturalism of the A and read it as a divine message to their community, announcing the accession of Governor Winthrop to the status of Angel. The inclusion of the Puritans' interpretation here clarifies the peculiarity of Dimmesdale's own. He shares their habit of finding symbols latent with divine meaning in nature, but he perverts that practice by finding "a revelation, addressed to himself alone" rather than to the whole of God's chosen community. In the morbid egotism of his guilt he assumes that "the firmament itself should appear no more than a fitting page for his soul's history and fate" (198). His is a further way in which we might read the celestial sign.

As the last paragraph indicates, "The Minister's Vigil" concludes with a drama of interpretation. We see how the characters understand the letter, and we see their understandings as proceeding from a whole way of making sense of experience. But what is most interesting about this drama is that we are implicated in it. For finally, when the characters are done with it, we have the fact of the A in the sky left over, unexplained. Hawthorne in effect withdraws his narrative's mediating veil and makes us undergo his own and his characters' central experience of direct and unaided encounter with the flaming symbol. And as we are forced to decide what to make of it the characters' modes of vision become the matter not of detached observation but of our own urgent choice. We are left alone to complete the episode's reality and meaning as we may, and as we do so, Hawthorne's demonstration of the implications of the available options ensures that we will be highly self-conscious about our own procedure as an imaginative act of a certain sort. A final purpose of the symbolic mode of *The Scarlet Letter*, therefore, is to complicate our perception of the story in such a way as to turn it in on itself.

An episode like this one illustrates the most important difference between *The Scarlet Letter* and the realistic novels with which it shares some features. Hawthorne includes all the interacting facets of individual and social life that compose their presented reality, but he refuses to exclude from his novel the presence of a magical or supernatural order. [. . .]

[. . .] The novel contains within it the materials for another novel, the Puritans' version of its characters, events, and significance. Their version is a lurid romance. Pearl is, to them, a demon offspring; Hester's letter emits an infernal light and heat; Dimmesdale is an angel, and Chillingworth a "diabolical agent" who, like Satan in the Book of Job, "had the Divine permission, for a season, to burrow into the clergyman's intimacy, and plot against his soul" (177). The phrases "there was a rumor" and "some averred" with which Hawthorne introduces these details are reminiscent of the "some will say" and "some maintain" in Wordsworth poems like "The Thorn" and "Lucy Gray." Both authors include the ghostly surmises of superstitious rumor in their narratives as a way of regaining access to a suppressed stratum of imaginative experience. Hawthorne's surmises help him to show the workings of the Puritan imagination from within. They see their world as a strife between supernatural and subterranean powers of good and evil, and they see this strife as governed by a providential order. At the same time, Hawthorne consciously distances himself from their raw magic, accepting it as indicative of a psychological, not theological, truth. Rather than rejecting outright the notion that the A burns Hester with infernal fire, he notes that it does indeed sear her bosom, with shame. Similarly he suggests that Mistress Hibbins, rather than being an actual witch, may simply be mad, and at another point he speculates that insanity may be the psychological equivalent of damnation, "that eternal alienation from the Good and True" (223).

Hawthorne's invocations of the magical formulas of a more primitive and archaic sort of fiction and his conversion of their significance into psychological terms is part of a larger effort in *The Scarlet Letter*, an effort to resuscitate something like the Puritans' ideas of evil, sin, and damnation as serious concepts that can be used in a more secular treatment of human experience. [. . .] Consider, for a moment, the character of Chillingworth. The Puritans believe that the fire in his laboratory is brought from hell, and just after he records this rumor Hawthorne himself adopts a closely related image.

> Sometimes, a light glimmered out of the physician's eyes, burning blue and ominous, like the reflection of a furnace, or, let us say, like one of those gleams of ghastly fire that darted from Bunyan's awful door-way in the hill-side, and quivered on the pilgrim's face. (178)

The "let us say" implies a degree of detachment in this invocation of the Puritans' demonic imagery. But what is curious about the characterization of Chillingworth is the extent to which Hawthorne makes use of the Puritans' imaginative mode in presenting him. When he meets Hester at the seaside "there came a glare of red light out of his eyes; as if the old man's soul were on fire" (207). The vulgar are not alone in seeing him as Satan's emissary; Hester, Pearl, and Dimmesdale all associate him with the Black Man, and he appears as the arch-fiend in the last two scaffold scenes.

There is, of course, a psychological truth contained in this diabolical imagery. "In a word, old Roger Chillingworth was a striking evidence of a man's faculty of transforming himself into a devil, if he will only, for a reasonable space of time, undertake a devil's office" (207). Giving himself up completely to his one evil purpose, Chillingworth brings about his own dehumanization and makes himself "more wretched than his victim" (187). And his malignity is not motiveless. His character has, as have the others, a psychological complexity and etiology of its own.

[. . .] Hester's mode of existence is at the furthest extreme from Chillingworth's. [. . .] When she does accept Puritan designations she does so out of a process of mind that belies their meaning. Thus in the beautiful chapter "Hester at Her Needle" Hawthorne observes with fine tact the process by which she comes to reject the pleasures of her art as sinful. She senses that her art might be a way of expressing, and thus of soothing, her repressed passion, and in order to protect her love she rejects—and labels as sin—whatever might help her to sublimate it. [. . .] Her effort to retain her passion intact leads her, in the chapter "Hester and Pearl," to commit a conscious deception. In the face of Pearl's earnest questionings Hester senses that Pearl might be capable of becoming a confidante, a friend, and thus of helping her to "overcome the passion, once so wild, and even yet neither dead nor asleep" (214). In telling Pearl that she wears the scarlet letter for the sake of its gold thread she is not true, to Pearl, to her badge, or to herself. But her falseness here is another strategy by which she attempts to maintain all the elements of her true self in suspension. She cannot achieve in her life the full expression of her complex self that she has wrought into her symbol, but she instinctively and covertly moves to keep this alive as a possibility.

Hawthorne writes that "the tendency of her fate and fortunes had been to set her free" (228). Her freedom is a mixed state of lucidity and self-deception, integrity and falsehood, love and hate: she experiences herself as being, like her letter, a "mesh of good and evil" (132). What is most exciting about Hester is her openness to all the varieties of experience—intellectual, imaginative, emotional—that the continuing emergency of her life brings to her. When she meets Chillingworth at the seaside she has a clear vision of what he has become; she perceives her own share of the responsibility for his transformation; she desperately insists on the possibility of a free act of forgiveness; and she recoils with bitterness from his grim refusal. No other character in the book is capable of this range of feeling. When she decides to go to Dimmesdale's aid she is prompted by her love, by her perception of his weakness, and by her recognition of the responsibility she has incurred for his destruction by promising to keep Chillingworth's identity secret. In defining a duty for herself she generates an ethical imperative out of a clear insight into the whole range of contradictory desires and obligations that confront her. Again, no other character in the book is capable of the adventure of free ethical choice that Hester undertakes here.

Hawthorne lavishes on Hester all of the psychological analysis that he deliberately withholds from Chillingworth. He endows her with the complex reality of a whole self as he becomes increasingly content simply to present Chillingworth's diabolical face. This is what creates the discrepancy between their ontological statuses, and it should be obvious by now that this discrepancy is neither careless nor purposeless. The way in which we are asked to believe in them as characters is a function of the way in which they believe in themselves. Chillingworth relinquishes his own freedom and adopts, in a perverted because atheistic way, the deterministic outlook of the Puritans. A dark necessity, he tells Hester, rules their fates: "Let the black flower blossom as it may!" (210). As he does so he gives up his complexity of being and becomes a rigidified figure of diabolical evil, a character in the sort of providential romance that the Puritans imagine. Hester is allowed the freedom and variegated selfhood of a character in a more realistic mode because she first opens herself to the full complexity of her existence. It is as if in deciding how they will understand themselves and their world the characters also get to decide what sort of literary reality their author will let them acquire; the different fictional modes in which they are realized become explicit reflections of their own imaginative outlooks.

[. . .] The chapters leading up to "The Revelation of the Scarlet Letter" are superb examples of Hawthorne's narrative art. Everything that has appeared in the book is gathered together in preparation for a fateful climax. The descriptions of the crowd, of the procession, and of Dimmesdale's sermon and its effects are among the most beautiful and thorough passages of social observation in the book, and at the same time we never forget that this public spectacle is postponing a critical event in the book's private drama. As the ministers and the magistrates leave the church the action becomes genuinely suspenseful. Everything is done in slow motion. Dimmesdale totters; he rejects Reverend Wilson's aid; he advances to the scaffold; Bellingham comes forward to assist him, but he is warned back by Dimmesdale's look. The martial music plays on, but Dimmesdale pauses. And now, with grim theatricality, he stages a ceremonious spectacle of his own, the spectacle of exposure of sin that he has acted out in his mind and on the scaffold at night. Supported by Hester, and with Pearl between them, he acts out a scene in which he is both avenger and sinner, exposer and concealer, agent and victim of God's wrath.

In this scene a dogmatic and theological and a secular and humanistic imagination come into passionate conflict one last time. Dimmesdale's outlook here is that of the Puritans raised to a ghastly pitch. He sees Chillingworth as the tempter and fiend; he speaks of the lurid gleam of Hester's letter; he sees the drama of his own life as a strife between God and the Devil, and his revelation as a "plea of guilty at the bar of Eternal Justice" (264). Set against his grim exultation and the narrow fixity of his orthodox interpretation are Hester's despair and her desperate attempts to broaden and thus deny the categories of his thought: "Shall we not spend our immortal life together? Surely, surely we have ransomed one another, with all this woe!" (267). Their debate is fully dramatic. Behind each of their claims we are aware of the personal psychic processes that inform their attitudes.

We realize that Dimmesdale's orthodoxy, here as before, is perverted in the image of his own guilt-obsessed mind. He is as masochistically obsessed with passing a self-destructive judgment on himself as he was in "The Minister's Vigil." And his is here, as it was there, an egotistical interpretation of the providential design: "behold me here, the one sinner of the world!" (265). We also realize that Hester is giving expression to her own guilty fantasy of a heavenly consummation, and that her affirmation that human love provides its own sanctifications and ransoms, like her bold claim in the forest that their love had a consecration of its own, is a desperate one, and one that does not square with the full complexity of the aftermath of their adultery. Each one's version of what their experience means is qualified by our awareness of his character, but these versions are allowed to stand side by side, without further comment. The narrator refuses to press the question of the truth or falsity of their statements beyond what they themselves have attained. If we try to do so we must return to Hester's answer: "I know not! I know not!" (264).

Dimmesdale concludes his confession with a fierce shriek [then] "With a convulsive motion he tore away the ministerial band from before his breast. It was revealed!" (265). But no sooner does he make his revelation than the author draws the curtain before our eyes: "But it were irreverent to describe that revelation." And, having dismissed the ghastly miracle, he continues with his narration of the scene.

By now we have grown accustomed to seeing the scarlet letter announce itself as a symbol in the middle of a fully dramatic scene. But this demurrer on Hawthorne's part is nonetheless startling. It is hard to say which is more surprising: the fact that he insists on including as the climax of his scene such a strange and wondrous revelation, or the fact that, having done so, he then refuses to show it forth. Why should he so carefully arouse the sort of curiosity that he does here and then so pointedly cheat it out of its gratification?

This final scene brings to a head a conflict of narrative methods that has run all through the book. Dimmesdale's uncovering of his red stigma stands as the culmination of a carefully cultivated line of suspense — Hawthorne has teased and teased us with allusions to this mystery. In constructing his plot around the concealed presence of this physical sign he gives his book the shape of a ghostly romance; it operates by a magical order of causal determinism in which internal conditions are externalized as physical appearances. This line of suspense is the narrative's equivalent to the fictional mode in which Chillingworth is envisioned, and again Hawthorne associates this mode with Puritan mental fictions. As Dimmesdale presents it the symbol is fraught with providential significance, a wonder-working token of God's justice to sinners. And just as Chillingworth's fictional mode plays against Hester's, so too another kind of suspense is set against that of Hawthorne's romance plot. This interests us not in supernatural manifestations, or in what God has wrought, or in anything that admits of a determinate meaning, but rather in what choice Dimmesdale will make, what role his decision will play in his own psychic life, and what effect his choice will have on the other characters. This is the suspense of a more realistic novel; it invites us to see the story's meaning in its drama, in the texture of the characters' experience and in their exercise of their human freedom.

Hawthorne can and does give us the sort of scene that the latter kind of interest demands, but he insists on including a more mysterious and magical drama as well, and he refuses to make it easy for us to ignore it. [. . .] [He] offers no explanation of his own for his story's omitted climax. Instead he reports the explanations of various spectators—that the letter on Dimmesdale's chest was the result of self-inflicted penitential torture, that it was magically produced by Chillingworth's potent necromancy, that it was the work of "the ever active tooth of remorse, gnawing from the inmost heart outwardly" (268). There is a fourth account as well, that of certain "highly respectable witnesses," according to whom there was no scarlet letter and Dimmesdale had no hidden personal guilt to conceal. To these witnesses Dimmesdale stood on the scaffold with the adulteress and her child to express in parabolic form the lesson that "in the view of Infinite Purity, we are all sinners alike" (268).

Hawthorne releases us from his narrative authority and allows us to choose among these, or to adopt whatever other explanation we like. And while at first his multiple choice seems simply to make the meaning and even the factuality of Dimmesdale's revelation ambiguous, the dimensions and the point of the ambiguity are not at all imprecise. Each of these choices gives the scene significance in terms of an implicit view of the nature of human guilt and evil. By absconding with his book's climax and providing these alternate versions of it instead, he allows us to construct our own conclusion, to see something or nothing on Dimmesdale's chest, but either one on the condition that we be aware of the nature of the vision that will make what we see meaningful to us. Our final moment of direct confrontation with the scarlet letter has the same purpose as the earlier ones did, but now that purpose is more obvious: it leaves us alone to complete the novel by determining its reality and its meaning as we think best, and to be conscious of our imaginative procedure as we do so.

Finally Hawthorne's multiple choices provide one last clue to the purpose of his use of romance in The Scarlet Letter. From what we have seen of the Puritans in the novel the fourth choice sounds less like their reaction than like that of highly respectable readers of a later age. In its unwillingness to admit mysteries like Dimmesdale's letter to its consciousness it partakes of what Hawthorne calls "our modern incredulity" (148). And in ceasing to believe in any form of magic it also ceases to adhere to a concept of sin as anything more than a comfortably universal phenomenon, lacking individual manifestations. In its light we see what the first three views have in common. They are all willing to accept the mysterious letter as a reality, and they all accept as a reality the "deep life-matter" (264) of guilt or evil from which they see it as springing. Hawthorne's own willingness to enter into the enchantments of romance and his eagerness to make us experience romance's magic all through *The Scarlet Letter* is a form of resistance to the trivializations latent in the secularism of an age that places "gilded volumes on the centre-table" (160) where the Puritans placed more serious literature and an age that makes adultery a matter of "mocking infamy and ridicule" (121). It is his way of regaining access to the mysteries of the psychic life, the reality of which both the Puritans and his own more secular fiction attest to in their own ways.

The Access of Power

Gloria C. Erlich

Gloria C. Erlich discusses Hawthorne's "access to power" in the course of writing "The Custom-House" and *The Scarlet Letter* soon after being ejected from the civil service job that had entrapped his imagination. In and beyond the bristling "contrarieties" of "The Custom-House," Erlich finds traces of the author himself and even of his parents (the mother who had just died and the long-dead father he had never really known) in *The Scarlet Letter*. As she also argues, "maternal presence and paternal absence" generate Hawthorne's first novel. [ED.]

[. . .] Like many a man in his forties, Hawthorne as Surveyor found himself with a seemingly assured income that he did not dare relinquish, but

---

From *Family Themes and Hawthorne's Fiction: The Tenacious Web.* New Brunswick: Rutgers UP, 1984. (All parenthetical references are to this New Riverside Edition.)

trapped in a life structure that suppressed the most valued part of his personality, "that one talent which is death to hide." As a conscientious husband and father who had known poverty, he was unlikely ever to have resigned his Custom House post. It is little wonder, then, that eventually he came to regard loss of this sinecure as an act of Providence, an act, that is, of an ironic Providence comparable to that afforded a "person who should entertain an idea of committing suicide, and, altogether beyond his hopes, meet with the good hap to be murdered" (115).

A major difference between the essays "Mosses from an Old Manse" and "The Custom-House" lies in the energy released by Hawthorne's knowledge of having arrived at his mature powers. No longer a gentlemanly reviver of faded pictures of the past, he is, in his major phase, a knowing master of the past in its dynamic relation to the present. "The Custom-House" is energetic not only in its prose but in its dynamic balance of opposing forces.

Instead of a genial guided tour of Salem and its port, we get a picture bristling with contrarieties. The town is drab and ugly, about as attractive "as a disarranged checkerboard," but the author is deeply attached to it. The wharf, once a scene of vigorous traffic, now is dilapidated and overgrown with grass. The American eagle poised over the Custom House entrance is a figure electric with the central polarities of the essay itself. This symbol of government is fierce, truculent, and threatening, but many seek to shelter themselves under its wing. Her bosom may appear to have "all the softness and snugness of an eider-down pillow," but she will very likely "fling off her nestling with a scratch of her claw, a dab of her beak, or a rankling wound from her barbed arrows" (88). We shall return to this symbol of unreliable protection, for its paradoxes are not yet exhausted.

The first view of the Custom House itself does more than evoke a colorful picture of past activity in contrast to present decline. Instead, the author presents figures of the past, the shipmaster, the owner, the merchant, and the young clerk in relationship to each other and to time. He shows the young clerk evolving into the merchant by prematurely buying shares in his master's cargo, and the homebound and the outwardbound sailors as emblems of a continuing cycle of life.

Because Hawthorne's mother communicated to him her dread that he might be lost at sea like his father, he was the first male Hawthorne in many generations not to become a sailor. In becoming a writer rather than a sailor he not only failed his ancestors, he also broke the chain of generational continuity: "From father to son, for above a hundred years, they followed the sea; a gray-headed shipmaster, in each generation, retiring from the quarter-deck to the homestead, while a boy of fourteen took the hereditary place before the mast, confronting the salt spray and the gale, which had blustered against his sire and grandsire. The boy, also, in due time, passed from the forecastle to the cabin, spent a tempestuous manhood, and returned from his world-wanderings, to grow old, and die, and mingle his dust with the natal earth" (92–93). By failing to share his father's vocation, Hawthorne lost an opportunity for identifying with the father who left so little positive trace on his life. Surveying the port of Salem was as close as he ever came to commanding a ship. Perhaps presiding over an important scene of his father's life helped close the rift between the generations and returned to him some portion of his father's power.

The authority he exercised over sea captains may have provided some small sense of having surpassed his father. Surely the narrator of "The Custom-House" expresses a curious pride in having under his orders such a "patriarchal body of veterans." This Nathaniel Hawthorne who himself so feared the contempt of his virile Puritan ancestors was amused "to behold the terrors that attended my advent; to see a furrowed cheek, weather-beaten by half a century of storm, turn ashy pale at the glance of so harmless an individual as myself" (95).

Authority over patriarchal figures very much like his father serves to remedy Hawthorne's sense of triviality. He enjoys the exercise of power, a feeling of having arrived at seniority, of being of the dominant generation. "The Custom-House" traces a process of integration of past selves, a drawing together of "identity fragments," and marks the forging for a time at least of a unified, independent, and powerful self that can safely comprehend both the dreaded Surveyor and the "harmless individual."

As the master of patriarchal elders, the Surveyor assumes a benign paternalism; he becomes the protector of childish old men as well as the judge of their worth. He experiences himself as a dominant adult by shielding elderly father figures from their own weakness. In perceiving and rendering various ways of growing old as epitomized by the Inspector and the Collector, the narrator anticipates his own coming decline and takes note of better and worse ways of aging. This close study of aging men has great import for one who is on the slippery peak of middle age. He derives from it not only a warning about time but a poignant picture of death-in-life, or stagnation, which makes the passing moment all the more precious. Figures of old men wallowing in torpid dependency are warnings to himself, fearful negative identities to him who enjoys a similar dependent relationship to Uncle Sam. *Carpe Diem!* [. . .]

Hawthorne may have felt destructive toward the gourmand Inspector, but he turned the energy of this anger to creative use by subtly relating the cruel picture of squandered life to his own temptation toward self-indulgence. Having truly depicted stagnation, he roused himself into a fury of creativity. He directed his portrait of the Inspector against his own tendency to indolence. With caricatures of enervated civil servants no longer capable of self-reliance, he combated his own attraction toward and fear of dependency. Instead of sketching characters for picturesque local color, he directed them toward energizing himself as narrator.

In contrast to that of the vapid Inspector, the reverent portrait of the Collector is an idealization of old age as a brooding, inward Tiresias figure apparently based less on observation than on imaginative projection. Already unapproachable because turned inward on his own memory, the Collector lends himself to affectionate contemplation and idealization. The narrator imputes to him ideal manliness, bravery, endurance, integrity, kindness, elegance, as well as "a young girl's appreciation of the floral tribe" (101). Attributed to this inaccessible, slumbrous old idol are all the contrary traits that if harmonized would make up a complete human being. The combination of military ferocity with feminine elegance and love of flowers suggests the integration of masculine and feminine traits that students of adult development believe takes place in middle and late adulthood. Because of the totally imputed rather than observed characterization of the Collector, this sketch stands out from the realistic portion of the essay and prepares us for the coming sketch of the narrator's spiritual father, Mr. Surveyor Pue.

Both the Inspector and the Collector spend their time in recollection of their pasts, one of past dinners, the other of past heroic deeds. The attic of the Custom House is full of dreary records of the past on which the author tries "exerting [his] fancy, sluggish with little use, to raise up from these dry bones an image" of Salem's brighter days. The gift of a usable vision of the past comes from the ghost of Hawthorne's predecessor, Mr. Surveyor Pue, an historic figure whom he adopts as his "official ancestor." Reminiscent of the ghost of Hamlet's father, the ghost of the former Surveyor charges his successor to complete his untold story of Hester Prynne and to give Mr. Pue his rightful credit. Surveyor Hawthorne accepts the commission in a spirit of filial duty and reverence.

In pledging filial obedience to Mr. Surveyor Pue, Hawthorne ignores his own father and bypasses his forefathers and guardian, to create the ghostly father he needs. This former Surveyor of customs who could also value and preserve in writing the story of Hester Prynne incorporates the author's own hitherto unresolved anti-theses, the man of affairs who is also a man of letters. In creating this paternal source of his own invention, Hawthorne engenders himself as master of his own talent, an author finally capable of producing a major, life-justifying work.

This essay so charged with a sense of time, of past recapitulated and laid to rest, of valediction to all that was prelude as Hawthorne looked forward to the future as an author in full possession of his powers, this autobiographical address to the reader of what bound him to a Salem he neither liked nor enjoyed, makes no mention of Hawthorne's truest links to his "natal spot." With exquisite tact and evasion he speaks neither of father nor mother, any more than he does of sisters, uncles, and aunts. He talks of forefathers and generations of fathers and sons, of patriarchal veterans in the Custom House, and of a filial duty to Mr. Pue, but of no actual father.

Nor does he mention the mother whose recent death nevertheless pervades the work. Instead, the residue of his grief emerges from the language: "the sensuous sympathy of dust for dust," dry bones, rigid corpses, decapitation, murder, ghosts. When the narrator, exploring the debris of the past in the Custom House attic, is about to discover Surveyor Pue's parchment, the language of death and stagnation gathers and condenses:

> ... the names of vessels that had long ago *foundered at sea* or *rotted at the wharves,* and those of merchants, *never heard of* now on 'Change, nor very readily decipherable on their mossy *tombstones;* glancing at such matters with the saddened, weary, half-reluctant interest which we bestow on the *corpse of dead activity*—and exerting my fancy, sluggish with little use, to *raise up from these dry bones* an image of the old town's brighter aspect. . . . I chanced to lay my hands on a small package. (106; italics added)

"The Custom-House" is death- and ghost-ridden, but real parents are notably absent from the text. Parents and children are left for symbolic treatment in *The Scarlet Letter.*

Nevertheless, parents real and surrogate leave their traces in "The Custom-House" in indirect but powerful ways. The presence of Hawthorne's mother emerges in his preference for the word "natal" over "native" in such phrases as "natal spot" or "as if the natal soil were an earthly paradise." In saying that drab Salem was for him "the inevitable center of the universe," the navel, as it were, of his emotional world, he fuses the natal and the native aspects of his birthplace. Thus separation from Salem marks a late stage of his individuation, the completion of a major transition.

Although such mothers as Hawthorne depicted in his works are clearly mothers, fathers are represented in diffuse and fragmented ways. Hester Prynne is established early and prominently as a solitary mother, but the novel depicts father-figures instead of fathers. We have Roger Chillingworth, Puritan elders and divines, a plurality of authority figures. Pearl's search among these figures for her true father may well be a major subtext of *The Scarlet Letter.*

Maternal presence and paternal absence are the positive and negative poles that generate this historical romance. With Hester standing on the scaffold like an image of the virgin mother, or "Divine Maternity" as the narrator terms it, the absence of a father becomes the dominant question for the community, the clergy, the governor, and most of all for the child. In response to the paternity question posed in the marketplace by the clergy, Hester refuses to assign Pearl an earthly father but consigns her instead to a greater one: "My child must seek a heavenly Father; she shall never know an earthly one!" (134). By suggesting the paradoxical notion that the illegitimate child may be of divine origin, both Hester and the narrator raise the factual issue of paternity to social, psychological, and metaphysical dimensions.

The tricky question of who "made" Pearl is played out on all three levels. In chapter six the perennial childish question of "where Pearl comes from" becomes a serious challenge when the evasive mother hesitates before providing the catechetically correct answer, "Thy Heavenly Father sent thee!" (156). Hester's evasion causes Pearl to deny that she has a heavenly father and to demand an answer more satisfying to her estranged reality.

Her steadfast refusal of a heavenly father without an earthly one generates her recalcitrant behavior when the town fathers test Pearl's knowledge of catechism to determine Hester's fitness to raise the child. To the first question, "Who art thou?" Pearl answers significantly, "I am mother's child . . . and my name is Pearl" (164), a response embodying the reality of her experience, the child of a mother only, no last name. To the question "Who made thee?", resonant enough for any child but especially so for a bastard, she perversely asserts that she has not been made but plucked from the wild rose tree by the prison door. This confirmation that Hester is not properly educating Pearl raises the danger of losing custody of the child. Fearing this, Hester demands menacingly that Dimmesdale "look to it" that mother and child not be parted, thus rousing the biological father to behave protectively.

Pearl's perverse refusal to acknowledge a heavenly father without being acknowledged by an earthly one thus provokes what she has been yearning for all along, a paternal response. Her behavior also activates her biological family, compelling intense interaction between mother and father and between father and daughter. Dimmesdale's protective act subdues Pearl's wildness and impels her gently to lay her cheek against his hand. His hesitation before responding to this tenderness is observed not only by the hyper-acute child but by ever-vigilant Chillingworth, who immediately revives the dormant question of the identity of Pearl's father.

This chapter, which connects the mystery of creation to the unsolved paternity question, is taut with multiple meanings. Three years later than the marketplace scene, it reassembles all the principal characters to reenact the earlier events with the difference that Pearl is now not an infant but a conscious agent. In a heightened version of their first public interview, her mother and father communicate directly to each other in a double language designed to deceive the world. Thus in Hester's charge that the minister defend her claim to the child, she iterates three times in one paragraph, "Thou knowest me better than these men can. . . . Thou knowest. . . . Thou knowest" (166), apparently referring to pastoral familiarity but meaning also carnal knowledge.

Every irony is wrung out of the catechetical question of who "made" Pearl, but now Pearl's unconscious needs are stage-managing the scene, bringing the parents into relationship, stimulating a renewed inquiry into paternity, evoking responses to her deepest needs. This uncanny infant manipulates the script from here on and so manages events that the narrative concludes with acknowledgment by her father. Hester never seeks to stand up publicly with the minister and finally does so only reluctantly, whereas Pearl, who seeks this persistently throughout the book, flies to his embrace. The grand finale of both the surface plot of adult actions and the underlying plot directed by the child is the public restoration on the scaffold at noonday of the true biological family.

Pearl's eldritch quality stems directly from the intensity of her search for paternal recognition. Lacking overt clues, she developed uncanny intuitive gifts. She had to search through her mother to discern her father, to sift and study Hester's relationship to men, to become an observer of the slightest gestures and behaviors of her elders. Pearl, that bundle of searching intuition, is, like Hester and Dimmesdale, a projection of aspects of the author.

The world looked to Pearl much as it did to the child Nathaniel Hawthorne, who scarcely knew his father. His chaste widowed mother must have seemed to him like the virgin mother, complete within herself. Eventually seeking the father every child must have, he, like Pearl, had to search through the mother for the missing male parent. And like Pearl, he found not one man in indisputable possession, but two, one a biological father who failed to claim his wife and child, the other a man somehow related to the mother with authority of an indeterminate sort over both mother and child. This unwarranted authority was, as appears in chapter three, sufficient to separate mother and child for the sake of the boy's education—the kind of separation threatened by Governor Bellingham after Pearl's faulty response to the catechism. In Pearl's case, the true father intervened to protect the mother-child relationship from tampering by would-be surrogate fathers—a development that young Nathaniel must have wished for in vain. Viewing the action of *The Scarlet Letter* from Pearl's perspective, that of a child trying to piece together its basic family constellation, to locate its father and account for the puzzling intruder, we find her early *Umwelt* much like that of her creator.

When Pearl's quest is fulfilled by her father's public embrace, she gains a father only to lose him. She attains not a father's care or solicitude, only the knowledge of who her father *was*, essentially all that Hawthorne had — knowledge of a lost father. Release of Pearl's gender identity and humanity depends on acknowledgment from her biological father; her material fortunes, however, depend just as surely on the inheritance bequeathed her by Roger Chillingworth, her mother's shadowy former husband. Chillingworth endows Pearl with the means for a larger destiny than her mother alone could have supplied, and he thereby assumes a genuine aspect of the fatherly role, that of provider.

This fragmenting of the biological and the sustaining aspects of fatherhood was a critical feature of Hawthorne's childhood experience. We must imagine how he tried to construe his family constellation both before and after his father's death. Probably content at first to be the only male in the family, he suddenly found himself surrounded by Manning relatives. While still trying to discern his mother's relationship to her parents, sisters, and brothers, he found one brother, Robert Manning, taking over the affairs of all the Hawthornes. Robert Manning was generous with love, interest, and material benefits, but Nathaniel grew to resent benefactions that he felt to be intrusive coming from someone other than a father. He became excessively sensitive about dependency on the Mannings in general and on Uncle Robert in particular.

Sensitivity about dependency fuels the animus against civil service permeating "The Custom-House." In the early part, unreliable parenting is symbolized by a maternal eagle, which promises protection and downy warmth, but will sooner or later "fling off her nestlings with . . . a rankling wound from her barbed arrows" (89). But in a long shrill paragraph leading into the "decapitation," Hawthorne symbolizes the federal government as male and an uncle. Through the agency of the civil service, Uncle Sam encourages dependency so far into the adulthood of the public servant that "his own proper strength departs from him." The debilitated office-holder is sure to be ejected eventually, having become a person who "for ever afterwards looks wistfully about him in quest of support external to himself" (113). At this stage, all he can hope for is restoration to office.

Such pervasive effects does Hawthorne attribute to government employment on the character, manhood, and vitality of the civil servant, that the reader senses motivation by an uncle more influential than Uncle Sam and a dependency characteristic established far earlier than middle life. [. . .]

[. . .] [E]ven though Hawthorne was later to seek the support of Uncle Sam's arm, he left the Custom House in 1849 with the exhilaration of one who feels he has thrown off such support just in time to salvage his independence and manhood. Rebounding with an energy equal to the threat of entrapment, he severed his ties to Salem by offensive statements about the government and his colleagues. It felt like a rebirth, and for a while it was. [. . .]

[How Culture Empowers Symbolic Form]

Sacvan Bercovitch

Sacvan Bercovitch's introduction to his book *The Office of* The Scarlet Letter argues that when Hawthorne says, "The scarlet letter had not done its office," he "invests the letter with a discrete function." Combining aesthetic interpretation with cultural argument, Bercovitch asserts that at the end of the novel, Hester not only accepts the letter but consents to its discipline, becoming "an agent of socialization" for the discontented individuals who seek her counsel. Thus she represents what Bercovitch calls the liberal "ideology of America." [ED.]

"The Scarlet Letter had not done its office": Hawthorne's stern, evasive one-line paragraph, midway through the novel, deserves the emphasis he gives it (205). The sentence links our various views of Hester Prynne—on the pillory and in the forest, in relation to the townspeople, her husband, her lover, her daughter, herself. It seems to confirm what we are often told, that Hawthorne's meanings are endless and open-ended. To speak of an office not done, especially without specifying the office, implies a commitment to process, a principled indefiniteness. But in fact Hawthorne is saying just the opposite. His very emphasis on the negative, the "not done," invests the letter with a discrete function, an office whose fulfillment (in due time) will be the mark of narrative closure. It reminds us, as does everything else about the novel, from title to plot, that the letter has a purpose and a goal. And to speak of an unfulfilled office when fulfillment is

From *The Office of* The Scarlet Letter. Baltimore: Johns Hopkins, 1991. (All parenthetical references are to this New Riverside Edition.)

under way, not *yet* done, is to imply teleology. Hawthorne's meanings may be endless, but they are not open-ended. On the contrary, they are designed to create a specific set of anticipations, to shape our understanding of what follows in some definite way.

"The scarlet letter had not done its office": on the one hand, process; on the other hand, purpose and telos. The coherence of the symbol lies in its capacity to combine both. It has a certain end, we might say, in the double sense of "certain," as certainty and as something still to be ascertained. The office of the letter is to identify one with the other—to make certainty a form of process, and the prospect of certain meanings a form of closure and control.

With that double prospect in view, Hester returns to New England. "Here had been her sin," Hawthorne writes, "here, her sorrow; and here was yet to be her penitence" (271). Again, process and closure have been combined, only now with a *certain* end in view—penitence—as earlier Dimmesdale has an end in view when he prophesies a certain "glorious destiny" for "this newly chosen people of the Lord" (261) and as Hester does later when she foresees an age of love to come. Once, long before, she transformed the A into a symbol for able, admirable. Now she transforms herself, able and admirable as she is, into an agent of socialization. Her cottage becomes a meeting ground for dissidents—particularly, unhappy young women chafing (as Hester had) under Puritan restrictions—and she takes the opportunity to make it a counseling center for patience and faith. In effect, she urges upon them a morphology of penitence (not unlike the official Puritan "preparation for salvation"): self-control, self-doubt, self-denial, a true sight of sin, and hope in the future, involving some apodictic revelation to come. Hester's "badge of shame" becomes the "mystic" token of integration (164, 108).

This is not some formulaic Victorian happy ending. In the first place, the ending is not happy. What brings Hester home, the necessity that serves in some measure (as Hawthorne promises at the start) to "relieve the darkening close" of his tale (120), is no deus ex machina. It is the narrative mechanism itself, in all its "sad" and "sombre" implications (271, 272). Hawthorne sums them up through the emblem on the lovers' tombstone—the "engraved escutcheon . . . relieved by one ever-glowing point of light gloomier than the shadow" (272)—an emblem that enforces our sense of closure precisely by sustaining narrative tension, for, like Hester's final penitence to be, the gloom that finally is to provide relief also returns us to the ambiguities of Hester's ordeal.

In these and other ways, Hawthorne's fusion of process and telos transmutes opposition into complementarity. Hester's return effectually reconciles the various antinomies that surround her throughout the novel: nature and culture, sacred and profane, light and shadow, memory and hope, repression and desire, angel and adulteress, her dream of love and the demands of history and community. It also draws together author and subject, for, as the letter's unfulfilled office midway through the story anticipates Hester's return, so the return of Hester anticipates Hawthorne's recovery of Puritan New England. Here had been her penitence, and here was yet to be *The Scarlet Letter: A Romance.* At the start Hawthorne reverses the disruptive effects of political office — the Democratic party defeat that cost him his tenure at the Salem Customs House — by reaching back through the A to national origins. At the end, reversing the alienating effects of her symbol, Hester looks forward to a "brighter period" (271) that relates her most intimate hopes to moral and social progress. In each case, the gesture enacts the symbolic method I noted, process and telos combined. And in each case the method reflects the strategies of what we have come to term "the American ideology."

The term requires a more precise definition, which I will elaborate, but, even in its vague implications — pertaining to the norms of the dominant culture — ideology, as Hawthorne suggests, is a rich and intricate system of meanings. *The Scarlet Letter* is a story of socialization in which the point of socialization is not to conform, but to consent. Anyone can submit; the socialized believe. It is not enough to have the letter imposed; you have to do it yourself, and that involves the total self — past, present, and future; private and public; thought and passion and action, or, if necessary, inaction. This is essentially the office of the A as the Puritan magistrates intended it and as Hester finally adopts it, from her own far more tolerant but not altogether different outlook. And we can assume that the letter's "deeper meanings" correspond. *Allegoria,* as Saint Augustine taught, is a function of *littera-historia.* By that time-honored principle of exegesis, the A is first and last a cultural artifact, a symbol that expresses the needs of the society within and for which it was produced. I refer to Hawthorne's society, of course, but I would also include Puritan New England, insofar as it may be said to have contributed to the development of antebellum ideology, and our period as well, insofar as it may be said to build on ideological continuities from Hawthorne's time.

By "Hawthorne's society" and "antebellum ideology" I mean the complex of social practices and cultural ideals that we associate with the liberal Northern United States from 1820 to the Civil War. I am aware of the many differences within that society and of the many problems in applying such generalities as "Jacksonian" to the Northern states. My concern lies with the broad patterns of life and thought that nonetheless bound together those diverse interests, groups, and regions (as events demonstrated), and within which, moreover, diversity itself was celebrated as part of a strategy of cultural cohesion. As an anticonsensus historian reports in a survey of the scholarship:

[T]he recent literature argues that politicians and lawmakers of all persuasions (including southern politicians . . .) were becoming increasingly enamored of liberal concepts . . . [and] came increasingly to interpret the republican framework as one or another form of liberal capitalist polity and economy.[1]

This study is in part a commentary on that engulfing process of interpretation—a process, let me add, that reaches back to "the republican framework." "The name of American," said George Washington in his Farewell Address (September 17, 1796), "must always exalt [your] just pride . . . more than any appellation derived from local discriminations. With slight shades of difference, you have the same Religion, Manners, Habits, and political Principles."

The "name of American" was an interpretative fiction in 1796 no less than it was in 1776 (or for that matter two centuries earlier, when it had served the opposite-but-complementary office of interpreting away differences between the religions, manners, habits, and political principles of the people we now again call Native Americans). But by mid-century it had become the cornerstone of a New World liberal identity that extended from the free enterprise vision of "American Economy" to the multidenominational varieties of "American Religion," and that included the "Shiloh" mission of "Young America in Literature," which Melville in 1850 ascribed to Hawthorne. In all this the name of American worked not only to displace the very real (and deepening) differences within the country, but equally—within the country's reigning liberal constituency—to display difference of all kinds as proof of a victorious pluralism. The result was a quasi-dialectic between exclusion and expansion that established, defined, and processually secured the boundaries of union, a "new nation" replete with mythic past and "manifest" future. Hawthorne and his contemporaries traced this cultural genealogy to Puritan New England, as did many of the leaders of both revolutionary and republican America. Their rhetoric of descent (simultaneously a rhetoric of ascent and consent) is central to the dynamics of cohesion in the movement from republican to Jacksonian America.

The scarlet letter functions in this sense as cultural genealogy; it functions, too, as it moves from the mid-nineteenth-century customs house

---

[1] Sean Wilentz, "On Class and Politics in Jacksonian America," in *The Promise of American History: Progress and Prospects.* Ed. Stanley I. Katler and Stanley N. Katz (Baltimore: Johns Hopkins University Press, 1983). [ED.]

back to its Puritan origins, to recall a major cultural shift from "civic" to individualistic norms. Historians have described this shift in conflictual terms, as entailing massive realignments of social, economic, and regional power. I am indebted to their descriptions, as the following chapters testify. My own focus, however, lies elsewhere—on the forces that recast conflict and change (potentially, the sort of radical upheavals that virtually everywhere else, in both the Old World and the New, led to the collapse of liberal revolutions) into a triumph of the American ideology. I have in mind the sustained liberal commitment of those who spoke for the Republic: the shared values, symbols, and beliefs that at once fueled and circumscribed the debates between Thomas Jefferson and John Adams, Thomas Paine and Timothy Dwight, Andrew Jackson and John Quincy Adams, Ralph Waldo Emerson and Daniel Webster, Abraham Lincoln and Stephen Douglas. Those debates can be said to mark the organic development from "classical" to "marketplace" liberalism. And in turn that quintessentially ideological development can be said to have guided the nation, through a civil war of unprecedented violence and destruction, from the era of liberal expansion to that of liberal incorporation.

I use "liberal" here and throughout this study as a catchall term to convey the continuing relation between social process and cultural symbology. [. . .]

[. . .] In this long view the office of the scarlet letter pertains both to the symbol in the text and to the symbol as the text. My purpose, accordingly, is to integrate ideological and aesthetic criticism. Ideology in its narrow sense works to empty objects of historical content—particularly, in our time, objects of art. It depoliticizes them in order to refill them with its own timeless and universal claims. I want to repoliticize *The Scarlet Letter* (in Aristotle's broad sense of the political) by turning the text inside out and the context outside in: to explain the novel's aesthetic design in terms of cultural strategies of control and to allow the culture to reveal itself in all its radical potentiality through its representation in the text.

Hence my emphasis on what I call, for lack of a better term, cultural symbology. I mean by it neither the "superstructures" posited by social science (where "ideology" is synonymous with false consciousness or *parti pris*) nor the fabled realm of the transcendent (our post-Romantic kingdom of God)—but the system of symbolic meanings that encompasses text and context alike, simultaneously nourishing the imagination and marking its boundaries. It is a highly volatile system, built upon multilayered connections between dominant patterns of cultural expression and their distinctive uses in exceptional works of art, as Hester's exotic letter connects to a wide range of Puritan *canonica*, from the Pentateuch to the illustrated catechism of the New England primer. Cultural symbology at once denies aesthetic autonomy and highlights the difference between aesthetics and the political or institutional forms usually associated with ideology. It reminds us that aesthetic representations are inescapably political, just as literature necessarily assumes an institutional form. It also reminds us that they are flexible enough to accommodate upheaval and transformation, that this flexibility may extend in extraordinary cases across time and place, and that, at a certain pitch of intensity, this transhistorical appeal may become the vehicle not only of elusiveness and indeterminacy but also of personal agency and social subversion.

The model I have in mind is, of course, the scarlet letter itself. The terms in which I just outlined its office as cultural work are intended in the loose sense of practical criticism—what might be called an ethnography of literary context. The boundaries I refer to include cross-cultural influences and conflicting modes of expression and belief. Their relation to ideology is variable and possibly disruptive. Ideology itself, in the anthropological sense I intend, involves a network of complex reciprocities between social construction and textual creation. And although I assume a basic contextual coherence—a system within which such terms as "cross-cultural," "conflicting," and "variable" make sense—I do so primarily by reference to a singular symbolic work of art. My point is not to demystify *The Scarlet Letter*. It is to call into question—that is, to problematize so as to seek knowledge from—its extraordinary powers of mystification. To understand the novel historically is to recognize that we learn most about background and sources from its aesthetic techniques. And to appreciate it aesthetically is to recognize that what is richest and most compelling about the novel lies in its profound ideological engagement—profound enough to allow us to trace the issues it masks; ideologically engaged enough to have made this darkest of Hawthorne's novels (as it has often been described) a vehicle of continuity at a time of cultural disruption and social change.

I think here not only of the continuities inscribed in the novel, from Puritan to antebellum New England and beyond, but of the widespread response to *The Scarlet Letter*. From the start readers acclaimed the novel for its representative national qualities. "Our literature has given the world no truer product of the American soil," declared Young America's literary pundit, Evert Duyckinck, upon the novel's appearance in 1850, and in one form or another his judgment was echoed by virtually every important nineteenth—century critic through William Dean Howells and Duyckinck's Gilded Age successor, the Brahmin literary entrepreneur Horace Scudder. It is not too much to say that *The Scarlet Letter* began the institutionalization of an American literary tradition. Of the three "immortals" officially enshrined in 1900 as the founders of American literature—Washington Irving, Henry Wadsworth Longfellow, and Hawthorne—only

Hawthorne survived the twentieth-century revaluation of the canon. And of the several books that contemporaries singled out as his masterpiece — *Mosses from an Old Manse, The Scarlet Letter, The House of the Seven Gables,* and *The Marble Faun*—only *The Scarlet Letter,* our first instant classic, has retained its appeal for subsequent generations of readers.

It is worth emphasizing the political import of this process. At mid-century Hawthorne's novel was the chief authority by which the new nation claimed independence in the realm of belles lettres. It "represented both what was essentially American," according to contemporary reviewers, "and what was 'best' by . . . universal criteria." By the turn of the century *The Scarlet Letter* was the centerpiece in the "general incorporation of literature into education," as expressing the "national spirit" in its "consummate" form — "the embodiment of what Americans share, the chief incarnation of the ethos that gives them existence as people . . . [and therefore for educational purposes,] the channel through which that ethos is disseminated, and . . . the means by which outsiders are brought inside it." [2]

The apotheosis of that tradition-making rite of passage came with Henry James's biography of 1879, which celebrates Hawthorne as "the most valuable example of the American genius." *The Scarlet Letter,* writes James, is

> the finest piece of imaginative writing yet put forth in the country. There was a consciousness of this in the welcome that was given it — a satisfaction in the idea of America having produced a novel that belonged to literature, and to the forefront of it. Something might at last be sent to Europe as exquisite in quality as anything that had been received, and the best of it was that the thing was absolutely American. . . . [*The Scarlet Letter*] will continue to be, for other generations than ours, his most substantial title to fame.[3]

James's acclaim was the elite mark of sanctification. The broad consensus to which he refers — reaching backward to the novel's first "welcome" and forward to its future "fame" — was being systematically enlarged throughout this time by an intricate network of belletristic, social, and economic institutions, including publishing houses, political and cultural reviews, salons, home libraries, public events, university lectures, and high school texts.

These facts do not point toward a conspiracy theory of canon formation. Nor do they imply that literature is a form of co-optation. They suggest that the power of the text, in all its extraordinary intensity and multivalence, is inseparable from context and function. Culture works through a variety of agencies, forces, and pressures, some of these mutually contradictory. But

---

[2] See Brodhead, *The School of Hawthorne,* (53, 58 – 60). [ED.]
[3] See pages 284 – 86 in this volume. [ED.]

basically it seeks to perpetuate itself through strategies of cohesion, and (in modern instances) it does so most effectively through particular rhetorical forms, designed to instate particular sets of norms and beliefs.

Literature participates in this design. It is nourished by the same values, sustained by the same institutions, and informed by the same codes of personal and communal identity through which culture works. In the case of *The Scarlet Letter*—as in that of all our mid-nineteenth-century classics, including Harriet Beecher Stowe's *Uncle Tom's Cabin* (1851–52) and Frederick Douglass's *The Narrative of the Life of Frederick Douglass* (1845)—the source of that reciprocity may be simply stated. It lies in the premises of American liberalism: "America," a national symbol denoting not only a national identity (as in Washington's Farewell Address) but also a literary ideal, and "liberalism," an interpretative framework denoting not only general habits of the heart and mind but also a particular economy, free enterprise capitalism in the antebellum North. Let me recall the powerful link between the two. "America" is to New World liberalism as the doctrine of the divine right of kings is to medieval monarchy. Open competition, group pluralism, voluntarism, private enterprise, personal rights, community by contract and consent, equality under the law, mobility, free opportunity, individualism—all the tenets of modern liberal society find their apotheosis in the symbol of America. The process by which the United States usurped America for itself, symbolically, is also the process by which liberalism established its political and economic dominance.

This double process took effect between the Revolution and the Civil War, and its aesthetic triumph is marked by the American literary renaissance. The locus classicus is 1850, the year of *The Scarlet Letter*—also of Susan Warner's *Wide, Wide World*, our amplest inside narrative of liberal domesticity, and Herman Melville's *Moby-Dick*, still the most searching critique we have of free enterprise democracy.[4] Of these, Hawthorne's

---

[4] In a separate, much broader work, concerning the development of liberal institutions in antebellum America (including the institution of literature), I explore these and other texts as complementary, conflicting, or alternative sites of culture formation and/or cultural critique. In doing so, I take up aspects of Hawthorne's writing that are treated here only in passing: for example, issues of gender (as in Warner's novel) and varieties of countercultural work (in the tradition of Melville). *The Scarlet Letter* has been used to discuss these concerns, most recently and most fully from a feminist perspective in important book-length studies by Lauren Berlant and Emily Budick. [The works referred to here are Berlant's *The Anatomy of National Fantasy: Hawthorne, Utopia, and Everyday Life* (1991) and Budick's *Engendering Romance: Women Writers and the Hawthorne Tradition, 1850–1990* (1994). ED.] My present purpose is to offer *within the author's frame of discourse* a certain kind of contextual close reading—that is, a cultural *explication de texte* in which ideological analysis is a form of "intrinsic criticism," and vice versa.

novel is the prime instance of literature as cultural work. It represents not only a set of ideologically mediated realities but also the ways and means of mediation. To some extent this is true of the other two novels as well, but each of them stands in a relatively tangential relation to society: Warner's by definition of "the woman's sphere" and Melville's because of his profoundly marginal perspective. *The Scarlet Letter* has proved our most enduring classic because it is the liberal example par excellence of art as ideological mimesis. To understand the office of the A, to appreciate its subtle combinings of process and closure, is to see how culture empowers symbolic form, including forms of dissent, and how symbols participate in the dynamics of culture, including the dynamics of constraint. [. . .]

Romance as Revision
The Scarlet Letter

Richard H. Millington

The following excerpt from Richard Millington's book *Practicing Romance* examines patterns of repetition in "The Custom-House" and *The Scarlet Letter* as Hawthorne's mode of pitting a community's constraints on the individual against that individual's freedom despite those constraints. Drawing on the "established gender distinctions" of his own day, Millington says, Hawthorne interrogated the relationship between his characters' inner and outer lives and their engagements with their community. Millington argues that "The Custom-House" "rewrites Hester's tragedy of irretrievable loss as Hawthorne's comedy of escape." [ED.]

In the territory of *The Scarlet Letter* and in the precinct of "The Custom-House" appended to it, things happen at least twice. Most strikingly, the plot of the romance ends by returning Hester and Dimmesdale to the moment of transgression that has generated its action. Attached to this pattern of return is a whole set of recurrences, from the famous trips to the scaffold, to Dimmesdale's pseudoconfessions, to Pearl's persistent questions

---

From *Practicing Romance: Narrative Form and Cultural Engagement in Hawthorne's Fiction*. Princeton: Princeton UP, 1992. (All parenthetical references are to this New Riverside Edition.)

about the letter, to the ghost stories that link the musings of "The Custom-House." Together, these circlings back make manifest a drama of cultural affiliation; the book's remarkable examination of the psychology of guilt is best understood as an attempt to locate, between the pulses of private feeling, the meaning of living within a community. *The Scarlet Letter* begins the work of romance by raising a question about the career of the self within a culture: is a life the repetitive playing out of the constrained relation between a given inner nature and the structure of the community one inhabits, or is there some room for freedom in our place of mind and in the forms of relation that constitute our social life? Our attempt to understand the particular answer that *The Scarlet Letter* poses to it might start from the shape of the plot: when the originating moment of transgression, itself elided from the book, returns, it returns with a difference. Its consequences have been lived out, fully revealed, and its meaning for Hester and Dimmesdale and for us as readers will be defined by acts of choice and interpretation rather than the inarticulate logic of passion. This essay argues that the working out of this distinction between constraint and choice — and the establishment of a possibility I will be calling revision — is at the heart of the book and the essence of Hawthorne's practice of romance.

[. . .] "The Custom-House" at once enacts and recommends a particular stance toward the experience of inhabiting a community, a way of thinking that I will be calling "revisionary." It establishes, that is, the spirit in which the book it introduces should be read. Hawthorne's essay begins with the fact of cultural attachment; his reasons for taking the job of Surveyor lie "chiefly" in a "strange, indolent, unjoyous attachment for my native town," a relation not of "love, but instinct" (93). The gap between his actual reasons for taking this post — a desperate need for cash — and the version we encounter here should remind us that the Hawthorne of "The Custom-House" is himself an invention, and that his creator is introducing us to *The Scarlet Letter* by constructing a story about his affiliation to the community that enfolds him, and by asking whether the joyless and unchosen forms of his attachment might be revised. This interrogation unfolds along two axes: what forms of connection to its past does the community make possible; and what configurations of selfhood does it allow? In each case, a significant, freeing way of living one's cultural attachment must be rescued from the dangers of constriction and enervation that characterize the life of the customhouse. In performing this work of rescue, the tactics of the essay — the acts of mind it performs and invites — are as important as the stories it tells.

"The Custom-House" unfolds as a series of ghost stories, and it is through these recurrent hauntings that our possibilities for significant connection to the past are explored. In the first of these encounters, the character Hawthorne invents for himself meets his Puritan ancestors. His willingness to take upon himself and expiate the "shame" of their persecutory excesses—an offer that implies a significant moral connection between generations—yields only inhibition in return, as his ghostly for-bears deliver an authoritative condemnation of story telling as a form of work. Despite this repudiation, Hawthorne persists in claiming that a link to these censorious ancestors remains: "strong traits of their nature have intertwined themselves with mine" (93). One of the central tasks of "The Custom-House" is to work out the form of the writer's engagement in his familial and communal history.

To enter the customhouse proper is to enter the order of life implied by the unchosen form of cultural affiliation—"not love, but instinct"—that attaches Hawthorne to Salem. The aged officers of the customs live out an evacuated selfhood held in place by the pointless repetition of stories and jokes that have been stripped of meaning, denatured to "passwords and countersigns." This aspect of the customhouse is presided over by the Permanent Inspector, who lives a life of instinctual gratification and for whom memory is reduced to the afterglow of past meals. His one unhappiness, in a parody of Hawthorne's ancestral haunting, is the memory of a promising-looking goose that proved to be too tough to cut. Like their leader, the aged functionaries have been unable to summon any meaning from the past: they "had gathered nothing worth preservation from their varied experience of life" (96).

The other patriarch of the customhouse is haunted by himself. Within the customhouse's archives of self, the General represents both the achievement of meaningful action and the fear that such a possibility is lost. He lives a rich but incommunicable inner life, full of the memories of a heroic past. His access to the present—and its access to him—is obscured by age's "veil of dim obstruction" (101). For Hawthorne the Surveyor, trying to reconstruct like an archaeologist the structure of his character, General Miller comes to represent, through the legend of his battlefield heroics, the revolutionary generation and the circumstances that so adequately answered their ambitions: he is as out of place among the "inkstands" and other writerly paraphernalia of the customhouse as "an old sword." He thus haunts Hawthorne as well as himself, his inward-turning presence a reminder, along with the essay's parodies of fame and hints of literary oblivion, of the dwindling scope of the present.

These customhouse portraits imply a culture of enervation and a form of affiliation to its history reduced to empty repetition on the one hand and a frustrating sense of loss on the other. But out of these materials the essay composes a different story about our relation to the past, a form of connection not inhibitory, empty, or elegiac but—at least potentially—invigorating. The story of the genesis of *The Scarlet Letter* that Hawthorne tells is in striking ways a revision of the stories of lost connection he has been telling. In a story told under the protection of a liberating "as if," he substitutes his official predecessor, Surveyor Pue, for his skeptical ancestors, and an energizing reconstruction of the past for the repetition and nostalgia we have witnessed.

Hawthorne's discovery of what will become *The Scarlet Letter* begins with the kind of emotional enervation that marked his return to Salem. He glances through the customhouse's detritus of discarded papers "with the saddened, weary, half-reluctant interest which we bestow on the corpse of dead activity" (106) until he locates a different kind of document, not "official" but "of a private nature" (107). This relic of the unofficial activities of his "official ancestor"—his work as a preserver of stories—animates a form of connection between them that evades the intellectual practices and emotional range of the customhouse. As he examines the letter itself, he moves from "accurate measurement," the mode of attention that belongs to the customhouse, to visual inspection and intellectual analysis, and finally to a form of connection that leaves mere "Surveyorship" entirely behind: placing the letter on his breast, he experiences "a sensation, not altogether physical, yet almost so, as of burning heat" (108). Hawthorne is careful to identify this moment of sympathetic exchange, in which the external becomes internal, as the indispensable moment in his account of the origin of his book: "the reader may smile, but must not doubt my word" (108).

This moment of connection not only generates *The Scarlet Letter*, which Hawthorne represents as a completion or filling out—a revision, in effect—of the "outline" he inherits from Surveyor Pue; it produces the appearance of the Surveyor himself. This newest in the essay's series of hauntings works to supply what the essay's previous versions of ancestral connection lacked. In place of the legacy of inhibition offered by his actual ancestors, Surveyor Pue offers through his manuscript a connection to the past that at once originates within the customhouse and offers a way out of its habits of heart and mind—a different cultural location, as it were. And the "I will" with which Hawthorne formally accepts Pue's commission reframes in its form General Miller's legendary act of heroic speech: "I'll try, Sir." Hawthorne's act of revision, then, animates the null relation to history that had belonged to the customhouse, and it covertly attaches the aura of heroic action to story telling.

This sequence of hauntings provides, in several ways, a model for the transformation of a cultural attachment gone wrong. Hawthorne's invention of the story of Surveyor Pue and his literary legacy substitutes for the inhibitory authority of the Puritan forefathers a different kind of connection, a "private" relationship that keeps alive the direct experience of meaning—the heart's heat of the letter—almost lost among the repetitions, erasures, and dead documents that constitute history within the customhouse. Authority, we must notice, is being rewritten rather than erased, for Surveyor Pue makes his own demands upon the fidelity of his legatee: *his* story must be told, he must be credited as the source. More subtly, we might see in the rewriting of this tale of authority an answer to the question with which we began: how have those Puritan ghosts inter-twined themselves into our storyteller's nature? Hawthorne's imitation of the General's heroic act of burden bearing—itself a version of his offer to take on his ancestral "shame"—implicitly claims that story telling is not idle but central, performing the crucial work of recovering or rescuing an evanescent meaning. By claiming, though by a liberatingly oblique route, a crucial cultural role for fiction, Hawthorne acknowledges that the ancestral question—"what mode of glorifying God, or being serviceable to mankind in his day and generation" (92) is writing storybooks?—is in fact the right one to ask. Finally, the very method Hawthorne employs in composing the essay, with its movement away from inhibition and enervation by recomposing similar narrative elements, suggests that one's mode of life within a community and a freer form of cultural affiliation will be a reworked, reimagined, "revised" thing—not, *pace* Emerson, an act of untrammeled invention.

The striking and curious thing about this story of liberating revision, though, is that its immediate yield is not freedom but constraint, in the form of a writer's block. This block is dramatically illustrated by still another haunting. In an ironic take on the scene of ancestral repudiation, the characters of his would-be romance refuse animation, rejecting him for the taint of practicality that brought him to the customhouse in the first place: as a mere wage-earner, "the little power you might once have possessed over the tribe of unrealities is gone!" (110). And the essay's famous invocations of the moonlit "neutral territory" of romance, where imagination finds its scope and power, are all written as conditions contrary-to-fact: they record an imaginative reawakening that is *not* happening. Though the writer's relation to the past, and to the figures of authority who preside over it, has been successfully reimagined and reclaimed, the essay clearly has more work to do. Hawthorne thus turns his attention to the present condition of his relation to his community.

The Hawthorne of the essay is haunted by an anxiety about the effect of his sojourn in the customhouse upon his character. He notes, early on, that his imagination has been deadened by his surveyorship, and he wonders whether too much of the customary life might permanently alter his character. He immediately erases his worries with a curious claim of immunity from the influence of external circumstances: it lies entirely "at [his] own option" to recover his past imaginativeness. He accompanies this confident notion with the assertion of a kind of imaginative election: "There was always a prophetic instinct, a low whisper in my ear, that, within no long period, and whenever a new change of custom should be essential to my good, a change would come" (103). Implicit in these assertions is a theory about the nature of selfhood and its interactions with the community that surrounds it. The Surveyor assuages his anxiety about self-loss, that is, with the notion that there exists an inviolable margin of free selfhood, an unencumberable form of property in the self, immune from the effects of living in the customhouse of culture. The saving "change of custom" does indeed come with his dismissal from his post, but not before he suffers, in the shock of the writer's block, the loss of his absolutist fantasy about the inviolability of the private self.

Hawthorne's inability to write wrests from him a more chastened, complex understanding of the relation between self and culture. This revision emerges in a new account of the effects of inhabiting the customhouse: "I had ceased to be a writer of tolerably poor tales and essays, and had become a tolerably good Surveyor of the Customs. That was all. But, nevertheless, it is anything but agreeable to be haunted by a suspicion that one's intellect is dwindling away; or exhaling, without your consciousness, like ether out of a phial; so that at every glance, you find a smaller and less volatile residuum" (112). This enervation of the self, a kind of internalization of the prevailing customhouse atmosphere, is assigned interesting origins. The customhouse officer, as a viewer rather than a maker, "does not share in the united effort of mankind" (112). Hawthorne attributes his loss of self, then, to his sequestration from culturally valuable work—the kind of work that writing, in the Surveyor Pue vignette, had seemed. Moreover, a job in the customhouse places the officer in a dependent relation to the too-paternal government—like his relation to his ancestors, this is another bad authority relationship—and each payment extracts some of the self's "proper strength . . . its sturdy force, its courage and constancy, its truth, its self-reliance, and all that gives emphasis to manly character" (113). And here Hawthorne acknowledges that his previous belief in the easy recoverability of independent selfhood was too optimistic. He admits that a moment of no return will arrive, after which even ejection from office will only produce fantasies of reacquiring it. He finds himself calculating "how much longer I could stay in the Custom-House and yet go forth a man" (113).

Hawthorne's dismissal from office of course rescues him from this frightening fate. Once out of office, Surveyor Pue's story at last comes to life.

With the resurgence of his imaginative powers, the sojourn in the custom-house becomes a healthy break from the literary life and the unimaginative Surveyor is revealed merely to be Hawthorne's "figurative" self; the writer regains his position as "the real human being," and *The Scarlet Letter* gets written. But a careful reading of the essay will insist that we notice that Hawthorne's rescue is an accident that, in the euphoria of his relief, is being celebrated as if it had been a choice—a choice, he is careful to point out, he would not have made. The ending of "The Custom-House," for all of its comic brio, reminds us of the narrowness of its author's escape and of the necessity of choosing—not merely acceding to—the forms our cultural attachments take. Hawthorne's close call, it seems to me, is acknowledged both in the description he supplies of the experience of writing *The Scarlet Letter*—its somberness is the mark of "the period of hardly accomplished revolution and still seething turmoil, in which the story shaped itself" (116)—which suggests a degree of struggle with his Surveyor-self that belies the serenity of the essay's account of his escape, and in the imagery of decapitation and death that finds its way into his comic ending.

A "real human being," a freeing, imaginative relation to the community and its history, and a valid form of work are all recovered during the course of the essay, but this vindication does not take place because that self was invulnerable to the power of the customary all along. Rather, the essay locates a significant relation to the community in the precarious balancing act I have been calling "revision," in acts of choice that do not leave the community behind but maneuver among its structures: in the way the essay proceeds by writing the inhibition out of the available stories about the past, or the way Hawthorne and Surveyor Pue meet on the ground of sympathetic connection created by the story of the scarlet letter. Hawthorne must indeed get out of the customhouse and its atmosphere of enervation in order to write his romance, but it would be a mistake to conclude that the essay is suggesting that there is an "outside" of cultural affiliation in which the writer and his reader might freely roam. For the story that points the way out of "The Custom-House" is found within it, and Hawthorne aspires to do work that will "share in the united effort of mankind." The essay recommends not romantic escape but a kind of revisionary aplomb; during the course of the essay, writer and reader, as it were, hold the experience of belonging to one's culture up to the light and see the forms of connection and meaning that are possible. Through this joint act of mind—through the acknowledgment that selfhood is not an inviolable essence but a form of relation, that freedom is achieved not by acts of transcendence but by acts of revision—the interesting terrain of choice, located in the interstices of the cultural field, becomes habitable. We become, in a phrase that balances fidelity and freedom, "citizens of somewhere else."

CULTURE AND THE CONDITIONS OF MEANING

I have suggested that *The Scarlet Letter* is engaged in providing a rigorous answer to the authoritative question that Hawthorne's ghostly ancestors asked in "The Custom-House": "A writer of story-books! What kind of a business in life,—what mode of glorifying God, or being serviceable to mankind in this day and generation,—may that be?" (92). Hawthorne answers that question by exploring, in a systematic and specific way, the relation between the shape of the self and the condition of the culture it inhabits. This first sustained romance promises to be "serviceable to mankind" by offering a lucid seeing of the conditions of meaning that attend social life, so that our relation to those conditions might become actively chosen, and so that we might see, in the fullest way, what connects us to the lives of others. [. . .] [T]he book begins by asking us to attend to the way Puritan Boston is organized and to the kinds of behavior and expression it sponsors or provokes. Its opening sequence provides us [. . .] with an account of the Puritan community as [. . .] an animate system actively engaged in the generation of meaning.

Hawthorne begins his description of Puritan Boston with a theorem about the construction of communities: "The founders of a new colony, whatever Utopia of human virtue and happiness they might originally project, have invariably recognized it among their earliest practical necessities to allot a portion of the virgin soil as a cemetery and another portion as the site of a prison" (119). Along with its reminder of the nonnegotiable fact of death, this version of the act of establishment implies that the joint action that calls a community into being will inevitably include an act of suppression: that, as the life of a community unfolds, its meaning will in part be established and its boundaries in effect defined by what it chooses to punish. The prison, along with the larger "penal machine" (124) it represents, is thus a form of cultural expression—"the black flower of civilized society" (119)—that will yield to analysis. When Hester and Pearl emerge from the prison door, what we witness is most crucially a drama of cultural definition.

In Hawthorne's representation of Hester's punishment, her transgression is treated less as a genuine threat to the community than as an opportunity for Puritan Boston to define—and thus to fortify—itself. [. . .] The letter is exposed to the gaze of the townspeople and the discourse of the authorities so as to establish its significance as a cultural boundary; the penal machine is engaged in the work of fixing Hester's new communal meaning. This punitive ceremony, then, strengthens the community by allowing it to proclaim again the kind of community it is. And the Puritan authorities continue to promote this opportunity for communal definition long after the initial ceremony is over, making Hester the text of sermons and the occasion for impromptu street-corner exhortations. Their sentence is thus said to be "undying" and "ever-active" (146). Even for those directly involved in the transgression—and this is a paradox I will be exploring later in the essay—Hester's exposure has the effect of both isolating them from the community and revealing the intensity of their affiliation to it, as though the transgression had itself become the site of a meaning too compelling to leave behind. Thus the one constant in Hester's, Dimmesdale's, and Chillingworth's reactions to the letter is an odd loyalty to the scene of their misery.

For all the power of this disciplinary ritual, the meanings it generates are not univocal. [. . .] Hester's transgression and its punishment reveal the existence of two crucially different forms of and potentials for meaning within the community. The first of these ways of meaning might be said to sponsor the punitive spectacle that I have been discussing, and Hawthorne's spatial representation of the scene of punishment shows us its structure. Hester's meaning is established and enforced by the authority figures who occupy the meetinghouse balcony that looms over her position on the scaffold; the townspeople assembled below her give their assent, as members of this community, to the meaning implicit in her punishment. This version of communal meaning is, then, hierarchical and protected by a power of enforcement. It establishes one meaning by suppressing others, as the narrator's comment that a Papist in the audience might have seen Hester as a version of the Madonna reminds us. [. . .]

Even within this authoritative spectacle, though, we hear whispers of other kinds of voices and notice traces of a differently constituted kind of meaning. One of the first of these is the soft voice of the youngest of the women Hawthorne places in the audience. Unlike her more vindictive companions, who focus their attention on the outward sign and relative severity of Hester's public punishment, this woman understands Hester's experience in terms of its internal effect, claiming that Hester has felt each stitch of the letter's embroidery "in her heart" (124). The act of sympathy that produces this perspective implies a form of communal connection that is not authorized from above but conducted on the same cultural level and generated by an exchange of emotion. As befits its unofficial status, this kind of meaning manifests itself as a barely articulated undercurrent: in the capacity for sympathy located in the "larger and warmer heart of the multitude" (132) and absent from the Puritan elders; in the "one accord of sympathy" (134) created by the latent emotional power of Dimmesdale's plea that Hester reveal the father; later in the book, in the acuity that lets the "uninstructed multitude," by virtue of the "intuitions of its great and warm heart" (177), grasp the perversity of Chillingworth's attachment to

Dimmesdale that official Boston cannot see; and, most significantly, in the kind of response Dimmesdale's preaching awakens, which depends not on the content of the sermons but on his capacity to speak "the heart's native language" through the tones and rhythms of his voice. This alternative form of meaning, which possesses significant cultural power of its own, also emerges in certain "wild" or heterodox meanings that the text occasionally puts in our way, like the beautiful rosebush that grows by the prison door, reputedly in the footsteps of the "sainted"—rambunctious adjective— Anne Hutchinson (120).

In his representation of the Puritan community as a system of mean- ing, Hawthorne is not suggesting a simple opposition between these two paths toward meaning, though *The Scarlet Letter* sets out to teach the ways of sympathy and to discipline the authoritarian impulse. Rather, their in- terpenetration within the life of this culture suggests that the original im- position of authoritative meaning that founded the community at the same time gave shape to a striving to express or include what official culture sup- presses or discounts, as though to fill an empty communal space and an- swer an ignored human capacity. This, I think, is the implication of one of the curious aftereffects of Hester's punishment, her capacity to sense the presence of "hidden sin" (147) or forbidden desires in her fellow citizens; she has become attuned to the community of heterodox emotion that shares Boston with its official culture.

A number of propositions crucial to our understanding of the life of a culture accompany Hawthorne's theory of the "double" nature of com- munal meaning and emerge from his way of describing Puritan Boston. Hawthorne's narrator is, in his insistence on cultural comparisons, an an- thropologist before his time. He continually imports into his narrative the perspectives of different communities: the Papist's view of Hester as Madonna, the Indians and mariners who observe the election day holiday, the many references to the folk traditions of the "Merrie England" the Puritans have left behind. Most interesting in its effect is his ongoing com- parison of Puritan Boston to the middle-class culture of his nineteenth- century audience. He observes, for example, the differences between the public boldness, emotional bluntness, and physical vigor of the Puritan women and the sensitivity and physical delicacy of their nineteenth-century descendants: "every successive mother has transmitted to her child a fainter bloom, a more delicate and briefer beauty, and a slighter physical frame" (121). He notices the difference in authority styles, comparing the Puritan respect for experience and stability to his era's admiration for the vagaries of "talent" (253). At times he uses a contemporary perspective to criti- cize the cruelty of Puritan social discipline, as in his description of the hor- rible exposure inflicted by the pillory: "There can be no outrage, methinks, against our common nature . . . more flagrant than to forbid the culprit to hide his face for shame" (125). An implicit act of comparison informs his tactics of representing character as well, for some of these Puritan characters display distinctly nineteenth-century characteristics. Thus the woman in the crowd able to sympathize with Hester displays the delicacy of frame and sensibility that Hawthorne has connected to his own era (she confirms her cultural advancement by dying during the course of the book). Dimmesdale especially betrays striking signs of nineteenth-century sentimentality (along with the requisite physical frailty), responding to Hester's refusal to name the father in the canonical vocabulary of middle-class America's celebration of female heroism: "Wondrous strength and generosity of a woman's Heart!" (134).

Taken together, the effects of this ongoing comparison between the Puritan community and other cultural arrangements, especially those of his own middle-class America, are complex and crucial to an understanding of what Hawthorne is up to in *The Scarlet Letter*. As the fair distribution of both appealing and unappealing characteristics indicates, the book carries no brief for either the sixteenth century or the nineteenth. Yet its perspective on cultural differences is not simply neutral or relativistic. Any set of cultural arrangements will confer genuine gains and losses, will sponsor or suppress different forms of pleasure, kindness, and cruelty. The narrator thus admires the high seriousness of Puritan social discipline *and* prefers the respect for private emotion accorded by the middle-class notion of privacy; the complacent association of "progress" with the present day is undermined by the evidence of declining energy that suggests that our current enlightenment enforces its own hidden suppressions. These versions of cultural comparison finally produce in the reader the sense that a culture is a structure of meaning that is not "natural" or automatic but locally variable, historically changing, and thus both inescapable (one is always in relation to one's cultural system) and humanly revisable—as the changing meaning of Hester's letter within the Puritan community makes clear. And the final reverberation of Hawthorne's cultural portraiture is this: the nineteenth-century middle-class culture that he writes from and to, and makes a presence within the book, is also revisable and always also the subject of *The Scarlet Letter*.

The presence of identifiable nineteenth-century traits in these Puritan characters, in addition to inducing readerly acts of cultural comparison, suggests that character, at any given moment within the history of a community, will be in flux—that there will be a variety of places for people to occupy within a particular cultural field. This range of responses or play of structures of selfhood lets us identify another important aspect of Hawthorne's account of the conditions of communal meaning: character is portrayed throughout the book not as an independent "nature" or free-standing psychology but as a changeable form of relation to the community. In effect, character is another form of meaning within a community, a specific way of negotiating the cultural terrain. [. . .] A character's inner life begins with a given set of capacities—Hester's "rich, voluptuous, Oriental characteristic" (145); Dimmesdale's hunger for an authoritative creed; Chillingworth's analytic predilections—but this "nature" unfolds in response to the ideological structures and forms of expression available within the community one inhabits. This conception of selfhood as a relationship between a complex psyche and a complex culture implies neither determinism nor a transcendent personal freedom but a much more complicated transaction, in which both choice and limitation are real. One may choose one's forms and gestures of affiliation, be they pious or rebellious, but those gestures will always be given by, and will always mean within, the community's structure of meaning.

It is in Hawthorne's depiction of Pearl that this view of character as a form of meaning within a community is most evident, precisely because Pearl's link to her community is so loosely established. Her nature is said to lack "reference and adaptation to the world into which she was born" (150), like a sign unplaced within a language. [. . .] For all her capriciousness and hostility to authority, Pearl is not a wild child; she is seeking, throughout the book, to find a way of meaning that can make sense of her experience.

One can see the various elements of Hawthorne's attention to the community's ways of meaning at work in the "The Governor's Hall" episode, where Hester fights to retain custody of Pearl. Hawthorne's depiction of the Governor's stately house makes it clear that Hester has entered the world according to authority. She is greeted by an indentured servant, a man, as the narrator reminds us, converted by decree into a piece of property, "as much a commodity of bargain and sale as an ox, or a joint-stool" (159). The most notable feature of the Governor's decor is the gallery of ancestral portraits that line the entrance hall. This display of ghostly "sternness and severity" produces an inhibitory effect reminiscent of Hawthorne's encounter with his own ancestral enforcers in "The Custom-House": Bellingham's forebears seem to gaze "with harsh and intolerant criticism at the pursuits and enjoyments of living men" (160). The most striking illustration of Hester's entry into the precincts of the authoritative and of the power of a culture's way of seeing to give its own twist to the local air is her reflection in the convex breastplate of the Governor's armor. She appears there exactly as she looks from the official point of view: all letter, as though her very shape had conformed to her new cultural function. Hester receives a confirmation of the power of ideology to define the real when she encounters the Governor himself. As John Wilson jokes about the scarlet-clad Pearl's membership in the clan of elves and fairies they left behind in England, the Governor's magisterial interpretive grid descends, censoring Wilson's playfulness, erasing the culture of holiday he refers to, and producing his own reading of Pearl's significance: "Nay, we might have judged that such a child's mother must needs be a scarlet woman and a worthy type of her of Babylon!" (164).

In giving us this dispute over who might best take charge of Pearl's "Christian nurture," Hawthorne is placing us in the most revealing cultural territory, for it is through its way of nurturing and disciplining its children that a community works to preserve and replicate itself. [. . . A] sense of cultural mission motivates the Governor's authoritative question to Hester—"Were it not, thinkest thou, for thy little one's temporal and eternal welfare, that she be taken out of thy charge, and clad soberly, and disciplined strictly, and instructed in the truths of heaven and earth?" (164). [. . .]

Hester's answer to the Governor speaks a truth out of Boston's other cultural dispensation, the community of meaning constituted by interchange rather than authority. She makes the extraordinary claim that her right to her child inheres in the very experience of wearing the letter: "See ye not, she is the scarlet letter, only capable of being loved, and so endowed with a million-fold the power of retribution for my sin?" (166). Hester's plea depends for its force on the logic of emotional exchange that I have been describing. It is Pearl's capacity to receive love—to be more than the culturally inflected sign of sin that she is for the elders—that guarantees Hester's fidelity, in raising the child, to the ethical vision her adultery has violated. Hester's remark, cryptic though it is, suggests that she confronts in her daughter's wildness and alienation, at every moment, the costs of her transgression; and she measures, in her hopes for Pearl, the value of the human connection that she, through her sin, has forfeited. Hence Hester's feeling that Pearl is the only thing "keep[ing] her heart alive" (166).

It is a sign of the gap between Hester's way of meaning and that of the Governor and the Reverend Wilson that they find her statement utterly incomprehensible. We get an illustration of the real—rather than the official—importance of Dimmesdale to this community when Hester turns to him to plead her case on the grounds that he has "sympathies which these men lack" (166)—that he has access, that is, to the world of meaning from which she speaks. The argument that Dimmesdale mounts on her behalf is a remarkable piece of cultural mediation. He translates Hester's language of the "heart" into the vocabulary of authority: by presenting Pearl not as a sign of forbidden passion but as an expression of the divine intention, he recasts Hester's bid for emotional survival into a struggle to save her own soul. Dimmesdale thus accommodates Hester's need to the theocratic way of seeing, and he does so without simply violating or erasing her meaning. Dimmesdale's successful mediation should be seen as a moment of cultural enlargement and strengthening, in which the authoritative vision that governs the community expands to include a difficult emotional truth. Wilson and Bellingham are not duped by Dimmesdale's plea, but given a way to discover and express their own capacity for sympathy. This moment looks forward to the community's awed and generous response to the tableau of suffering that closes the book, and it lets us see the complexity of the relationships and meanings that constitute, for Hawthorne, the life of a culture.

CHARACTER AND CULTURAL AFFILIATION

Hawthorne's representation of character in *The Scarlet Letter* should be understood not simply as psychological exploration but as an interrogation of the form taken by one's affiliation to a particular community: character is the subtlest and most complicated expression of the meaning that a culture makes. In portraying the different ways that Hester Prynne and Arthur Dimmesdale respond to their transgression, Hawthorne distinguishes between two structures of mind. Against Hester's persistent rebelliousness, speculative freedom, and capacity to love, he poses Dimmesdale's inner drama of self-entrapment: his compulsive acts of penance, his increasing passivity, his encompassing narcissism. These two psychologies simultaneously represent two forms of relation to the communal structure of Puritan Boston, for Hester's externally imposed punishment at last confers an inner freedom that makes her a profound critic of the community she inhabits, while Dimmesdale's guilt confines him ever more stringently to the authoritarian vision of the Puritan theocracy. *The Scarlet Letter*, then, is the history of two strategies available to consciousness in response to the guilt that expresses its affiliation to the community it inhabits: Hester's subversion of conscience, and Dimmesdale's entrapment by it—even his embracing of it.

[. . .] Hester's capacity to love as the source of her subversiveness and the essence of the distinction between her and her erstwhile lovers is Hawthorne's contribution to the thinking about the nature of male and female character that was so absorbing a subject in antebellum America. Dimmesdale and Chillingworth, careerists both, build their lives upon stories that are primarily about themselves, and in those stories emotional need assumes the guise of abstract principle and is fueled by ambition. For Dimmesdale the story of his adultery is not about him and Hester but about his private election and his right to public eminence. Chillingworth disguises his wounding and the career of his rage as a philosophical inquiry into the manifestations of the guilty heart and adopts a determinism that diffuses personal responsibility for his vendetta. It is precisely Hester's willingness to build her life upon her bonds to others that saves her from the self-absorption, despair, and abstraction that her isolation invites—that keeps her, from Hawthorne's point of view, alive as a woman and, paradoxically, freer in her relation to the community than her self-regarding lovers.

Hawthorne uses these established gender distinctions, it seems to me, to think about how cultural transformation might occur. Hester is just at the point of falling into a despair that might take the form of a rebellion against male authority conducted, like Anne Hutchinson's, on abstract grounds when Chillingworth's victimization of Dimmesdale at last gives her, along with her care of Pearl, a pathway for her passion, "an object that appeared worthy of any exertion and sacrifice for its attainment" (205). This moment, when Hester's "heart . . . come[s] uppermost," begins as a celebration, canonical to antebellum gender discourse, of the womanly capacity for sympathy, but we should notice where Hester's emotions take her. When Hester resolves to rescue the minister from the patriarchal camp, she moves from speculation to action, thus becoming subversive in a more dangerous way than in her theoretical musings. As she knows from her own experience, the authority structure of Puritan Boston and the forms of male ambition it endorses depend upon love's subordination to abstract principles, and she is acting as though meaning were grounded not on principle but on love. And since the minister vividly represents the self-poisoning suppressions and closet egoism that attend the version of male character that paternalistic cultures—like antebellum America—seem to produce, Hester's attempt to steal Dimmesdale for her world is a step toward realizing her revolutionary vision of a transformed cultural life: a world in which "the very nature of the opposite sex, or its long hereditary habit, which has become like nature" (205) and the culture that supports that "habit" might be transformed and "the whole relation between man and woman" might be reestablished "on a surer ground of mutual happiness" (271). [. . .]

[. . .] In contending that Hester's return at once models and is designed to occasion the achievement by the reader, via interpretation, of a substantially freer, authentically critical relation to the community, I am countering an influential body of readings, built upon the fact of her return and her assumption of the role of counselor to unhappy women, that accuse Hawthorne of attempting to contain or escape the radical possibilities let loose in Hester's character. [. . .]

[. . .] More largely, I do not think that one's estimate of the cultural effect or ambitions of the book depends upon answering the undecidable question of whether Hester is *really* revolutionary or upon Hawthorne's own political affiliations. [. . .]

I began this essay by suggesting that things happen at least twice within the world of *The Scarlet Letter*. From the vantage point of its close, this pattern of repetition becomes visible as a series of achieved and failed acts of revision: from Hawthorne's replacement of his inhibitory ancestors with Surveyor Pue; to Hester's opening gesture, in which she strides toward her punishment "as if by her own free-will" (122); to Pearl's verdant imitation of her mother's scarlet letter; to Dimmesdale's failed confessions and Chillingworth's refusal to forgive; to the displacement of Dimmesdale's midnight appearance on the scaffold by the tableau of disclosure that brings the action to its close. "The Custom-House" itself, from the standpoint of the end of the book, is as revisionary as it is introductory, for it rewrites Hester's tragedy of irretrievable loss as Hawthorne's comedy of escape. This revisionary relation between story and introduction insists that our reading accommodate both the tragic stasis of the final scene and the resilience of the "decapitated" but vital Surveyor, that we locate in the overdetermined scene of cultural meaning both the scaffold of limitation and room to maneuver. [. . .]

Domesticity as Redemption

Walter Herbert

Walter Herbert's book *Dearest Beloved* explores the marriage of Nathaniel and Sophia Hawthorne in the context of the sexual politics that shaped them both, and his section on *The Scarlet Letter* focuses on the joys and torments of domestic intimacy. The following excerpt discusses Hester and Dimmesdale as they conform to or deviate from the nineteenth-century ideals of "true womanhood" and "essential manhood," particularly during their forest encounter and in the final scaffold scene. Herbert also discusses Chillingworth's roles in the domestic drama and probes Pearl's relationship to both of her parents (who do not "provide adequate nurture"); and he

---

From *Dearest Beloved: The Hawthornes and the Making of the Middle-Class Family*. Berkeley: U of California P, 1993. (All parenthetical references are to this New Riverside Edition.)

connects Pearl's "peremptory force" and conflicted character to Hawthorne's ponderings about his daughter Una. [ED.]

As a woman "stained" with sin, Hester represents the classic opposite of domestic purity. Instead of sublimating male desire into worship, her nature has "a rich, voluptuous, Oriental characteristic" (145). Roger's addiction to voyeuristic cruelty and Arthur's addiction to exhibitionist guilt are correlative transformations of the passion she stirs up. Yet even as Hester plays her part in this system of interlocking emotional contradictions, Hawthorne gives her qualities of the "true womanhood" that promises to place the relation of the sexes on a new footing. Like the brief description of the young woman at the scaffold, her story is a harbinger of the redemption she foretells in her old age but will not live to see. Hawthorne seeks, that is, to contain his material within the rhetoric of the domestic ideal, even as he lays open the dilemmas intrinsic to that ideal. This pervading metabolism of meanings—in which domesticity is established in the act of being subverted—strongly contributes to the cultural power *The Scarlet Letter* has been found to possess.

The narrative intimates that Roger and Arthur are indissolubly united, yet it manifestly presents them as two different men between whom Hester may choose. Hester eventually decides, not surprisingly, to keep faith with Arthur, breaking the promise she had given Roger to keep their "former" marriage a secret. She confirms her commitment, that is, to marriage as a sacred communion of souls, and her relationship to Arthur is a parable of redemptive spiritual intercourse.

[. . .] She is preserved from the wilder excesses of rebellion by the devotion she pours into the rearing of Pearl; and in her relation to the community at large she displays compassionate self-sacrifice. Hawthorne speaks of her uncomplaining submission to the abuse she received from the public and celebrates the "blameless purity" of her life. Sickbed and deathbed scenes best reveal her distinctive feminine virtue; there "Hester's nature showed itself warm and rich; a well-spring of human tenderness, unfailing to every real demand, and inexhaustible by the largest" (202). The townsfolk begin to tell each other that the scarlet A "meant Able; so strong was Hester Prynne, with a woman's strength" (202).

The reciprocal magic touch, in which Hester recovers her womanhood and, in the consummate exercise of her woman's strength, makes a "man" out of Arthur Dimmesdale, is enacted in the forest. As Hester sees Arthur approaching, she observes his "nerveless despondency" (220); and the ensuing scene reveals that he has lost the ascribed masculine qualities of public initiative and self-possession, of rational judgment and resolute will. When Dimmesdale learns that Roger "was" Hester's husband, he collapses altogether and turns to Hester for guidance. "Think for me, Hester! Thou art strong. Resolve for me!" (226). Hester has already contrived the plan that she now persuades Arthur to adopt. She wants them to leave the colony for a better life elsewhere; in the course of pursuing this objective, she asserts her psychological dominion over him. "'Is the world then so narrow?' exclaimed Hester Prynne, fixing her deep eyes on the minister's, and instinctively exercising a magnetic power over a spirit so shattered and subdued, that it could hardly hold itself erect" (226).

This encounter does not bring Arthur under her power for long, however. Instead of complying with her plan, he conceives and executes a plan of his own to extend and, indeed, to culminate his public responsibilities. Hester is startled and dismayed, after the Election Day sermon, when Arthur approaches the scaffold to proclaim his guilt. Yet something within her compels her to acquiesce: "slowly, as if impelled by inevitable fate, and against her strongest will" (263), Hester joins him. Innate womanly submission undermines the long-practiced assertion of her will now that Arthur assumes command. She has rendered him capable of fulfilling his manhood, which includes taking charge of her, and he continues to depend on her "woman's strength," now subordinated to the purpose he has chosen without consulting her. As they mount the scaffold together, they form a tableau in which the domestic vision of natural genders is triumphant: essential manhood and essential womanhood have been mutually re-created and are reciprocally confirmed. "Come hither now, and twine thy strength about me! Thy strength, Hester; but let it be guided by the will which God hath granted me!" (263–64).

Pearl's redemption occurs at this moment of confession and expiation and fulfillment. The child has inherited Hester's defiance and seems to anticipate that she too will eventually be at odds with the world. Instead of playing with the children of the town, Pearl invents imaginary playmates, whom she regards with vehement hostility: "She never created a friend, but seemed always to be sowing broadcast the dragon's teeth, whence sprung a harvest of armed enemies, against whom she rushed to battle. It was inexpressibly sad—then what depth of sorrow to a mother, who felt in her own heart the cause!—to observe, in one so young, this constant recognition of an adverse world, and so fierce a training of the energies that were to make good her cause, in the contest that must ensue" (154).

Just as Hester's rebellion puts her at odds with her own "womanly" nature, so Pearl's character is a battleground. She is an agent of Hester's punishment, upholding the validity of the order Hester violates: her preoccupation with the scarlet letter, her persistent allusions to it, and her eerily apt questions to Hester about Arthur fill out her character as an enforcer of the lawful order of society. Yet she herself "could not be made amenable to rules" (150).

This contradictory situation comes to a head in the forest after Hester has removed the scarlet letter from her breast and the severe cap from her head, so that her dark hair flows voluptuously down over her shoulders, stirring Arthur to a resumption of his manhood. Having agreed to flee the colony, they call the child to join them, but instead of responding with sympathy, Pearl throws a tantrum that is at once commanding and uncontrolled. "Assuming a singular air of authority, Pearl stretched out her hand, with the small forefinger extended, and pointing evidently towards her mother's breast," and then "stamped her foot with a yet more imperious look and gesture." When Hester sternly repeats her demand, Pearl "suddenly burst into a fit of passion, gesticulating violently, and throwing her small figure into the most extravagant contortions. She accompanied this wild outbreak with piercing shrieks" (234–35) whereupon Hester gives in and restores the letter.

Pearl's peremptory force, here as elsewhere, recalls what Hawthorne saw in [his daughter] Una; his notebook entries complain that she was often "exceedingly ungracious in her mode of asking, or rather demanding favors. For instance, wishing to have a story read to her, she has just said, 'Now I'm going to have some reading'; and she always seems to adopt the imperative mood, in this manner. She uses it to me, I think, more than to her mother, and, from what I observe of some of her collateral predecessors, I believe it to be an hereditary trait to assume the government of her father" (*American Notebooks* 414).

Pearl gains control of others by losing control of herself, a stratagem Una found successful with her father. Hawthorne's journal returns again and again to the "tempestuous" protests that erupt when Una's will is crossed (*American Notebooks* 411). [. . .] When Hawthorne was overawed by Una's fury, [. . .] he looked to Sophia to calm her, and Arthur Dimmesdale is likewise intimidated by Pearl. "I know nothing that I would not sooner encounter than this passion in a child," he says to Hester. "In Pearl's young beauty, as in the wrinkled witch, it has a preternatural effect. Pacify her, if thou lovest me" (235).

Pearl's hysterical insistence on maintaining decorum carries the note of inward desperation that was audible in Una's outbursts. Sophia once read aloud a story titled "The Bear and the Skrattel," and her imitation of the Skrattel's unearthly shrill voice set Una off. "Little Una cries 'No; no!' with a kind of dread," Hawthorne noted, and he then specifies with an unnerving serenity the chronic distress of which this outcry gave evidence. "It is rather singular that she should so strongly oppose herself to whatever is unbeautiful or even unusual, while she is continually doing unbeautiful things in her own person. I think, if she were to see a little girl who behaved in all respects like herself, it would be a continual horror and misery to her, and would ultimately drive her mad" (*American Notebooks* 419).

Hawthorne uncannily predicts the psychic breakdowns that befell Una in later years, yet he could see that the child's mental torment was already severe. It could hardly have escaped him that she was doomed to her own company. More startling than Hawthorne's insight, however, is the tone of detached inquiry in which he pursues the "rather singular" puzzle of Una's inward war. Just as Dimmesdale's terror at Pearl's rage bespeaks Una's power to disconcert her father, so this cold diagnosis—with a vengeful impulse lurking beneath its objective surface—discloses Hawthorne's kinship with Chillingworth.

In Pearl these contradictions are resolved as Hester helps Arthur mount the scaffold: "The great scene of grief, in which the wild infant bore a part, had developed all her sympathies; and as her tears fell upon her father's cheek, they were the pledge that she would grow up amid human joy and sorrow, nor for ever do battle with the world, but be a woman in it" (267). The child's "manlike" imperiousness gives way to tears of sympathy, and the "elflike" impersonal remoteness gives way to warm human relations. Like Pinocchio, Pearl is transformed from an unnatural creature, endowed with life but not truly human, into a "real little girl." Hawthorne expresses the confidence, as the narrative closes, that "her wild, rich nature had been softened and subdued, and made capable of a woman's gentle happiness" (278).

As many critics have observed, however, Pearl's prospective domestic felicity is not located in the United States or in any other clearly definable place. It is supported by a fabulous inheritance, which makes her "the richest heiress of her day," and Hawthorne is careful to point out that the seals on her letters have "bearings unknown to English heraldry" (270). Hawthorne's conclusion exempts Pearl from the dilemmas that the book portrays but does not resolve them.

Even the concluding scaffold scene, where Pearl's redemption takes place, testifies to the interior disharmonies of the domestic ideal. The completed family group obeys Pearl's demand that Dimmesdale acknowledge her and her mother before the community. Yet that tableau also includes Chillingworth, "as one intimately connected with the drama of guilt and sorrow in which they had all been actors" (264). While Chillingworth concedes that Dimmesdale has finally escaped his vengeance, his claim on Dimmesdale's conscience is vindicated—not dismissed—by the clergyman's final confession. The self-divided manhood represented by Arthur and Roger is not healed at the final scaffold scene; it comes to a crisis that neither man survives.

Hawthorne establishes a special relation between Pearl and Chillingworth that probes issues beyond the dilemmas of split manhood and of "true womanhood," namely the responsibilities of child rearing. The sin of Hester and Arthur is not only their defiance of Roger's legal claim; their soul-marriage fails to provide adequate nurture for Pearl. Hester refuses the injunction to break the child's will by a "frequent application of the rod" and instead "sought to impose a tender, but strict, control over the infant immortality that was committed to her charge" (91–92). Yet Pearl's stubborn waywardness makes a mockery of sentimental blandishments. She is an incorrigible, like the slave child Topsy, in *Uncle Tom's Cabin,* who becomes tractable only when little Eva's death brings tears to her eyes, like those Pearl sheds over the expiring Arthur. Hester "grew acquainted with a certain peculiar look, that warned her when it would be labor thrown away to insist, persuade, or plead. It was a look so intelligent, yet inexplicable, so perverse, sometimes so malicious, . . . that Hester could not help questioning . . . whether Pearl was a human child" (151). Unlike Topsy, who has been beaten into hardness of heart, Pearl is demonically rebellious because her father does not acknowledge her.

Hawthorne repeatedly asserts the connection between Roger's claim and Pearl's need. As Hester refuses to name her lover, Roger calls from the crowd, "Speak, woman! . . . Speak; and give your child a father" (124). In the midnight scaffold scene, when Hester and Pearl join hand in hand with Arthur, Pearl gestures toward Roger standing alone in the shadows, and includes him in the family group. Roger bequeaths his fortune to Pearl, a circumstance all the more striking in view of Arthur's failure to make provision for his child's support at any point in the narrative.

It never dawns on Arthur, despite his orgy of guilt over falling into sin, that he has any moral or material responsibility for his child. When the magistrates propose to remove Pearl from Hester's care, Arthur defends Hester's "indefeasible rights" by invoking "a quality of awful sacredness in the relation between this mother and this child" (168). Yet the Reverend Wilson underscores the material responsibility that Arthur ignores, the need for "a father's kindness towards the poor, deserted babe" (170). As

David Leverenz rightly noted, the relation of Pearl and Arthur presents a sharply intensified version of domesticity, in which the mother is over-present and the father is absent, busy attaining distinction in the world (274). As Dimmesdale marches toward the Election Day ceremony where he will consummate his career, Hester becomes miserably aware of the gulf that stands between them: Dimmesdale seems "so unattainable in his worldly position, and still more so in that far vista of his unsympathizing thoughts" (255). Dimmesdale's prospective worldly triumph will be fueled by the emotional energies awakened by his conversation with Hester in the forest Yet to Hester, that renewal of their self-consecrating love evapo-rates. "Her spirit sank with the idea that all must have been a delusion, and that . . . there could be no real bond betwixt the clergyman and her-self" (255). This moment dramatizes a paradox that has existed from the outset of the narrative, in which Hester and Dimmesdale are bound by a compelling intimate tie yet live solitary and apart. The daily experience of their communion of souls is, for the most part, an alien proximity in which each keeps a pained and guilty silence. Hester "could scarcely forgive him" Hawthorne tells us, "for being able so completely to withdraw himself from their mutual world; while she groped darkly, and stretched forth her cold hands, and found him not" (255).

This marriage-defining wretchedness besieges them even at the fullest dramatization of their marital bond. In the forest scene where Hester and Arthur re-enact their self-consecration, Hawthorne presents a collision between the claims of their relationship and the obligations represented by Pearl. Instead of staging a triumph of "natural" genders over social con-vention, this conflict pits nature against nature.

The renewal of marital communion begins as Arthur "put forth his hand, chill as death, and touched the chill hand of Hester Prynne." The two engage in commonplace small talk, which opens "the doors of inter-course," so that they could move onward, "step by step, into the themes that were brooding deepest in their hearts" (221). Their spiritual and sex-ual bond comes slowly back to life, until at length Hester removes the let-ter from her bosom and throws it away, whereupon "there played around her mouth, and beamed out of her eyes, a radiant and tender smile, that seemed gushing from the very heart of womanhood" (230). As we have seen, the "womanhood" expressed here is not submissive and angelic do-mesticity, but the triumph of Hester's purposeful intelligence, releasing the full wealth of her sexual power. She has persuaded Arthur to begin a new life in a new place and has promised to sustain him with her strength and courage.

This moment of androgynous consummation is blessed by a flood of sunshine. "Such was the sympathy of Nature—that wild, heathen Nature of the forest, never subjugated by human law, nor illumined by higher truth—with the bliss of these two spirits! Love, whether newly born, or aroused from a deathlike slumber, must always create a sunshine, filling the heart so full of radiance, that it overflows upon the outward world" (231). Yet this validation of their mutual world is soon crosscut by Pearl's refusal to accept it, and Hawthorne specifies this refusal as equally blessed by Nature.

During her parents' conversation, Pearl enters a prelapsarian communion with creatures of the forest: a partridge, a pigeon, a squirrel, and a fox. Even a wolf lets her pat its head. "The mother-forest, and these wild things which it nourished, all recognized a kindred wildness in the human child" (232). Decking herself out with flowers and greenery, Pearl becomes "a nymph-child, or an infant dryad, or whatever else was in closest sympathy with the antique wood" (232). So adorned, Pearl fulfills her parents' sacred union. "It was with a feeling which neither of them had ever before experienced, that they sat and watched Pearl's slow advance. In her was visible the tie that united them. She had been offered to the world, these seven years past, as the living hieroglyphic, in which was revealed the secret they so darkly sought to hide,—all written in this symbol. . . . Pearl was the oneness of their being" (233).

Yet the child of nature is excluded from the relationship whose nature she embodies. "Another inmate had been admitted within the circle of the mother's feelings, and so modified the aspect of them all, that Pearl, the returning wanderer, could not find her wonted place, and hardly knew where she was" (234). Pearl accordingly demands that the letter, with its "withering spell" be restored. Hester loses her power to animate Arthur's natural manhood as "the warmth and richness of her womanhood departed, like fading sunshine; and a gray shadow seemed to fall across her" (237). The soul-marriage of Arthur and Hester is again marked as adulterous, not by outmoded marital legislation or the self-division of self-made men, but by a logic that asserts itself when sexual intercourse is made a sacrament of the marital bond. The spiritual communion of the two souls is checked by the offspring that its enactment produces.

Running through the forest episode is an emblem of this native dissonance, a little brook that almost never flows clear in the sunlight because it is obstructed by fallen branches, boulders, and the roots of great trees. These obstacles, as natural as the stream itself, "choked up the current, and compelled it to form eddies and black depths" (218). The stream has a wordless voice, like Dimmesdale's sorrowful and haunting undertone; it "still kept telling its unintelligible secret of some very mournful mystery that had happened—or making a prophetic lamentation about something that was yet to happen—within the verge of the dismal forest" (219–20). At the conclusion of the episode, after the communion of souls has been revived and self-stifled, Hawthorne tells us that "the melancholy brook would add this other tale to the mystery with which its little heart was already overburdened, and whereof it still kept up a murmuring babble, with not a whit more cheerfulness of tone than for ages heretofore" (238).

This device will serve as an emblem of Hawthorne's literary power, by which the miseries attendant on a specific form of marital intimacy are made to appear the blight that man was born for. The brook ceaselessly intimates a sorrow arising from the nature of nature and offers a mild and rueful comfort more compelling than Arthur's triumphant confession or Hester's messianic vision of a future day. The voice of the brook will not cancel the torments intrinsic to the domestic ideal but will keep saying them forever: "kind, quiet, soothing, but melancholy, like the voice of a young child that was spending its infancy without playfulness, and knew not how to be merry among sad acquaintance and events of sombre hue" (219). The allusion here to Una's psychic disorder and early sorrow marks the paradox of Hawthorne's greatest art. The most luminous passages, whose wave fronts seem to travel across the relativities of history at an absolute speed and to create a radiance independent of any local reference, are entangled with the painful contingencies amid which they originate.

Hawthorne's masterwork occasioned a communion between Nathaniel and Sophia from which the rhetoric of domestic bliss was notably absent. Nathaniel later recalled "my emotions when I read the last scene of the Scarlet Letter to my wife, just after writing it—tried to read it, rather, for my voice swelled and heaved, as if I were tossed up and down on an ocean, as it subsided after a storm. But I was in a very nervous state, then, having gone through a great diversity and severity of emotion, for many months past. I think I have never overcome my own adamant in any other instance" (*English Notebooks* 225). That Nathaniel should consummate the months of creative torment in the image of an ocean storm is uncannily suited to its sources in himself, recalling his lost ship-captain father and the unresolvable grief that lay at the root of his lifelong struggle with the meaning of manliness. The "adamant" that allowed him to hold this suffering at bay, and thus to maintain the working coherence of his own mind, was relaxed for a moment here, so that it was almost impossible for him to read his own words. Yet the image also implies that the struggle had reached a pause; what Nathaniel feels is the subsiding.

Sophia was likewise filled with distress. "It broke her heart," her husband wrote the following day, "and sent her to bed with a grievous headache." His adamant now restored, Nathaniel considered Sophia's anguish "a triumphant success" (*Letters, 1843–1853* 311). When Sophia likewise regained her composure, she sent a letter to her sister Mary: "I do not know what you will think of the Romance," she wrote. "It is most powerful, & contains a moral as terrific & stunning as a thunder bolt. It shows that the Law cannot be broken" (*Letters, 1843–1853*, 313).

Sophia and Nathaniel were brought together and set apart by the same text, which each felt to be overpowering. Sophia contains her celebration in an assertion of unbreakable moral law, as though anyone reading it would receive the same thunderbolt of truth. Yet in admitting she has no idea what her sister will think, Sophia indicates her awareness of having passed through a distinctively personal and intimate experience. She was herself prospectively designated by Hawthorne's description—which he read to her that night—of the "angel" of the coming revelation who will show "how sacred love should make us happy, by the truest test of a life successful to such an end." Yet her headache was hardly caused by this compliment, even if she took it ironically. The thunderbolt lay in Hawthorne's compelling depiction of the burdens that were entailed on women by this ideal, the burdens borne by Hester Prynne. [. . .]

CHRONOLOGY

1804   Born July 4 in Salem, Massachusetts, the second child and only son of Nathaniel Hathorne (a sea captain) and Elizabeth Manning Hathorne.

1808   Captain Hathorne dies of yellow fever in Surinam. His widow and three children move to her parents' house on Herbert Street.

1813   Lamed by a ballplaying accident for over a year, Nathaniel immerses himself in books.

1816–19   Lives with his mother and sisters on the Manning property in the lakeside wilderness of Raymond, Maine.

1819–21   Recalled to Salem to prepare for college.

1821–25   Attends Bowdoin College in Brunswick, Maine; classmates include Henry Wadsworth Longfellow, Horatio Bridge, and Franklin Pierce.

1825–37   Returns to Herbert Street to pursue a literary career. Reads widely in New England history. Pays for anonymous publication of *Fanshawe* and publishes over forty tales and sketches. In 1836, edits the *American Magazine of Useful and Entertaining Knowledge* and writes his first children's book, *Peter Parley's Universal History.*

1837–38   *Twice-Told Tales* is published with his name on the cover (after Bridge secretly guarantees the publisher against loss), and Longfellow reviews it enthusiastically. Meets Sophia Peabody. They become secretly engaged at the end of 1838.

1839–41   Works as measurer of salt and coal at the Boston Custom House. Publishes three children's books: *Grandfather's Chair, Famous Old People,* and *Liberty Tree.*

1841   In April he joins the utopian community of Brook Farm, hoping to begin married life there with Sophia, but farm work proves incompatible with writing and he leaves in November.

1842–45   Marries Sophia in July and moves into the Old Manse in Concord, where friends include Ralph Waldo Emerson and Henry David Thoreau. Daughter Una born in 1844. Publishes nearly two dozen tales and sketches, an expanded volume of *Twice-Told Tales*, and *Biographical Stories for Children*.

1846–49   Surveyor of customs at the Port of Salem. In 1846 *Mosses from an Old Manse* is published, and son Julian is born. Ousted as surveyor in June 1849. Mother dies in July. Begins writing *The Scarlet Letter* in September.

1850   *The Scarlet Letter* is published. Moves to Lenox, Massachusetts, and begins friendship with Herman Melville (who dedicates *Moby-Dick* to him).

1851   *The House of the Seven Gables*, *The Snow-Image and Other Twice-Told Tales*, *True Stories from History and Biography*, and *A Wonder Book for Girls and Boys* are published. Moves to West Newton. Daughter Rose is born.

1852   Moves to the Wayside in Concord (the only house he ever owns). *The Blithedale Romance* and a campaign biography for Franklin Pierce are published.

1853   *Tanglewood Tales for Girls and Boys* is published. President Pierce appoints Hawthorne consul to Liverpool.

1853–57   American consul in Liverpool.

1857–59   Travels on the continent and lives in Rome and Florence. Begins *The Marble Faun* (published in 1860).

1860–64   Returns to America and works on three romances that he never completes, "The Ancestral Footstep," "Etherege," and "Grimshawe" (recently included in *The American Claimant Manuscripts*, Volume 12 of the Centenary Edition [1977]). Publishes a report on wartime Washington and a series of sketches drawn from his English notebooks (collected as *Our Old Home* [1863]). Dies in his sleep on 19 May 1864 in Plymouth, New Hampshire.

WORKS CITED

Abbott, Anne. "[The Magic Power of Hawthorne's Style.]" *Critical Essays on Hawthorne's* The Scarlet Letter. Ed. David B. Kesterson. Boston: Hall, 1988. 31–35. Originally published in *North American Review* (July 1850).

Baym, Nina. *The Shape of Hawthorne's Career*. Ithaca: Cornell UP, 1976.

Bercovitch, Sacvan. *The Office of the Scarlet Letter*. Baltimore: Johns Hopkins UP, 1991.

Brodhead, Richard H. *Hawthorne, Melville, and the Novel*. Chicago: U of Chicago P, 1976.

——. *The School of Hawthorne*. New York: Oxford UP, 1986.

Brownson, Orestes. "[An Unfit Subject for Literature.]" *Critical Essays on Hawthorne's* The Scarlet Letter. Ed. David B. Kesterson. Boston: Hall, 1988. 36–39. Originally published in *Brownson's Quarterly Review* (Oct. 1850).

Chase, Richard. *The American Novel and Its Traditions*. Garden City: Doubleday, 1957.

Crews, Frederick C. *The Sins of the Fathers: Hawthorne's Psychological Themes*. New York: Oxford UP, 1966.

Duyckinck, Evert A. *Critical Essays on Hawthorne's* The Scarlet Letter. Ed. David B. Kesterson. Boston: Hall, 1988. 24–25. Originally published in *Literary World* (Mar. 1850).

Erlich, Gloria C. *Family Themes and Hawthorne's Fiction: The Tenacious Web*. New Brunswick: Rutgers UP, 1984.

Feidelson, Charles, Jr. "*The Scarlet Letter*." *Hawthorne Centenary Essays*. Ed. Roy Harvey Pierce. Columbus: Ohio State UP, 1964. 31–77.

Fields, James T. *Yesterdays with Authors*. Boston: Houghton, 1871.

Gollin, Rita K. *Nathaniel Hawthorne and the Truth of Dreams*. Baton Rouge: Louisiana State UP, 1979.

Hawthorne, Nathaniel. *The American Notebooks*. Ed. Claude M. Simpson. Columbus: Ohio State UP, 1972.

———. *The Blithedale Romance*. Ed. William Charvat et al. Columbus: Ohio State UP, 1964.

———. *The English Notebooks*. Ed. Thomas Woodson and Bill Ellis. Columbus: Ohio State UP, 1997.

———. *Miscellaneous Prose and Verse*. Ed. Thomas Woodson, Claude M. Simpson, and L. Neal Smith. Columbus: Ohio State UP, 1994.

———. *The Letters, 1843–1853*. Ed. Thomas Woodson, L. Neal Smith, and Norman Holmes Pearson. Columbus: Ohio State UP, 1985.

———. *The Letters, 1853–1856*. Ed. Thomas Woodson, L. Neal Smith, and Norman Holmes Pearson. Columbus: Ohio State UP, 1988.

———. *Twice-Told Tales*. Ed. Bill Ellis and Claude M. Simpson. Columbus: Ohio State UP, 1974.

Herbert, Walter. *Dearest Beloved: The Hawthornes and the Making of the Middle-Class Family*. Berkeley: U of California P, 1993.

James, Henry. *Hawthorne*. London: MacMillan, 1879.

Leverenz, David. *Manhood and the American Renaissance*. Ithaca: Cornell UP, 1989.

Matthiessen, F. O. *American Renaissance: Art and Expression in the Age of Emerson and Whitman*. New York: Oxford UP, 1941.

Millington, Richard H. *Practicing Romance: Narrative Form and Cultural Engagement in Hawthorne's Fiction*. Princeton: Princeton UP, 1992.

Reynolds, Larry J. "*The Scarlet Letter* and Revolutions Abroad." *American Literature* 57 (1985): 44–67.

Ryskamp, Charles. "The New England Sources of *The Scarlet Letter*." *American Literature* 31 (1959): 244–67.

Waggoner, Hyatt H. *The Presence of Hawthorne*. Baton Rouge: Louisiana State UP, 1979.

Whipple, Edwin Percy. "[A True Artist's Certainty of Touch and Expression]," *Critical Essays on Hawthorne's* The Scarlet Letter. Ed. David B. Kesterson. Boston: Hall, 1988. 27–29. Originally published in *Graham's Magazine* (May 1850).

Winship, Michael. "Publishing *The Scarlet Letter* in the Nineteenth-Century United States." Adapted from a paper delivered at the Nathaniel Hawthorne Conference. Boston. June 2000.

Woodberry, George E. *Nathaniel Hawthorne*. American Men of Letters 15. Boston: Houghton, 1902.

FOR FURTHER READING

Arac, Jonathan. "The Politics of *The Scarlet Letter.*" *Ideology and Classic American Literature.* Ed. Sacvan Bercovitch and Myra Jehlen. Cambridge: Harvard UP, 1986.

Bell, Michael. *Hawthorne and the Historical Romance of New England.* Princeton: Princeton UP, 1971.

Bell, Millicent. *Hawthorne's View of the Artist.* New York: New York State UP, 1962.

Budick, Emily Miller. *Fiction and Historical Consciousness: The American Romance Tradition.* New Haven: Yale UP, 1999.

Carton, Evan. *The Rhetoric of American Romance: Dialectic and Identity in Emerson, Dickinson, Poe, and Hawthorne.* Baltimore: Johns Hopkins UP, 1985.

Dauber, Kenneth. *Rediscovering Hawthorne.* Princeton: Princeton UP, 1977.

Dryden, Edgar. *Nathaniel Hawthorne: The Poetics of Enchantment.* Ithaca: Cornell UP, 1977.

Feidelson, Charles. *Symbolism and Classic American Literature.* Chicago: U of Chicago P, 1983.

Fogle, Richard Harter. *Hawthorne's Fiction: The Light and the Dark.* Norman: U of Oklahoma P, 1952.

Hawthorne, Nathaniel. *Mosses from an Old Manse.* Ed. William Charvat et al. Columbus: Ohio State UP, 1974.

Idol, John L., Jr., and Buford Jones, eds. *Nathaniel Hawthorne: The Contemporary Reviews.* Cambridge: Cambridge UP, 1994.

Male, Roy R. *Hawthorne's Tragic Vision.* Austin: U of Texas P, 1957.

Martin, Terence. *Nathaniel Hawthorne.* Boston: Twayne, 1983.

Mellow, James R. *Nathaniel Hawthorne in His Times*. Boston: Houghton, 1980.

Mizruchi, Susan L. *The Power of Historical Knowledge: Narrating the Past in Hawthorne, James, and Dreiser*. Princeton: Princeton UP, 1988.

Newberry, Frederick. *Hawthorne's Divided Loyalties: England and America in His Works*. Rutherford: Fairleigh Dickinson UP, 1987.

Nissenbaum, Stephen. "The Firing of Nathaniel Hawthorne." *Essex Institute Historical Collections* 114 (1978): 57–86.

Schubert, Leland. *Hawthorne, the Artist: Fine Art Devices in Fiction*. Chapel Hill: U of North Carolina P, 1944.

Stewart, Randall. *Nathaniel Hawthorne: A Biography*. New York: Oxford UP, 1948.

Turner, Arlin. *Nathaniel Hawthorne: A Biography*. New York: Oxford UP, 1980.

Waggoner, Hyatt H. *Hawthorne: A Critical Study*. Cambridge: Harvard UP, 1955.

RELATED WEB SITES

http://eldred.ne.mediaone.net/nh/hawthorne.html
This well-constructed site run by Eric Eldred of the Eldritch Press includes texts of Hawthorne's fiction and nonfiction (good texts, though not the now-standard but copyrighted Centenary editions). It includes links to biographical and critical studies from Hawthorne's time to our own, portraits of Hawthorne, and illustrations of his works, as well as a wide range of information about, for example, film and opera versions of *The Scarlet Letter* and other Hawthorne-related projects (including conferences of the Nathaniel Hawthorne Society).

http://pearl.nscc.mass.edu
This ambitious "Hawthorne in Salem" Web site, still in progress, is funded by the National Endowment for the Humanities and sponsored by North Shore Community College in Danvers, Massachusetts, and three Salem institutions: the Peabody Essex Museum, the Salem Maritime National Historic Site, and The House of the Seven Gables. It offers a wide compendium of materials relating to Hawthorne, his writings about Salem, and Salem itself.

http://etext.virginia.edu/salem/witchcraft/index.html
This site, run by the University of Virginia and entitled "Witchcraft in Salem Village," includes documents from the Salem witchcraft trials, maps, and other materials related to that event.

http://www.classicreader.com/author.php/aut.24/
This site contains texts of Hawthorne's four novels and thirty-six of his short stories (without identifying their editions).

CREDITS